CAREER WOMEN AND CHILDBEARING

A Psychological Analysis of the Decision Process

CAREER WOMEN AND CHILDBEARING

A Psychological Analysis of the Decision Process

Carole A. Wilk

VNR VAN NOSTRAND REINHOLD COMPANY
——————————————— New York

Copyright © 1986 by Van Nostrand Reinhold Company Inc.

Library of Congress Catalog Card Number: 85-9216
ISBN: 0-442-29352-6

Manufactured in the United States of America

Published by Van Nostrand Reinhold Company Inc.
115 Fifth Avenue
New York, New York 10003

Van Nostrand Reinhold Company Limited
Molly Millars Lane
Wokingham, Berkshire RG11 2PY, England

Van Nostrand Reinhold
480 Latrobe Street
Melbourne, Victoria 3000, Australia

Macmillan of Canada
Division of Gage Publishing Limited
164 Commander Boulevard
Agincourt, Ontario MIS 3C7, Canada

15   14   13   12   11   10   9   8   7   6   5   4   3   2   1

Library of Congress Cataloging in Publication Data

Wilk, Carole A.
   Career Women and Childbearing

   Includes index.
   1. Motherhood.   2. Married people—Employment.
3. Feminine Development.   I. Title.
HQ759.W52   1986   306.8′743   85-9216
ISBN 0-442-29352-6

*This book is dedicated, with love,
to my parents, my children, and
especially to my husband, Arthur.*

PREFACE

For a period of about ten years, from 1970 to 1980, as Co-Director of a counseling service for women, I worked with women who were dealing with psychological pressures arising from individual adult developmental transitions as well as from the broader social implications of the women's movement. For many, the primary issue was a career vs. family conflict.

Many women, especially those who were about 25-35, whose education and early career experience had led them to believe that a life-long career was reasonable, also expected to "grow up, get married and live happily ever after." Although this combination of expectations represented a break with tradition, a growing number of young, well-educated women decided to combine career and family goals in a dual-career lifestyle. Over the course of a few years, the number of dual-career couples has grown large enough to constitute a new middle class norm.

As I became more familiar with the complicated issues that confront dual-career couples—issues dealing with their needs to balance individual career and personal growth, with needs for intimacy and security—I recognized that the difficulties involved in working out the dual-career lifestyle are vastly compounded when there are children in the family. For those without children, the decision about whether or when to have a baby was often difficult and conflictual. The more I got to know young career oriented women who were at the childbearing decision stage (both in my clinical work and in the research for this book), the more I recognized that the need to reach a satisfying childbearing decision is the central organizing psychological focus. In due course, however, either with or without help, most women and couples ultimately reach a decision either to have children or to remain childless. But some dual-career women, ambivalent about many aspects of their complex lives, report feeling unable to reach a decision about whether or not they wish to become a mother. Reluctant to challenge and/or reject the maternal model, yet unsure about their parenting interest and/or capacity, these women describe an extreme degree of stress surrounding what they feel to be a societal double bind which says, in effect, "have children and be a 'real' woman" vs. "keep your mind on your career and be a 'real' professional."

How do we understand the differences between women who can reach a satisfying childbearing decision and those who feel confused, ambivalent, and undecided? In the clinical setting, what help can the therapist offer? As I looked to previous research for a theoretical framework from which I could conceptualize the issues involved, I found that although there was research on dual-career couples with children, and research on traditional couples who decide to become parents, and research on the general topic of women and mothering, there was no research on this particular dilemma faced by the young dual-career couple.

This book is written for and about dual-career women and couples who are dealing with the decision about whether or not they will have children. I have described the way in which the adult, female childbearing decision is affected by very early (infantile) developmental processes and outcomes, and have introduced a psychosocial childbearing decision model. I believe this information will be useful both to those working in an academic setting and to those working in a therapeutic setting, and will help develop an informed perspective among both professionals and clients who feel themselves to be "stuck" at this point.

CAROLE A. WILK, Ph.D.
Highland Park, Illinois

ACKNOWLEDGEMENT

I would like to thank all the dual-career women whose lives and childbearing decisions served as the basis for the present analysis. I'm grateful for their cooperation, courage and insight. Their willingness to participate in such an extensive exploration of such an intimate process helped me develop an understanding and appreciation of the complexities of their childbearing decision. Throughout this text I have disguised their identities. Their stories, however, are presented exactly as they emerged.

CONTENTS

INTRODUCTION

This book analyzes the childbearing decision process of a very special group of childless women. They are part of a rapidly growing, new middle class norm—the dual-career couple.

Dual-career couples depart from tradition in the sense that both members of the couple have a strong professional orientation, and derive a significant portion of their adult self-concept in reflection of their work. In trying to balance marriage and career, in trying to find a satisfying blend of independence/dependence, and autonomy/intimacy, the dual-career couple must deal with a complex and unprecedented series of issues and pressures. Perhaps the most difficult problem they face is the decision concerning whether or when they will have children.

My purpose here is twofold. First, I will present a theoretical model of the dual-career childbearing decision; then I will illustrate the utility of this model in a discussion of anticipated clinical issues and treatment strategies.

Although I will use the dual-career couple as a general frame of reference, and try to develop a genuine understanding of both the positive and negative aspects of this new family system, my primary focus is on the woman in the couple. Without minimizing the significance of the husband's contribution to the childbearing decision, and the impact on the relationship resulting from his dual-career position, [1] the fact is that dual-career women are evolving a new social role in establishing the wife/mother/career combination. (Husband/father/career is, of course, well established). We need to know more about this dual-career woman, to know her both psychologically and socially, to know her intrapsychic position, her development and current personality, her external, career life, her intimate, personal life, her other significant relationships, her goals, and her dreams. We need to deepen our knowledge of her in order to understand the childbearing dilemma.

We will see that for many women, given relative stability in their marriage and in their work, and in spite of the anticipated difficulties, the choice eventually becomes clear: children are seen as critical to a full and happy life and the major conflicts relate to timing and finances. [2] Other women, equally decisive, realize that they have no interest in becoming a mother, and view the addition of a child as an unwelcome complication to an otherwise satisfying lifestyle.

However, there is a third group of dual-career women, who seem unable to resolve the childbearing dilemma. Ambivalent about many aspects of their lives, these women are conflicted about whether or when they wish to have a child, conflicted about their wish and/or ability to balance the anticipated wife/mother/career combination, conflicted about how they will change, and how their relationships and lifestyle will change. In contrast to other dual-career women, this ambivalent group feels unable to reach a satisfying decision.

We will analyze the lives and childbearing intentions of these three distinct groups of childless dual-career women: those who have decided to have children sometime in the future; those who have decided not to have children; and those who are unable to come to a decision. Most of the analysis of clinical issues will concentrate on the latter group, the ambivalent women.

Unlike previous generations, in which most middle class, white women (such as those discussed here) considered motherhood and careers to be mutually exclusive simultaneous pursuits, it is well known that many women today question the idea that the "good" mother needs to be the exclusive caretaker (of children and spouse) and therefore must relinquish and/or postpone professional ambitions. Questions about the nature of the motherhood role and about its relationship to mature femininity and individuation, lead some women to wonder whether that role is one they wish to seek. In so challenging previous cultural assumptions about the inevitable nature of motherhood, these women differ radically from their predecessors.

Young women today are the first generation for whom the issue of whether or not to have children is clearly seen as a choice. A national opinion poll (1980) reported that although 94% of American women favored marriage, 82% said that, " . . . children are not an essential ingredient in a full and happy marriage . . . "[3] It seems that many women are breaking out of the pattern to "grow up, get married and have children." These women are saying yes to marriage and only maybe to children.[4]

Whereas traditionally the childless couple was labeled as somehow "deviant" and was presumed to be sterile (in most cases, the wife was "blamed" for somehow not being adequately female), today, voluntary childlessness is openly discussed and viewed by increasing numbers of couples as the appropriate decision.

A 1980 Census Report indicates that 11% of the total female population expects to remain childless as contrasted to a 1% expectation in 1955. College educated women (typical dual-career women) have an even higher level of intended childlessness, approximately 17%.[5] As we will see, however, alongside the apparent acceptance of voluntary childlessness, there is a cultural undercurrent—a psychosocial bias—which is unequivocally pronatalist. In light of the social acclaim that many women received for their career/achievement oriented, nontraditional, early adult decisions, this pronatalist bias is experienced by many young women as a confusing double message. As these women look for models against which to measure their plans for work, relationships, and children, they find that there are no social precedents for their experience. They report feeling cut off from any generational continuity, from any consensually validated "social time clock."[6]

The experience of their parents does not provide an acceptable guide. Parents are described, for the most part, in stereotypic, traditional roles—father in a career while mother raises the children.* Rejecting that prototype, they find themselves burdened, and at times overwhelmed by the pressure of living with the unknown consequences of a host of new adult decisions . . . about relationships, about personal ambition, and about children.

Although they do not see themselves as pioneers (as we will see, the people studied for this book deny that they have set out to change the social structure) nevertheless, as a group, their expectations, views, and perspectives are in many ways critically different from those of previous generations.

SUBJECTS

This book is based on an intensive study of a relatively small group of childless dual-career women.** The subjects were 24 white, middle class, childless, dual-career women, ranging in age from 27–35 (average age 30), who had been married an average of 4 years. (Two couples were living together in what they described as a permanent relationship.) All the subjects were employed full-time, and had been working in their career field an average of eight years. Without exception, all the women considered their work to be extremely important. All subjects had at least a B.A. degree; thirteen women had an M.A. or professional degree.

---

*Although most of the mothers of the women studied here worked outside the home at some time, daughter (and mother) discounted this work since it was not considered central to her self concept.

**It should be mentioned at this point, that in addition to the study of dual-career women at the childbearing decision stage, over the past five years, I have also worked with dual-career couples who are at other life stages. Therefore, from time to time I will refer to couples with young children, as well as to midlife dual-career couples.

(Please see Appendix A for further description of subjects.)

Prior to the study, the women indicated that they held one of the following positions in terms of the decision to have children:

A–*Ambivalent Group.* Women who describe themselves as uncertain about whether or not they intend to have children.

B–*Baby Group.* Women who have decided to have children sometime in the future.

C–*Childless Group.* Women who have decided to remain voluntarily childless.

Race

Minority women were included in two pilot studies which were conducted as preparation for the present research (1978 and 1979). However, the number of new elements that were introduced by virtue of the unique experiences of professional minority women, suggested that a much larger study was required in order to adequately address all these separate issues. Therefore, the present study was limited to white dual-career women.

Nature of Career Commitment

Dual-career women, according to the definition being used, formulate a portion of their self-concept out of a sense of their professional identity. Included in this professional self-image is the intention of pursuing a life-long career, regardless of childbearing intentions. Only those women whose career commitments were described in this way were selected as subjects.

Subjects' Fields of Work

- Advertising
- College Teaching
- Computer Science
- Elementary Education
- Health Systems Management
- Hospital Administration
- Library Science
- Music
- Personnel Management
- Planning
- Pre-School Education

- Psychology–Psychotherapy
- Sales
- Special Education
- Systems Analysis
- University Administration

Age

I selected a group of women who were presumed to be as close as possible to the biological age limit in terms of their ability to conceive and bear children. It was reasoned that, whereas younger dual-career women might very well deal with these same questions, the pressure for a decision was probably felt more intensely by those who were in the age 30 group. Therefore, only women between the ages of 27–35 were invited to participate in this study.

As the childbearing decision is seen more and more as a deliberate choice (the "whether" question), the issue of timing (the "when" question) becomes critical. There are reports in the press that focus either on the glories of "elderly primagravidas," or on the difficulties in over-30 conception.[7] An excellent study by Daniels and Weingarten, compares the experience of early and late timed parenthood.[8] These works have tended to focus on the relationship between the age of the mother and the development of the child. In contrast, the present study concentrates on the childbearing decision process itself, on the psychological environment of the woman who wants to reach a decision, and on women's feelings about the "right" age to have children.

Spouse

Although this analysis will focus on the female perspective, recognizing the significance of the spouse's contribution to the decision about whether or when to have children, I conducted a limited number of interviews with men in each of the three groups. The purpose was to explore the degree of congruence between the male and female perspectives, as well as to discover whether the interview strategy failed to uncover issues seen as critical by spouses. These data must be treated very cautiously, since the inquiry was so limited. However, they suggest some issues which warrant future study.

METHODOLOGY

A qualitative methodology was selected for this study of childbearing decisions, due to two factors: a) the lack of any base line data from which a theoretical model of the dual-career childbearing decision could be generated;* and b) the intimate nature of the subject matter. These factors influenced not only the kind of data required, but also the strategy of the search.

Questions of one's relationship to spouse and childbearing decisions, sexual identity, self-image, and relationship to parents, are of such an extremely sensitive nature, that a frank examination is impossible unless there is an atmosphere of trust. In my research I used a one-to-one extended interview schedule to establish the necessary rapport. By using an open-ended, flexible interview guide, appropriate to a qualitative design, it was also possible to achieve the necessary degree of spontaneity to allow each subject to explore and pursue the issues at hand according to his or her own unique timetable and ability to do so without undue stress.**

Instrumentation

The selection of instrumentation was governed by my wish to obtain both conscious and preconscious/unconscious material. I used three separate measures.

An interview series, which lasted approximately 6–8 hours, was selected to help develop a picture of the subjects' conscious view of themes and issues. To tap preconscious/unconscious material, the women were also given two projective measures; a sentence completion test, and a new TAT series, which was developed especially for this research. This new test, the MTAT © Midlife Thematic Apperception Test, consists of twelve pictures, all focused on issues relevant to adult female development.†[12]

By analyzing this combination of conscious and pre/unconscious material, I was able to develop a picture of how the subject perceived her life structure, the pressures of which she was aware, as well as some of the underlying dynamic and developmental factors of which she was probably unaware. As we will see below, efforts were made throughout the process of data analysis to compare the conscious and pre/unconscious material. For some, especially the women who were in the ambivalent group, it became apparent that there was a wide discrepancy between conscious reports and pre/unconscious contents. We will discuss these discrepancies in Part II.

---

*Although there has been recent work on the issue of voluntary childlessness[9] and on college student attitudes toward parenting,[10] there is no data on the dual-career couple in terms of childbearing decisions. General studies of dual-career issues may be found in several sources.[11]

**In those cases where the material provoked an extreme degree of stress, provisions were made for counseling and/or referral.

†MTAT, Copyright 1979 by Carole A. Wilk and Marcia H. Wilk. All rights reserved.

LIMITATIONS

The reader is cautioned that both the data collection and analysis may have been affected by the fact that I was the sole investigator. Furthermore, I am a member of a dual-career couple and the mother of three adult children. Recognizing the possibility of unintended bias, the protocols were also analyzed in a blind review procedure by a second person, who is unmarried and has no children.

As indicated at the outset of the Introduction, this analysis is focused on professional dual-career couples. Nonprofessional couples may or may not have similar issues as they try to make a decision about children. However, I am not able to offer any conclusions about the childbearing decision-making process faced by the millions of couples where both partners are employed full-time in nonprofessional occupations.

PLAN OF THE BOOK

In Part I, the reader will be introduced to the dual-career childbearing decision model. Focusing primarily on the dual-career woman, we'll analyze the elements of the childbearing decision as seen through her eyes and as told largely in her words. An analysis of the determinants of the childbearing decision will enable us to differentiate between women who plan to have children, those who intend to remain childless, and those who are ambivalent.

The questions raised by the ambivalent position will be explored fully in Part II. We will ask, Why are these women ambivalent? Why are they unable to reach a personally satisfying decision about children? What are they like intrapsychically? Are their relationships, careers, and personalities different from those who seem unconflicted in terms of childbearing decisions? In Part III these same questions will be reframed in terms of the clinical issues they suggest. It is assumed that the people in this group—that is, those who are the most conflicted about their childbearing decision—are the most apt to seek treatment. In order to develop effective treatment strategies, clinicians need to be aware of the unique dynamics of this very difficult decision.

In spite of the growing number of dual-career couples, and the apparent openmindedness regarding childbearing intentions, as I began my study, it became clear that very little was known about the specific elements of this particular childbearing decision. As a clinician looking for some theoretical understanding of the issues, I found that there were no base line data, and no framework to guide the treatment of couples dealing with this dilemma. Prior work on the decision to have children does not take into account the new issues related to the dual-career structure.

Two major elements will serve as our prism throughout. First, the psychosocial texture, which facilitates, influences, enables, thwarts, enhances, inhibits, and complicates the dual-career family system; and second, the individual psychological position of each dual-career participant.

We'll begin Part I by introducing a typical dual-career couple, Barbara and Jim. Barbara is 27 and Jim is 32. They have been married for four years.

REFERENCES

1. Davis, B. & Manning, L. "Men in Dual-Career Families: Career Aspirations and Parenting." In, Gilbert, L. (Chair) *Meeting Parental Role Responsibilities in a Changing Society: The Dual-career Family.* Symposium presented to the American Psychological Association Annual Convention, Los Angeles, CA. August, 1981.
2. Daniels, P. and Weingarten, K. *Sooner or Later: The Timing of Parenthood in Adult Lives.* New York: W. W. Norton, 1980.
3. Roper Organization. *Virginia Slims American Women's Opinion Poll.* 1980 Survey.
4. Campbell, A. "The American Way of Mating, Marriage Si, Children, Only Maybe." *Psychology Today*, May 1975, 37–44.
5. *Fertility of American Women.* June, 1980. U. S. Department of Commerce, Bureau of the Census, 1980.
   Women at Work, U. S. Department of Labor, Bureau of Labor Statistics, April, 1983.
6. Neugarten,B. (Ed) *Middle Age and Aging*, Chicago: University of Chicago Press, 1968.
7. *Time*, February 22, 1982; 52–59.
   N. Y. Times, Editorial, February 21, 1982.
8. Daniels and Weingarten. *Sooner or Later.*
9. Veevers, J. E. "Voluntary Childlessness: A Neglected Area of Family Study." *Family Coordinator*, April, 1973, 22, 199–205.
   Veevers, J. E. "The Moral Careers of Voluntary Childless Wives: Notes on the Defense of a Variant World View." *Family Coordinator*, October, 1975, 24, (4) 473–487.
   Veevers, J. E. "Life Style of Voluntary Childlessness." In Larson, L. (Ed) *The Canadian Family in Comparative Prospective.* Toronto: Prentice Hall, 1976.
   Houseknecht, S. "Reference Group Support for Voluntary Childlessness: Evidence for Conformity," *Journal of Marriage and the Family*, May, 1977, 285–292.
10. Gerson, M. J. "The Lure of Motherhood." *Journal of College Placement*, Spring, 1980, 29–31.
11. Rapoport, R. and R. *Dual-Career Families.* Harmondsworth, England: Penguin Books, 1971.
    Rapoport, R. and R. *Dual-Career Families Re-Examined.* New York: Harper and Row, 1976.
    Rapoport, R. and R., Bumstead, J. (Eds.) *Working Couples.* New York: Harper and Row, 1978.
    Johnson, C. L. and F. A. "Attitudes Towards Parenting in Dual-Career Families," *American Journal of Psychiatry,* April, 1978, 134 (4) 391–395.
    Safilios-Rothschild, C. and Dijkers, M. "Handling Unconventional Asymmetries." In Rapoport et al, (Eds) *Working Couples.* New York: Harper and Row, 1978.
    Hall, D. T. and F. S. *The Two-Career Couple.* Reading, MA: Addison Wesley, 1979.
12. Wilk, Carole A. "The Development and Preliminary Testing of the MTAT, Midlife Thematic Apperception Test." in Cytrynbaum, S. (Chair) *Midlife Development: A Research Agenda for the 1980s.* Symposium presented to the American Educational Research Association, Los Angeles, California, April, 1981.

Part I
Dual-Career
Childbearing
Decision Model

1
CHILDLESS DUAL-CAREER COUPLES

BARBARA AND JIM

I have chosen to launch this analysis with the story of Barbara and Jim, because their experience, the dynamics of their relationship, and their individual personality characteristics can be used to illustrate many of the issues that we must understand. Furthermore, Barbara and Jim are the only couple who were followed from the time they were ambivalent about children, until they had reached a satisfying childbearing decision.

As we previously stated, Barbara is 27 and Jim is 32. They have been married four years.

I first met with Barbara and Jim one evening about a year after they had moved into their condominium. It was a beautifully furnished apartment in meticulous order. When we talked on the phone, Barbara expressed a keen interest in participating in my study, saying that she and Jim had not reached a decision about having children. She greeted me with enthusiasm. Barbara is petite, dark haired, and was dressed in an elegantly casual jump suit. Jim, large and gangly, appeared somewhat reserved at the outset, but soon relaxed and contributed equally to the initial discussion. Barbara and Jim were interviewed together for the first session, then Barbara continued the discussion without Jim. As their story unfolded over the course of a series of meetings, I developed a picture of their complicated lifestyle, their history, their careers, and their thoughts about children.

Family Background

Barbara's parents, hardworking and ambitious, wanted the lives of their two daughters to be better than their own. Her mother, a high school graduate, worked as a bookkeeping clerk in the company where her father was employed as the accountant. Barbara said they often told her that during their courtship, they dreamed of having a family and becoming financially secure. When Barbara's sister Janet was born, her mother retired as a book-keeper, and became a full-time wife/mother/housekeeper. Barbara was born two years later.

Growing up, Barbara reports that Janet seemed to know how to please mother. She was pretty, liked to dress up, and was happy to learn how to sew and cook. On the other hand, Barbara says she was a tomboy—always a problem to her mother. She recalled a family Christmas picture, taken when she was about 5 years old, in which she and Janet are standing side by side, holding their Christmas toys. Janet was smiling, dressed in frills and party shoes, whereas Barbara, looking somewhat beligerent, posed in her old clothes and gym shoes. She said, "My Dad agreed with me—getting dressed up was silly and a waste of time. I remember when I was young he would help me work on puzzles and read books to me. I could always make him laugh, and as I grew up, we'd always joke together; but he had high goals for me. As for my mother, I just couldn't seem to figure out what I was supposed to do."

Barbara recalls, "We had some battles as I was growing up, but they are both very proud of me now. My mother can't quite understand why we don't have children yet, but she only mentions this now and then. Once in a while they interfere. Like when we were buying this condo. They came over in a panic one night and insisted that we couldn't afford it and would be getting in over our heads. I was really furious at that."

Jim's family background is quite different from Barbara's. He never knew his parents. After spending several years at an orphanage, he was raised by an aunt who had five children of her own. Thus, he says, his self-sufficiency was forced on him. A bright child, Jim did very well in school, managed to always have a part time job, and was able to get through college on a combination of scholarships and hard work. He recalls that his aunt was loving and approved of him, and seemed content with whatever he wanted to do.

Barbara and Jim reported that when they first met, they were attracted to each other because they recognized some of their own independence and self-confidence in the other. Jim, not having a family of his own, was more anxious to marry than Barbara, who first wanted to get established in her career. Before they were married they talked about whether or not they wanted children. Jim recalls, "Well, we both said, it's really Barbara's life that would change the most . . . so we just sort of put that aside. We knew it was important, but not the most important thing for us. What was probably most important was that we both knew what we wanted to do professionally and we knew we were willing to work hard to get it. We had a lot of respect for each other's professional ambitions. I think now, it was really lucky that we aren't in the same field though. We're both too competitive!''

Careers and Lifestyle

Barbara, employed full-time as a speech pathologist, attends an evening MBA program specializing in hospital administration. She is hoping her clinical experience will help her administrative career. Jim has just completed law school. Following his life-long pattern, he has been working full-time and going to school evenings. He was recently hired by a major Chicago law firm and he is very happy with his job. They are both heavily invested in their career development, are enthusiastic about their work, and thrive on the "pressure cooker environment."

Traditional marriage patterns assumed a male dominance in terms of professional achievement, and a female reflected identity, mostly derived from "vicarious achievement"[1] in terms of the husband's socioeconomic position (that is, she achieved status and recognition through her relationships, rather than as an individual, e.g., as "the V. P.'s wife" or "the mother of that precocious child"). Barbara and Jim, however, have started marriage with a different set of assumptions. For example: Barbara and Jim have an almost equal record of individual achievements and successes as measured by academic rewards and significant professional entry positions. Both assume they will continue this path. Both look to their marriage for a permanent, intimate relationship, as well as for enhancement of their individuation and for support of their growing, independent identity.

Barbara and Jim are bright, vigorous, and happy with their marriage and their complicated life. They see marriage as a vehicle to support their mutual and individual development. They believe that they have a better chance to achieve professional goals, now that they have "settled" the search for a relationship. "We've had a struggle, though," said Barbara, "and we still have some very rough times . . . because I care more about how this place looks than Jim does." She hesitated a moment. "It's motivated by the fear that my mother might drop in, I guess. But I resent being the only one who cleans. We finally realized that we just have to be able to talk about it, rather than expect that the other one can guess. Before we figured that out, I would walk around here grumbling about how overworked I was. Now Jim and I are both overworked," she added with a laugh. "We used to argue about money all the time. I think that's pretty much settled now, though, since we both have gotten a couple of raises. Another thing we had to work out was what to do about Jim's offer from a really good firm in

New York. I'm so involved here, in my job and at school, that I just couldn't see moving right now. But we worried about that for a long time. I guess I still feel insecure about that . . . whether he feels any resentment toward me . . . I know the question of moving will come up again, though . . . "

As was obvious from their surroundings, Barbara and Jim have grown accustomed to a living standard based on two good incomes. They are able to afford the condominium, to dine out frequently, to take regular vacations, and even to get away for weekends when their work permits.

"Of course," said Jim, "if we were to start a family, we'd probably have to do so by the time Barbara is about 30. Then everything would change." (Their target of age 30 reflects a trend among young, dual-career couples who postpone the birth of the first child until the wife is about 30 years old.[2]).

The traditional assumption, even for highly educated, professional women, was that when the first child was born, the mother would stop working, stay home, and raise the baby, at least through the infancy stage.[3] However, Barbara and Jim are questioning many traditional assumptions, beginning with the assumption that they will have children. They are aware that the option not to have children is becoming more acceptable; that a growing number of other dual-career couples have made the decision to remain childless. (According to the U.S. Census Bureau, the number of couples planning voluntary childlessness increased from 1% in 1955 to 11% in 1980.)[4]

Barbara and Jim ask themselves, Do we want to alter the lifestyle we've created by having children? Can we afford to live on one income? What would we be missing if we decided not to have children? On the other hand, if we do have kids, what kinds of major marriage and career shifts will result, and can we handle the strain on each of us and on the relationship?

For Barbara and Jim there is never any question about whether she'd go back to work . . . it is a question of when and under what conditions. A major worry is about child care—could they find someone they could trust? Not knowing what to believe in terms of theories of early infant development, they wonder what would happen to the baby's development if Barbara went right back to work within a few months after the baby's birth. On the other hand, if she "gives up" her work for a longer period of time, will she resent the baby because of that? What would that resentment do to the baby's super-sensitive antennae? Barbara has some friends who tell her that after their baby was born, they couldn't bear to leave the baby every day. If she does not go back to work for example, for six months or a year, what would happen to her career?

Barbara is quite aware of the reality that her employer will probably not wait an open-ended period of time until she feels her primary early mothering tasks are completed. There is no such thing as one extra wide step on the career ladder, labeled "FOR NEW MOTHERS." In fact, she knows that once she drops out for a substantial length of time, she will have a very tough time ever rising to the top—no matter how competent she is, or how enlightened the organization is.[5] The conventional career expectation is built on the assumption that in order to pursue a serious career, one must be single minded about that work.

Barbara and Jim have each launched what looks like a conventional career track, and have already started to define her or his self-concept through a professional identity. They recognize that conventional career expectations are based on the ideal of a one-career marriage . . . traditionally a male career enhanced by a female support system.[6]

As all dual-career couples do, Barbara and Jim face problems associated with trying to pursue a conventional career without a backup support system. However, the issues become vastly more complicated, especially for Barbara, as she starts to consider whether this fledgling conventional career and professional identity can be maintained along with a maternal identity. Barbara has doubts—deep and distressing doubts—about her ability, or her desire to be a mother; to give totally of herself to another. Even as she (hesitatingly) expressed these thoughts, she wondered whether that made her seem strange and different from "normal" women. Searching for reassurance, she finds that some of her friends seem similarly unsure. She's certain about one thing—she does not want to follow her mother's example. She says, "My mother really was smart and had a lot to offer. But she didn't know how to use her capacities, so she concentrated too much on us. The results, for me anyway, weren't all that great. I can't see myself giving up my goals, or having just family goals, the way she did. It wouldn't be good for me," or, she added, "for the child."

Barbara acknowledges that her career identity (which was already well established by the time she started to be serious about her childbearing decision) presumes a 100% commitment. Even if she can arrange less than 100% of the child care responsibility, Barbara feels that a 100% emotional investment is critical. She knows many women who expect themselves to manage the 200% position. The superwoman syndrome and its pitfalls are well known. But which part of that 200% can she change? And how will she react to that change? What will it do to her self image and to their relationship?

Since Barbara and Jim's dilemma is shared by so many contemporary childless dual-career couples, we can use their experience to illustrate some general, dual-career themes, which I, as well as other researchers, have observed. In order to position Barbara and Jim's struggle within the appropriate socio-historical context, we need to go back for a moment, and consider how the dual-career family system developed.

DEVELOPMENT OF THE DUAL-CAREER SYSTEM

In the popular press, dual-career couples are often portrayed as attractive, stylish, superpeople, who manage to combine a heroic professional life with an intensely satisfying marital relationship. They have time to spend with their families, enjoy a wide circle of friends, and of course, play tennis and jog regularly! Another version (equally inaccurate) describes the dual-career couple as perpetually worn out and irritable, distracted from each other by the demands of their work, competing in every aspect of their lives, unhappy, and about to give up on marriage. Of course, neither image gives us a picture of the way most dual-career couples live. Given the growing number of couples like Barbara and Jim, we need to have a more accurate view of what they are like, both as individuals and as a couple; of the nature of their relationship; and of the pressures and pleasures they ascribe to the dual-career modality.

The dual-career phenomenon is a system made possible (perhaps inevitable) by the power of the women's revolution, combined with economic pressures. Over the course of relatively a few years this upheaval has precipitated major social changes which have become so much a part of our lives that it's easy to overlook their significance and impact. The most visible sign of this revolution is the rapid increase in the number of married women employed outside the home. According to the U.S. Dept. of Labor, by 1982 more than 66% of all U.S. families had more than one income. Thus, the dual-career couple, although unique in its emphasis on equal professional identity, is in fact, a small percentage of a much larger social movement.

The women's revolution has had a critical impact on our attitude toward the relationship between work and family life. Consider the following: In 1982, 59% of the women in the U.S. with children under 18 were in the labor force; the prediction is that by the end of the eighty's, more than 70% of this group will be working outside the home. The biggest single group of women workers is made up of married women with young children. Moreover, 50% of all mothers with preschool children were employed in 1982 as compared to 28% as recently as 1970.[7]

The rigid separation of work and family life is considered a by-product of the industrial revolution and the emergence of the Protestant work ethic. It was both cost effective and morally justified to separate domestic and commercial enterprises. Though this separation notion has been labeled as more a myth than a reality by sociologists[8] who point to the considerable overlapping of functions that has always existed, for our purposes (i.e., focusing on the psychological implication of the idealized if not actual separation) the consequences of this split are significant.

For the middle class, or those who aspired to be middle class, this separation permitted the female to be idealized and sentimentalized. Bound to the home by what was seen as her predominantly nurturant, supportive, expressive, passive, inwardly creative *nature*, she was educated and socialized within this model. This, too served to separate, distance, and remove the female from the male world, and thus relieve anxieties based on fears of female power.[9] Competition, aggression, drive, and externalized action were considered male characteristics. Sex-stereotyped roles, which segregated and dictated adult behaviors, were internalized as "natural." However, the women's revolution has caused these "natural" labels to be questioned and re-evaluated. The climate created by this revolution has legitimized the challenge to previously accepted social "truths" regarding the inevitable nature of sexually circumscribed roles. Today, both men and women are encouraged (some say pressured) to re-examine gender determined, individual developmental timetables. However, this re-examination often triggers conflicting emotions in both men and women.

Thus, we have evolved a set of challenges to the notion that independence and external achievement are male characteristics that are unavailable to females, and that interdependence and preoccupation with nurturance and family are female characteristics that are unavailable to males.

Given our knowledge of individual psychological development, we know that each person must deal with these challenges in reflection of his or her early intrapsychic processes and previously internalized social learning. For some, contemporary challenges are experienced as personally empowering opportunities; for others, they feel overwhelmingly stressful. To see how these conflicting social and intrapsychic messages impact on the dual-career childbearing decision we now return to Barbara and Jim to further analyze their dilemma. First, we'll discuss some issues related to family background and general family expectations; then we will look at the complex dual-career lifestyle; and, finally some areas of conflict and resolution and some dual-career success stories.

Family Background

Mother. The fact that Barbara's mother had worked as a bookkeeping clerk before Janet was born and did not return to nonfamily work, had a great influence on Barbara's adult career decisions. Her determination not to follow her mother's example, reflects both her own wish as well as what she believes to be her mother's point of view.

First, feeling dissatisfied with her relationship to mother, Barbara suggests that she would have been better off had her mother been occupied with something besides the family. In this sentence, we should probably read "sister" for family. For Barbara, we recall, revealed overtones of jealousy and competition for mother's love. This pattern was repeated in every case I studied where the dual-career woman had an older sister. That is, the older sister's primary identification was with the mother, and the dual-career subject's primary identification, as we will see, was with the father.

Second, Barbara suggests that mother herself was dissatisfied with her life. By the time her mother was 30, the two children were in school. In Barbara's view, her mother was then at a loss—unable to refocus beyond the family, and unable to utilize her energies and intelligence. Barbara's reaction seems to confirm some recent research. It has been reported that having a working mother, whether it is the wife's or the husband's mother, is related to the dual-career woman's decision to have a career.[10] Studies of professional women found that almost half of the mothers of dual-career women had extensive work histories.[11] Even if not working themselves, the mothers of dual-career women generally endorsed the idea of women with children working outside the home.[12]

In the present study, more than half the mothers worked outside the home. Interestingly, regardless of whether they had worked outside the home or not, the only mothers who did not support a daughter's intention to combine work and children were Group B mothers, thus indicating some confirmation of traditional stereotypic expectations, and perhaps some residual conflict over their own maternal functioning, or their feelings about having "sacrificed" their career goals.

The women in this study are the daughters of middle-class or would-be middle-class women. Raised in a climate that endorsed total and exclusive maternal investment in child development, we must keep in mind that, although many mothers worked outside the home, the value ascribed to this work reflected the traditional cultural position—that is, the unspoken assumption was that women who could do so, would, of course, elect not to work. Only in a few cases, which will be illustrated below, did the mother attach enough importance to her external orientation so as to suggest to the daughter that a woman's exclusive professional identity was acceptable.

In spite of some tenacious myths that refer to the damaging effects of maternal employment, research has not found a correlation between working mothers and the incidence of emotional and/or behavioral problems in their children. That is, problems are found as often in children of non-working mothers as they are in children of working mothers.[13] As has been said so often, the nature and quality of the maternal-child interaction and the home environment in general, are more likely to have an impact on childhood outcomes than the number of hours that mother is home. Therefore, we can expect that dual-career mothers, who are satisfied with their lives, will see their daughters growing up with the belief that wife/mother/ career is possible. Bardwick,[14] noting that although today's midlife daughters do not look to their mothers as role models, predicted that because of the generalized social climate of women's career acceptance, today's young dual-career mothers and their daughters will develop a different set of expectations.

Father. Let's now consider some elements of Barbara's identification with father. Her father read to her, did puzzles with her, supported her verbal development, and rewarded her for her accomplishments with his added attention. Furthermore, by his example—that is, by the fact that he regularly came in and out of the home environment without loss of love or family role—he became an ego resource and a safe behavior model.[15]

In the literature it has been reported that the father's attitude toward his daughter and his treatment of her as a child have important bearing on her later decisions about work and family. We will expand on this idea below. Fathers of dual-career women relate to their daughters in predominantly verbal ways, (e.g., by rewarding verbal behavior), as well as by appreciating their femininity.[16] The father-daughter relationship, and the ego-strength provided by the father, enabled the daughter to feel safe in sacrificing some of her early dependency.[17]

Some authors have reported that dual-career fathers pressured their daughters into behaving as if they were boys. "He treated me as if I were a boy . . . ," said one dual-career woman, in reference to achievement expectations.[18] As we will see, this paternal expectation sets up contrary outcomes. Some dual-career women, feeling support for their achievement motivation, believe that their combination of personal and professional goals will gain their father's (later, husband's) approval.[19] Others react to the affirmation of achievement, externalization, competition, and aggression—the stereotypic masculine characteristics—as if it implies a rejection of the feminine aspects of themselves.

Spouse's Attitude

The dual-career husband's active and vigorous support of the dual-career philosophy, and his positive attitude toward his wife's career are critical for a successful dual-career marital system.[20]

In a longitudinal analysis of the labor market experiences of women, it was reported that "Of all the marital and family characteristics that have been investigated, the one that bears the most pronounced relationship with wives' career status is the respondents' perception of her husband's attitude toward her working."[21]

Some of the research on the family background of dual-career men gives us a clue as to the origins of this masculine disposition. Dual-career husbands are frequently described as having had a warm relationship with their mother[22] thus enabling them to see women as nonfearful, valuable, and independent.

Jim, described above, grew up confident of his aunt's approval. He knew that whatever he did would be acceptable to her. Thus we assume he was able to perceive women as nonthreatening, and could deal with Barbara's professional ambition in a nondefensive way.

All the husbands in the present study actively supported their wives' career ambitions. Beyond the obvious financial benefits, this attitude seemed to reflect a basic endorsement of the value of her professional work.[23] Identification of this attitude is not meant to imply, however, the absence of any home/career conflict; but rather, that *without* a basic attitude of encouragement and respect for the woman's achievement goals, realization of a stable, dual-career structure would be impossible.

It is a bit soon to know how men will respond to the long range effects of their wives' lifetime employment.[24] However, it has been found that dual-career husbands, more than their traditional counterparts, will try to adapt to their wives' schedules and career demands.[25]

In a few cases in the present study, the wives' career requirements took precedence over the husbands'. We saw that Barbara's wish to remain in her present career/graduate school program influenced Jim's decision not to accept a new job in New York. In two other cases, the husband, dissatisfied with a teaching career, wanted to look for a job change, in a new geographical location, However, in both cases, the wife's satisfaction with her career was so strong, that they decided they would not move (at least for the time being). In a few cases, the woman's income added a degree of security which enabled the husband to take greater career risks.[26] Other men, however, felt somewhat threatened by their spouse's higher earning power and status.[27] It comes as no surprise to find that issues related to income disparity often served to mask an underlying power struggle. (We'll return to this issue in Chapter 3.) However, there seems to be no support for the idea that a successful career woman is an automatic threat to the spouse's self image or to the establishment of a dual-career balance. Once again, it is not her professional status or income per se, which seems to be the critical factor, but rather the underlying meaning and value attributed by both partners to her work. For Barbara and Jim, his supportive attitude toward her career was clearly evident even before their marriage. They said it was simple—Barbara's work was as important as Jim's.

Over the course of their four-year history, Barbara and Jim alternated in terms of who was holding the dominant income producing responsibility and who took the personal/educational role. Jim's decision to enter law school meant not only that they would have the additional educational costs, but that he would have to cut down somewhat on his working hours. During some of this period, Barbara was the primary wage earner. As Jim entered his third year of law school, he was able to increase his work hours and salary, at which time Barbara went back to school for her MBA. Thus, they more or less "took turns"' in pursuit of career goals, as well as in the major responsibility for family support. (Similar patterns of successive career emphasis have been noted by others.[28]) Without this joint willingness to support the other's goals, the dual-career system could not be maintained.

Lifestyle

In describing the lifestyle of the dual-career couple, we must keep in mind the significance they attribute to their professional orientation and their high emotional investment in their work. As we will see, the pull between concentration on work versus concentration on spouse was often experienced as a source of conflict. Many couples talked about difficult pressure periods when work seemed to take all of one spouse's available energy and the other was left feeling like an outsider, alienated, and ignored.

As we try to focus on the lifestyles of these childless, dual-career individuals, we need to keep in mind some basic descriptors. The women studied were about 30 years old; all had at least a bachelor's degree; more than half had an advanced degree; they had been married about four years; and they'd been working professionally for about eight years. Therefore, we know that before their relationship was established, they already had a fairly good start in their respective fields. Without exception, they worked hard, with an intensity that reflected their total commitment. As a result, they had progressed rapidly and were well beyond the entry level in terms of responsibility and salary. More critically, perhaps, they knew they could support themselves. Also important in terms of their ability to establish an interdependent relationship, those studied all had quite a bit of experience living apart from their original families. All had lived independently for many years.* As Barbara and Jim told me, when they first met they admired in each other what they recognized as their own need for independence and high achievement.

---

*Three women had been previously married.

When the people in this study talked about the quality of their personal lives, what seemed uppermost in their minds was that they felt responsible only to their spouse. And they prized that exclusive concentration. They valued their freedom and spontaneity. They could decide to meet after work and not come home; they could lazy around all weekend if they so chose; they could take an extra assignment that included some heavy travel; they could take off for a weekend; sometimes they could focus on each other without distraction. Other times, work was an acceptable distraction which helped diffuse conflicts between them. If they were so inclined, they could follow independent interests; or they could spend every free moment together. Some women talked about their ability to be dependent, to let down their superwoman image, and to welcome the opportunity to let the other person take care of them.[29]

Although many of the couples said, for example, " . . . we're not ready for a decision yet . . . ," and perhaps succeeded in putting the subject off for a few years, nevertheless, the question of whether or when to have a child was always in the background, needing to be addressed. Until a childbearing decision was reached, this issue remained pervasive, affecting the psychological climate of their lives as well as concrete career and lifestyle decisions.

Day to Day Living.   Given their independence, high achievement needs, and professional commitment, how do these couples work out the day to day events—the mundane elements that make up such a large part of our lives? As I considered this question, one thing became quite clear. This group is really not interested in becoming pioneers.[30] Though they may very well be critical of some aspects of traditional marriage, they have not set out to change the world. They see themselves doing what they feel is appropriate for them, for their relationship, and for their individual careers. For example, although they have more money than their parents did at their age and do not automatically agree that children and a home in the suburbs are the only acceptable goals in life, in many ways they appear to be very much like their parents. For instance, I found that some couples work constantly—others don't; some (like Barbara and Jim) live in elegant surroundings—others seemed rather messy; some couples have money in the bank—others don't; some want to spend free time with extended families—others resent time spent with families; some plan every minute of free time—others want to be spontaneous; some know how to play—others don't; some know how to defuse potential explosions in their relationship—others don't. In other words, dual-career couples are not different than traditional couples in many basic ways. The variety is infinite, and any attempt to lump dual-career couples into a neat sociological and psychological group, or to describe a typical dual-career lifestyle is futile. However, in terms of the value attributed to the woman's career, these couples are strikingly different from traditional couples; and these differences affect many other aspects of their lives. For example, if the dual-career wife's work is considered as important as her husband's, and equal time and energy are committed to that work, then what about the ordinary things (e.g. sewing on a missing button, picking up the cleaning, buying a mother's day present, grocery shopping, staying home when the new furniture is delivered, paying the bills, taking the car in to be repaired, etc.)? Interestingly, the resolution of these everyday questions, often provided a clue to larger issues of marital satisfaction.[31]

Areas of Conflict.   As with other couples, this family must work out issues involving power and control, competition, relationships to others, (family and nonfamily), and management of money and chores. Because they are also caught up in the pursuit of their individual professional goals, they must also work out the balance between demands of home vs. career.

Domestic Responsibilities.   Out of the 24 subjects in this study, 18 were satisfied with the way household chores were shared, and 6 reported that they were quite dissatisfied. Those who were satisfied said that it had taken a conscious effort on the part of both partners to arrive at a suitable balance. You will remember that Barbara described her unhappiness with Jim's attitude toward housekeeping as one of their major stress points.

A recent book by D & F Hall[32] discussing stress and the two career family, identified four types of dual-career relationships. These types are: 1) *Accommodaters*—the group most like the traditional marriage, where one partner is high in career involvement and low in home involvement, and the other is high in home involvement and low in career involvement; 2) *Adversaries*—the most stressful types—are both high in career involvement and low in home involvement, although they value home order; 3) *Allies*—experience little conflict, since both are either high or low in work and family; and 4) *Acrobats*—both high in all roles (these are the supercouples, the model for everyone else!) Thinking about what we know of Barbara and Jim, we might label them Adversaries, since both have high career involvement, though only Barbara values home order.

Though all the couples I met had started marriage with a sincere intention to split the domestic chores, the lack of a traditional back up person, proved a strain that often resulted in the eruption of some unconsiously held traditional expectations. Many dual-career studies, including this one, have found that regardless of the female's level of career achievement, or demands of time, travel etc., even the most nontraditional couples revert back to a stereotypic separation of domestic roles and tasks once they are home together.*[33]

Many women who were dissatisfied with the way domestic chores were shared, told me that before they were married their spouse seemed to have no problem doing the laundry, the cooking, etc.; he had been accustomed to doing these things in his own apartment. But soon after they were married, they both fell into a more traditional distribution of routine jobs; she feeling responsible for cleaning, shopping, cooking, and laundry, and he for home maintenance, keeping the car in shape, etc.

Several subjects resented what they described as a disproportionate share of work at home, and were really angry that somehow their plan to share the work had gotten lost. For example, Marlis (A)**said, " . . . it became the great housework issue . . . from the day we were married . . . he assumed that all the life support activities were mine . . . " Though they may have been angry at themselves for participating in such a system, it became evident, in both subtle and obvious ways, that whether or not they actually did more domestic work, women *felt* responsible for the way their home appeared. Oddly enough, even though many couples could afford to do so, only 2 of the 24 couples employed domestic help. Some said that they couldn't find the right person, others didn't want to spend the money.

Finances.   With two salaries, dual-career couples have a relatively high combined income. Yet many reported that financial issues were the greatest source of conflict between them.

Like most people, their basic expenses had grown with their income. For Barbara and Jim, it was the condominium; for others an expensive apartment; in a few cases, investment in a house. They took several breaks a year, including at least one long and relatively luxurious vacation. They both needed an appropriate professional wardrobe; they needed to furnish their home; and they needed funds for leisure activities and entertainment. They felt they needed all their income and often argued about the ways to use discretionary funds. (For example, Jim was an opera buff, and wanted to keep up their opera series; Barbara found it too extravagant.)

Career Pressure.   In their climb up the career ladder, dual-career individuals deal with the same career issues as any young, highly motivated employee. However, one particularly stressful issue arises from a promotion offer which requires relocation to another city. For most, the assumption

---

*In another study of couples with children this was really easy to see. She felt that the responsibility for child care arrangements was hers.

**Throughout the text, subjects will be described by name as well as according to their childbearing decision, i.e., A = Ambivalent Group, B = Baby Group, C = Childless Group.

was that only one partner would move, especially for a trial period. The special problems of the commuting dual-career couple—they each live in different cities during the work week and see each other only on weekends—has been described frequently.[34] One couple in the present study (they were both musicians) had seriously contemplated such a commuting schedule. However, Alice (C) said, "After much soul searching I decided not to take the offer with the X Symphony Orchestra. It would have been the end of our relationship. We tried that for a few months three years ago, and it doesn't work for us. We need to be able to come home and share the things that have happened . . . and we need that every day. Too much goes unsaid otherwise and pressures mount up. We tried the weekend reunions and the reunions were great, but it was all the unsaid things and feelings that added a tremendous amount of tension . . . "

One dual-career expert, in discussing the pressures of career mobility: " . . . the best strategy for the corporation is to assist the couple . . . by maintaining flexible career development tracks and having spouse involvement in career planning."[35]

Given the number of young professional couples, it would seem that the organizations in which they are employed would be sensitive to some of their special problems. However, this corporate sensitivity is not generally evident. In fact, the attitudes of managers were found to be a significant barrier to women who want to balance careers and motherhood. In a study of a thousand managers, a question related to promotions and leaves of absence was given to subjects.[36] Half of the group received a leave of absence request from a "Ruth B"; the other half, from a "Ralph B." Even when "Ralph" said, " . . . my first duty is to my family . . . ," they were offered a leave or a promotion; when the women said this, they received no offers.

Organization theorists[37] have noted that rewards regarded as significant by employees have shifted from exclusive focus on extrinsic rewards, to a multi-dimensional focus that includes intrinsic rewards such as geographic location, family life-style, and overall life-structure. It seems though, according to the people I have observed, that the majority of organizations continue to structure themselves around traditional rewards and traditional career development concepts. Dual-career couples run into problems with the traditional system as they try to formulate new family/work patterns.

Success Styles

Having mentioned some issues related to dual-career stress, it would be unfortunate if these comments left you with a predominantly negative impression. In spite of the complexities, pressures, risks, and anxieties inherent in creating this new adult norm, the general evaluation made by those engaged in the dual-career process is well expressed by one of the dual-career subjects. She said, " . . . it's tough, but, if you can make it, it sure is worth it!" Again and again I was told that the payoffs more than balanced the problems.

Let me outline some characteristics of successful dual-career couples. By successful, I refer to those couples who believe that they have achieved a satisfying balance between their individual career objectives and their relationships to each other and to others. The most fortunate couples were those for whom the dual-career relationship served, in a synergistic fashion, to enhance opportunities for personal growth and individuation. Even for these people, though, it was not without a deliberate effort. Good health—physical and emotional—seems to be critical to success.

Sense of Limitations.   The successful couples have come a long way from what may have been an initial omnipotent sense of wanting everything. There now seems to be a recognition of limitations and of compromises. One woman expressed this in responding to a question of how they made the dual-career marriage work: "You have to be an over-achiever, highly motivated, but not a super-achiever. Because the super-achiever would probably make sacrifices in the relationship, and that would upset the balance. The super-achiever would not have the flexibility required to combine several goals at once; and be able to bend from time to time—that's what makes it work."

Barbara (A) said, "You can't do it all. You have to sacrifice. You have to make choices. I have missed a lot along the way, like really being frivolous with my time. I could never do that. But it was a conscious choice."

Holly (B) summarized the recognition of limitations. She said, " . . . It's been a combination of internal pressure plus the circumstances that on the one hand made things possible and on the other made things impossible; opened up here and closed off there . . . not a feeling of crusading, but more a feeling of doing what I had to do, and delighted that I was able . . . From back there when I found out that I could earn a living . . . the feeling has been one of wider possibilities and freeing up of confidence and strength in me that made whatever riskiness there was, well worth it . . . it felt good. At this point in my life . . . to begin to be in harmony with limitations . . . to accept limitations . . . to recognize when they're there, finally, but not too soon. To believe in the possibility of accomplishment and the possibility of limitations."

Careful Use of Time.   Given the expected level of both logistical and emotional overload, all our couples were conscious of how they used their time. All couples emphasized that there was never enough time—not for each other, for their extended family, or for leisure or for friends; so the allocation of nonwork time was of critical importance. The high success couples had reached an agreement on priorities and organization. For most couples the sense of organization was very tight. Karen (C) said, "The only way we can make this happen is because we share a sense of what's important, and we're organized around this sense of what has to come first."

Flexibility.   Though it may seem contradictory, along with a characteristically efficient use of time, our subjects also saw the importance of flexibility. Using an informal measure of flexibility, I found that all subjects who reported a high level of satisfaction with their lives, work, and spouse, described themselves as "flexible" or "very flexible." These people regarded their flexibility as critical to their ability to manage. It will be seen below, that flexibility was also found to be related to the childbearing decision.

Ability to Communicate.   Without exception, all success couples value a good system of communication and a conscious pattern of honest talk, which was established at the very beginning of their relationship. Jane's (A) comment is typical: "I realized that open communication is the only way I can survive. I think a lot of people feel that if someone loves me, they'll know . . . If you love me, you'll know why I'm mad . . . you'll know what's upsetting me. Now my position is . . . you can't get into another person's head . . . know what they went through during the day. It has nothing to do with love . . . that's a communication need . . . we have to keep talking . . . otherwise it starts to show up in your behavior and you misread what it is . . . "
Subjects said that they found they had to take time to talk out everything, everyday domestic things as well as the deeper issues related to conscious and unconscious responses to work and/or family problems. One midlife dual-career woman, who was part of a separate study, described the formalization of this on-going dialogue. She said in spite of their difficulties, they were both committed to trying to make their dual-career marriage last: "We renegotiated our marriage. My going back to school necessitated some changes . . . my husband and I sat down one Sunday and we renegotiated everything . . . we went through every single thing that needed to be done, even including affection and support . . . and we developed a contract . . . it was about five pages long . . . as we signed it . . . " For most dual-career couples, though, communication is spontaneous and constant. For example, Julie (B) said, "We confront issues all the time and try not to deny even what hurts. For instance, by talking he helped me reduce the guilt

level for not being able to spend as much time with him and with my mother, who is recently widowed, as I'd like . . . what was happening was that everyone was telling me what I was 'supposed' to do, and I guess I must have unconsciously agreed with them. I was beginning to feel awful, and especially to doubt myself. But when we talk, it helps me get clear on what's happening and what we are about."

Relationship First. Although, as indicated from the outset, all of our subjects are highly motivated to achieve independent career success, when pressed to consider priorities, the general response was that the relationship must come first; and if it is sufficiently empathic, then sensitivity to each other's career requirements will naturally emerge. Said Joyce (B), "I would not sacrifice a relationship for a career, because I think in some ways, relationships are harder to come by . . . There has to be an awareness in both partners that each has respect for the other and for what they do. Independence and basic security that when one partner spends less time with the family . . . it does not mean the family has become less important."

Many couples talked about their respect for each other. Julie (B), said, " . . . each of us has so many resources . . . though we spend a lot of time together, we have really strong other lives. We're aware that sometimes the other life seems to run away with us, but we get through these times because we respect each other." Out of this sense of respect for each other, emerges the joint perspective, which Rapoport referred to in some of the very earliest dual-career studies.[38] The successful dual-career couples reported that the most critical element in their lives was this sense of mutuality and the development of a joint perspective. As we will see throughout this analysis, interdependence—the capacitiy to be both dependent and independent—is characteristic of those who are satisfied with their dual-career system.

In reviewing the elements that are common to the successful dual-career couples in the present study, we find that although each member of the couple is highly achievement oriented, in terms of personal goals, they are able to recognize their limitations and make sacrifices in the service of their relationship; they are generally sensitive to the need to structure time; they see their ability to be flexible as a highly significant element in their system; they follow life long patterns of open communication with each other; and they give top priority to their relationship to each other.

At this point, you have developed a general picture of the complicated and challenging dual-career lifestyle. Barbara and Jim can be thought of as a representative dual-career couple, whose nontraditional career, family, and lifestyle expectations are beginning to emerge as a new middle class standard, and whose questions raise far-reaching psychological, social, and political questions. As we proceed, we will come back to Barbara and Jim, and follow them as they finally arrive at a childbearing decision.

Now we turn our attention away from the couple, and focus instead on the individual dual-career woman. We want to know as much as we can about her—her personality, her dreams, her goals, and her ambitions. In order to understand her childbearing decision, we need to know who she is, what she cares about, and what matters to her.

REFERENCES

1. Lipman-Bluman, J. "How Ideology Shapes Women's Lives." *Scientific America.* 1972, 226 (1) 34–42.
2. Rapoport, R., and R. *Dual-Career Families.* Harmondsworth, England: Penguin Books, 1971.
   Hoffman L., and Nye, I., (eds.) *Working Mothers.* San Francisco: Jossey-Bass, 1974.
   Hall, D. T., and F. S. *The Two-Career Couple.* Reading, MA: Addison-Wesley, 1979.
   Daniels, P., and Weingarten, K. *Sooner or Later: The Timing of Parenthood in Adult Lives.* New York: W. W. Norton, 1980.
3. Epstein, C. *Women's Place.* Berkeley, CA: University of California Press, 1970.
4. U.S. Census, Department of Labor, Bureau of Labor Statistics, 1981, 1983.
5. Rapoport, *Dual Career Families.*
   Kanter, R. M. *Work and Family in the U.S.* New York: Russell Sage Foundation, 1977.
6. Ibid.
7. Department of Labor, Bureau of Labor Statistics, February, 1981, October, 1982.
8. Kanter, R. M. *Men and Women of the Corporation.* New York: Basic Books, 1977.
   Bernard, J. *Women, Wives and Mothers: Values and Options.* Chicago, IL: Aldine Press, 1975.
9. Lerner, H. "Early Origins of Envy and Devaluation of Women." *Bulletin of the Menninger Clinic.* November, 1974, 38, 538.
10. Holmstrom, L. *The Two Career Family.* Cambridge: Schenkman Publishing Co., 1972. p. 202.
    Rapoport, *Dual-Career Families.*
11. Holmstrom, *The Two Career Family.*
12. Hopkins, J. "A Comparison of Wives of Dual-Career and Single-Career Families." *Dissertation Abstracts International.* 1977, 38, (2) Section A.
13. Kagan, J. "Day Care Given a Clean Bill of Health." *American Psychological Association Monitor.* April, 1976, 4.
14. Bardwick, J. *In Transition.* New York: Holt, Rinehart & Winston, 1979.
15. Lamb, Michael E., ed. *The Role of the Father in Child Development.* New York: John Wiley & Sons, Inc., 1981.
16. Kahn, C. "Women's Choice of Dual Role: Brief Notes on a Developmental Determinant" In *Career and Motherhood,* edited by Roland and Harris. New York: Human Sciences Press, 1959.
17. Bernstein, D. "Female Identity Synthesis." In *Career and Motherhood,* op. cit.
18. Rapoport, *Dual-Career Families,* p. 38.
19. *Psychology of Women Quarterly,* Winter, 1981, p. 218.
20. Rapoport, *Dual-Career Families.*
    Parnes et al. *Dual-Careers: A Longitudinal Analysis of the Labor Market Experiences of Women.* Columbus, Ohio: Ohio State University Press, 1975.
21. Ibid., p. 65.
    Bielby, D. "Factors Affecting Career Commitment of Female College Graduates." *Dissertation Abstracts International.* June, 1976, 36 (12-B) pt. 1.

St. John-Parsons, D. "Continuous Dual-Career Families: A Case Study." *Psychology of Women Quarterly.* Fall, 1978, 3, (1) 30–42.

22. Rapoport, R., and R. *Dual-Career Families Re-Examined.* New York: Harper and Row, 1976.

23. Beilby, "Career Commitment of Female Graduates."
St. John-Parsons, "Continuous Dual-Career Families."
Hopkins, "Comparison of Wives of Dual-Career Families."

24. Burke, R., and Wier, T. "Relationship of Wives' Employment to Husband, Wife, Pair Satisfaction and Performance." *Journal of Marriage and the Family.* May, 1976, 38, (2) 279–288.

25. Rapoport, *Dual-Career Families Re-examined.*

26. Ibid., p. 242.

27. Garland, T. N. "The Better Half? The Male in the Dual Profession Family." In *Toward a Sociology of Women,* Lexington, MA: Xerox College Publishing Co., 1972.

28. Rapoport, *Dual-Career Families Re-Examined.*
Hall, *The Two Career Couple.*

29. Also reported in Bardwick, J. *In Transition.* 1979.

30. Rapoport, *Dual-Career Families Re-examined.*

31. Ibid.

32. Hall, *Two Career Couple.*

33. Rapoport, *Dual-Career Families Re-examined.*
Bryson, R., and B., and Johnson, M. "Family Size Satisfaction and Productivity in Dual Career Couples." *Psychology of Women Quarterly.* Fall, 1978, 3, (1), Special Issue, 67–77.
Johnson, C. L., and F. A. "Attitudes Toward Parenting in Dual-Career Families." *American Journal of Psychiatry.* April, 1978, 134, (4) 391–395.
Weingarten, K. "The Employment Patterns of Professional Couples." *Psychology of Women Quarterly.* Fall, 1978, 3, (1).

34. Bird, Caroline. *The Two-Paycheck Marriage.* New York: Rawson, Wade, Inc., 1979.
Hall, *Two Career Couple.*
Peterson et. al., eds. *The Two-Career Family: A Symposium Report.* Washington, D.C.: University Press, 1978.
Business Week, September 3, 1978.

35. Hall, D. T., and F. S., "Dual Careers: How Do Couples and Companies Cope with the Problems." *Organization Dynamics,* Spring, 1978, p. 70.
Berger, M., Foster, and Wallston. "You and Me Against the World: Dual-Career Couples and Joint Job Seeking." *Journal of Research and Development in Education.* Summer 1977, 10, 30–37.

36. Rosen, B. et. al. "Dual Career Marital Adjustment: Potential Effects of Discriminating Managerial Attitudes." *Journal of Marriage and the Family.* August, 1975, 565.

37. Kanter, *Men and Women of the Corporation.*
Schein, E. H. *Career Dynamics: Matching Individuals and Organizational Needs.* Reading, MA: Addison-Wesley, 1978.
Bailyn, L. "Accommodation of Work to Family," In *Working Couples.,* edited by R. and R. Rapoport. New York: Harper & Row, 1978.

38. Rapoport, *Dual-Career Families.*

2
THE CHILDLESS DUAL-CAREER WOMAN

Our goal in this chapter is to begin to see the dual-career woman the way she sees herself. We want to understand her personality, dreams, goals, fears, and pleasures. Positioning her experiences within the larger social setting, we'll start with a focus on her adult self-concept and professional orientation; on issues related to her self-confidence and self-esteem, and her sense of femininity and sexual identity. Then we will look at how she relates to others—especially her spouse and her colleagues.

HOW SHE SEES HERSELF

Professional Self Image

Having worked an average of eight years and been married an average of four years, our subjects had well established career identities by the time they were married. Their professional sense of self is strong and commanding. Regardless of their decisions about children, or in some cases, about the permanence of their relationship, these women all view a lifelong commitment to their work as a given. Eighteen out of the twenty-four women reported a high level of career satisfaction.

In order to understand how our subjects' career orientation and professional self-image developed, we need to look back to their early development, the school years, the family setting and general social climate, and the economic and political events which colored the world into which they were born and grew to adulthood.

The parents of these women were themselves children of the Great Depression. Growing up during World War II, they formed much of their early adult lives around that experience—the anxiety, the disbelief and the complexity that grew out of the new atomic era. Their response—that is, their reflexive move back into the home, and into the child-centered family-togetherness, daddy-goes-to-work mommy-stays-home model—has been well documented.[1] But two revolutionary movements—the women's movement, and the technological explosion (compounded by the trauma of Vietnam.)—caused dramatic changes. These changes brought about a world of new expectations, opportunities, challenges, questions, fears, and possibilities, which began to affect our subjects even before they entered school.

The space age created a climate that valued educational excellence and competition. With the influx of readily available funds for schools in the post-Sputnik era, there was a revitalization of interest in encouraging bright children (even girls) to develop all of their intellectual capacities. Our subjects were these bright children. They did well in school, were placed in accelerated classes, were rewarded, and encouraged (pushed?) to be competitive and to achieve as much as possible. As we come to know these women, we will see that not only did they do what was expected of them (by family, teachers, peers), but they also frequently outdid the others. They accumulated records of individual accomplishment, which continued beyond their early school days, into high school and college. They saw themselves as high achievers and as independent. For them, competition, risk-taking, and assertive behavior felt comfortable and consistent with their self-concept. They believed that they performed best when pressured to succeed. Success, very often in the form of external, public rewards seemed natural, and became part of their internalized performance expectation.

Our subjects' development during high school was powerfully influenced by the Vietnam crisis. Many of these fast-track kids became the Vietnam flower children. Whether they participated in active protest or not, dissent against the "established" system was validated. The loss of faith in authority and the loss of confidence in the legitimacy of traditional systems of restraint spilled over from the political/military domain (Watergate and Vietnam), to the personal/sexual/moral spheres. It became the rule, legitimate and expected, to challenge tradition. Frequently, the most familiar traditions, those closest and best known, were attacked first. Thus, parents' roles, values, behaviors, relationships, and lifestyles became a prime target. Our subjects looked critically at their parents; many felt a need to be different, especially a need to be different from mother. This challenge to tradition coincided with the growing power of the women's movement. The struggle to change the traditional secondary position of women, to formulate a new definition of the feminine role, to allow women to develop according to unique, individual timetables rather than to a prior set of social expectations, developed into a dominant social movement. Women's achievements—personal and professional—were sanctioned. The early educational message, which had encouraged excellence for our subjects as school children, was stated again in terms of adult expectations. Within an astonishingly short period of time, the "vicarious achievement" ethic[2] was rejected.

As a reminder of just how fast so many deeply entrenched systems have changed, consider for example, the issue of women's participation in traditionally male occupations. When our subjects were about 10 years old, the percentage of women medical school graduates was 5.5%; by the time they entered college it was 9.6%, and by 1980 it was 24.8%.[3] However, the very pace that has made such occupational advances possible for women has contributed to the stress experienced by so many dual-career subjects. Changing all the rules so fast, without an opportunity to establish new norms or to test out new combinations of work and family, means that although the participants have a much greater range of choice, and have much more freedom to make autonomous decisions, they also are under enormous additional pressure. No longer are there rigidly prescribed, time-bound adult stages to follow. Life plans need to be developed according to individual (couples) needs. The increased accountability implied in the new freedom carries a far greater degree of individual responsibility for the outcome of decisions. Throughout this book, we will see how this expanded sense of personal responsibility was experienced in different ways by different women.

Having grown into adulthood with an image of themselves as competent, confident, and capable; having the benefit of good training and education; having a newly expanded range of professional opportunities available; having the freedom generated by the women's movement, which encouraged individual feminine achievement, and the pill which enabled them to regulate pregnancy; and finally, having found that they were (more or less) welcomed into the professional domain of their choice, our subjects plunged into their careers with vigor and enthusiasm. They started out on a career track modeled after the masculine pattern. We recall that the early feminist position, in rejecting the stereotypic denigration of femininity, was interpreted to imply that the male career path was the route to success. Though this has gradually grown to include a recognition of the value of both traditional feminine and masculine activities,[4] when our subjects were starting out professionally, they followed the traditional male pattern.

The women in all three groups are very special, and they made this fact known wherever they worked. Bright, alert, attractive, used to competition, and conditioned to success, they seemed to be able to be at the right place at the right time, for training opportunities, for hearing about that extra job that needed to be done, for figuring out how to balance the need for visibility with the need for restraint, etc.—these women clearly got off to a fast start professionally. As one subject told me, Merryl (C), " . . . This is how it happened. I was always willing to work hard, always ready to take an extra assignment, to stay late. I tried never to forget to do my homework, always to be prepared. I knew how to listen, wasn't afraid to ask questions, was thoroughly invested in my work. I deliberately made it known that I was a winner, I knew it and so did they . . . or at least I acted as if I knew it . . . " After a pause, Merryl continued, " . . . But now, sometimes, I'm afraid I'll slip—make a serious mistake. Then my whole cover will be blown."

Self-Confidence

Merryl's statement above, expresses a feeling that I soon discovered was shared by many dual-career women.* That is, although they appear self-confident and totally "in charge," in truth, they actually feel defenseless, filled with self-doubt, insecure about their ability, their relationships, and themselves. This fluctuating self-confidence, and a fear (sometimes expressed as a "fear of being found out") was typical of women labeled successful by the usual external criteria of education, experience, income, and status. Nevertheless, the presence of a pervasive, persistent, nagging self-doubt, forces them to question their competence and keeps them always on guard. The fear of being found out refers to the dread the women talked about, of one day "slipping"—of one day dropping their super smooth cover and being seen by all the world for the scared, incompetent, insecure person they "really" were.[6]

It was astonishing to discover how widespread this fear of being found out is! And it was precisely those women who looked to the world as if they knew exactly what they were doing, and who had accumulated the external evidence to convince others that they were on the right track (that is, they had the right academic credentials; they had an upwardly mobile career; they had more than an average income; personally, they had succeeded in establishing a significant loving relationship, etc.), who remained unconvinced themselves. They talked about the feelings they had—of having to walk carefully, of having to watch out that someone might get a glimpse of what they were really feeling—of how scared they "really" were. The dissonance, the lack of congruence, between their externally projected self-confidence and the gut level sense of fear and insecurity, was experienced more acutely by some women than others. For some, especially those who were in the ambivalent group, the dissonance was particularly vivid.

The search for the origins of this lack of self-confidence in so able and successful an adult group of women, led to an exploration of underlying factors related to dependency and autonomy. We'll expand on these issues as we move into the discussion of the ambivalent women in Part II.

Let me illustrate the path I followed in formulating these conclusions about the fear of being found out. In addition to the conscious statements

---

*This was also found to be true for midlife dual-career women.[5]

offered during the interviews, I found evidence of this fear in some of the projective responses. For example, to MTAT Card II (illustration of a woman looking at diploma and family pictures), one subject said, "There's something very tentative about her . . . I sense a place in her that's a little shattered, a little afraid . . . she's like a thermos bottle that looks good on the outside, but on the inside it's shattered."

Another subject, responding to a group scene (MTAT Card III) said, "Now, that's strange, but all these people have masks on . . . they don't want to be seen for who they really are . . . "

Judy's (B) statement provides another kind of clue. She said, " . . . I still blame my mother. I know so many women like me. They look professionally competent, but boy—are they scared inside."

These images—the thermos bottle that looks good on the outside but is shattered on the inside, the people who wear masks in order not to be seen, and finally, the reference to the mother/daughter relationship as the source of the problem—led me to wonder whether or not the integrated ego, which had been assumed from the external representation, was actually frail, and structurally inadequate. On examining the underlying factors, I first wondered whether these indications of self doubt were an expression of a fear of success (FOS), the phenomenon described by Horner in 1968, and discussed with much controversy since then.[7] FOS or M-S (Motive to Avoid Success) was defined by Horner as neither a will nor a need to fail, but rather an experienced anxiety, resulting from ambivalent feelings about the consequences of success in a competitive achievement situation. These feelings were further translated into a lower performance capability, particularly in a male/female competitive setting. The basic hypothesis was that, " . . . femininity and individual achievement . . . are desirable, but are mutually exclusive goals."[8]

One author commented that FOS studies are important because, " . . . they relate women's orientation toward achievement to the relationship of the self (including super ego and ego ideal) with significant others, primarily in terms of the early emotional experience with the nuclear family."[9] As we continue with this analysis, we will keep in mind this association between achievement and primitive images of self vis a vis significant others.

Gender role orientation was at one point considered to be crucial to understanding the FOS phenomena. " . . . failure to take gender role variables into account may help to explain the dramatic fluctuation obtained in M-S imagery across studies," said O'Leary and Hammock in 1975.[10] More recently, however, two separate literature reviews[11] concluded that there was not enough support for the hypothesis that there are gender differences in FOS. Individual differences and traditional versus nontraditional orientation accounted for greater differences in FOS than did gender.[12]

Recent studies of feminine achievement-motivation suggest that formerly rigid boundaries regarding gender appropriate behavior have been shifting over the last decade, so that superimposed on early internalization of traditional male/female role expectations, are a series of contemporary hypotheses; e.g., perhaps women are both achieving and affiliative; perhaps independence and competition, the other sides of dependence and cooperation are mutually compatible and situation-specific styles. Apparently men also worry about success and apparently some women can be unconflicted in a success situation.[13]

Contrary to the FOS prediction, dual-career women do not turn away from success, but rather deliberately seek it out. Furthermore, in their pursuit of a double goal (i.e., a success in both career and relationships), they reject the basic assumption that femininity and career achievement are mutually exclusive goals. However, along with a success orientation, underlying fluctuating self-confidence remained. Therefore, the fear of being found out was examined further. The pattern that emerged was a process of undervaluing the self either by 1) a form of self-sabotage; 2) a feeling that they have somehow "tricked" others; or 3) a feeling that they must continuously seek validation of themselves through others' approval.

Denise's (C) experience illustrates the third process. She is a very attractive sophisticated 35 year old executive, and one of very few female officers in her company. Though she graduated from college with a degree in education, she quickly decided that business was more interesting than teaching. She worked her way up through the ranks and now manages a large department and a sizeable budget. Recently she initiated a unique profit center within her organization which is getting rave reviews and is the focus of attention. She has been married for 2 years, has no children, and lives in a city condominium. She said, " . . . sometimes I still feel like the small town girl misplaced in a big company like X. I have the feeling that I don't belong . . . afraid they'll find out . . . very different from the self-confident image I want to present. I want others to see only the outside—to say she's in control, competent and capable."

The significance to Denise (C) of having others see only the outside, the importance of looking good, of presenting a perfect appearance, becomes more understandable when we look deeper into her personal history and psychological development. Some of the dynamic origins of her insecurity can be traced to the early development of the self in relation to her mother. She was the first girl after two boys. She tells us, " . . . No matter what I did as a kid, it wasn't good enough. Mother just wasn't satisfied. I always felt that if my mother had had her choice, she wouldn't have had kids . . . the sense that I was a burden to her . . . that her life would have been much better if I wasn't there."

As a child, feeling mother's withdrawal and rejection, Denise turned to her father whose attention focused on her appearance, her femininity, her prettiness, her smallness—the way she was different from the other siblings. She seems to have internalized this approval based on her appearance, as verification that the other parts of herself were unacceptable and inadequate.

Her parents were divorced before she was three, and she remembers feeling abandoned and believing that somehow she was responsible. Losing her father at this age also suggests that the stage was set for idealization of the desired, but unavailable paternal object.

As she was growing up, she wanted to live up to the stereotypic popular girl image (i.e., to be the high school cheerleader, to date the football hero, to dress right). She always tried to look right, to be pretty, and to act her role. For Denise, a gulf grew between the external self she could show the world—the protective but fragile shell of her good looks—and the inner self, which had to remain hidden because, as imperfect, it was unacceptable. Denise's need to hide her real self from the world is evident throughout. For example, to MTAT III (group scene) she says, "These people don't want to be here. You can tell by their eyes . . . they're concerned . . . their body language is closed . . . they haven't warmed up at all . . . they won't . . . " To MTAT Card IV, (woman and aging parents) Denise responded, "She feels like a stranger . . . like an outsider . . . she is distant . . . she doesn't fit in . . . "

Recalling that Denise felt that she was unacceptable to her mother, it is assumed that there was an unsuccessful identification with mother, which may have influenced her sense of autonomy, as well as her developing femininity. She recalls feeling ambivalent about her sexual attractiveness. Although she had boyfriends growing up and dated frequently as an adult, she always felt afraid to reveal anything but her superficial attractiveness.

"Before I met my husband I felt that no man, if he really got to know me and know the insecure person I was underneath the surface, would find me acceptable."

Thus Denise's inability to rely on herself for a realistic appraisal of her competence and achievement stems developmentally from an early sense of maternal rejection and paternal superficial (and impermanent) approval. She is somewhat aware now of an inadequacy, an emptiness, which she can't seem to fill, regardless of her level of external success. And it is this feeling of emptiness that she is afraid will be "found out."*

At this point let's return to our general description of the dual-career

---

*These conclusions (re fear of being found out) will be expanded in Chapter 8.

woman and consider some issues related to her conception of femininity and sexual identity.

The Concept of Female, Femininity, and Sexual Identity

As we consider the nature of the contemporary social/psychological conception of the female, we are struck by an apparent contradiction. Women are simultaneously glorified and devalued. We react, consciously and unconsciously, to women as if they are extremely powerful/weak, awe-inspiring/despised, and vengeful/compassionate. Young women trying to establish a sense of themselves as female, receive an array of opposing prescriptions that reflect this antithesis.

Theoretical Note. There is a general agreement in the literature that our conscious and unconscious concept of the "female" reflects the early Greek mythological portrayal of woman as the "other"—as either Great Mother or overwhelmingly powerful and mysterious.[14] Themes of mother/son antagonism, ambivalence, and tension pervade the early Greek myths.[15]

Freud struggled with this dichotomous concept of the female but never settled on a clear statement of the psychological meaning of male and female.[16] Freud's inconclusive and controversial positions regarding feminine development have been the target of innumerable analyses.*

Shafer (1977) comments," . . . for Freud, psychosexual outcomes other than reproductive generativity are called illness . . . "[20] The pairing of full feminine identity with motherhood, which forms the basis for contemporary pronatalism, was reported by Deutsch[21] who identified three characteristically female orientations: narcissism, passivity, and masochism, and by Benedek[22] who wrote that women have an instinctual need to mother. According to this school of thought, early (infantile) bisexuality, which included aggression and externalization, is converted to the service of femininity thus leaving the characteristics of aggression and externalization as exclusively male. This concept is reflected in the "parental imperative" notion as stated by Gutmann,[23] which refers to adult parental role formation. The theme of female passivity, labeled as a "receptive readiness" by Deutsch,[24] is echoed in the Eriksonian observation that girls are more concerned with inner space—with interiors—than are boys.[25]

The present study argues with this position, finding little substantiation

---

*The most controversial debates focus on: the theory of penis envy;[17] the concept that superego and morality development differ for men and women;[18] the norm that equates female sexuality with motherhood.[19]

for the Freudian functionalist conclusions, or for the rigid masochistic/ passive theories of female sexual development. Nancy Chodorow, in a brilliant social/psychological analysis of mothering, presents a careful exposition that reaches a restatement of Freudian theory, which is closer to my findings.[26] Chodorow argues with the Freudian conclusion that gender differences result from the " . . . presence or absence of masculinity . . . " but agrees with Freud that gender identity develops out of genital differences.[27] Chodorow comments, "Most contemporary analysts agree that passivity, masochism, and narcissism are all psychological defenses found in both women and men, and have the same object-relational origins in each, in the early infant-mother relationship."[28] She continues, "The psycho-analytic account shows . . . how women and men come to create the kinds of interpersonal relationships which make it likely that women will remain in the domestic sphere . . . and will . . . mother the next generation."[29]

Returning to the question of the origin of the almost universal process which results in feminine devaluation, object relations theorists tell us that both the glorification and the fear of women stem from the very earliest infant/mother relationship. [30] They trace this basic and generalized anxiety regarding women to the infantile process of splitting. In this process, the maternal object is separated—split into that part which the infant perceives as good (that part which provides physical satisfaction and anticipates the infant's requirements) vs that part which the infant perceives as bad (withdrawing, and thus unavailable and hateful, the "other"). In this process the maternal figure, the female image, is split, perhaps never to be reintegrated. Furthermore, Klein[31] characterizes infantile female identification as an awareness and rejection of mother as an inadequate sexual object, which ultimately leads to a devaluing of self as female.

Cognitive theorists find that, having made certain prior gender identifications, which Kohlberg point out require a " . . . necessary maturation of cognitive capacities . . . which are . . . the key to gender identity . . . "[32] the child then goes on to learn the expected behaviors. That is, the child is socialized according to gender appropriate behaviors. Once sufficient maturation has enabled the child to develop the capacity to learn this socially defined gender identity, the underlying primitive ambivalence toward the female is already well established. The learning process, however, serves to reinforce the ambivalence.

Women in positions of authority (and, as we will see, many dual-career women in this study fall into this category) are particularly vulnerable to conflicts that may be traced to this devaluing and ambivalence. Many authors have examined the psychological experiences and responses to women in positions of authority.[33] Describing the origins of the devaluing, contempt and stereotypic fears which often surround women in authority, one author points out that, " . . . in most cultures (the female) is much devalued; the frequent exhaltation and idealization of women hardly masks the underlying contempt . . . "[34] She claims that the devaluing of women, as well as culturally accepted stereotypes of women, " . . . stem in large part from a defensive handling of the powerful and persistent effects of early infant/mother relationship."[35] Through the process of devaluation, a process shared by women and men, the feared object is rendered less powerful, less threatening.

The feminine concept of self-as-less, is described by Bardwick as a pervasive sense of inferiority experienced by women.[36] Stewart[37] points out that, " . . . although traditional female goals are not valued . . . women are sanctioned for not succeeding in them . . . ", further emphasizing the contradictions of traditional expectations.

Sexual Identity—Some Definitions

The stereotypic definition of traditional femininity suggested a few years ago by Bardwick is as follows: " . . . Our entire culture sees women as understanding, tender, generous, loving, moral, nurturant, kind and patient . . . as well as incapable of responsibility, dependent, inconsistent, emotionally weak, intuitive (rather than intelligent), anxious, fearful and childish."[38] Thus, traditionally, femininity is defined by both positive and negative descriptors. Recent, nontraditional concepts of masculine and feminine include a more androgynous, value-free definition.[39] It is generally agreed, however, that nurturance (defined as those attitudes and behaviors that organize one's psychic and physical energies in the service of satisfying the needs of another individual) is viewed as central to the traditional concept of femininity.

The concept of gender identity refers to the privately experienced, conscious and unconscious perception of one's individuality as biologically male or female. The term gender role refers to the total range of behaviors that label, for oneself and others, the degree to which one is masculine, feminine, or undecided.[40] Sexuality, commonly understood as referring to the biological and functional aspects of sexual responses and behaviors, is not usually specified in the traditional definition of femininity (nor for that matter in the traditional definition of masculinity) even though it is generally implied.

Sexual identity refers to the social/sexual self-concept based on an interaction and combination of innate biological characteristics, unique psychodynamic development, plus external socially assigned and reinforced attitudes and behaviors. Sexual identity in large part reflects the stimulation and interaction with the social environment[41] and serves to provide standards by which we judge interpersonal behavior.[42]

New Definition of Femininity

Based on my research, I would like to propose a change in the traditional definition which equates femininity with nurturance. It is more accurate to describe nurturance and sexuality as separate aspects of the feminine (or masculine) self concept. Whereas, all the subjects identified themselves as sexually female, in terms of female gender identification and heterosexual self-concept, only certain women evidenced a nurturant self-concept. Those who planned to have children were both sexual and nurturant; those who elected to remain childless found a nurturant self-concept ego-dystonic; and those who were ambivalent about children were ambivalent about nurturance as well. In the following chapters we will discuss this new definition at some length.

At this point, however, I would like to suggest that the expanded definition of femininity, as described above, leads to speculation about the nature of masculinity and especially masculine nurturance. Studies of midlife men[43] describe a phenomena whereby at midlife, men find themselves struggling to integrate the feminine aspects of their psyche. These opposite aspects of one's sexual self concept are referred to in the literature as the *contrasexual opposite*. There are some data[44] which describe an increase in nurturance among much younger groups of men. As new masculine roles become possible we find evidence that this integrative effort occurs at a much younger age than previously documented. For example, in dual-career couples, we have seen an increase in the masculine assumption of previously labeled "feminine" functions (e.g., child care, cooking, housekeeping, etc.), ranging all the way from total reversal of traditional roles (where the male stays home with the children and the female works away from home), to the more common situation of shared responsibility for childcare and domestic responsibilities. Overall, it has become more culturally acceptable for the male to function in a nurturant capacity.

Nurturance, like sexual behaviors, can be seen to have greater variability among members of the same sex than between the sexes, and can also be seen as varying widely throughout the individual's unique developmental cycle. Nurturance, previously held as feminine, (just as aggression was held as masculine) can be more usefully described as an orientation toward interpersonal caretaking, and as a composite of feelings, attitudes, and behaviors which is available to both sexes in greater or lesser degrees of intensity at differing stages of development.

No evidence has been found that in dual-career families women were becoming psychologically and/or sexually more masculine, or that men were becoming more feminine.[45] However, dual-career women are more likely than non-dual-career women to describe themselves as masculine.[46]

Self as Different

With striking uniformity, all the women in this study spontaneously described themselves as somehow "different." They felt they were different from other girls as children and adolescents, and continued to feel different from other women in college and early career days. Given our focus on the question of childbearing, we must consider whether or not the feeling of being different from other women affects their decision about children.

Some women recalled that their mother pressured them to be different. Mothers who were dissatisfied with their own lives, their maternal role and especially with their relationship to spouse and to men in general, often (though probably unconsciously) gave their daughters permission to remain childless. The impact of this maternal message will be explored in greater depth in Chapter 4.

Several women, reflecting stereotypic masculine labeling, and the generally shared preference for such, believed they were more masculine than feminine. For example, Paula (A) said: " . . . and I'm much more ambitious than most women . . . have a lot higher goals . . . I am much more thoughtful . . . others can be satisfied with certain things, and can accept that they're not going to have anything more . . . I can't do that. I think there are more men like me than there are women . . . because of the socialization process." Many women traced a preference for masculine identification to their early relationship with father. Said Barbara (A), "My father and I are more alike than my mother and I. You see, my Dad didn't have any sons, so I used to go everywhere with him. He probably had a greater impact than my mother did. It was the way he treated me . . . less emotionally." Larla (C) said: "There's a long-standing need I have to be different . . . definitely came from my father. That there were ordinary people and not ordinary . . . and that we were not ordinary. This echoes over the years. It's true though, I do get what I want. I don't have to give in to social pressures. But there are probably not many women who are as independent as I am." Louise (A) "I wanted to be an architect. But in junior high I had a teacher who told me not to think about that, because that was for boys. I remember I decided then to be different from other girls."

In spite of their stated feeling of being different from other women, as we noted above, women who have crossed conventional sex-barriers in their occupational life, seem to have a need to revert back to sexually stereotyped roles and tasks after their work day is over.[47] Interestingly, it was also found that although they accept this responsibility, they become angry at the overload this produces.

This pattern of reverting to traditional roles after work, was seen over and over in our subjects. Said Kay, (C), "Everyone says you're supposed to be the housewife, no matter what else you do . . . it's all that internal crap . . . if you ask any woman no matter what her job is, she'll tell you how it feels . . . we're all influenced by that stereotype to an extent that we don't even realize."

Especially evident in that group of women who achieve high occupational status and generate a high income, are signs of what is labeled the search for a new affirmation of femininity.[48] It is not clear whether this is a defense against actual or fantasied disapproval from self or significant male figures, or a more positive ability to accept feelings defined as feminine. Bardwick notes, "In this transitional period, occupationally successful women are very likely to permit or want small symbols of male protectiveness."[49]

Some dual-career subjects, male and female, told me that they welcomed the idea of "being taken care of" by a loved person; that it in no way conflicted with the concept of themselves as being competent, powerful and independent. For example, Denise (C) said, "One of the things we like to do for each other is take care of one another. Certain things he does for me I like and depend on. I have a protective instinct toward him and he does for me. But that doesn't change our idea of independence. I've always had my own discipline and my own structure." Another woman said, "Three years ago I finally got hold of being me . . . independent, but able to be dependent. Accepting the fact that I can use support, but I can also be supportive." However, for others, there was fear and a sense of conflict between their need for independence and impulses toward dependency. Margaret (B) " . . . there is that fear, that if I let myself be taken care of, then I would ultimately lose my sense of discipline and would become a captive. But there are lots of times when I would love dearly to be taken care of . . . but it's both feelings."

For some, the pursuit of the socially designated power position led to a fantasied "superwoman" ideal. For example, Kay (C) said she told herself, "Hey superwoman! You can handle it! You see, I had been treated all my life as the superwoman. I was always the overachiever. I always had to try to do even more, to please my mother. In everything I did. I was always different from the other girls . . . In school and church . . . lead in school plays, wrote the school newspaper . . . 4.0 grade point . . . everything. It would hurt if I wasn't achieving. I would just hate myself if I didn't at least try for everything . . . But I'm beginning to realize that I have my limitations . . . I really question whether or not I'll ever reach that spot I have in mind . . . whether it's worth it . . . or what I have to give up." One hears the underlying conflict in this kind of statement. The need to be different (i.e., not like mother) forces Kay to question her identification with traditional femininity, especially with nurturance which is so universally equated with feminine behavior. Whether or not mother actually was nurturant, the internalized ideal of the "perfect" mother is "perfect" nurturance. When nurturance as a self concept feels uncomfortable, they ask themselves, does this need to be different reflect an underlying masculine orientation? These questions inevitably must come up against the pressure from other (perhaps early feminized) aspects of themselves (for example, Kay's thoughts about . . . "what I'll have to give up . . . "), which may or may not be denied, but which form a significant part of the self.

For most women, these feelings of being different emerge from time to time, but do not become disruptive. For those in the ambivalent group, even more than the childless group, the feeling is one of uneasiness, as if there is some still undiscovered aspect of the self. It is useful to repeat, however, that regardless of this sense of being different, and regardless of the status of their professional development, the stability of their relationship or their parenthood motivation, all of the women in this study considered themselves to be sexually feminine.

HOW SHE RELATES TO OTHERS

Spouse

Because of the spouse's dominant role, as the "significant other," the interaction between the marital partners became the vehicle for the individual's personal developmental struggle. Issues of independence, control, and separation were continuously played out. In this section we will hear some of the thoughts expressed by dual-career women as they talked about their relationship to their husbands.

All the women in this study described their husband as the single most important person in their lives. Family and friends, in varying degrees of intimacy, formed a secondary, remote ring around this primary unit. For some, professional colleagues, often one special individual, took the place of family and friends, serving as people with whom to share dreams, hopes, and confidences. Religious affiliations, which had served a significant socializing function in earlier generations, seemed quite remote to this group. Very few had time for memberships in non-work associations, clubs, or volunteer organizations.

As I mentioned before, by the time they were thirty, these women had lived most of their adult lives as independent, single persons. This was true for their spouses as well. For example, Alyssa (A) said, "Mike was 28 when we met and pretty much a confirmed bachelor. We spent a lot of time together and he couldn't believe that he could spend so much time with a woman.'' For some, perhaps most, this extended period of independence gave them a secure sense of personal strength and provided a concrete validation of autonomy. Other women, however, saw this time as a holding period—a transitional stage until they established a permanent relationship, and a time in which they remained developmentally inactive.[50]

The more their career pressures intensified, the more our subjects looked to their marriage to provide a safe haven—an environment of acceptance, security, and protection. Sometimes this happened, other times it did not. Alice (C): '' . . . He's very good for me. If I have a problem at the office, our home is such a safe refuge. Both our personalities make that refuge. I enjoy being with him an awful lot . . . '' Karen (C): "This makes the relationship a haven because we both understand what the other is going through . . . we are always in the same room, very close. He is not just my spouse, he is my best friend and I really enjoy him . . . '' Diane (A) saw her husband as a resource to help her with career problems. Diane said, "I would say that the marriage has enhanced my career. Michael and I spend a lot of time talking about what is going on there . . . he's more ambitious than I am, so he can see certain things I probably would miss . . . and that helps me make the right moves . . . ''

Many dual-career couples seem to be able to work out a system wherein they take turns being the supportive back-up person—take turns in the sense of bending when the other's career and personal needs have to be recognized.[51] For example, Diane (A) said, "Right now Michael's career is taking a big change . . . he's leaving the organization he's been with for several years and going out on his own. So I try not to get in his way too often, in the sense of having too many big issues of my own . . . '' In contrast, other subjects reported that when their relationship felt troubled, they invested more energy into their work, especially into the other people at work.

Mutual Support/Interdependence. According to some participants, the dual-career system enables them to do things that they never could do independently. Julie (B) said, "He allows me to be a much better person than I was alone. I know that I can be cranky and neurotic and see a lot of negatives. And I'm so grateful that this person allows me to be anything I want . . . and then I want to be the best I can . . . '' Karen (C): "There are things I want to do, that are important for me. I want to go to New York for a conference for example. It is never a question of checking with him, but rather asking him if he'd like to join me." Louise (A), talking about her husband: "He has this nurturing thing and a guilt thing as well. He thinks I'm naive and very vulnerable, and people can take advantage of me. I'm not . . . I can handle myself a lot better than he thinks I can. But he seems to want to keep on having that image of me. I think it's good for his male ego.''

Dominance and Control.   For those whose marriage did not seem to be on a firm footing, almost any issue—dominance, control, independence, finances, lack of communication, domestic inequities—could become the arena for disagreement. Many women were very much aware of an ongoing power struggle between themselves and their spouse. For example, Marlis (A) said, ''The power struggle is always going on . . . but I don't want to . . . couldn't win. I finally found someone I cannot dominate. At the same time he's very supportive. For example, when I was so upset about this job, he told me not to tolerate some of the nonsense around here . . . made me feel good because he was so much on my side . . . '' Marlis continued, ''But we fight all the time . . . mainly issues of control. He isn't afraid of me . . . he needs a lot of psychic space . . . the great attraction is that he is not intimidated by me. But I have to fight all the time to have my space . . . ''

Colleagues/Mentor

As mentioned above, given the hectic pace of the average dual-career life-style, and the limited time for friends, family, or leisure activities, profes-sional colleagues assume a very important position in terms of significant relationships. In this section we will first consider one such colleague, the mentor, and then comment briefly on relationships with other women.

The Mentor.   We have noted that out subjects began their career in what they described as a masculine pattern. Therefore, it is interesting to look at the question of mentoring, which is described by Levinson as such an important early aspect of a successful (male) career. According to Levinson, '' . . . the mentor is ordinarily several years older, and a person of greater experience and seniority in the world the young man is entering . . . ''[52]* Levinson states that the mentor's most important function is '' . . . to sup-port and facilitate the realization of the Dream.'' (meaning the *Occupa-tional Dream*).

   Wendy Stewart's study of women's early adult development found that women who gave a high priority to an Occupational Dream sought out

---

*Levinson's work is based on a male population. He comments, however, '' . . . in principle a mentor may be either the same or cross-gender. A relationship with a female mentor can be an enormously valuable experience for a young man, as I know from my own experience.''[53]

a relationship with a senior male or female in their organization who became a mentor. In contrast, women whose primary Dream was related to marriage/family themes, chose to form a relationship with a Special Man as part of their Dream.[54] (Also see Chapter 9 below) Most of our subjects were obviously in the first group, in the sense that the Occupational Dream formed a significant portion of their early adult self concept. They were very conscious of the importance of the mentor role and talked about their search for a mentor. Given the lack of sufficient numbers of women in senior organizational positions, it comes as no surprise that females were not often found as mentors. Several women had a positive experience with a male mentor; only a few had received mentoring from a woman; others felt themselves to be in a mentoring role.

Male Mentor.   Alice (C) said, "Oh, yes, I've had several mentors. The chairman of the music department in college took an interest . . . motivated me and was really wonderful in helping me get orchestral experience, even though I was quite young." Julie (B): "I found a mentor, a guy with whom I worked who is still my boss . . . he said to me, 'three years from now you are going to be something' . . . He helped to give me self confidence. Then it wasn't hard for me to fall into things . . . it was easy. It just seemed to happen, but he was there." Marla (C): "My mentor, George, . . . he cared enough to confront me about some things about my behavior . . . I will be eternally grateful to him for that."

Women as Mentors.   Lois (B) reflecting on her relationship with her supervisor: "She is really a big inspiration for me . . . very open and flexible. And has really done a lot for me personally, too." Joyce (B): "As I went along there would be certain women I admired, maybe her personality or her independent life. But I have never had any long range mentor. I have never seen any women serving as a mentor for anybody else here, either . . . " Kay (C) was bitter about what she felt to be sexual discrimination re mentoring. "I have no mentor here. None of the women do, although in time, I see myself going into that role. The men have mentors and networks, and women have to have them if we're going to survive."

Self as Mentor.   Kay's suggestion that she wished to serve as mentor, was especially well stated by Julie (B) as follows: "I am a mentor person, I try to be. Well I would hope that I turn out to be the kind of person who would do as well as other people have done for me. To remember how it felt to be in a position where you needed help . . . those feelings of nobody caring . . . and pull you out of that . . . and not expecting anything in return really. Just try to clear the path for the person and some day they will look over their shoulder and realize what happened." Louise (A): "I've had a couple of mentors. But in my job now, I have no mentor. There are no other women at the top here, and so I feel rather isolated in that respect. It's lonely . . . I do try to give support now, to the younger women coming up." Margaret (B): "As far as I'm concerned, it doesn't make any difference whether it's male or female mentoring. I'd be happy to show someone the ropes. A lot of times I've found older employees feel kind of threatened. The new people move faster than they did . . . and probably know more than they did at that point. So they're more reluctant to reach out and help. They feel so competitive. But I feel that, well, I guess I'm feeling pretty secure, so why not try to give that to someone else?"

Relationship to Other Women

Although very few of the women who participated in this study identified themselves as active feminists, they were conscious of their special relationship to other women. A few women had close friends who were also in a dual-career marriage and who shared similar problems. The sharing of uncertainties, especially relating to their childbearing dilemma, was particularly meaningful.

Diane (A) focused on the problems of relating to women at other levels in her organization: "I think what happens is that when women move up in the organization they do not want to feel that they are in any way associated with where they have come from, which is the lower levels. That has never been part of my modus operandi. I really believe that in order to succeed you have to get everybody on your side . . . " Julie (B), a supervisor in a large P.R. firm, said: "I am actually much more sensitive about the women I supervise than the men. And it's because I am closer to them. They are my friends and my cohorts. The people with whom I go shopping and go to lunch. Most of the men I work with I didn't have a relationship with before they worked for me, and so it made it a little easier. They came in and knew I was going to be their boss and accepted that and we have a real nice respectful relationship. We are friends but it is as though we are not as intimate as I am with the women who work in this same position. The supervisor's role is more difficult with the women, because I project myself into their personal life, so it is harder. But I do the role of supervisor and I try to do it considerately. I am not sure I am quite secure about that yet."

Lee (C) had negative feelings about working with women: "I think women working for a woman is very difficult . . . it's also a problem because I was much younger. The woman that I fired was probably 40 and I was 23 years old." Talking about competitive feelings for other women, Marlis (A) said,

"No, I don't feel the competitiveness, I think I feel like an obligation or a responsibility to share whatever you know, whatever good things that have happened to me. I think that gives me a responsibility to share that with other women."

Several subjects talked about the way they have changed over the years in terms of their relationship with other women. Kay (C) said, "I think I saw myself more in competition with other women than I feel today. I think I saw myself either not measuring up to them or surpassing them. But not being, hey, we're different, but that's okay." Marlis (A) repeated this idea: "I do feel as though now I'm more open, I'm more approachable, and more real." For Marla (C) the difference was a reflection of her own increased feelings of competence: "First of all, I try to be a little bit more responsible for my friends now. I had few friends when I was younger . . . I feel equal to my really good friends now. My good friends in college I definitely felt inferior to intellectually. I don't feel that way anymore. I recognize differences in intellectual capacity. There are times when I want the companionship of my women friends very much now which I don't remember thinking or feeling before."

SUMMARY

In this chapter we have discussed several personal characteristics of dual-career women. First focusing on her self-concept, then on some of her relationships, we have presented a portrait of the age thirty, dual-career, childless woman as a stable, generally well-functioning individual. Although we have seen she is somewhat insecure on certain levels, she presents herself as competent, flexible, and dynamic.

In the course of getting to know what she believed to be important, it became clear that issues related to her childbearing decision were uniformly regarded as significant. In the following chapters, we will discuss some of the elements of the childbearing decision, and will introduce a decision model which was developed from analysis of these data. Following the presentation of the decision model, Chapter 5 discusses some of the differences between women who plan to have children, vs those who intend to remain childless or who are so far unable to make a decision.

REFERENCES

1. Friedan, Betty. *The Feminine Mystique.* New York: W. W. Norton, 1963.
2. Lipman-Blumen, J. "How Ideology Shapes Women's Lives." *Scientific America.* 1972, 226, (1) 34–42.
3. *Journal of the American Medical Association.* December 25, 1981.

4. Bem, S. L. "The Measurement of Psychological Androgyny." *Journal of Consulting and Clinical Psychology.* 1974, 42, 155–162.
5. Wilk, C. "Coping and Adaptation in Midlife Dual-Career Families." In Cytrynbaum, S. (Chair) Symposium: *Midlife Development: Influence of Gender, Personality and Social Systems.* Presented to the American Psychological Association Annual Convention, New York, 1979.
6. Downing, C. *Cinderella Complex.* New York: Pocket Books, 1981.
7. Horner, M. "Toward an Understanding of Achievement Related Conflicts in Women." In *Women and Achievement.* edited by Mednick, Tangri, and Hoffman. New York: Wiley, 1976.
8. Ibid., page 206.
9. Podoretz, H. "Women and Career Goals: Some Developmental Vicissitudes." In *Career and Motherhood.* edited by A. Roland and H. Harris. New York: Human Sciences Press, 1979, page 148.
10. O'Leary, V., and Hammock, B. "Sex Role Orientation and Achievement Context as Determinants of the Motive to Avoid Success." *Sex Roles.* 1975, 1, 225–268.
11. O'Leary, V. and Depner, C. "Understanding Feminine Careerism: FOS and New Directions." *Sex Roles.* 1976, 2, (3) 259–268.
12. Tresemer, D. "The Cumulative Record of Research on FOS." *Sex Roles.* 1976, 2, (3) 217–135.
13. Bem, S. L. "Sex-Role Adaptability: One Consequence of Psychological Androgyny." *Journal of Personality and Social Psychology.* 1975, 1, (4) 634–43.
   Spence, J. T., and Helmreich, R. *Masculinity and Femininity: Their Psychological Dimensions, Correlates, and Antecedents.* Austin, TX: University of Texas Press, 1978.
14. Horney, K. *Feminine Psychology.* New York: W. W. Norton and Co., 1967.
   Hillman, J. *Re-Visioning Psychology.* New York: Harper Colophon, 1975.
   Williams, J. *Psychology of Women.* New York: W. W. Norton and Co., 1977.
   Blum, H., ed. *Female Psychology.* New York: International Universities Press, Inc., 1977.
   Slater, P. *Footholds.* New York: D. P. Dutton, 1977.
15. Ibid.
   Newmann, E. *The Psychological Stages of Feminine Development.* New York: Spring Publications, 1959.
16. Freud, S. "Female Sexuality." *The Complete Psychological Works.* Standard Edition, 223–243. London: Hogarth Press, 1931, 21.
   Freud, S., "Femininity." *New Introductory Lectures.* (Translated by J. Strachey), 112–135. New York: Norton, 1933, 1965.
17. Horney, *Feminine Psychology.*
   Thompson, C. *Interpersonal Psychoanalysis: The Selected Papers of Clara M. Thompson.* New York: Basic Books, 1949.
   Bernard, J. *Women, Wives, and Mothers: Values and Options.* Chicago: Aldine Press, 1975.
   Chodorow, N. *The Reproduction of Mothering: Psychoanalysis and The Sociology of Gender.* Berkeley, CA: University of California Press, 1978.
18. Shafer, R. "Problems in Freud's Psychology of Women." In *Female Psychology.* Edited by H. Blum. New York: International Universities Press, 1977.
   Blum, *Female Psychology.*
   Kohlberg, L. "Development of Moral Character and Moral Ideology." In *Review of Child Development Research,* edited by M. and L. Hoffman. New York: Russell Sage Foundation, 1964.
   Gilligan, C. *In A Different Voice.* Cambridge, MA: Harvard University Press, 1982.

19. Deutsch, H. *The Psychology of Women*. New York: Grune & Stratton, 1944.
    Benedek, T. "Parenthood as a Developmental Phase: A Contribution to Libido Theory," *Journal of American Psychoanalytic Association*. 1959, 7 (3), 389–417.
    Bardwick, J. *Psychology of Women*. New York: Harper & Row, 1971.
20. Shafer, "Problems in Freud's Psychology of Women," p. 345.
21. Deutsch, *The Psychology of Women*.
22. Benedek, "Parenthood as a Developmental Phase."
23. Gutmann, D. "Parenthood: A Key to the Comparative Study of the Life Cycle." In *Life-Span Developmental Psychology*. edited by P. Datan and L. Ginsberg. New York: Academic Press, 1975.
24. Deutsch, *The Psychology of Women*.
25. Erikson, E. "Inner and Outer Space: Reflections on Womanhood." In *A Modern Introduction to the Family,* edited by Bell and Vogel. New York: Free Press, 1968.
    Bardwick, *Psychology of Women*.
26. Chodorow, *Reproduction of Mothering*.
    Also see:
    Bardwick, J. *In Transition*. New York: Holt, Rinehart & Winston, 1979.
    Shafer, "Problems in Freud's Psychology of Women."
    Hoffman, L. and Nye, I., eds. *Working Mothers*. San Francisco: Jossey-Bass, 1974.
    Maccoby, E., and Jacklin, E. *The Psychology of Sex Differences*. San Francisco: Stanford University Press, 1974.
    Bem, "Sex-Role Adaptability: One Consequence of Psychological Androgyny."
27. Chodorow, *The Reproduction of Mothering*. p. 158.
28. Ibid., p. 165.
29. Ibid., p. 38.
30. Klein, M. *Love, Hate and Reparation*. New York: Dell Publishing, 1975.
    Kernberg, O. *Borderline Conditions and Pathological Narcissism*. New York: Jason Aronson, 1975.
    Menzies I. "A Case Study in the Functioning of Social Systems as a Defense Against Anxiety." In *Group Relations Reader,* edited by A. Coleman and W. Bexton. Sausalito, CA: Grex Publishing, 1975.
31. Klein, *Love, Hate and Reparation*.
32. Kohlberg, "Development of Moral Character." p. 13.
33. Bayes, M., and Newton, P. "Women In Authority: A Socio-psychological Analysis." Paper presented to First Annual Scientific Meeting of A. K. Rice Institute, April, 1976.
    Cytrynbaum, S., and Brandt, L. "Women In Authority: Dilemmas for Male and Female Subordinates." Paper presented to the American Psychological Association Annual Convention, New York, September, 1979.
    Kanter, R. M. *Men and Women of the Corporation*. New York: Basic Books, 1977.
34. Lerner, H. "Early Origins of Envy and Devaluation of Women." *Bulletin of the Menninger Clinic*. November, 1974, 38, p. 537.
35. Ibid., p. 540.
36. Bardwick, *In Transition*.
37. Stewart, W. "A Psychological Study of the Formation of the Early Adult Life in Women." Ph.D. Diss., Columbia University, 1977.
38. Bardwick, *In Transition*. p. 37.
39. Bem, "Measurement of Psychological Androgyny."
    Spence and Helmreich, *Masculinity and Femininity*.
40. Ibid.
41. Ibid.

42. Yorburg, B. *Sexual Identity.* New York: John Wiley and Sons, 1975.
43. Cytrynbaum, S. et al. "Gender and Adult Midlife Development: A Critical Appraisal."
    Paper presented to the American Psychological Association Annual Convention, Toronto,
    Canada, 1978.
    Levinson, D. et al. *The Seasons of a Man's Life.* New York: Alfred A. Knopf, 1978.
    Vaillant, G. *Adaptation to Life.* Boston: Little Brown and Co., 1977.
44. Wilk, C. "Coping and Adaptation in Midlife Dual-Career Families." In Cytrynbaum, S.
    (Chair) Symposium: Midlife Development: Influence of Gender, Personality and Social
    Systems. Presented to the American Psychological Association Annual Convention, New
    York, 1979.
45. Fogarty, M., and Rapoport, R. and R. *Sex, Career and Family.* London: George Allen
    and Unwin, Ltd., 1971.
46. Hopkins, J. "A Comparison of Wives of Dual-Career and Single-Career Families" Diss.
    Abstracts International, 1977, 38 (2) Section A.
47. St. John-Parsons, D. "Continuous Dual-Career Families: A Case Study." *Psychology of
    Women Quarterly.* Fall, 1978, 3, (1) 30–42.
48. Kanter, *Men and Women of the Corporation.*
    Bird, C. *The Two-Paycheck Marriage.* New York: Rawson, Wade, Inc., 1979.
49. Bardwick, *In Transition.* p. 117.
50. Levinson, *The Season's of a Man's Life.*
51. Hall, D. T. and F. S. *The Two-Career Couple.* Reading MA: Addison Wesley, 1979.
52. Levinson, *The Seasons of a Man's Life.* p. 97.
53. Ibid., p. 98.
54. Stewart, W. *Formation of Early Adult Life in Women.* p. 60.

3
ELEMENTS OF THE CHILDBEARING DECISION

As I gradually got to know what was important to these dual-career subjects, one fact became very clear. The decision about whether or when to have children had been thought about, talked about, cried about, intellectualized about, avoided, confronted, resolved (in some cases), and suspended (in other cases) by every couple in this study in varying degrees of intensity. Most couples had worked on this issue before they were married. As they shared with me the process they had followed (in some cases, of course, the process was ongoing), I recognized that, regardless of the outcome, all three groups had certain common concerns. In this chapter we listen as these women discuss these concerns in terms of both conscious and pre/unconscious elements. First, we'll discuss their attitudes toward issues of age, career, finances, lifestyle, relationship to spouse, and non-rational elements. We then turn to a consideration of certain intrapsychic elements that impact on their decision.

CONSCIOUS ELEMENTS

Age

Interestingly, there seems to be a variable maximum age limit in the planning for the first child. That is, women in their late twenties said that by age thirty they would make this decision; thirty year old women said they had until thirty-five to make this decision; and thirty-three to thirty-five year old women felt they could postpone the decision until they were in their late thirties or early forties. The older women discussed the diagnostic usefulness of amniocentesis, as support for delaying a decision. Yet, since all subjects were about the same age (average age for Group A was 31; for Group B was 30; for Group C was 32), it's evident that age alone was not a decision determinant. For example, Lois (B) (age twenty-nine) said, "But I have a real thing about getting pregnant over thirty and thirty-two . . .

just the dangers of being pregnant when you're older . . . " Jane (A) (age thirty-two) said, "I know it's there. It's like time running out. You have to know your decision. I think we're pro-children—personally pro-children. We're not adamantly against children or anything like that . . . but the pressure is the fact that I'm thirty-two. If you have your children after that you're too old biologically." Merryl (C) (age thirty-five) said, "When I was twenty-eight, I said, I'm a career woman. I don't want to stop my career. My gynecologist said, 'you'll probably be one of those who gets pregnant when you're forty-three'; and I said, NOT ME . . . and pretty much made a conscious decision we were not going to have a child and told our families." (At age thirty-two, Merryl had a tubal ligation.) Holly (B) (age thirty-four) said, "For me, age thirty-five is a kind of crossroads for two reasons . . . thirty-five career-wise seems really going from a younger person to a middle-aged person . . . and then having a child after that would affect our lives . . . we'd be so settled . . . " Diane (A) (age thirty-three) not only pushes the age to "sometime in the forties," but points out some of the age-related implications in terms of career stage: "You can keep postponing it up until a certain point, and a lot of my friends talk about a biological clock presumably after thirty-five something magical happens . . . it's more difficult to have a child . . . it's a higher risk for the mother. It's a higher risk for the child. The cutoff for me would be sometime in my forties. I think as you get older your career makes it more difficult to have a child. I know five years ago when I was in a comparatively low place in the organization, it would have been a much easier time for me than now, because I have greater responsibilities. There's much more demand where my time's concerned, much more stress . . . and I travel approximately once a month."

Career Issues—The "Right Time" Question

There was very little agreement about the "right" time to take off for a baby. For example, Julie (B), having reached a senior management position, believed that she could take some time off for a baby and still come back into the organization without losing ground. On the other hand, Diane, (A) having worked for several years, felt pressured to stay with her career because she had achieved a position of responsibility in her organization. Although some younger dual-career women suggest that children first, then career, is the best plan, others felt they needed to become more fully established in order to be able to take time out without losing too much. For example, Jane (A): "I can't see having a child and not being part of the child's life. The decision to have a baby means the decision not to work, for awhile, anyway . . . and then the question is, could I come back?"

A study that compared early and late timing motherhood concludes that there is no " . . . single 'right time' "[1] to have children. The authors note that those who spend many years in a career before they have children seem to have an advantage over those who don't have a significant record of experience. However, they remind us that there are many variables that compound this process. Since the dual-career system is so new, we really don't have enough experience to assess the long range career impact of taking an extended time-out.

Several other career related problems emerged as women anticipated the difficulties of combining careers with motherhood. Louise (A) focused on her appearance, on how she'd look in a business setting, if she were pregnant: "The other thing is I'm not going to be a really dynamic seminar speaker if I'm eight months pregnant." Diane (A), anticipated a negative attitude from the men in her organization: " . . . the kid begins to fight with your ability to do the job; and even though you are able to put out the same amount of work, again I think there is a big hurdle that men have to get over in terms of their perception of what's effective for women to do and what's not acceptable. It's acceptable for men, for instance, to leave work and go off golfing because an army buddy is in town, but it's not acceptable for a woman to go home because the kid is sick."

I found that career concerns often masked other, less conscious themes. For example, to understand Diane's (A) ambivalence, it is helpful to consider some unconscious elements of her conflict which are reflected in the following MTAT response: Card VII (two women with a baby crawling on the floor between them) " . . . so she opted to have a child late and dropped out of the job market . . . now her friend is visiting . . . but the friend is ambivalent about the fact that the mother has dropped out of the job market . . . their conversation is unsatisfactory . . . the mother tries to get the child interested in another toy but that lasts only for a few seconds . . . later when she tells her husband about the afternoon, he can tell how unhappy she is . . . even though they waited to have a child, before she dropped out . . . " The themes here—the inability to talk, the child's demanding presence, her stated unhappiness and finally her triple reference to dropping out—reveal some of the underlying conflict. Therefore, although Diane is consciously aware of elements of competition and perhaps discriminatory treatment of women in business, part of her ambivalence arises out of these unconscious issues.

Group B women who reported a uniformly high level of satisfaction with their career did not seem to feel that their overall professional growth would be dramatically changed with the addition of a baby, but they did feel that their current work could very well evolve into something different. Several Group B women found it reasonable to consider less than full-time work— some kind of self-employment, or some kind of close-to-home arrangement. For example, Julie (B) said, "Well I think I am very lucky. Maybe it is because I am where I never thought I would be in the first place. I think timing has a lot to do with the decisions you make in life, and this is a good time for me right now. I am still young . . . it seems right and the next logical step. Yet, I need intellectual stimulation. I'm spoiled—I need that interaction. I need my peer group around me. I know I couldn't sit around and talk about baby food all day. I don't know if I'll stop working. I'm sure I'll never be a full-time housewife. I'm sure I'll never not do something. I might, though, have my own business. I would enjoy it."

For all women in this study, questions of continuing career commitment were related not only to issues of self-fulfillment and personal achievement, but also to financial considerations.

Finances

Karen (C) said, "The biggest problem dual-career couples can have is money. I think so, I really do. It brings out the worst in us . . . competition, power issues . . . it's our biggest hassle." Finances were a problem for everybody. But as the pressure to reach a childbearing decision increased, financial considerations became critical.

Some couples who had become dependent on two incomes said that although the increased income enabled them to establish a satisfactory lifestyle—to buy a house, take trips, eat dinner out often—it also served to limit their freedom to change. They felt locked into their work, unable to alter their lifestyle. This was particularly true when career or family decisions would result in having to give up one income. Kay (C) said, "For us, the really big issue in marriage is money . . . our income goes amazingly quickly; and it's a sizable income for a family of two. Yet our bills always seem to get ahead of us . . . particularly now because of our investment in a house. So even if I'd like to start thinking about a career move, I'm afraid to rock the boat."

Most couples pooled their incomes, and then developed some idiosyncratic system for maintaining a sense of individual contribution. Many women talked about the relationship between their income and their feeling of independence. For example, Margaret (B) said, "We share expenses down the middle . . . collect our slips on all expenses, and then at the end of the month we split it up. Never been a problem, though our friends don't understand. My financial independence is very important to me. If I am able to save some money, I don't want to pool it. Then if he's less frugal, I don't want my money going down the drain."

Some women in this study who were earning more money than their spouses, managed this without any stress. (It has been reported that approximately 16% of wives in dual-career families earn more money than their husbands.)[2] For others, however, such as Lois (B), the difference between her income and his was clearly a sore point. Lois (B) and her husband are both teachers. She's been in the school system longer, has somewhat better academic credentials, and earns about $5,000 a year more than he does. She said, "Usually we don't even think about that. But last winter when it was so cold, he kept turning down the heat, and I wanted it up a little . . . and we kept arguing, and I really got so mad and screamed that I could do whatever I liked because I was paying the bills. He just couldn't stand my saying that . . . it was awful . . . we were so bitter. It took us a long time to get over that . . . we don't talk about it much . . . but it's still there." That this outburst may have been symptomatic of other issues is revealed through some themes in Lois' projective responses. In response to MTAT Card II (woman in office, looking at diploma and pictures of family): " . . . she looks rigid, like there's something wrong . . . she looks uncomfortable . . . she seems to be in this place she doesn't quite fit in . . . she's got this problem and needs to talk to somebody about that . . . she knows she needs help, because of the way she feels . . . " To Card III (group scene), she says, " . . . I don't know . . . I was going to say there was some conflict of some kind . . . " Obviously, Lois is experiencing some kind of stress. We need to know more about her, but her responses—" . . . something wrong . . . being in a place she doesn't quite fit . . . needing help . . . conflict of some kind . . . "—suggest that there may be some other problems here.

Financial concerns were specifically related to the childbearing decision for many Group A and B women. Lisa (A) and Fred had recently moved into a new house. For them, the uninterrupted availability of two incomes was critical: " . . . And it finally came out—'what will happen if you get pregnant?' And I answered, it's not going to happen because we need both incomes to pay for this mortgage . . . that's not going to happen, Fred."

Most women talked about the high cost of acceptable childcare. Lisa (A) continued, "If we were financially able to hire someone to stay with the baby who I felt comfortable with, if I could be assured that the baby was receiving the right environment and stimulus from this person during the day and I didn't have those mechanical things to do on an ongoing basis . . . I guess I want the best of two worlds . . . have the baby and keep my job too."

There were four women in Group B who felt they were at a point where they could handle the financial impact of going from two incomes to one. For example, Julie (B): "We're lucky because we can afford to give up one income for awhile." Barbara (A): "We have figured it out, and financially, we're at the point where we could make it on just one salary." Judy

(B): " . . . Then we said, when will we ever have enough money? We realize we'll never get the house the way we'd like it . . . so then it became another question. That is, were we ready to change our lives; and so we began to talk about that . . . " Thus, Judy introduces another common element that impacted on their decision; that is, a question of lifestyle.

Lifestyle

Although all these women have an established, child-free lifestyle, they differed in their response to the anticipated changes a child would necessitate. Group A suffered in their exploration of changing lifestyles. Group B viewed the changes as acceptable. And Group C found those changes unacceptable.

Denise's comments are illustrative of the Group C position. Denise (C): " . . . It's been a very simple decision and maybe we haven't looked at all sides of it and we haven't thought about it the way we should, but for us, it's really a question of lifestyle. It's a lifestyle decision . . . In terms of where I'm at right now in my life. I really love what I'm doing. I really love coming here to work and having the freedom to do what I'm doing; and having to give that up would cause a lot of resentment toward whatever, or whoever, was responsible. And I know that would translate . . . the child would be a victim of that . . . there really is not a place in my life for children . . . that isn't to say, I don't say I don't like children. I love children and really enjoy being around them. But in terms of fitting them into my life, I can't see it . . . Lifestyle was the major consideration."

Quality of the Marital Relationship

As we said above in Chapter 2, all women said that their spouse was the most important person in their lives. The nature of their relationship, the level of interdependence, the degree of intimacy, their mutual and combined capacity for growth, the confidence that their relationship could withstand the instrusive new-baby demands, the anticipated need to share, and the stirrings of jealousy toward the yet unborn rival, all affected the child-bearing-decision.

One thing was certain—children were out of the question for those who felt that their relationship was shaky. Marlis (A): "Before I could become pregnant . . . I'd need to feel that this relationship was absolutely secure—that I could count on it for ten years . . . I don't know that it is that . . . " Lisa (A): "I would not be confident now to bring a child into our marriage; not even if tomorrow we inherited $1 million and I could stay home. I wouldn't do it. I don't feel secure enough that this is going to be a long-lasting relationship. To have children the one priority I have is to feel that the marriage is more solid than it is right now."

Some subjects said that part of the hesitancy about children was based on the recognition that their spouse would not share the childcare responsibilities. For instance, Larla (C): "Over the years, I have gotten more and more specific in my questions to Tom, such as would you be willing to give up half your life to take care of a child, and he says, absolutely not; so it doesn't make any sense to me for Tom to say on the one hand that under no circumstances would he stay home and cut back his number of working hours, and on the other hand to tell me I'm selfish because I'm not willing to have a baby." Jane (A), looking at what she regards as an unsatisfactory division of domestic responsibilities, worries that childcare responsibilities would follow the same pattern. "Yes, it will be fine if he wants to play with the baby, great, but . . . when it comes to cleaning, feeding, running to the doctor . . . would be my responsibility."

On the other hand, women in Group B who were generally satisfied with the way their domestic chores were shared, felt that their spouse would share equally in all aspects of parenting. Barbara (A): "Jim's been ready for several years. I was the one who had certain goals to reach first—like this degree—before I was ready. But I always knew how he felt, and how he'd share in the responsibility. But the other thing I knew is that it's really my life that's going to change the most; but at this point . . . I'm ready for those changes."

More than half the women in Groups A and C felt that although their spouse had "veto" power, they had the larger voice in making the decision about children. It is not by chance that all the following examples include the word "burden." This responsibility was viewed as an extremely heavy weight. Diane (A): "If we have a decision, the decision will be 60% mine and 40% my husband's, and the reason I say that is I believe he has more of a veto decision, but the decision would ultimately have to rest with me. I feel the burden rests much more heavily on the shoulders of the woman than that of the man . . . I also think the psychological burden is with the woman." Francine (C): " . . . It was really mostly up to me, because if I had said I wanted to have a child, Mitch would have been open to it. As it was, I knew he was also against having children . . . so in that way, it was easier . . . but the burden of this decision was on me. Now except for the hassles from my mother, I feel pretty satisfied with my decision." Francine's reference to her mother echoed a common observation. Many parents and friends try to pressure the ambivalent and voluntarily childless groups. Francine's mother was most outspoken and direct. She said, "What did I do so badly? Why don't you want to be like me?" The emotional impact of this kind of pressure brings us to the final issue to be presented in this section, which I refer to as a non-rational element.

A Non-Rational Element

Most subjects were aware that there was an aspect of their decision which was not clearly thought out in a rational fashion, but rather was based on a "gut feeling." For some, the non-rational press arose out of feelings of stress and ambiguity. For example, Diane (A): "I think the decision to have a child is more an emotional one than a rational one. I talked with a friend of mine who was pregnant and she talked about what she was going through. I told her I thought the obstacle was logistics, and she said I wonder if that is a cover for emotional feelings that you don't want to deal with . . . there's probably a lot in what she said." Larla (C), having decided not to have children said, "I am not really comfortable with it yet. That's the thing. It is a major decision . . . it's normal to have children . . . the deviance taps into old labels . . . 'selfish,' 'can't give,' 'rigid,' . . . but I can't see myself with the mess of a child . . . I still have that baggage and it's hard for me to imagine that I cold (sic) dropped it off." Larla's unusual usage of the word "cold" reflects an unconscious fear of isolation and rejection, which was even more apparent in her projective responses. To MTAT IV (daughter and aging parents) she said, " . . . there's never a lot of emotional display . . . there's no expression . . . can't see her eyes . . . they are tight and not giving . . . " It seems for Larla, the decision not to have a child stirs up feelings of rejection and loss, of which she is only somewhat aware.

Marlis (A), for whom planning and control are very important, offered an extremely poignant statement of the nature of her conflict. "How have I put children in a category of things that cannot be controlled? But I feel I don't . . . I don't know. Everything else seems to come first . . . whether I want it to or not. Everything like work and school and all the things I can control. They all seem very important; they have to be settled immediately. I can get from one day to the next . . . Relationships with men and children seem like things that just happen . . . I have managed men, but I don't control them. I would like to say that I will be pregnant next year or maybe the year after . . . I would like to be able to say . . . but I think we are not going to decide . . . I am terribly afraid that we are not going to decide . . . I am afraid I have stalled too long and our world would have to change too much."

In contrast to these conflictual statements, many women in Group B said to me that they had reached a point where they stopped waiting for the "right time." They said that having children is simply a part of life; an experience they are anticipating with excitement and pleasure. Joyce (B):

"I want to have the experience of going through a pregnancy, but I think more, it is watching children grow with some kind of input . . . I think it is the interest and enjoyment in children as they get older—watching them develop and the enjoyment of seeing them develop." Julie (B), expresses this position very well: "I just think it's a part of life. It's enriching and it's like a miracle . . . it's like nothing else you can co . . . you can have a job . . . and be successful . . . but I think it is one of the most rewarding things in your life you can undertake . . . it's scary and it's devastatingly frightening . . . in my opinion, it's the only irreversible decision in your life you can make. Marriage can end in divorce, but you can't walk away from a child, . . . we think we'll be great for our kids . . . and the kids will know that." I have labeled these last few statements "non-rational," referring to the aspect of the childbearing decision that was not determined by an intellectual, rational process, but which was of an unconscious/preconscious origin. In the course of attempting to probe more deeply into these factors, I came to understand that there was a relationship between several very early intrapsychic processes and the adult childbearing decision.

INTRAPSYCHIC ELEMENTS

When I compared these subjects in terms of very early developmental processes and relationships, I discovered that all the women in Group A (Ambivalent) and all but one woman in Group B (Baby) recalled a loving, special feeling of approval from father. In contrast, all Group C (Childless) women described father's abandonment or rejection. However, the quality of this early relationship with father did not seem related to either a positive or negative identification with mother.

Relationship to Father

As these women talked about their earliest memories of their relationship to their father, it was evident that certain women felt that they held a very special position in the family vis-a-vis their father. (see Chart I) These subjects reflected what I have termed the "chosen one" feeling. For example, Lisa (A) said, "I was my father's pride and joy. He took me to school . . . when my father came home he would spend at least two hours with me. On Saturdays I would usually follow him everywhere . . . " Lois (B), whose father died when she was a very young child, said, "I don't remember my father that well, but I know he and I always used to go out for doughnuts after church . . . and he worked a lot . . . he was a private detective, and he had odd hours, but he always had time for me . . . "

CHART I

RELATIONSHIP TO FATHER AND MOTHER
MOTHER'S ATTITUDE TOWARD MEN

SUBJECT	RELATIONSHIP TO FATHER		RELATIONSHIP TO MOTHER			MOTHER'S ATTITUDE TOWARD MEN	
	"Chosen One"	Unloved or Abandoned	Loving	Love you, only if*	Unloved or Abandoned	Positive	Negative
Group A							
Marlis	X			X			X
Jane	X				X		X
Paula	X		X			X	
Alyssa	X			X		X	
Lisa	X				X		X
Louise	X			X		X	
Diane	X		X			X	
Barbara	X			X		X	
Group B							
Holly	X		X			X	
Lois	X		X			X	
Judy		X			X		X
Julie	X				X	X	
Becky	X		X			X	
Joyce	X		X			X	
Margaret	X		X			X	
Barbara	X			X		X	
Group C							
Karen		X	X				X
Larla		X			X		X
Kay		X			X		X
Merryl		X	X				X
Denise		X			X		X
Lee		X			X		X
Alice		X		X		X	
Francine		X			X		X

*"Only if . . . you're perfect; only if you meet my needs." (This category was not found in relationships to father.)

Key: A = Ambivalent Group
      B = Baby Group
      C = Childless Group

In the memories described above, father is always viewed as available and loving, choosing to do special things with the child. Some women compared this relationship with their father with the way he treated their siblings. Jane (A): "My mother and my sister seemed to get along a lot better, and I got along with my dad. I was his . . . or at least, I thought I was, sort of chosen . . . and I loved it. We did everything. I'd follow him around, even to putty the windows . . . everywhere . . . I saw myself as being a partner. I was always hanging around with boys, too, though.''

Jane's comments, illustrating her feeling that her sister and mother were alike, and that she was like her father, were repeated by every subject who had an older sister, as I noted above. Jane also seems to recognize that she was identifying with *all* the males in her life—not just her father. Although we can see this is a positive memory, Jane's projective response to Card III (group scene) is indicative of some discrepancy between conscious and unconscious themes, as she says, " . . . is he supposed to be a priest? Everyone is supposed to be listening to him . . . but whatever he says, I know I'll disagree . . . he's trying to take over and I don't want that to happen . . . '' Thus Jane reveals a possible conflict underlying her response to father's total acceptance. Perhaps she questions the price she is expected to pay for that approval.

Some women suggested a recognition of underlying oedipal issues, as manifested in the following: Marlis (A): ''In those elementary school years, I felt real close to him. We had our weekend excursions to the library. We had cookouts and he had a shop. He liked to build things and I can remember helping him. On weekends I always hung around with my father. His deal was that he was going to teach his girl to be a lady. He was concerned with manners and deportment in a way that my mother never was. He talked to me, and he criticized me if I didn't behave nicely, but not too hard . . . I do remember one episode and that I remember it so clearly must mean something. Something really good had happened, I don't remember what. My father hugged me, and when he hugged me, I bit him on the arm . . . not hard. He didn't seem to notice, he was too busy hugging me. (Question: What significance did that have?) I don't think my parents were sleeping together by then. My mother hated it. No touching or hugging. My mother would recoil if my father even patted her. By the time I was a grown-up, she didn't even want a friendly pat. I didn't see any sexuality between them.''

In the following material Louise (A) reveals strong oedipal issues. She infuses a projected aspect of the earlier father/daughter struggle into an ongoing unresolved guilt vis-a-vis mother. To MTAT IV (woman and aging parents) she said, " . . . the old man looks at her with these sort of dark adoring eyes, and sort of laps after her everywhere she goes . . . the man is absolutely enthralled with her and worries about her constantly . . . the daughter wants their approval . . . but the mother is reserved . . . something has happened . . . and they don't really talk about it . . . '' Conscious and unconscious themes of paternal approval combined with negative feelings about the relationship with mother, are related to certain aspects of the conflict affecting Louise's decisions about having children. (We will return to these issues below in discussing the formation of the individual's sense of femininity.)

The point here is that all women in Group A, and 7 out of the 8 in Group B saw themselves as either the "chosen one" or very accepted by father. In contrast, *none* of the Group C women recalled feeling this sense of being the chosen one. Their comments are illustrative. Lee (C): "My father would threaten us a few times and snap his belt, but he would never hit us . . . he didn't know us well enough to hit us. I certainly could never talk to my father early in my life and I never did."

Francine and Merryl reacted in a very physical way to their fear of father: Francine (C): "I was afraid of him . . . in fact, if I'd come home and see his car in the driveway, my stomach would just tie up in knots." Merryl (C): "I always had to be careful . . . he would come home drunk . . . he was never violent, but there were confrontations between him and my mother and it would just knot my stomach . . . it would just knot my stomach up terribly, and I would retreat and feel awful." Karen (C) remembers her father as a rather shadowy, remote figure, scary and unavailable: "In my early memories, my father was rather scary. He would work literally sometimes 23 hours a day. He had his own small business, heating and plumbing and air conditioning . . . so I just didn't see him very much . . . I don't think I can give you an incident that we shared together closely."

The picture here of father as distant and unavailable was repeated in Karen's response to Card IV (woman and aging parents). " . . . there's a conflict here . . . the younger person is angry at the other two . . . she's telling them about her divorce . . . they think it's terrible . . . she realizes that she had expected this reaction . . . so negative . . . from her father anyway . . . she doesn't stay there . . . she just leaves . . . "

In her response to Card VI (man and woman shaking hands) we hear Karen's wish to dominate, humiliate the father, to punish him for his rejection and to blame him for her failings. She tells a story of a father, whose daughter was having problems in school, and who was called to school for a conference with the teacher: " . . . the child is acting up in class and is causing a disruption . . . she used to be bright and used to work well . . . The father is uncomfortable in this situation because the teacher is a young woman . . . younger than he is . . . and he's just trying to ignore the fact that his daughter is having difficulties . . . so it's not a very pleasant meeting because the teacher must be firm about trying to understand the daughter's problem, particularly between him and his wife . . . " Manifesting her fantasy of taking over the mother's role, in this projection, Karen is both the daughter and the teacher. In both roles, the father is seen as inadequate.

Alice, another woman in Group C, felt that she had to compete with her sister for father's love, which was ultimately denied. She said, "My sister was the special one, she could understand the tools to use . . . and I'm sure my father built up a jealousy between me and my sister and my brother who is four years younger . . . I avoided confrontation. I avoided him . . . because I learned that where I was concerned, it just didn't do any good." These memories of rejection color Alice's unconscious wish to retaliate and hurt the father as she was hurt. This is evident in her response to MTAT Card IV (woman and aging parents): " . . . two elderly people who don't look particularly happy . . . I don't feel any particular affinity . . . the man in particular seems unhappy . . . and the kind of look on her face . . . sort of like self-satisfaction . . . and it is hurting her parents and she is almost enjoying it . . . it looks to me like she is a little smug and is watching them be hurt and watching them be displeased and it almost gives her satisfaction . . . "

Summarizing, both conscious and unconscious material revealed that Group A and B recall feeling either as if they were the "chosen one," or else very much accepted by father. However, Group C women indicated consciously that they never felt accepted or loved by their fathers; their unconscious themes are bitter and filled with wishes for revenge. Given these stark differences in memories of early relationship to father, the question arose as to whether there would be any association between these feelings and identification with mother.

Relationship to Mother

Before we analyze the differences between women who felt loved by mother vs those who felt rejected, let's look again at Chart I on page 52. As can be seen, two women in Group A, five women in Group B, and two women in Group C described a loving relationship with their mother. Six women in the study had established what I have termed a "conditional love" relationship with mother. That is, they felt that she would love them only if they behaved a certain way; only if they followed her wishes; only if they were "perfect"; only if they met her needs. Most of Group B recalled a loving relationship with mother and most of Group C felt unloved or abandoned. It's important to note here that two of the Group C women were able to establish a positive identification with mother, although they felt rejected by father. Thus, there does not seem to be an inevitable link between the feelings of acceptance or rejection by father, and either a positive or negative identification with mother.

Loving Relationship to Mother.   I examined the nature of the loving relationship to mother to see if there were any qualitative differences between Groups A, B, and C. The dominant patterns used to describe positive relationships for Groups A and B include some of the following: a mother more than a wife; patient; creative; security in her rules; sacrifice; dependable; gave us her energy; wise; handles sibling relationships well. The dominant patterns used to describe the positive relationships for Group C include: accomplished; outgoing; professional; good business woman. Thus, positive mothers from Group A and B are described in terms of the way they relate to the child. The positive mothers in Group C are described in the way they related to the world. These trends become quite vivid as we examine the statements of the subjects, as well as their preconscious and unconscious material.

Paula's (A) admiration for her mother is clear. Talking about her mother she said, " . . . she had always given totally of herself . . . and that is my role model . . . tireless constant energy . . . givingness . . . When I was about five, I told my mother I was going to run away . . . and her attitude was, okay, I will help you pack. And she did . . . it was very heavy! She had enormous insight . . . she knew exactly what to do. I never got across the street! I didn't even get out the front door the suitcase was so big and heavy!"

Holly (B) felt secure in mother's stability and structure: "Basically she was a rule follower, and so I'm still a rule follower. I mean I feel guilty when I take a donut out of the cafeteria. Rules are, you are not supposed to take food into the office. But there was a lot of security in her rules and in her organized life . . . I know I'm probably trying to be like her in that way . . . "

Lois (B) felt she was like her mother in many ways. She talked about her mother's love of, " . . . making creative things for us . . . I'm like that too. That's one reason I know I could find so many things to do if I stayed home with a baby. I'd like that."

Comparing Self to Others.   Many subjects compared their relationship to mother with that of their siblings'. Some felt that mother's love for them was not threatened by another sibling. For example, Becky's (B) earliest memories of mother are associated with her brother: "I remember her handing me my baby brother to hold, which was a big thrill. I've asked my mother a million times how I was so accepting of having a new brother. Evidently she reassured me that I was still important to her."

As mentioned before, I found that all subjects who had an older sister felt that the older sister was more like mother than they were, and could more easily gain mother's love. Louise (A), somewhat unsure of her role vis-a-vis mother, remembers feeling very competitive toward her sister, (and mother). Louise began Card IV (woman and aging parents) by rejecting the existence of the mother; mother was added as an afterthought, as the story unfolded. By omitting reference to the mother, Louise suggests an unconscious wish to remove her from the family triangle. She says, " . . . This is a young girl with her father . . . " In Card X (younger woman looking up at older woman) Louise (A) reveals not only her wish to reverse roles, to control and dominate the mother, but also a sense of her unfulfilled need for nurturance. She says, " . . . she's trying to teach me something . . . I will just keep feeding her questions and gain as much as I can from her . . . I would have exhausted her . . . "

Marlis (A) understood that mother's love was contingent on her performance. If she was achieving, if she was "being perfect" she had mother's love. Marlis (A): "There was no question about my father's love. But my mother's love felt contingent . . . enormous pressure from my mother to just do a little better. She didn't know I felt so unworthy all the time. I couldn't be good enough. As she saw it, she was encouraging me. As I saw it, no matter how hard I tried, I was a disaster in her eyes. . . . You see she needed for me to be perfect . . . and now I seem to need that for myself."

The four Group A women, who fall into the only-if-you're-perfect love category, believed that in spite of their own conflict with mother, the family was the center of the mother's life. For example, Alyssa (A) refers to her mother in the following statement as more of a mother than a wife. She says, "My mom was always the mother . . . she took being a mother seriously, and I saw her more as a mother than as a wife." Alyssa's response to MTAT Card IV (woman and aging parents) illustrates that perhaps under conscious affirmation there is some discrepancy: " . . . they are all unhappy . . . uncomfortable with each other . . . the daughter is asking for their approval, but that is withheld by the mother." Another response shows us, however, that Alyssa tries to find a way to restore the balance: Card X (younger woman looking up at older woman), " . . . the daughter is competent . . . their relationship is good, but the mother loves the daughter more than the daughter loves the mother . . . they may have had their problems, but on the whole they think alike . . . " These examples have illustrated that, although the relationship to mother is consciously described by Group A and B women as loving (in seven cases) or as conditional (in five cases), there is somewhat more discrepancy between conscious reporting and unconscious themes in Group A women than in Group B. The direction of the relationship, however, is always from mother to daughter.

Identification with External Orientation. In contrast to the interpersonal process, which was characteristic of groups A and B, the two group C women who identified strongly and positively with mother emphasized mother's career identity, independence, and external orientation. Karen (C): "My mother ran a grocery store until I was about five. She must have had it for about 10 or 15 years, and so she spent a lot of time in the store in the front of our house. It was her store . . . my dad worked elsewhere, and she did fine. It was a situation that if you needed her you could run into the store and get her." Merryl (C): "Well, my mother, I saw her as a woman who was . . . I mean she was quiet and she was sweet but she was also . . . she'd take on the leadership of everything. She took on the leadership of a Brownie troop, she'd join the PTA, she had the neighborhood get-together. So she was an outgoing woman, and an accomplished woman. She also had a profession . . . a nursing profession. I clearly understood that woman worked. My aunt worked. She was a professional woman. All the women around me worked."

Unhappy Relationship to Mother.   Two women in group A, two in Group B, and five in group C who described a painful early relationship with mother, said that mother's focus was on either their siblings or their father. In other words, the mother's love was deflected from the subject, but still contained within the family system.

Jane (A) remembers vying with her sister for mother's attention and feeling the need to fight for her place. She uses the word "battle." Jane says, "I probably didn't like her (sister) because she was probably in my way. With five kids you are battling for your territory. The way she got along with my mother bothered me at various times. My relationship was not anything with my mother. It was a battle."

Judy (B), the only member of B Group who recalls an unhappy relationship with both father and mother, relates this unhappiness to the fact that her natural father and mother were divorced when she was one year old, and she was adopted by a step father who strongly rejected her: "I remember a lot of quarreling and my being thrown onto a bed." Judy continued, "When she had had enough of my step father, where she just couldn't take his aggravation—complaining about the kids . . . then she would agree with him . . . and you would think, Oh my gosh . . . you really thought she was on your side . . . and you really felt you had somebody. And you didn't. She was gone." Judy's unconscious wish for reparation, her continuing search for a positive response from mother, can be seen in the story she tells in MTAT Card VII (two women, baby crawling between them). Judy describes a mother coming to visit the daughter and her baby: " . . . the girl seems very ill at ease . . . the mother seems to be a very stern, strict woman . . . there are no feelings . . . just small talk . . . she had hoped it would be different with the baby . . . but the mother has no feelings about how it is . . . she doesn't ask how she's feeling to be a mother . . . " Judy refers to a lack of feeling three times in this short response. We hear her say that in spite of her hopes that this time it might be different, the mother continues the lifelong pattern, that is, mother continues to re-fuse to give her what she wants.

We note that the five women in Group C who described a painful rela-tionship to mother also saw mother as concentrating primarily on other family members (as Groups A and B did) rather than externally; on some sort of work or on something else in the environment.

Mother's Attitude Toward Men. In considering mother's attitude to-ward men, it was very interesting to see that although three mothers in Group A and one in Group B were anti-male, seven mothers in Group C were extremely negative toward their own spouse and, in general, devalued the males with whom they come in contact. For example, Merryl (C) said, "My mother and my aunt weren't particularly interested in men . . . I had this really negative attitude toward men, too, particularly after my parents were divorced . . . so I got the message from them, but I didn't know how to handle it . . . it comes out even today though. Now most men, men who are very powerful and who exercise that power . . . I feel intimidated by them. I lose all sense of my wisdom and age . . . I feel much younger. I act like a child . . . like I did in high school." Kay (C): "My mother was very young when my father died but she never remarried . . . or even dated . . . she wasn't interested in men." Denise (C): "My mother always felt that it was his (father's) fault that she was miserable."

In Chapter 8 we'll come back to a discussion of the possible impact of mother's attitude toward men, in terms of daughter's childbearing decision.

Other Mother/Daughter Issues. There were three other important ele-ments of the relationship with mother which emerged from the analysis of the data. The first concerns the focus on independence and career orien-tation, the second on sexual competition, and the third on the message about children.

Independence and Career Orientation. Across all three groups there were some women who traced their independence and career orientation to a resolve to be different from mother. For example, Diane (A) developed a resolve to avoid some of her mother's dissatisfaction: "My mother was a little bit frustrated . . . she had the feeling that I am not really being fulfilled because I am a housewife and a woman . . . that sort of thing." Louise (A): "Well, I think she always wanted to be more independent. Her sense of self value centered around the family. And when I recognized that that was happening . . . it made me think about what I was going to do with my life." Marlis (A) recalls that her mother actively urged her to become independent: "My mother wanted me to have a profession so I would be independent . . . she felt strongly about the fact that she didn't have that."

Sexual Competition.   Several women reported that as they reached adolescence they became engaged in a competitive struggle with their mother, and that their developing sexuality was perceived as a threat. For example, Julie (B): "I know she is sorry for a lot of things. I forgive her but at the same time I wish she had been more mature, so that we could talk about things. By the time I was twelve I understood a lot of things, I understood what the resentment was about. But I was going to be a woman regardless. I was no longer a little girl she could dress up and would do everything she wanted me to do . . . the reaction I got was always very negative, always on the verge of disgust, always the negative comment. Very threatened by my beginning relationship with boys . . . " Lee (C) felt that her mother resented her daughter's sexual development. Issues of sexual competition finally led to a complete breakdown between them: "After her divorce, she wanted to be young again. Lost a lot of weight, dyed her hair, all new clothes, and she was unhappy that here she was at this stage of life. I think she resented the fact that she wasn't young, and I was dating. She had lost her youth and never had gotten enjoyment out of her youth and she resented it."

Message About Children.   Many subjects said that mother's message was, " . . . grow up, get married, and have kids. That's it . . . be like me." Although some women partially accepted this directive, others like Lisa (A) resented her mother's assumption that if she did those things, that was enough. Lisa said, "She's very different from me . . . She believes that you should get married, buy a house and have a family, and the man works. For example, when we were getting married (she had literally given up on my ever getting married!) and she said 'now that you are getting married you will stop going to school every night.' And I said 'no I won't stop going to school,' and she said, 'But what do you need it for now'?"

Reflecting on mother's early message about the position of children in one's life, Marlis (A) remembers her mother's belief, " . . . that somewhere along in this independent life you get married, because you have to have children . . . Marriage is an unpleasant and unnecessary event you have to go through in order to have children. What was important was having children. Marriage was trivial . . . In retrospect, I feel that she believed that marriage was a sad but inevitable fate."

Alyssa (A) feels that she will have her mother's support if she decides against having children: "And I said that Mike and I have decided that we might not have any kids . . . and her comment was that she knew some very happy people who did not have children. I guess she sees me happy now, married, whereas when I was single she sensed my unrest. She felt I would be happier married and hoped that I would be married some day. If she saw me unhappy and wanting kids . . . she might feel differently."

Francine (C) feels that even today as an adult she does not have her mother's approval primarily because of her choice not to have a child. Francine said she feels a "sort of irrational guilt" as her mother asks her, " . . . why can't you be like me . . . what did I do that was so bad?"

The analysis so far indicates the following:

1. There are sharp distinctions in perception of early relationships with the father. Women in Groups A and B generally reported feeling accepted and loved by their father. Women in Group C felt rejected by father.
2. There was no apparent relationship between the feelings of rejection by father and either positive or negative identification with mother.
3. Of those who experienced a positive identification with mother, there are clear distinctions between Groups A, B, and C. Positive feelings for Group A and B were generated because of the way mother related to them. Positive feelings for Group C were associated with mother's external orientation.
4. Half of the subjects in Group A, and one in each of the other groups reflected what has been termed a conditional maternal love. All of the Group A and B conditionally loved, were nevertheless self-labeled as "chosen" by father.
5. Those women in all three groups who had strong negative feelings toward their mother were focused on their own experience of inadequacy. They felt that mother's rejection was due to their failure, rather than as a result of mother's need, either internal or external. They believed that mother's love was reserved for other family members.
6. There was a greater discrepancy between conscious reporting and unconscious themes in Group A than in either Group B or C.
7. Exploration of subject's perception of mother's attitudes indicated that seven out of the eight mothers in Group C had a pervasively negative attitude toward men, as compared to three mothers in Group A and one mother in Group B.

These apparent differences in the nature and outcome of significant early relationships, led me to the next developmental question: Are there any differences in the content and process of feminine identification that characterize and separate the three groups under analysis?

FEMININE IDENTIFICATION
AND THE CHILDBEARING DECISION

The adult sense of femininity is the product of a vast array of variables, including biological (chromosomal, genital/reproductive, hormonal); sociological (gender/sex role), and psychological (unconscious/conscious, cognitive, etc.) aspects. Adding to this complexity, the women I studied have apparently separated their sense of self as female into two distinct aspects: sexuality and nurturance. By understanding the nature of this separation, we gain another clue to the complicated childbearing decision process.

External Female Characteristics

Some women in all the groups talked about the significance of a feminine appearance. Louise (A) and Paula (A) had differing perspectives on the importance of a feminine appearance. Louise (A) places importance on external appearances" . . . To look pretty and feminine can be used to advantage . . . " For example, in Card VI (handshake between woman and man) she says " . . . he thinks she's just an attractive, sweet young thing . . . she really should have on a business suit . . . she's cultivating the relationship and is really in complete control but she really should not have worn that dress . . . he's pleased with the flirting aspect and does not understand what's really going on . . . " Paula (A) said, "I am probably a non-romantic practical woman . . . I take care of myself and my femininity . . . I enjoy being a woman, but the usual trappings of being pretty . . . that's not it." Julie (B) talked about the changes over the years in the way she dealt with the issues of sexuality and appearance. "When I was in my early 20's I was self-conscious about my sexuality. But I know I used my sexuality in a way to get men to depend on me, professionally and individually . . . I became defensive about my sexuality in a business setting. But today I don't have to be defensive about my success or my appearance because by and large at age 31 people do not resent me for being where I am . . . but I think some people believe that I must have done something. Like when I was in high school and the teacher said you can't be beautiful and smart. I thought to myself, I'll be damned if I would change." Denise (C) said, "To me femininity has to do with being stylish and being smart and looking sophisticated and all that. The attractive, sexual woman is feminine to me."

Gender Issues:

Identification with Masculine Activities.   Subjects in all three groups recalled a period in their lives when they sought identification with masculine activities. For example, Louise (A) said, "Of course we played with dolls, but really would have preferred the mechanical toys . . . " Margaret (B): "I didn't see myself as a rebel in wanting what they had; I saw myself going after something that would be a natural sort of thing." Kay (C): "One of my biggest trips as a kid was being able to play tag with the boys and beat them. I never played with the girls. Boys did all the good things."

Competition.   'Some subjects expressed deeply conflicted feelings about their spouse's and/or male colleagues' image of them as female vs their own view of femininity. For example, Lisa (A) talked about the conflicts between traditional male expectations of feminine submissiveness and her professional self-image: "I have had some very conflicting message in myself about that, that is, sexuality. I know that sometimes it is very hard for me to go from the daily routine, as strong as I have to be to get through the day . . . and then Fred wants to make love. You cannot be submissive during the business day, you know. Then to just turn around . . . . it's a hard transition . . . it's a matter of my having a really hard time being this little kitten person . . . because it doesn't fit into the things I've had to do all day . . . " To card VI (handshake) Lisa says, " . . . he just isn't taking her seriously . . . he's just sitting there and making it as hard for her as he can . . . " To MTAT XII (male watching female walk away) she punishes him (i.e., all men) by leaving him: " . . . I don't want to make this a divorce story . . . but, she's going off to her . . . something she is happy with . . . and he doesn't know what he wants to do . . . he's standing there watching her leave and feeling a great sense of aloneness that somehow she is not sharing his problem because she is happy with herself . . . he can't get it together. But he is bringing her down, and she has a lot going for her. It seems she's done all the giving, but at this point she leaves him."

Karen (C) refers to the way her concept of femininity has changed over the years: "I remember at the X corporation a woman trying to go up the ladder. She was a very male figure. She was not my role model at all. She was tall and overbearing. Impressive, but she was not my role model of what a woman has to be to rise to the top. If that is what it takes to get there, I thought, I don't want it. And when you get to a point of being successful because you are good, did you strip yourself of being a woman?

Were you one of the 'boys?' That used to bother me, and it worried me. How do you find that balance between the two?'' She continued, ''When I was younger, I used to play the male/female thing. But now I want to be myself. And if you have to deal with me in business, you have to deal with me like I am, not stripped of my femininity . . . ''

Karen's projective responses are consistent with these themes. For example, to MTAT Card VIII (woman standing behind seated male) she says, '' . . . they have a good relationship. It is open and caring . . . they are straight with each other and really are themselves . . . ''

Fears

Although all the subjects in this study identified themselves as sexually feminine, some women in all three groups shared Marlis' (A) feelings that sexuality was a frightening topic. Marlis: ''I didn't want to talk about this (sexuality) when it first came up . . . sexuality makes me anxious . . . it's a whole new rock to be turned over and those little crawlies . . . I don't want to talk about it.'' (As we analyze the ambivalent women, in Part II, we'll return to this statement, and its implications.) In spite of her stated fears, Marlis's MTAT themes describe women who are dominant and superior, and who use their sexuality seductively. For example, to Card VI (handshake between woman and man) she says, '' . . . it's her office and she is good at what she does . . . he is going to be a bit of a problem and she knows it because he has no style . . . she feels superior to him, and has her mind on the next appointment even while he's there . . . ''

Becky's (B) fears of sexuality were revealed in both interview and projective responses: ''As a kid of course, I knew that other girls did that, but I was very convinced that it was wrong . . . I would have nightmares . . . I wondered if I would scream and fall apart . . . I'd have fantasies about all the things that could happen . . . embarrassed . . . afraid of my sexuality.'' Sexual tension is suggested in MTAT card III (group scene): ''They don't know each other . . . the kind of body language that says don't come too close . . . don't come near me . . . and just the fact that he is hovering over these women and the situation where they are very rigid . . . '' In response to Card V (woman looking out of window) she says, ''She's looking out at the rain . . . and feeling so indecisive . . . and she knows it will be colder and darker when she leaves . . . but . . . she decided she won't see him. She'd rather do something by herself than go out into the cold again . . . '' Notice all the negatives in this short response—indecisive, colder, darker, leaving, won't see him, go out into the cold.

For Lee (C) sexuality and guilt are closely associated: ''For me, there was always a lot of guilt . . . and fear. The terrible, terrible guilt and what a terrible person I was to have those feelings. I was afraid I was going to have to put up with it just as my mother had told me." Jane (A): "My mother was busy teaching me that sex is this unfortunate business . . . but there is something wrong with you if you kind of like it . . . " (Please note: For a full discussion of the impact of mother's attitude toward sexuality, see Chapter 8).

Separation of Sexuality and Nurturance

In examining the subjects' associations regarding femininity and nurturance I found clear differences between the groups.

Group A. Lisa speaks for several Group A women in terms of separating feminity and nurturance. "That's the myth . . . that's what I'm separating . . . that women should have or should want to have children . . . and should want to care for them. I don't feel that way at all . . . "

Lisa sounds pretty convincing. Yet, some discrepancy emerges between this conscious report and the unconscious themes which appear throughout her MTAT stories. For example, in response to Card II (woman looking at pictures of male and children) she says, " . . . she's very serious . . . wants to make the right decision . . . wondering if this is making her happy . . . vs. what she should/could have done . . . she wonders . . . if this is all there is . . . but then . . . there are the children . . . " And in response to Card IV (woman and aging parents) she says, " . . . this woman is all alone, rather than with a husband . . . she has no husband . . . " In Card V (woman looking out of the window; note: there are no other cues in this picture), " . . . she is afraid not to have the baby . . . that would be a harder emotional problem . . . and she has had other emotional problems in the past and she knows how hard it is to come back . . . from these setbacks and guilt feelings . . . and somehow I think it will be easier to deal with being a mother . . . than going the other route. I feel sorry for her. I am not sure she is making the right decision, but I would probably make that decision."

From these statements, which clearly show the difference between what she says in the interview vs what she says in response to the projectives, we get a sense of conflict between Lisa's overt rejection of nurturance and her uncertainty about having children.

Group B. On the whole, women in Group B expressed the view that feminity and motherhood—that is, nurturance—were significantly associated for them. For example, Lois (B) said, " . . . I do feel that my femininity and my ability to be a mother are the same. Because one time I went to the doctor and he gave me the impression that maybe one day I wouldn't be able to have kids and I thought I was going to die . . . I just couldn't stand it. I just felt I wasn't able to be all I wanted to be . . . '' Julie (B) had very strong feelings about childbirth as a verification of her femininity. She had had a baby when she was about 18 years old and had given that baby up for adoption: "Even in that situation I felt maternal and feminine. Maybe even more because of that experience I look forward to having a baby and being able to raise it and love it . . . '' Holly (B): "We're trying to become pregnant right now. My idea of myself as a female is closely associated with my long standing goal of some day having kids . . . ''

Group C. All the Group C woman had thought about the relationship between their femininity and their decision not to have children. Frequently the focus was on the issue of nurturance. Alice (C): "Femininity is . . . a relationship between male and female . . . I don't consider myself unfeminine for not having children. I don't necessarily consider myself a sex object either.''

Alice's general satisfaction with her sense of herself and her life choices comes through in her MTAT stories. In MTAT VII (two woman and crawling baby) she says, " . . . they knew each other a long time ago . . . they are still friends, but the child has created this gap between them. She is hesitant to talk about her life and her work . . . and the things she is doing for fear of making the other one lonely . . . her friend wants to try to go back but she can't.'' To Card II (woman looking at pictures of male and children, degree on the wall) she says, " . . . I would probably be more interested in the degree than she . . . it's interesting to me, take the children out if you want to . . . '' In this last statement, she reveals a bit of a sense of dissonance in terms of the existence of children, and offers her solution, i.e., don't have children.

Denise (C): "Femininity is . . . I don't worry about my femininity. I don't think it will make me less female if I don't have children and I don't think it makes you more female if you do. Whatever femininity is to me, not being a mother is not in conflict.'' Karen (C): "Any nurturance needs I might have are satisfied by my relationship with my husband . . . femininity and nurturance are certainly not linked for me. Look at some of the nurses in this hospital. Could hardly see more unfeminine women.'' Francine (C) "Femininity is being a sexual woman. Not mothering. In fact, I think you become less sexual as you become maternal.''

Chart II presents my conceptualization of the content and process of fem-

CHART II
THE CONTENT AND PROCESS OF FEMININE IDENTIFICATION AND ITS RELATIONSHIP TO CHILDBEARING INTENTIONS

	PRE-OEDIPAL SEPARATION/ INDIVIDUATION	OEDIPAL RESOLUTION	FEMININE SELF-CONCEPT		IDENTIFICATION WITH MOTHERHOOD	
			SEXUAL	NURTURANT		
GROUP A	Developmental Tasks Unresolved	Satisfactory Resolution	Yes	????	????	GROUP A
GROUP B	Satisfactory Resolution	Satisfactory Resolution	Yes	Yes	Yes	GROUP B
GROUP C	Conflicted Outcome	Unsatisfactory Resolution	Yes	No	No	GROUP C

Key: A = Ambivalent Group
       B = Baby Group
       C = Childless Group

inine identification, and its relationship to the childbearing decision. This chart is, in effect, a summary of our analysis of the data regarding early relationships to mother and father, and the subsequent development of a feminine self concept.

As indicated on the chart, the process begins with the mother/infant relationship and focuses on issues of separation/individuation. From what we have learned, Group B women experienced a satisfactory pre-oedipal relationship. However, for many in Groups A and C, it seems that there was no clear resolution of the pre-oedipal separation struggle. The required developmental tasks remain incomplete. In some cases (especially Group C) separation apparently was experienced more in the nature of rejection and abandonment than in helping to build a positive and autonomous sense of self-as-dependable object. In many Group A women, we saw that separation was tied to an unobtainable perfection, and thus became impossible to achieve. We assume that some elements of future guilt and self doublt may spring from this position. Daughter, as "not perfect" was forever tied to that attempt, and in the process, forever tied to mother.*

The finding that many ambivalent women had a conflictual relationship with mother, led to a reexamination of the pre-oedipal position, and its possible link to the childbearing decision.**

In terms of the childbearing decision, I have concluded that the Group A woman is ambivalent partially in reflection of her own dependency conflict. The inability to relinquish the maternal dependent relationship, renders her unable to become the dependable object herself.

Proceeding from the pre-oedipal to the oedipal position, we recall that Group A and B women were characterized as having felt that they had a special relationship with father—that they were the "chosen ones." We thus assume that they emerged from the oedipal period in a satisfactory manner, feeling themselves verified as females. They then were free to establish a feminine identification with mother as model.

I found that Group A (identifying with sexuality) is ambivalent insofar as accepting a nurturant orientation. This group is also ambivalent in terms of identification with the motherhood role.

---

*Part II will elaborate on these issues.

**A word of caution. It would be an error to conclude that the ambivalent daughter's lack of identification with a nurturant self concept can be directly attributed to her mother's handling of her as an infant. As we know, there is rarely a clear cut or single determinant for the development of any psychological position. The way in which the infant daughter perceived and responded to her human and nonhuman environment is very likely to be of as much significance as the actual maternal behavior.

Group B, experiencing their feminity as both sexual and nurturant, identified with mother in the sense of validation of motherhood.

Group C, on the other hand, felt rejected and inadequate in their relationship with father, thus suggesting an unsatisfactory resolution of oedipal
issues. Equating femininity with sexuality but not nurturance, they reject
identification with mother in terms of motherhood as a valid self-concept.
(Though not indicated on this chart, note that some Group C women established a positive identification with mother, based on identification with
mother's external orientation.)

To recapitulate, the content and process of feminine identification, and
the outcome of the childbearing decision, differed for each group studied.
Defining femininity as both sexual and nurturant, all subjects described
their femininity as sexual in nature. However, only Group B included nurturance in their self-concept. Group A remained ambivalent about the nurturant factor, and Group C rejected nurturance as a critical component of
femininity.

Women who were unconflicted in terms of wanting children, seemed to
progress from satisfactory early separation/individuation to paternal validation of self as female, to feminine identification embodying motherhood
(nurturance) and sexuality. Failure to establish positive early separation led
to adult ambivalence regarding motherhood. Failure to establish paternal
verification, was related to a feminine identification as exclusively sexual.

Although it is possible to entertain rival hypotheses as to the interpretation of these findings concerning the development of feminine identification, these data do not fit the classical theory of feminine development,
in which the female is seen as oriented toward passivity and masochism; [3]
as having an instinctual need to nurture; [4] and as being preoccupied with
interiority. [5] Full femininity, according to these theorists, is inextricably
bound to the maternal (nurturant) function.

The present study indicates that apparently only certain contemporary
women (in this case, Group B) identify comfortably with the nurturant
component of femininity. Other women, as we have seen, have a need to
separate sexuality from a maternal orientation. Some of this latter group
(Group A) reported a high level of ambivalence in terms of accepting a
nurturant self-concept, whereas others (Group C) at present report no dissonance between rejection of nurturance and identification with femininity.*

Many questions emerge from the new concept of femininity developed

---

*The question of how a sexual self-concept is established in Group C women remains unclear,
and is an area requiring further research. Some comments on this are found below.

in this study. For example, it will be particularly interesting to observe the middle and later life developmental outcomes for women, who at age 30, hold a nonnurturant self-concept. There is some evidence from the study of the midlife process of integration of contrasexual opposites, [6] that professional women appear at midlife, [7] and even earlier, [8] to confront certain developmental tasks which have previously been thought of as characteristically masculine. The mechanics underlying this process become more undertandable in view of the expanded definition of femininity developed in this study. It seems logical to assume that as these women, who have questioned and/or rejected the nurturant component at age 30 (as the ambivalent and childless women did) attempt to integrate previously unacknowledged aspects of self at midlife, they will appear to be struggling with "masculine" midlife tasks. It seems that an expanded, nonstereotypic definition of masculinity would be useful in future analysis of this process. For the present discussion, however, we will note that all subjects described a solid feminine self-concept regardless of the status of their child-bearing decision, or the relative salience of career vs. relationship. None of these women adopted a masculine orientation or assumed a masculine identification. Career success, independence and autonomy were experienced as harmonious and congruent with self image as female.

The conceptualizations in this chapter are presented as hypotheses about the formation of the sense of feminine identity, and about the development of the intention to bear children. Obviously, we need to continue to study these ideas before we can state with certainty that these processes are understood. However, the data presented so far, reflecting the analysis of both conscious and unconscious elements of the childbearing decision process, has led to the development of a model, which is useful because it illustrates the way in which marriage, career, and lifestyle issues are affected by certain individual psychological determinants, and how the interaction of these elements impacts on the childbearing decision. Chapter 4 introduces this dual-career childbearing decision model.

REFERENCES

1. Daniels, P. and Weingarten, K. *Sooner or Later: The Timing of Parenthood in Adult Lives.* New York: W.W. Norton, 1982. p. 304.
2. *Women at Work.* U.S. Department of Labor, Bureau of Labor Statistics, April, 1983.
3. Freud, S. "Female Sexuality" In *The Complete Psychological Works.* Standard Edition. London: Hogarth Press, 1931.
   Deutsch, H. *The Psychology of Women.* New York: Grune & Stratton, 1944.
4. Benedek, T. "Parenthood as a Developmental Phase: A Contribution to Libido Theory." *Journal of American Psychoanalytic Association.* 1959, 7, (3) 389–417.

5. Erikson, E. "Inner and Outer Space: Reflections on Womanhood." In *A Modern Introduction to the Family,* edited by Bell and Vogel. New York: Free Press, 1968.

6. Jung. C.G. "The Stages of Life." In *Structure and Dynamics of the Psyche.* (Translated by R.F.C.Hull) Princeton, NJ: Princeton University Press, 1969. Vol 8.

   Cytrynbaum, S. et al. "Midlife Development: A Personality and Social Systems Perspective." In *Aging in the 1980's,* edited by L. Poon. Washington, D.C.: American Psychological Association, 1980.

   Gutmann, D. "Parenthood: A Key to the Comparative Study of the Life Cycle." In *Life-Span Developmental Psychology,* edited by P. Datan and L. Ginsberg. New York: Academic Press, 1975.

7. Wilk, C. "Coping and Adaptation in Midlife Dual-Career Families." In Cytrynbaum, S. (Chair) Symposium: Midlife Development: Influence of Gender, Personality and Social Systems. Presented to the American Psychological Association Annual convention, New York, 1979.

8. Hennig, M. and Jardin, A. *The Managerial Woman.* Garden City, New York: Anchor Publishing, 1977.

4
A CHILDBEARING DECISION MODEL

Having come to know some of the issues that are important to dual-career couples, including certain conscious and pre/unconscious elements of the dual-career woman's decision about whether or when to have children, it is now possible to summarize these findings in the form of a conceptual model, which will allow us to analyze the dual-career childbearing decision.

Two pilot studies [1], which were undertaken in preparation for the present research, suggested that there were two stages in the development of a dual-career childbearing decision. In the first stage, which I had then labeled ambivalent, the couple avoided a decision either through overintellectualization or denial. In the second stage, the couple was able (more or less) to consider the inevitable changes in their relationship, in their lifestyle, and in their careers.

Although this two-stage model has some useful elements, additional work suggests that it is too narrow a theoretical framework. For example, I found that there were some couples who seemed unable to get through the first stage—who seemed never to be able to identify and/or resolve the various elements of the childbearing decision. In order to understand the nature of this apparent block, and to identify where in the decision process the difficulties arose, as well as to be able to follow the sequence for couples who were able to reach a satisfying decision, it was necessary to develop a conceptualization, which takes into account the interaction of a number of influencing systems, all of which impact on the outcome. A decision model framed in this fashion reflects the interaction of individual intrapsychic factors, as well as marriage, career, and lifestyle factors. A diagram of this model will be found below.*

---

*As with all the hypotheses presented here, these formulations are based on the feminine perspective. Although I believe this is a good starting point in thinking about the decision process, obviously, an appreciation of the masculine position is critical to the full understanding of this issue.

CHART III
A DUAL-CAREER CHILDBEARING DECISION MODEL

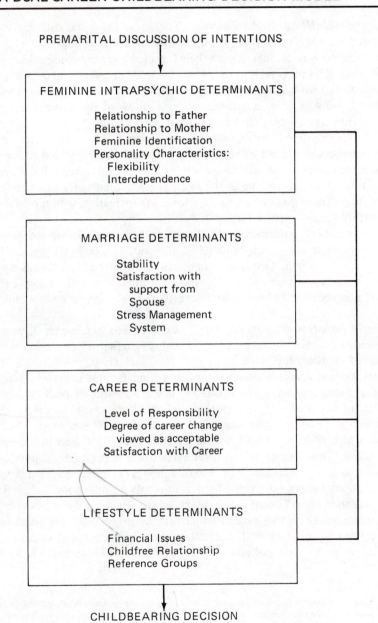

PREMARITAL DISCUSSION OF INTENTIONS

FEMININE INTRAPSYCHIC DETERMINANTS

    Relationship to Father
    Relationship to Mother
    Feminine Identification
    Personality Characteristics:
        Flexibility
        Interdependence

MARRIAGE DETERMINANTS

    Stability
    Satisfaction with
        support from
        Spouse
    Stress Management
        System

CAREER DETERMINANTS

    Level of Responsibility
    Degree of career change
        viewed as acceptable
    Satisfaction with Career

LIFESTYLE DETERMINANTS

    Financial Issues
    Childfree Relationship
    Reference Groups

CHILDBEARING DECISION

DETERMINANTS

Intratrapsychic Determinants

Early Relationship to Father. The most dramatic difference which I found between these three groups of dual-career women was in the nature of their early relationship with their father. I have concluded that resolution of oedipal issues is related to the adult female childbearing decision. I found that all Group C, the voluntarily childless, had early experiences suggesting that there was never a satisfactory resolution of the oedipal struggle, and that they never experienced a sense of paternal validation of their femininity. This negative early experience with father was in contrast to the positive experiences of almost all the women who had either decided to have a child or were still considering the question. Thus, developmentally, paternal validation of self as female at the oedipal level apparently permits the subsequent establishment of an ego-syntonic identification with motherhood and nurturance, as seen in Group B.*

Insufficient paternal verification was linked to deliberate rejection of motherhood as an acceptable self definition, as seen in Group C. However, for some women, Group A, successful oedipal resolution was apparently not sufficient in terms of adoption of a nurturant self concept; that is, it did not necessarily lead to an unconflicted decision to have a child.

Early Relationship to Mother. As discussed in Chapter 3, women who decided to have children generally had a satisfactory and relatively unconflicted relationship with mother. (See Chart II, page 67.) This group of women was identified as having progressed from a satisfactory resolution of pre-oedipal issues, to a satisfactory resolution of oedipal issues, to a mature feminine self concept that included both sexual and nurturant components. However, you will recall that I found several ambivalent women who although "chosen" by father, felt that they were unacceptable to mother. This finding led to a reanalysis of the pre-oedipal position. Both conscious reports and unconscious imagery indicated that ambivalent daughters have a reservoir of early, unresolved separation issues. This contrasts sharply to Group B daughters, whose histories do not document such issues. Based on these data, which will be more fully discussed in Part II below, I have concluded that unless there is a clear and unconflicted resolution of pre-oedipal issues of separation/individuation, the orientation

---

*Please note that I am drawing a distinction between women who make a conscious, voluntary decision to have children and others who, for various reasons, become mothers without deliberately electing to do so.

to later life identification with maternal (nurturant) functioning is ambivalent in some cases (Group A), and is negative in others (Group C).

Six out of the eight Group C women felt a sense of maternal rejection. However, in contrast to those who were still actively pursuing a satisfying resolution of the mother/daughter relationship, (and we know that Group A women were so engaged), I found that the Group C women had apparently integrated, (that is, they either denied or more or less accepted) the early maternal rejection. (Two women in Group A and two in Group B were rejected by mother.)

Traditional psychoanalytic theory concludes that there is a pre-oedipal prerequisite—a necessary condition enabling the infant to successfully traverse the oedipal struggle.[2] For example, Chodorow reminds us that " . . . (Freud) finds that a woman's pre-oedipal attachment to her mother largely determines both her subsequent oedipal attachment to her father and her later relationship to men in general."[3] My findings go on to suggest that the pre-oedipal mother/daughter relationship also affects the adult childbearing decision. However, in sharp contrast to the traditional conclusion that penis envy serves to catapult the daughter into the oedipal period, I am suggesting that it is through the act of distancing from the mother (female), and claiming herself as female and adequate (as a function of reflection of mother), that the oedipal stage is set. The oedipal turn to father, rather than a way of obtaining the desired penis, is more accurately seen as a major shift in relational orientation based on a degree of self confidence and autonomy.[4] *

It seems that an adequate degree of autonomy, the first threshold of self-confidence, must be established between mother and child prior to the oedipal stage. Without that degree of autonomy, the daughter is still so bound to her mother; so merged in the grip of primitive bonding, that she is unable to differentiate enough to seek and/or accept paternal attention.

Deutsch suggests that it is necessary for women to have a strong, non-aggressive identification with mother in order to wish to become a mother herself.[6] This study confirms Deutsch's statement concerning maternal orientation, though not her other conclusion that equates femininity with maternity. It is worth repeating that all the women studied here, regardless of pre-oedipal or oedipal outcomes, had achieved a cohesive, adult, feminine sexual identity. However, sexuality was separated from nurturance, in terms of the contents of the self concept.

Returning to the general findings concerning mother/daughter relation-

---

*For a feminist/psychoanalytic view of the female oedipal tasks and resolution, see Chodorow, Ch. 6 and 7.[5]

ships, there were sharp distinctions in the nature of the loving relationship, even in cases where a positive relationship to mother was established. Groups A and B generally felt that mother's loving relationship arose out of the interaction between mother and daughter. This contrasts to the two Group C women whose positive relationship with mother was based on mother's external orientation and daughter's more distant admiration and love of mother in this context. In examining the consequences of this externalization I conclude that since all the subjects are professional women, adult career orientation does not fully account for the impact of this early maternal focus. However, examination of the daughter's childbearing intentions suggests that by choosing the child-free status, the daughter seeks to duplicate the mother's external modeling, in a way that was not available to mother.

Feminine Identification.   Through an analysis of these subjects' responses, we have developed several hypotheses about the content and process of feminine identification as it appears in this group of childless, dual-career women. We have seen how differences in this aspect of the self concept relate to the childbearing decision.

First, it has been determined that there are clear differences between subjects in terms of the contents of feminine identification. Only the women in Group B include elements of both sexuality and nurturance in their feminine self concept. Ambivalent women and those who wish to remain childless, although firmly identifying with female sexuality, are either uncertain or reject the nurturant component. Thus, we conclude that in order to decide to have children, a woman must have a clear and unconflicted feminine self concept as both sexual and nurturant.

Second, the process whereby a woman accepts a sexual and nurturant feminine identification has been analyzed through examination of both preoedipal and oedipal determinants. Some of those who can be called "oedipal daughters" see themselves as both sexual and nurturant; however, other oedipal daughters, especially those who seem to have had an unsatisfactory resolution of the very earliest separation/individuation issues, find themselves, as adults, ambivalent about their nurturant orientation. Women who never experienced paternal verification in the sense of successfully resolving the oedipal conflict, (Group C) were also found to reject identification with nurturance.

This study has tended to both corroborate and refute certain classical assumptions of psychoanalytic theory regarding psychosexual developmental processes. Apparently, resolution of oedipal issues bears an association with the nature of feminine identification and subsequent childbearing decisions. The oedipal daughter's sense of having been "chosen" by father, thus establishing, at least temporarily, her supremacy over mother, seems to be a necessary condition for adult incorporation of a nurturant self concept. However, confirmation of feminine sexuality was not found to be associated with the outcome of pre-oedipal or oedipal development. It has been argued[7] that the strength of the pre-oedipal attachment to mother, which was either validated or disrupted by the resolution of the oedipal crisis, was developmentally related to female sexuality. Yet this study found no clear association between oedipal outcomes, the nature of subsequent attachment to mother, and the development of an adult heterosexual self concept.

Women who chose to remain child-free identified as positively with female sexuality as did those who considered motherhood to be ego-syntonic. Furthermore, no evidence was found to support the assumption that external (i.e., career) orientation or rejection of motherhood, was tantamount to acceptance of a masculine identification. The experience of these women, all of whom rejected the classical concept that females are inadequate and incomplete, in the sense of being "not quite male," has enabled us to conceptualize adult femininity in a new light.

Significant Personality Characteristics.

Flexibility.   Given the complexity of the dual-career lifestyle, it is easy to understand why all the dual-career subjects said that flexibility was an important personal characteristic. Reports from a symposium on the dual-career family[8] found that flexibility—the ability to alter course without undue stress—is the single most significant adaptive strategy for dual-career couples. I found that flexibility, both as a characteristic mode of individual response and as a lifestyle which the couple has evolved, was influential in the decision about whether or not to have children. However, I realized that although all subjects aspired to a flexible position, they did not uniformly describe themselves as flexible. Using a self rating scale of flexibility (1 = very rigid; 2 = somewhat rigid; 3 = somewhat flexible; 4 = flexible; 5 = very flexible), the following mean scores were reported:

	SELF	SPOUSE
Group A	2.5	3.0
Group B	4.0	3.5
Group C	3.0	3.5

Although there were some situational differences in the way subjects described their ability to be flexible (e.g., some said they were more flexible in their personal lives than on the job, and others just the opposite), clearly

Group B women, more than either A or C, think of themselves as being able to respond to change without too much stress. Not only are Group B women more flexible than the other women but, interestingly enough, they see themselves as more flexible than their spouses. It seems as if they (Group B) believe they can tolerate the pressures of interruption and unexpected change more easily than their husbands. Since it is the female combination of roles as wife/mother/career that is most apt to require the maximum degree of flexibility, and since neither Group A nor Group C women see themselves as very flexible, the conclusion is that this self concept is related to the decision to have children. Without this personality characteristic, the addition of the motherhood role is anticipated as either conflictual (as in Group A) or absolutely out of the question (as in Group C).

Interdependence.   How is interdependence, the ability to accept another as a resource while maintaining a sense of autonomy and independence, related to the decision to have children? Interdependence was seen to be more characteristic of Groups B and C women than Group A women. Though Group A women felt a need to be part of a "special group," the parameters of that unique group and the degree of mutual dependence remained vague and undefined.

As we have already seen, women in Group A have not yet resolved certain critical autonomy issues vis a vis mother. Therefore, we can assume that other relationships will recreate similar conflicts regarding dependence. These women could be expected to assume a counter-dependent stance—withholding, protective, and insecure—and in so doing, could either alienate the spouse (out of fear of engulfment) or overwhelm him in terms of expecting him to fill a lifetime of unsatisfied needs. In either case, the outcome is not interdependence as we have defined it. At the very least, such conflicts are likely to contribute to ambivalence regarding the dependency position.

Group B women were relatively unthreatened by an interdependent position, and manifested this not only in relation to spouse, but to colleagues, family, and friends. For Group C, interdependence formed around a satisfactory relationship to spouse and to a predominantly childless reference group.

Given the above data, I propose that there is a relationship between childbearing intentions and the nature and degree of interdependence which is desired and achieved as an adult. From what we have seen here, women who choose to have children feel the least threatened in terms of dependency issues, and experience the greatest congruence between demands of interdependence and personal needs.

Thus far we have discussed certain intrapsychic determinants which bear on the childbearing decision process, including the relationship to father and mother, feminine identification, and two important personality characteristics, which seem to discriminate between these three groups of subjects. The childbearing decision was further determined by the interaction between these psychological elements and the nature of the marital relationship.

Marriage Determinants

A sense of marital stability and permanence was required by women who said they wanted to have children. Only subjects who felt fully supported, both emotionally, in terms of genuine sensitivity and appreciation of professional and personal goals, and materially, in terms of a sense of shared financial and domestic responsibility, were able to reach an unconflicted decision either to have children or to remain child-free. At times, the pressure to reach a decision about children forced the couple into a confrontation with other, hidden conflicts in their relationship. (See Joyce, p. 81) For example, one couple seeking marital counseling (their story will be more fully examined in the chapter on Treatment Issues), gradually recognized that the wife's concentration on her husband's lack of financial responsibility, kept her from focusing on her own conflicted feelings about children. She was a nurse; he an executive recruiter, currently "between jobs." He had been out of work for more than six months. In therapy, they realized that her anger toward him stemmed in part from her conviction that his reluctance to find a job and to share the financial load equally, served to act as his way of ensuring that they were unable to have children, because they could not afford to do so. Until this issue was clarified, they were not able to confront the other, more unconscious aspects of their conflict.

Those couples who seemed most comfortable with their dual-career system, described an established stress management system, which they routinely employed. Therefore, it is assumed that couples who do not have such a system, may not be able to reach a satisfying decision about having children.*

Career Determinants

A host of career related issues impact on the childbearing decision (e.g., the philosophy and professional demands of the particular setting, the accepted organizational career path, the attitude of colleagues, the history of

_____

*In Part III we will discuss some therapeutic implications of the stress management system.

other career mothers in that particular group, the individual's professional track record, the relationship between the individual and her supervisors, etc.). For example, considering the issue of the "right" time out, some women reported that the more responsibility they had, the more difficult it became to take time out for a baby. Others said quite the opposite, i.e., that until they had a position with a significant level of responsibility, a maternity leave meant they'd risk losing out on career growth within their organization.[9] Therefore, the conclusion is that although there may be a relationship between career level and the decision to have children, this relationship varies according to many other highly idiosyncratic issues.

Only Group B women envisioned career changes as being compatible with current self image. They were comfortable contemplating working in other fields, on a different schedule, etc. Other women experienced the idea of these kinds of career changes as ego threatening and conflictual. Those who defined themselves primarily in terms of professional identity, were fairly rigid in terms of their intention to maintain a career priority.

Lifestyle Determinants. All the subjects in this study have established a lifestyle based on a child-free relationship. This lifestyle is characterized by relative freedom and spontaneity, and by an intense focus on the relationship to each other. The decision to have a child therefore, was a decision to alter the existing lifestyle and relationship. Responses to these changes varied as subjects anticipated the consequences (only some of which were known) of that alteration.

Financial consequences, perhaps because they were the most tangible, were uppermost in terms of the lifestyle issues. Having established a system built on two incomes, the subject's decision to suspend one income, at least temporarily, had both practical and psychological implications. Recognizing that this is a group of high achievers, whose goals generally include financial as well as personal and professional growth and security, and who had reached a relatively affluent level in their early adulthood, the difficulties surrounding economic issues become more understandable.

As Groups A and B explored the financial implications of their childbearing decision, they felt extremely pressured in anticipation of the high costs of childcare. Consequently, they expressed a need to maintain themselves "on track" professionally, so as not to jeopardize their income level. However, this career pressure was described as being in conflict with their freedom to choose whether or not they could extend the period of time they would stay home with baby, and thus contributed an additional stress factor.

To summarize, the model presented here allows us to see that the decision to have a child grows out of an interaction between a series of intrapsychic

processes and outcomes, combined with individual personality characteristics, which are subsequently affected by the nature and quality of the marriage relationship, the individual's career level and professional self-concept
and a series of lifestyle issues.

At this point let's meet Joyce, one of the Group B women. Our purpose
is to illustrate the development of her childbearing decision, and to indicate
the ways in which the four determinants we have identified are integrated
in the course of this process.

A CASE STUDY: JOYCE/ GROUP B

Joyce is a tall, attractive 32 year old woman who works as a reference librarian at a university library. She has an M.A. in Library Science, was
married at age 26, and divorced at age 30. She's currently engaged and
planning to marry, in the next few months, a man she has been living with
for one year. Joyce is soft-spoken, has a good sense of humor, and laughs
easily.

Family Background/ Childhood

Joyce was raised in a small town in Iowa, where she lived with her sister
(a year and a half older; no other siblings) her mother and father, and
was surrounded by a close group of aunts, uncles, and cousins. Joyce reported that her parents were " . . . married late; my mother was 40 when
I was born. Before my sister was born, my mother had some clerical and
bookkeeping, but not as a career. Then when I was in high school, she
found a clerical job . . . never any strong career push for women in our
family."

Joyce's father died when she was three. Her memories of him are focused
on their shared sense of humor: "My father had a very good sense of humor, and I used to hear stories about how funny he was. And people would
tell me that we were alike . . . And I remember my father laughing if I said
something cute . . . something funny. He and I thought the same things
were funny, I guess."*

Joyce remembers that things were pretty hard for her mother for a while
after father died " . . . but that she had enough insurance and could get
by without working. I always felt that she could have developed her abilities
but instead what she did was take over a lot of responsibilities for us so
that we would just stay in school and get an education. She sheltered us

---

*The identification with father's verbal behavior has been noted before.[10]

. . . I think she was afraid of our leaving . . . getting too independent . . . and she would be alone.''

In describing her early relationship with her sister, Joyce remembers that they were very different from each other: "I was a skinny kid . . . blond hair which would stick out all over the place, and she was heavier and she always had this curly beautiful blond hair. I was not jealous of her hair until I was older. She was the feminine little girl, and I was the tomboy. Jane is more passive, she was never rebellious. What my mother had in mind for us, she pretty well had in mind for herself.''

Self-Image

"I really felt awkward and insecure when I was growing up. I felt very unattractive. I was really a fat little kid when I got to grade school, and kept the weight on through high school and then lost it. I know I wasn't attractive to other people or to myself. Not attractive to boys. I think a lot of it was insecurity . . . a shy nature. I thought I made friends because I was funny, and people would laugh . . . I also had the reputation, which I cultivated, of really studying hard, and really being very bright. I played the flute and that was different from the others, but even in that I was not really part of the regular music group.''

Joyce remembers that her mother was concerned about her shyness; about the fact that she had no social life: "I remember my mother telling me I should be more outgoing . . . and of course, I would have liked to be part of the popular set and gone to dances . . . didn't have boyfriends . . . sort of a passive existence. I hated it, the social thing in high school was a complete disaster. What I did was to do things like building floats for the class project . . . people were not hostile . . . it was just that I was typecast early . . . this is Joyce . . . and this is her role. I didn't see any way I could break out of it except to get into a different environment which is what I did in college.''

"I remember thinking that those boys didn't have any preconceived ideas of me as an ugly duckling, a wallflower, and an egghead. And I found out it was easy to make friends. I decided I should do something for my mother . . . I knew she had this traditional sort of TV idea, that if you were popular you went out with the football team. And I did, and it confirmed what I felt about them in high school, that they were stupid, and I stopped.''

Joyce talked about an early dream for herself, more or less following mother's expectations: "I probably had the same dream. I would go to college and do all these intellectual things, and afterward would marry someone like an English professor and have children . . . but I would be able to use my brains. I didn't really have a clear idea what I wanted to do after that, I just didn't question it. I just thought I would end up doing those things, get married, have children, and quit doing whatever I was doing, but then there was this fuzzy area after that . . . ''

Self as Different

Joyce grew up feeling she was different from other girls. As a little girl, she saw herself as the tomboy, and not like her sister who was pretty and feminine. In high school she felt different because she was not part of the popular social group. She found, though, that she could gain attention and acceptance in other ways, by doing well academically, but especially through her humor. Although she attended a small Lutheran college about ninety miles from her home ('' . . . there was a strong family tradition to go there and there were no options . . . ''), Joyce nevertheless felt it was important to break out of that mold: "I thought I should be getting a different experience, so I went to a free university for a semester."

At this point, feeling somewhat more socially self-confident, Joyce began to view herself as different in terms of life goals: "Even in high school, I had different interests. Besides the piano and the flute, I was pretty ambitious. A lot of kids in my high school just stayed in that area and had no ambitions except to get married after graduation . . . I just knew I had different goals."

Adult Self-Image

For a period of time in college, Joyce and her boyfriend were part of a '' . . . hippie-type commune . . . I think it was a matter of just breaking out, I suppose, this was part of my rebellion . . . I had just gotten to the point where I was out of the influence of my mother, and her response to that was that she was very upset . . . she had read about different types of people . . . and drugs and people dropping out and going crazy. I think she was concerned that I would do the same. But actually it wasn't that way at all. Remember by this time I was twenty-one years old, and I had a pretty well set, stable pattern. So I wasn't about to go off the deep end."

Joyce's mother developed a serious heart condition while Joyce was a senior in college. '' . . . So I went back to the college near home, even though I didn't want to . . . just simply because she was ill. I guess I took it more seriously than I realized then. It was just that my mother was sick and there was no one else and that family should be close . . . to be available to each other . . . and I did . . . ''

In terms of her current self-image, Joyce says of herself, ''I think of myself now as an achiever, but not an over-achiever. I have an ongoing goal which I have formulated more and more strongly over the years, and that is to combine a career and a family.''

Career

Joyce has been employed as a reference librarian for a period of six years. Before going to graduate school for a degree in library science, she worked in various library jobs to confirm what she recognized as a growing interest. ''My feeling is that librarians love what they are doing; it's low pressure and very satisfying. I have the skills and I have a lot of flexibility in my work and I like that.''

For Joyce, there was never any question about the fact that work was a significant part of her self-image. She had decided very early in life that she would develop a professional career which would guarantee both financial independence and personal satisfaction. ''. . . I would not give up something I enjoy doing for something that I didn't enjoy just because it was one step up in the ladder and it was for more money. To me, it isn't outside approval, it's more internal. For me, success is being good at what I do, having high standards. I don't measure success monetarily. I have enough money to do what I want, which is important to me . . . but I don't need a great deal. When I got this job, I felt very lucky.''

As we will see, Joyce's concept of success became a focal point of disagreement in her marriage.

Marriage

Joyce and her husband met while she was in college. She said, ''I think I was attracted to him because he was very aggressive and very social . . . incredible energy. I was really physically attracted to him. And he would do all these crazy things. It was exciting to me. I had never done anything like that and I thought why not . . . why did I always have to be so responsible? . . . why not do all these things?'' Thus, in Joyce's view, her first husband represented her own shadow side—those irresponsible parts of herself that she had always shut down. She continued, ''We had lived together since I was twenty-one. We got married when I was twenty-six. After my mother died, I took the money that I had gotten from her estate, and bought a car and drove around Europe for about four months. It was something we both wanted to do . . . we knew that when we got back he was going to start in graduate school.''

It was during the period when they were both at graduate school (and she continued to work at the library) that their marriage began to come apart: "I enjoyed what I was doing . . . but he continually pressured me to get a more prestigious job . . . to get more money."

Jim's career seemed to lack direction, just at the stage when Joyce felt satisfied and confident that she was on the right track. He had been in law school, then to school in social work, and then back to business school. " . . . So he was having a whole lot of trouble figuring out what he wanted . . . at the same time he was jealous and very critical of me."

Things came to a head over the issue of children: "We had always planned to have children but it was in the future. And we hadn't set a date. I thought it would be around the time I would be thirty . . . but when I reached thirty I began questioning whether I wanted to be married to my husband and I came to the conclusion that I didn't. I didn't want to have children with him and I didn't want to continue living with him. I didn't think he would be a good father and be able to share. He is very domineering and egotistical. I could deal with it on a one-to-one basis, but I didn't think I could deal with it with children. I wanted something that would be more equal and compatible."

Joyce and Jim were separated for a few months and then decided on a divorce which became final about a year ago.

Current Relationship

Joyce feels that the relationship she now has with Bob is stable, secure, and mutually satisfying: "He's the complete opposite of Jim. He's more mature, much more self-confident, and he doesn't have a temper, very calm. He has a lot of respect for what I do . . . he's an artisan, a carpenter. He has his own business . . . and he really enjoys what he is doing. I don't think that anything I would do would threaten him. He's secure and very independent." Joyce feels that his attitude has helped her become more comfortable with herself. She said, "I don't feel any pressure from him, career-wise, to do anything other then what I want to do. He's encouraging me to go back to being more creative . . . he's pleased when I start painting or drawing again, or sewing my own clothes. Jim never did, and I loved to do all those things."

Joyce and Bob are planning to get married this spring: "We both would love to have children. I feel that he will be very good with kids . . . He has some property upstate in New York, and we'll probably move there and we'll build a house there and we'll raise a family. But it's really close to the X University, so there will be an opportunity for me to continue my work."

Joyce made an interesting comment in considering the priority of career vs relationship. She said, "I think probably the relationship has to come first. I would not sacrifice the relationship because I think in some ways they are harder to come by than a career.''

Decision to Have a Child

Joyce intends to have her first child within the next year or so. She reported that about five years ago she had an abortion: " . . . and I think it hit me then that I really did want to have children . . . at that point I realized that I didn't want Jim as the father . . . that it would complicate things and not be good for the child or for me. My reaction then surprised me. I felt so strongly and was so unhappy. I knew I would have that abortion, but I was not happy about it, and I would not do it again.'' She continued, "Biologically I think a child will satisfy a basic need I have. I think I'd like to be pregnant. I like children . . . I'd like the experience of raising children and having children around . . . ''

Joyce has thought a great deal about the "right" age to have children: "At forty it becomes more dangerous . . . I think by thirty-five or six, given the medical knowledge, you don't take quite so many risks. But I think that now at age thirty-two, I know much more about what I want, and I know more about how I think children should be raised than I did at age 21 or 22 . . . I'm much more comfortable and confident about myself and my abilities.

Joyce's response to some of the MTAT cards gives us another perspective regarding her attitude toward children. To Card VII (two women talking and a baby crawling on the floor between them) she said, "They are enjoying their visit . . . they are both self-sufficient, they are both in careers, and the baby doesn't encumber either one. I don't see the baby as a burden . . . she wouldn't consider letting the baby hold her back from what she wants to do . . . '' By insisting that the baby is not a burden, Joyce seems to be denying some underlying fears that she may have in terms of both the unknown aspects of mothering and the difficulty of achieving her complicated double goals. Other signals point to some of her conflicted feelings, as well as to the direction of her decision. She said, e.g., to MTAT III, (group scene) " . . . the female is probably more high-powered than the male . . . '' and to Card V (woman looking out the window) she said, " . . . she decides to go on with her career and to put off her family.'' To Card IV (woman and aging parents) she says, " . . . she's not married and she does not have children and she doesn't know what way she is going.'' However, to MTAT II (woman in office, with pictures of male and children on desk; diploma on wall.) she says, " . . . this is part of her life . . . these two things, and she is thinking about her family right now, while she is in her office, and she feels great contentment.''

As much as she loves library science, Joyce believes that she would be satisfied with other work while her children are infants: "I don't think I can set out a rigid goal . . . this is the way it has to be . . . there are bound to be those fuzzy areas . . . for everything I want needs flexibility . . . and I am pretty flexible . . . " (She rates herself at a 4 on the flexibility scale and rates Bob at about three.) "There are certain things I want, certain needs, but how I fill them in is undetermined . . . yes I do want children . . . I do want to do work that I enjoy . . . I want everything . . . but I think that everything demands a great deal of flexibility . . . and tradition has been that you either have a career or you have children. Now I'm saying both . . . but I know that there will be compromises . . . I think that my generation . . . we have put off having children for so long that we have had an opportunity to have a career path and to enjoy it. And we will not give that up. But there are not many women ahead of us who were doing what we are doing, so the decisions are hard to make."

" . . . I think it's different what career you choose. Mine is academic and it's more flexible and my area has less pressure in it. But generally, in order to raise a family and have a life that encompasses two careers and children . . . there has to be an awareness for both partners that each has responsibilities to each other, to their kids and to their jobs. They have to have independence and basic security that when one partner spends less time with the family at one point, it does not mean that the family has become less important. I know that I can completely count on him, but I wouldn't be dependent on Bob for all my moral support, emotional support, or an evaluation of myself. And he wouldn't depend on me for that . . . We both have a sense of ourselves apart from our relationship."

Finally, after careful and deliberate analysis of all the issues, Joyce said, "I just know that I will have a career and I will have children . . . one way or another."

THE CHILDBEARING DECISION MODEL

Having come to know Joyce—how she feels about herself, her relationships, her dual-career lifestyle, and her professional history and goals—we are now in a position to look at her decision to have children in terms of the model we have proposed.

Intrapsychic Determinants

To understand Joyce dynamically, we must look first at her relationship to mother and father. Even though Joyce felt that she and her mother did not communicate well, she knew that mother's life was focused on her and that she had mother's love and attention. Although she feels somewhat critical of her mother's failure to use her potential energies and intelligence, Joyce recognizes that her mother herself was extremely satisfied with her mothering role. Her own feeling of compatibility with a maternal orientation is based on an identification with mother's nurturance. Thus, Joyce's need to be different from mother, in the sense of establishing a career and financial independence, did not extend to rejection of nurturant functioning and motherhood.

In terms of critical early separation issues, we have seen that although Joyce can function autonomously, she is not afraid of closeness—not afraid of losing herself in a dependent relationship. For example, we saw that she could leave the mother and go off to the university (contrary to family tradition). Still, when her mother was ill, she saw no problem in coming home to take care of her, and apparently felt no resentment in doing so.

We know she experienced herself as "chosen," as special to her father. They were alike. The conscious identification grew out of a similar approach to life based on humor. Because her father died when Joyce was so young, she retains an idealized conception of the father/daughter relationship. For Joyce, it is idealized approval. She remains the oedipal daughter. In the framework we have developed, Joyce thus established an early validation of self as female.

Feminine Identification

Joyce's definition of femininity includes aspects of both sexuality and nurturance. She feels that to take care of children, and to raise them, would be stimulating and rewarding. She believes that having children is a natural and desirable part of the female role, not to be missed.

Personality Characteristics

Flexibility.   Joyce rated herself at 4 on the flexibility scale. She says of her first marriage, that one way she recognized she had problems with Jim, was that he seemed to be falling into more and more rigid (tradition-bound) patterns and expectations, at the same time that her increasing self confidence allowed her to be more spontaneous.

Interdependence.   In her new relationship, Joyce recognizes her wish (and ability) to depend on Bob in a way that she was never able to do before. She says that their mutual dependence in no way interferes with her feelings of independence. Because he encourages her to resume the creative tasks which are so meaningful to her, she feels freed up and empowered.

Self as Different.   Although Joyce felt different from other women as a young girl, she has apparently not extended that difference to a need to change traditional marriage and child-raising expectations. Having made the decision to pursue career goals and to postpone children, she has recently formed a relationship with other career women in similar situations. Therefore, although she feels different from women in general, she has developed a reference group she respects and whose members have similar multiple goals.

Marriage Determinants

It is important to remember that Joyce said, " . . . . the relationship must come first . . . " With this emphasis we see that for her, the marital relationship is more important than individual goals, lifestyle issues, or career goals. Yet, she tells us that Bob values her work, in the same way as he does his own. As a result, Joyce feels approval, support, understanding, and respect.

We will remember that it was their disagreement over the issue of children, and Joyce's realization that Jim would not be the same kind of parent that she would be, that foreshadowed their divorce. Now, however, Joyce feels absolutely confident and secure in the love and stability of her present relationship. She feels that she can now be "more herself." (As we saw above, this includes a focus on being more creative, which she sees as more feminine.)

Career Determinants

Although a continuous career is viewed as being a significant part of her life, Joyce does not feel pressured to succeed according to any external criteria of money and power. She accepts the idea of an interrupted professional career, with full confidence that it would in no way alter her long range career goals.

Lifestyle Determinants

Financial competition, which surfaced in a destructive manner in her first marriage, is apparently not an issue in the present relationship. With Bob, Joyce has found the needed approval for her work, a shared interest in creative activities, and compatibility in values. In their lifestyle plans, that is, their intention to move to his property in upstate New York, build a house, raise a family, and resume her career as a university librarian, she and Bob have developed a joint, mutually satisfying series of goals. Significantly, they have also reached agreement on how to work toward these goals.

To recapitulate, examining Joyce's decision to have children in the framework of the proposed dual-career childbearing decision model, we have said that her decision is based on the following elements:

Intrapsychic Determinants

- Satisfactory separation from mother at the pre-oedipal level.
- Intrapsychic sense of paternal validation at the oedipal level.
- Feminine identification which includes sexuality and nurturance.
- Personality characteristics including high degree of flexibility and a capacity for interdependence.

Marriage Determinants

- Confidence in the stability and permanence of her marriage.

Career Determinants

- Satisfaction with career status and with the prospect of career change.

Lifestyle Determinants

- Satisfaction with lifestyle.

With this model as a guide, we're ready to look at some of the differences between the three groups of dual-career women. Chapter 5 will outline the differences between women who plan to have children vs. those who are either ambivalent or who intend to remain childless. We'll also return briefly to Barbara and Jim, whom we met in Chapter 1, when they were ambivalent.

REFERENCES

1. Wilk, C. Gender and Midlife Development. In Cytrynbaum et al., Paper presented to the American Psychological Association Annual Convention, Toronto, Canada, 1978.
   Wilk, C. "The Dual-Career Childbearing Decision." Unpublished Paper, 1979.
2. Freud, S. "Femininity." In *The Complete Psychological Works.* (Translated by J. Strachey). New York: Norton, 1933, 1965.
   Deutsch, H. *The Psychology of Women.* New York: Grune & Stratton, 1944.
   Chodorow, N. *The Reproduction of Mothering: Psychoanalysis and the Sociology of Gender.* Berkeley, CA: University of California Press, 1978.
3. Ibid., p. 96.
4. Ibid.
5. Ibid.

6. Deutsch, *The Psychology of Women.*
7. Freud, "Femininity."
   Deutsch, *Psychology of Women.*
8. Peterson et al., eds. *The Two Career Family: A Symposium Report.* Washington, D.C.: University Press, 1978.
9. Hall, D.T. and F.S. *The Two-Career Couple.* Reading, MA.: Addison Wesley, 1979. Daniels, P., and Weingarten, K. *Sooner or Later: The Timing of Parenthood in Adult Lives.* New York: W. W. Norton, 1980.
10. Lamb, M. ed. *The Role of the Father in Child Development.* New York: John Wiley & Sons, 1981. Especially see Chapter 11, Radin, N. "The Role of the Father in Cognitive, Academic and Intellectual Functioning."

5
DIFFERENCES BETWEEN GROUPS
A, B, AND C

Before we summarize some of the differences between these three groups of women, let's go back to Barbara and Jim, (the couple described in Chapter 1). As I mentioned earlier, they were the only couple I followed through two different stages of their childbearing decision.

Barbara and Jim were ambivalent about having children when we first met. When they were interviewed about 2 years later, they were trying to become pregnant. Several shifts in their conscious processes (perhaps unconscious as well) were evident. The most obvious change to me was the way that Barbara had stopped intellectualizing. At first, she had talked her way around everything, and was obviously afraid of her feelings. Now, however, she seemed able to acknowledge how difficult some of the inevitable changes would be. She talked about what she thought it would like to be pregnant, and what life with a new baby might be like.

(Psychological Shifts: Change in defensive structure; able to be more flexible, able to confront affective component; able to anticipate relationship to child without undue fear.)

We recall that Barbara had always thought of herself as special to her father, and somewhat conflicted about mother. She told us about the feeling she had, that mother might disapprove of her as a housekeeper—might disapprove of her as a woman. In some way, fortunately, Barbara had resolved this internal struggle with mother. Perhaps she was able to obtain the required unconditional love from Jim (remember, she felt that mother's love was available *only if* she met mother's needs), and thus worked through her feeling that no matter what she did, it was never good enough to please mother.*

The changes in Barbara were apparent when we met in her new house

---

*In Part II we'll return to a fuller analysis of some other aspects of this struggle with mother.

for the second series of interviews. Not only was she dressed more casually, and was (appropriately) unconcerned about ordinary clutter, but she seemed very relaxed with Jim, very pleased with their relationship, and in general, pleased with herself.

Barbara hinted that the closer she got to finishing up her degree, the more her mother had backed off. (We wonder whose attitude had changed?) Father remained very supportive of whatever she did. Barbara had been offered a job, which she said sounded pretty good. She talked about maybe taking the job for while, and then maybe trying to work out a part-time schedule after they had a baby.

(Intrapsychic Resolution: father kept as idealized affirmation of self as female; mother rendered less fearful, more realistic; self-concept more stabilized as autonomous).

Jim's career was really going well, (without his having to move). They had decided that they could manage on just his income until Barbara was ready to return to work. Jim mentioned that someone in his office had been able to arrange to be home with his baby on a regular schedule. Jim hoped to work out a similar arrangement.

In contrast to their earlier, rather grandiose plan for childcare, they were realistic in terms of their bottom line requirements, and knew several other dual-career couples who were dealing with the difficulties of finding appropriate childcare. Barbara and Jim seemed to have a network of friends who were dealing with similar problems, and they acted as a support group for each other. Barbara said, "I guess I feel better about myself on a lot of levels. We've been married long enough so that we know how to take care of each other, and how to be separate from each other. It was really hard for a long time, but I feel that I've made a pretty good start, professionally, so I'm in a position now to make a change if I want to . . . I'm beginning to grow up, I guess. I think I'm trying to be a bit more flexible about things around here, and still feel ok. I still care about how this house looks, but I also feel pretty confident about myself in other areas, so that if this is a mess at times, who cares? I suppose that's a change for me, isn't it?"

(Marriage Stability: relationship more intimate, less competitive; ability to take care of spouse seen as rehearsal for nurturant functions re child; belief that lifestyle can continue with only one income; network of friends who support and reinforce dual-career system. Self as more confident, and able to tolerate change.)

GROUP A—AMBIVALENT WOMEN

Why is it that some women, like Barbara, can resolve their dilemma and others cannot? In Part II we'll explore this ambivalence—its underlying psychodynamic origins and processes. At this point, however, we will offer a brief summary of the three groups, so that the reader can compare them.

Group A women can most accurately be described as ambivalent. These women, given to over-intellectualization (as Barbara had been), are highly cautious, uncomfortable with anticipated changes, and somewhat inflexible. They are neither fully satisfied with their career nor their relationship. Half the group orient their lives around a career; half around their relationship and/or self-image.

Viewed psychodynamically, although the members of this group apparently managed early psychosexual development in a satisfactory fashion, they failed somehow to identify solidly with mother. At the same time, however, they were reluctant to reject a maternal identification.

Group A women, who defined femininity as sexual (as all the subjects did in this study), felt they could not easily identify with nurturance as one component of femininity. This may explain how, as a group, they were unable to allow themselves to be dependent; that is, the conflict around the ability to give nurturance extends to the reverse ability to receive nurturance. However, Group A women were also unable to relinquish a dependent self-concept. Although there were some exceptions, significant interpersonal relationships and reference groups, both of which assume a degree of interdependence, were also difficult to maintain for these women.

Compared with the other Groups, Group A were the most conflicted, exhibited the highest levels of anxiety, and had the most poorly developed adaptive strategies. Analysis of Group A case material revealed more discrepancies between conscious reporting and unconscious themes than were found in either Group B or Group C.

GROUP B—THOSE WHO INTEND
TO HAVE CHILDREN

Women who plan to have children are perhaps the easiest group to understand, because their childbearing decision continues in the traditional pattern. That is "of course" they want to have children. They describe themselves as happily married, satisfied with their career; as more flexible than their spouse (you recall that Group B women were the only ones who saw themselves this way); and open to future changes in both lifestyle and profession. Though energetically committed to a continuous career (as all subjects were) they gave clear priority to their relationship and/or self-image.

Psychodynamically, this group seems to have emerged from the early psychosexual developmental stages with an affirmation of themselves as female. Apparently the women in this group identified with mother in terms of her role as nurturant caretaker, and accept the concept of motherhood as ego-syntonic. It was also noted that all but one subject in this group felt the influence of her mother's generally positive attitude toward men.

The ability to be dependent as well as interdependent was viewed as natural by Group B women, and not in conflict with a generally independent self-image. This ability may also be related to the development of a satisfactory system of stress management which was common to these women and their relationship.*

GROUP C—VOLUNTARY CHILDLESSNESS

The number of voluntarily childless women in America is large enough to constitute a new normative group. For example, in 1980, about 11% of all American women and 17% of college-educated women said that they intend to remain voluntarily childless.[1]**

I found that Group C, the voluntarily childless women, were generally more like Group B than Group A in terms of presenting fewer conflicts related to work and spouse. On the whole, they were very positive about their childbearing decision, and generally satisfied with their lifestyle and domestic balance.

Group C women were definite about the importance and priority of career issues, and generally were not open to changes in either career or lifestyle. Though highly sensitive to what they experienced as a coercive pronatalist bias,[2] these women viewed their child-free lifestyle as entirely appropriate. As indicated above, although they recognized that their choices did in fact represent a new and altered adult female role, they wished neither to judge nor be judged by traditional feminine models. Their choice to remain voluntarily childless was seen as personally empowering—as a personal growth decision. It was experienced as "freeing" in the sense of an affirmation of themselves, their professional career, and their relationship.

---

*In the last section of this book—clinical applications—we will focus again on some of the elements of the childbearing decision of Group B women. The treatment process described is intended to highlight (hopefully facilitate) the sequence of the decision, and illustrate some aspects of the process that are followed autonomously by the non-clinical subjects.

**For a discussion of research on issues related to voluntary childlessness, please see Appendix B.

However, in clear distinction to both Groups A and B, none of the Group C women could be described as oedipal daughters; that is, none of them experienced a sense of feminine affirmation through an early positive relationship with father. Their deeper images of father are bitter and filled with wishes for revenge. Although two women in this group identified strongly with mother, the identification is with her external orientation, rather than with any sort of dependency or nurturance. All but one mother in Group C were described as having a negative attitude toward men. These findings suggest a possible relationship between mother's rejection of men and daughter's decision to remain childless. Nevertheless, in spite of a negative maternal message, women in this group neither appear to have particularly conflicted relationships with men, nor do they seem to relate differently to men than do the other subjects in this study. They are comfortable with a feminine self-concept as sexual, and do not consider nurturance an integral component of their female self-concept.

Although they seem to reject a dependent mode, Group C women have formed a strong relationship with their spouse, and with specific reference groups, out of an ability to sustain an interdependent system based on shared, intellectualized responsibility. Anxiety for Group C women was primarily related to conflicts between demands of career vs. relationship, in contrast to Group A women whose stress was predominantly focused on the evolution from a childless to parent status. As we've seen, although Group B women experienced some of the same stress, they seemed able to manage the pressures more easily than Group A.

In this chapter we have summarized the differences between the childbearing decisions of Groups A, B, and C. Now we are in a position to turn our full attention to the ambivalent group. As I indicated earlier, I believe that these women, who feel they are unable to reach a satisfying childbearing decision, are the most difficult to understand, and the most likely to experience distress. The following chapters explore personality issues, psychodynamic factors, and developmental considerations.

REFERENCES

1. *Fertility of American Women:* June 1980. U.S. Department of Commerce, Bureau of the Census, October, 1982.
2. Bardwick, J. *Psychology of Women.* New York: Harper & Row, 1971.

Part II
The Ambivalent Woman

INTRODUCTION

As part of a university sponsored seminar on dual-career issues, I spoke to a group of women and men about what I had learned about the child-bearing decision. Several people described the evolution of their decision, either to have children or to remain childless. They talked about how much stress they had gone through until they finally reached a decision. Having settled that issue satisfactorily, they said they were now able to tackle other stressors in their complex dual-career system.

Another panelist at the seminar, a pediatrician, said that my remarks about the personality and the psychodynamic development of the ambivalent woman were too negative. Dr. A. said the description was pejorative, and she felt attacked. She paused, however, and then added that she herself was in the throes of deciding whether or when to have children, and that as she thought about it, my descriptors of the ambivalent position hit home. They suggested things about herself that she knew were true, but that she did not wish to acknowledge.

About one year later, I had the opportunity to meet Dr. A. again. Now four months pregnant, and very happy with her condition, she talked about her plans for combining parenthood with her medical career.* When I asked her how she had decided to become pregnant, she laughed and said, "Well, I just got a little careless about birth control." This statement, and its ap-

---

*Please note: Although in this example, Dr. A's decision was to become a parent, obviously, my choice of her as an example is not intended to indicate endorsement of this as the "correct" resolution.

parent casualness, seemed astonishing to me, in light of what I knew about her, especially the way she made other significant life decisions.

Dr. A had planned to be a doctor since she was four. The youngest of a family of high achievers, she followed the family pattern of being highly ambitious. She reports satisfactory relationships with both father and mother and felt their pride in her achievements. Yet, she also knew, from a very young age, that her mother viewed career women as not quite properly female. Her mother's message was that there are two kinds of women— the career women (implication: unhappy and unfulfilled), and the wife/mother (like me: happy and fulfilled).

Getting through her undergraduate years and medical school with single-minded dedication to her career, Dr. A. said that she ruled out a serious relationship for herself during that period. She felt she didn't have the time or the energy to work on both her professional development and a personal relationship. Thus we have an important clue to help understand Dr. A. She is a planner. Having planned to be a doctor all her life, she was able to carry through with her educational plans, and choose not to be distracted by the demands of a relationship.

After graduation from medical school, she met and married her husband, who is about ten years her senior. Dr. A. noted that her husband's mother had been a lifelong career woman who traveled extensively and left him in the care of others.

Based on a vague (unspoken) agreement not to have children yet, both she and her spouse plunged vigorously into demanding work. In addition to her primary work in a group medical practice, Dr. A. has written two books relating to her specialization, is in the midst of working on several articles for medical journals, does a considerable amount of public speaking, and is also completing a graduate degree in a related field. In addition, she is active in her community, and has time for friends, family, and lots of reading. How does it all get done? Lots of energy, good health, good planning, and a relaxed attitude. She says that she's kind of "laid back." Obviously, this is a super organized, extremely capable woman.

How does this organized planner, this methodical, careful intellectualizer, get careless about something as important as having children? How does she come to an accidental pregnancy? Dr. A. seemed surprised when I asked her this. Since our conversation was social, we let it go with her statement that she was more eager to have a child than her spouse was, and she supposed that her pregnancy was a way of pushing him a bit. She added a brief comment about wanting to see if she could really become pregnant.

As we talked, she said that my comments (the year before in our seminar) about the pattern that I discovered about early relationships of ambivalent dual-career women, held true for her: "I was special to my father, and somewhat conflicted regarding mother." She commented on the fact that her husband's mother was a lifelong career woman who traveled frequently. Consequently, Dr. A commented, her husband (as a child) was often placed with relatives for long periods of time. Whether this meant to Dr. A.'s husband, that children were not a good idea for a career woman such as his mother (since he was left behind), or whether this meant that women could combine family and career, was not fully explained. Since we know he was more reluctant than she to start a family, we assume that he has some negative feelings about children and career mothers. We could also speculate that he was seeking a woman who would concentrate on him, as opposed to a woman (mother) who divided her attentions between him and another focus.

How did Dr. A. arrive at her decision? How much does she resemble the ambivalent women studied here? Asking the same question in another way, are all Group A decisions going to be "accidental?" How can Dr. A. help us understand the position of other women who are unable to resolve this issue

Dr. A. is obviously functioning well, both personally and professionally. Apparently she was able to work her way through her ambivalence, and now feels comfortable with her decision. But what about those who are incapable of resolving this dilemma, and who remain conflicted, in spite of their attempts to deal with their feelings about parenthood, and to work through the psychological and practical barriers of the childbearing decision?

From what I have learned about ambivalent women, I believe that the stress surrounding their inability to reach a decision about children becomes the central organizing focus in their lives. At times, this conflict interferes with their normal level of functioning. When the ambivalent woman becomes aware of her distress, we may expect her to seek clinical treatment.

In Part II, we focus on the ambivalent position, the areas of conflict, and the identified stressors. We examine the personality development, history, and current functioning, in order to clarify both the intrapsychic and external processes and conflicts involved in the childbearing decision. As I stated before, the objective of this analysis is twofold: first, to help develop an informed perspective among clinicians who may work with these patients; second, to provide some information and help for the woman who feels "stuck" at this point, and unable to resolve her dilemma. Before proceeding to a description of the contents of Part II, I want to remind the reader of the methods by which my conclusions about ambivalence were reached.

Methods

Employing a grounded theory methodology, rather than starting from a series of hypotheses which had to be either proven or disproven, I was able to piece the evidence together as it emerged from the data, proceeding clue by clue, and gradually building a theoretical point of view. For example, the clues to the conflicted state of the ambivalent subjects began with their response to the very first question in the interview process. This was the only question that remained uniform throughout the work with each subject. From that point on, the subjects' responses guided my questions. The first question was: "Tell me about your life right now." Their responses can be illustrated as follows:

	Group A	Group B	Group C
"Tell me about your life right now"			
Career Focus	4	1	8
Relationship and/or Self Image Focus	4	7	0

Clearly, Group B answered in terms of their feelings about themselves or their relationship, and Group C women responded in terms of their careers. However, when we look at the first responses of Group A, they were split evenly between primary orientation to career and primary orientation to relationship and/or self.

I made it a practice not to interview an entire group in sequence. Therefore, the dramatic differences in responses to the first question—that is, the uniformity within Groups B and C and the even split in Group A— was not obvious to me until all interviews were completed and I began to compare the data. It was at that point that I recognized that the very first response of each subject, reflected her primary mode of self organization[1] and could be used as a key to unlock the meaning of all subsequent material.

In the course of analyzing the data, it became evident that for many ambivalent subjects, there was little consistency between interview and projective responses. This incongruence can be illustrated by the following responses given by Lisa (A).

Lisa, 28 years old, and the youngest of 11 children, has been married for four years and is employed in sales in a very large commercial insurance corporation. Though she is somewhat unsure about the stability of her marriage, she is very enthusiastic about her work, stating, " . . . I'm alive at work—creative and energetic . . . " In response to the sentence completion question, *"I believe that having children . . . "* Lisa said, "My marriage is too shaky right now . . . "

When Lisa talked about her feelings about herself as a woman and about what femininity, sexuality, and nurturance meant she said, "That's the myth . . . that's what I'm separating . . . that women should have or should want to have children . . . and should want to care for them. I don't feel that way at all . . . I guess I never viewed my mother as being feminine . . . and also my not having that much respect for her as a mother or as a woman." In this response we hear Lisa stating definitely, and with conviction, that women can be feminine without wanting to take care of children. ("I don't feel that way at all.") In fact, her next statement about her mother not being seen as feminine, implies that perhaps some femininity is lost with motherhood. Note that she immediately makes an association between her thoughts about children and her feelings about her mother, particularly mother's lack of femininity and her lack of respect for mother. Lisa's words tell us that she believes she can be more feminine without having children. These remarks reflect the conscious content and the conscious nature of the conflict regarding the mother. We begin to see some discrepancy between these conscious reports and the unconscious themes as we listen to Lisa's projective responses. For example, to Card II (woman looking at pictures of male and children) she says, " . . . she's very serious . . . wants to make the right decision . . . wondering if this is making her happy vs. what she could have done . . . she wonders . . . if this is all there is . . . but then . . . there are the children . . . " To Card IV (woman and aging parents) she says, " . . . this woman is alone rather than with a husband . . . she has no husband." To Card V (woman looking out the window) she says, " . . . she is afraid not to have the baby . . . that would be a harder emotional problem . . . and she has had other emotional problems in the past and she knows how hard it is to come back . . . from these setbacks and guilt feelings . . . and somehow I think it will be easier to deal with being a mother . . . than going the other route . . . I feel sorry for her . . . I am not sure she made the right decision, but I would probably make that decision . . . "

In her conscious responses Lisa appears sure of herself and definite about her opinion; that is, children get in the way of femininity. (Does she mean sexuality?) She says, "I don't feel that way at all. That women should want to have children." However, when we examine the content of the projective responses, we come to a different picture of Lisa. Here she is unsure; is wondering how it will be; is feeling the pressures of personal sacrifice and the fear of isolation. The issue of children taps into fears of abandonment and loss, as she sees the older woman alone, without a husband. In the last

MTAT illustrated here, Lisa's words reveal her orientation: "fear," "emotional," "hard," "setback," "guilt," "feel sorry for her," "not the right decision." From this brief illustration, the reader can see that, given this apparent discrepancy, a deeper probe of this response and of the subjective meaning attached to these words must be undertaken. At the outset, however, we know that these responses reflect conflictual material and, therefore we must be alert to discover their meaning.

Lisa's statements are significant for two separate reasons. Clearly, they provide a clue to her unique intrapsychic processes. But they also serve to raise a larger question, which develops from the association she makes between her thoughts about children (actually her ambivalence about children) and her conflictual relationship with her mother. This association, between ambivalence and the conflict vis a vis mother, was also found in other subjects.

According to classical theory,[2] a woman must have a strong, unconflicted identification with her mother in order to wish to become a mother herself. Here we apparently have clinical verification of this theoretical finding. The question arises: will this verification be found often enough in other subjects in order to provide a broader confirmation of the theory? Following this, we ask, will there be some other similarities between women who have these thoughts? Will they also be ambivalent about children? Or will they have been able to reach a childbearing decision? If so how did that happen? What else was occurring? What about the relationship? The work? The family history? How does this conflictual maternal/daughter relationship affect the childbearing decision in cases where there is no positive relationship with father? If the mother/daughter identification is conflicted, are there compensatory mechanisms, which daughter can employ, to resolve her ambivalence? What are these mechanisms? How can they be identified? Can therapeutic intervention aid in the individual's ability to utilize these mechanisms?

These speculations, and many others, have arisen from the preliminary analysis of a few sentences of one subject's protocol. As in all studies that follow a grounded theory modality, the task of the research from this point on becomes one of searching for further evidence, from this subject and others, which leads to clarification and, ultimately, either confirmation or rejection of the emerging theory.

PLAN FOR PART II

We begin the discussion of the ambivalent position in Chapter 6 with an extended case study. We will get to know Louise, age 33, married 11 years, and a professor of mathematics. Louise has not been able to decide about whether or when to have a child. She tells us that she feels "it's part of life" that she does not want to miss, and yet . . . she does not yet have a way to fit children into her complicated life. We'll come into Louise's life, get to know her psychologically, and try to understand her feelings about herself, her husband, her career, her family, and her dreams.

Our purpose in starting with a case study is to present the subsequent theoretical analysis of childbearing ambivalence, from the perspective of one individual's experience—to be able to relate the theory to the personal experience of one woman.

Chapter 7 focuses on several dimensions of the personality of the ambivalent woman. We analyze aspects of functioning related to autonomy, achievement, competition, flexibility, dominance, independence, and characteristic defenses. We ask, what's unique about this woman? How does she operate? What can we expect in terms of how she reacts—how she relates? How she feels? How she performs? In other words, this chapter talks about her behaviors and her responses to the external environment.

Chapter 8 explores some of the intrapsychic processes, the underlying dynamic forces that influence and determine her internal orientation. The chapter begins with analysis of pre-oedipal issues and asks whether we can see a relationship between a characteristic very early (pre-oepidal) mother/infant pattern and a later adult psychological position. Focusing on issues relating to separation/individuation, we provide support for the theory that the adult low self-image and lack of self-confidence has its roots in this phase of development.

From pre-oedipal issues we move on to consider the oedipal period, and the way in which the resolution of the oedipal constellation affects the later life orientation toward childbearing. As indicated in Part I, there was a marked difference in adult response to the content of the oedipal situation. Women in Groups A and B all recalled a special, loving relationship with father stemming from this early period. This relationship is what I refer to as the "chosen one" situation. On the other hand, all the women in Group C, those who intend to remain childless, indicated their dissatisfaction with father. Never feeling important to him or loved by him, instead, they recalled a strong sense of paternal rejection and abandonment. In this chapter, we try to establish, again through the words of our subjects (and through comparison of their protocols with those of the other two groups) that this sense of having been "chosen" is, by itself, not sufficient to cause the adult woman to wish to become a parent herself.

Following the discussion of pre-oedipal and oedipal elements, we move on to consider the question of the development of feminine identification as well as the larger issue of identity formation as an aspect of ego development. Is there a characteristic developmental process that can be used to understand the history of the ambivalent woman? Of clinical interest, is there something that we need to learn about these developmental processes in order to intervene in a reconstructive fashion?

In Chapter 9 we first consider developmental issues related to puberty, adolescence, menstruation, and young adulthood. Moving to adult issues, the discussion of parenthood as a developmental stage, probes the relationship between parenthood and the feelings about aging, the relationship between childbirth and dying, and the need for a legacy.

Throughout the discussion in Part II, the intent is to try to understand the separate elements of stress that the ambivalent woman might experience. Based on this discussion of the sources of such stress, Part III presents an analysis of clinical issues and treatment strategies.

REFERENCES

1. Stein, J. "Gender and Midlife Developmental Processes." In Cytrynbaum et al. Paper presented to the American Psychological Association Annual Convention, Toronto, Canada, 1978.
2. Freud, S. "Female Sexuality." In *The Complete Psychological Works*. Standard Edition, London: Hogarth Press, 1931.
   Deutsch, H. *The Psychology of Women*. New York: Grune & Stratton, 1944.

6
CASE STUDY—LOUISE

Louise (A), Ph.D. Professor of Mathematics; age 33; married 11 years; husband Bob is an attorney.

We met in Louise's office at the university where she teaches graduate level courses. Louise is quite short, and has rather long, beautifully groomed, dark hair. She was dressed that day in a rather conservative dark suit with a softly tailored blouse and very high heeled, elegant shoes. On her desk there were stacks of student files and a briefcase of material from the prior evening's consultation project. Louise speaks in a non-stop, slightly pressured fashion, with an excellent command of the language, and a lecture-type delivery. She answered all my questions with very extensive, thoughtful comments, which frequently lasted several minutes.

She maintained constant eye contact, smiled and laughed easily, and projected an air of confidence and well-being. Louise was very enthusiastic about discussing her views of dual-career marriages and her childbearing intentions.

Childhood

Louise grew up in downstate Illinois, the second daughter in a close family, which she describes as "average Catholic, not too strict." Her sister is three years older than she; there are no other children. Her upbringing and early childhood was very traditional. Her parents adhered to traditional, sex stereotyped roles: " . . . My mother was a typical mother in the sense that she didn't work; she stayed home. She's a very good homemaker—very domestic. And my father works. He's a plant engineer. He always worked in a factory and worked very hard. Both my parents are very sharp intellectually, but they are not educated beyond high school. So they instilled in us the idea that education was important and good. At the same time, they instilled the idea of traditional roles. So I learned how to do all the girl things . . . I could sew and cook when I was ten years old . . . but . . . with my dad . . . You see, he didn't have any sons and he used to take me with him down to the shop where he worked. He and I were really alike, and we did special things together. He treated me I think the way girls ought to be treated . . . as someone who is feminine and someone who should look pretty, who was a pretty little girl, and he was proud of that. As I grew up my father treated me more as a person than my mother did. We could always talk. It didn't get emotional like with my mother. I am like that too. My sister and my mother used to fight a lot. They were probably more alike in certain ways. And my father and I were more alike. My dad had high goals for me and gave me the feeling there was nothing I couldn't do. Of course, he was pretty strict too . . . and I really had to do my work.''

As Louise spoke of her father she revealed her sense of being special to him, a sense of being accepted by him as feminine and the sense of being treated as an equal. She also recognized that he thought she was smart and ambitious. She felt approval for this, as well as for "looking pretty". "My mother was a very dedicated mother and loved being a mother. My sister followed her in everything. I was more with my dad. When my sister and I grew up and we went off to school and got married and all that, my mother still has not recovered. She's proud of what we do but . . . she can't understand it. She'd be very happy if we were more traditional in the sense of having two or three kids and still nearby.''

Feeling that she's not really like her mother, Louise intimates that she had some questions in terms of identification with mother and the mothering role. Some feelings of ambivalence emerge as she described a favorite childhood fantasy: "I always used to project myself into that imaginary character. That character who was a female and was living in a big city, who was independent, and didn't have kids. She was always beautiful. Of course, when I was young when I played house . . . I was the mother. I used to build gas stations and buildings. I used to play mother and I used to play a great lady. I always used to be so female. I didn't project myself as a male. I was the female but I was the dominant person in whatever group we were in. Of course, I didn't know any better.'' A growing sense of ambivalence unfolds with the juxtaposition here of mother as the dominant person who nevertheless does masculine things such as build gas stations and buildings. First we saw a female with no children . . . then . . . "I was the mother . . . a great lady . . . ''

Later she said of her mother, "I think my mother always wanted to be more independent . . . but well . . . her sense of self-value centered around the family . . . and when we children grew up and didn't need her anymore, her sense of self-worth blew up in a puff of smoke. 'Now what am I good for? Now what do I do?' And had she had grandchildren, she would have done what everybody else does.''

Louise feels her mother's role in life left her without an enduring sense of self-worth, and that she herself, by not providing grandchildren, contributes to mother's dilemma. Throughout her story, references to mother reflect an undercurrent of guilt, which is always attached to the idea that somehow she still fails to please mother.

Early Self-Image. "As a kid I was more introverted and shy than my sister. I used to play by myself and I was a very serious student. I guess I believed then that everybody in the family played some sort of role; and the thing that I did, I was not supposed to rock the boat too much and I was supposed to do my work which was learning." (We heard earlier that she believed her role was also to identify with her father.)

Issues of Gender. "Even though my parents had well-defined roles for girls and boys, in certain areas we crossed the boundaries. For instance, I never felt there were things I couldn't do because I was a girl. I never felt inferior or different from boys intellectually." However, in school Louise felt that there was a lot of discrimination against girls, especially in the science courses to which she gravitated: "The teachers didn't treat us well. There were very few of us . . . they totally ignored us. I was really frustrated . . . it was as if they were saying, you can't do these things because you're a girl. And indeed so very few girls did and the ones who did were the ones who wore thick glasses and who weren't socially acceptable."

Louise easily achieved her goal of being socially acceptable. She was not only a high achiever in the academic sense, but she was accepted in social and peer activities and had a wide circle of girls and boys as friends: "I was always very active in school. I was the editor of the yearbook, and I was on student council, and I was involved in a lot of activities always . . . I felt that there should be a balance." At the same time, however, Louise recalls feeling that she was different from the other girls. She felt different in terms of body image as well as in terms of her family background: "I'm still very short, but as a kid I was always littler than I should have been for my age. I remember my parents were worried about that. Besides that I was very dark—dark hair and eyes, my sister was taller and lighter. We lived in a Swedish neighborhood and there were very few Italians. The others were all blond and blue-eyed and boy did I stick out . . . you see, we lived on the wrong side of the tracks and then moved . . . and so I really didn't fit in there . . . as I grew older, I also realized that there was some real prejudice against us, but then I didn't think of it that way."

Perhaps because she was always conscious of being seen as so tiny physically, Louise is very concerned about her physical image as an adult. She says, "as kids we always dressed well—really looked pretty when we all went out together.'' Appearances remain important to Louise. She believes women in business must be careful how they look. For example to MTAT card I (young woman wearing a dress) she says, . . . ''she really wishes she had worn a suit.'' To MTAT card VI (office scene; handshake between male and female) Louise says, ''she really is not experienced . . . first of all, she seems to have on a dress again. She really should have worn a business suit. That's the most versatile thing to wear . . . he thinks she's an attractive young thing . . . actually she's trying to sell him a system . . . '' Thus external feminine characteristics form an important part of Louise's female identification. We also hear her suggestion that the female has a hidden agenda—she uses her external attraction to further her private purpose.

Adult Self-Image

As an adult Louise sees herself as competent, strong, and independent. In talking about her career achievements, it's obvious that she's proud and very satisfied with her accomplishments. Although she takes pleasure in describing how well she does stereotypic female tasks, e.g., '' . . . I'd go into the kitchen and turn out three pies . . . it's fun,'' this aspect of herself is as highly structured as her professional self.

In terms of flexibility Louise describes herself as fairly rigid. (On a scale of 1 = very rigid, 5 = very flexible, she ranks herself at 2 and ranks her spouse at 3.) Her life is carefully organized and both she and her husband like to plan everything they do very carefully.

She continues to describe herself as different from other women: ''I think it's true what they say about it's lonely at the top . . . there aren't a lot of other women in my specialization . . . there are not many other equals who are at my level . . . so I don't have a wide circle of women who are in the same spot that I am . . . ''

Femininity

Throughout her story, Louise describes the conflict she feels between her identification as female vs. her role as successful career woman. We recall that even in school she characterized successful women as non-feminine. ''Later'', she said, ''when I was in business, I used to once in a while deliberately announce that I had to go shopping at lunch, in order to meet their (male) expectations of what women did, so that then when I had something to contribute professionally, the shock was diminished.''

Though Louise says she felt comfortable as supervisor of an all male work group, and totally in command of the work, she is very competitive with the men in her field, and resents what she describes as obvious sexual discrimination. In response to that attitude she says, "I'm probably typically manipulative, like a lot of women. I think we are conditioned to get what we want by pleasing others. I know a lot of times, I am devious. I will back off and go in another direction if I have to." Louise's MTAT themes are illustrative of this perspective, i.e., women are devious and manipulative, men are weak and vulnerable.

Card I (woman looking at a blank wall)—"This young lady is contemplating going in to see her boss. She's thinking, I wore a dress today and I look pretty feminine and that ought to help . . . when I get in there I'll sit down and cross my legs. Then we'll discuss the merits of the situation . . . but he's not going to put anything over on me. Because I know what all my fellow males (sic) are making and I'm going to be sure that I'm making the same. Of course he's a weak male and she can easily manipulate him, and she comes out with what she wants. She feels totally competent . . . as good as anybody . . . perhaps better than some of them . . . only she really wishes she had worn a business suit."

Card VIII (office setting—woman standing behind seated male) "Lady boss definitely . . . she has males working for her and she's doing her periodic motivation trip . . . she wants to make him feel as though she cares . . . and she does . . . she wants to feel as though she has a friend, because you know it's lonely at the top."

Career

Louise had determined as a child that she was going to achieve something professionally. "I was always the little kid who did her homework every day, and knew all the answers, and loved to answer all the questions . . . later on in college I became a math major because it was a nice clean science and didn't have any labs . . . and besides I was good at it. When I was in my fairly early college years I made some statement to the effect that I was interested in having a career . . . I was not going to finish school, work a couple of years, and then retire and become a full-time wife and mother. I always wanted to pursue some kind of lifetime, full-time career."

Louise talked about her feelings of competition and her strong resentment about women's traditional socialization: "I feel as though I guess I'm really paranoid about being second. It's a conflict in a sense of saying that you have to be supportive. And a wife always supports her husband . . . haven't you heard that? If your husband goes across the world you have to follow him. I think, what kind of bull is that? Why do I always have to be second? Why should I be second? Why is he better than I am? Then I start feeling guilty about it because I say you're such an uncompromising bitch. There's kind of a conflict of fighting for one's rights to be an equal human partner. This has been engraved since day one that women come second. So it's a balancing act trying to be nice and being fulfilled by both of those roles. But I can do it a lot better than I used to. I think women as a whole can do it a lot better than men because they've been conditioned to make that a part of themselves.''

Louise sees herself as a planner, but also a risk taker: "The biggest thing I learned is that if you want to succeed you've got to risk failure. You've got to expect it. When it happens you feel bad, but you just pull yourself together no matter how you feel about it . . . if you want to be successful the only way that I can see of doing it is not only to stick your toe in, but jump in all the way. But I don't go in unprepared. If you do you're sure to fail. And I don't like to fail. I feel very bad when I do. But the biggest fear I have is to get there and not have things prepared. For instance, my students are wonderful, but if I come in unprepared I'm going to lose them; and once you lose them, it's hard to get them back. What I mean about losing them is that they don't cooperate with you. They don't respect you. They start asking nasty questions and you can't control them. I don't want to lose control, that's the basis for everything; it's that I don't like to lose control. I like to be in control.''

Louise describes herself as very satisfied with her twelve year career and very ambitious to keep moving up. By the time she finished up her Ph.D. at age 28, she had been teaching at the university for a while, and was deeply committed to her special research. At one point in her career, she left teaching and went into business. She stayed five years: " . . . I learned a lot . . . had an absolutely marvelous time being a lady executive . . . and making a lot of money . . . and then decided to return to teaching . . . ''

She's extremely enthusiastic about her specialization, has been successful in publishing, and is well received in her professional association. She's currently finishing her second book and is filled with ideas for a private consulting venture.

Marriage

Louise and Bob have been married for eleven years. They met in high school (he was yearbook editor the year before she was) and dated all through college. They did not live together before marriage: "We were attracted to one another physically from the very beginning, but we didn't have a physical relationship that we couldn't handle . . . neither one of us was ready for that. In college I knew I wanted to marry Bob, but I certainly didn't want to marry him then, and he didn't want to marry me then either.''

Louise describes her husband as the most "interesting" person she's ever known. " . . . He's much more gregarious and social than I am . . . he's a great person to have at a party . . . we've had our ups and downs like a lot of other marriages. We like each other very much and we love each other.''

Louise reports domestic chores are shared about 70/30: "He helps me when I ask . . . but I have to ask.'' They do not argue about this, although she does feel resentment, especially when she's overloaded. The hardest times for her are " . . . when I have over-committed myself, and I have these problems meeting my obligations.''

She reports that most of their arguments are about her relationship to her parents, and her feelings that she (they) ought to spend more time with the parents. They also argue about " . . . past mistakes in not facing and handling problems and disagreements.''

Unlike many of the other subjects, this couple feels secure financially. Their combined income is over $50,000. They recently bought a city condo and have traveled in Europe and elsewhere buying furniture for it.

Louise talked about feelings of competition: "When I got my Ph.D., he would not even read one word, and refused to even look at any charts . . . he could have been helpful but he wasn't at all. And then when he passed the bar he went out by himself first to celebrate. I felt terrible. Then when I was in business and earning more money, people would always tease us, him particularly, about how it felt to have such a powerful wife . . . it presented some problems and we had to talk it out, because he had very strong feelings . . . the male ego thing. That's gotten a lot better now that he's doing well too.''

Decision about Having Children

Louise and Bob were married when she was 22 and he was 23. Louise stated, "When we were first married we assumed we would have children. We assumed that somewhere down the line we would make a decision as to when. But we did not initially consider having children, because it wouldn't be practical. We weren't psychologically ready for it—especially Bob—and besides, we were so young.''

Louise, as all the other subjects, had thought about the age factor in becoming pregnant: "Well now we're in the process of thinking about it because we're getting older . . . I'm 33 . . . and so pretty soon I wouldn't be able to have children that easily. I know that when you approach 35 it becomes more difficult. But I decided that I wasn't going to let that scare me into having kids. Because if it turns out that I'm 35 and I'm not ready then, well . . . I'll make another decision. I can always adopt* if I decide

---

*As mentioned above, all subjects have strong feeling about adoption; three quarters of the women in group A indicated they'd adopt if they decided they wanted to have a child and found they could not have a child naturally.

I'm too old . . . I don't want to be scared into having children. I just don't want to be scared and do something that I'm not ready for. And then if I'm too old, we'll get them some other way. There are other options." Three times in this statement, Louise expresses fear, conscious and unconscious, about having children. She says, "I don't want to be scared into it . . . I'm afraid I will not be ready . . . other options . . . " Some of these fears are related to the physical process of childbearing. Understanding her feelings about body image and her need to always look "pretty," her strong negative response to the physical aspects of pregnancy and childbirth comes as no surprise. She says, "I'm ready to be a father. I would love it if Bob could be the one to get pregnant, have the kid, have the morning sickness, and get fat—the whole bit. And he'd also be the one to stay home with the baby and feed it every four hours. That would be fine. I would come home and say, 'Oh what a beautiful baby,' and I'd hold it and love it for a few hours but not have the 24-hour responsibility. I'm ready for that part-time responsibility, but that responsibility is traditionally the father's role, and that would be fine with me. If I had a full-time housekeeper or whatever, then I could simulate that role, and I don't think I'd feel a bit guilty about it . . ."

Given their income level, the child care arrangement that Louise speaks of seems possible financially. However it's not conflict free, in terms of what Louise knows about mother-infant theories: "Psychologists say it's very important for the mother to be with the child for the first three years or whatever, and if you're not then it could do damage. I would hate to do damage to my child. I really don't think that I fully believe that though. But I would consider it as a possible problem. I would be willing to go through being pregnant and childbearing I suppose, but that's not the way I'd like it. I would be willing to go through it but I'm not enthralled with the idea. I look at it this way. I'm a busy woman. I have lots of things to do, and I don't really have time to be sick—like time for morning sickness. Believe me, I know I would have morning sickness too because I can't even take the pill without having morning sickness. My doctor has told me that. He said when you're pregnant just get ready for it, because you're not going to be in tip top shape; you're going to be sick. My mother was really sick and I know that's probably what's going to happen to me . . . I think about that a lot . . . because I would rather be building a consulting organization than having morning sickness right now." We get a strong sense that the conflict for Louise, contains a pull between what she wants and what she feels she ought to be doing.

Speculating as to whether she'd feel she was missing something if she didn't have children, Louise stated, "I have no real desire . . . the baby part doesn't appeal to me a whole lot . . . the changing of diapers and all

that sort of thing . . . I don't think I really need to go through that . . .
yet at the same time I wonder . . . I feel it's a natural part of life and if I
didn't have children I'd think I'd be passing up a part of life that I would
want to experience. I want to experience everything I can in life and that's
a very positive part. And I think I would enjoy being a mother. I think
that's a part of me that I haven't done yet and that I always intended to
do, and I don't think I'll let that slip through my fingers. If it means I have
to adopt a child of maybe three or four, well I'll do that then . . . "

When confronted with issues related to motherhood which were presented on the MTAT cards II and VII, Louise fell into an over intellectualized mode. She became the professor, doing research on human behavior. She said to MTAT Card II (woman in office; pictures of male and
children on desk; diploma on wall): "Oh, I see the conflict . . . the woman
is saying where did I go wrong?" According to Louise the hero feels better
because she's going to be in control by deliberately making a decision. But
Louise is unable to report what the decision is: " . . . whatever she does,
at least she will have the comfort of knowing that she deliberately made
that decision but I can't tell you what it is . . . "

To Card VII (two women, with a baby crawling between them) she says,
"This must be Margaret and me . . . I have some free time so I decided I
should practice my human interaction and see how she's doing. What does
a young mother with a six month old baby do in the afternoon? So . . .
we're chatting about everything in our various business activities . . . how
we're balancing everything and how she is handling little Allie . . . Margaret
feels a bit isolated . . . she feels as though I should have a kid; that I could
be exactly in the same boat as she is . . . But we're not talking much about
Allie . . . we're talking about business . . . " We see that even though the
visit is framed around the child, they still avoid discussing her decision and/
or issues of childrearing. As all Group A women did, Louise had certain
prior conditions that had to be met before she'd consider becoming pregnant.

Decision Criteria

"We have to feel that it's not going to interfere with the rest of our lives.
We have to feel that it's a positive rather than a negative step. And we have
to feel that it's—well that we're not going to feel compromised by it. Because if we are, then I don't think it would be a very good thing. When I
have children I want it to be positive, wonderful, and exciting. I don't want
it to be something that we're not excited about. And if we never reach the
point of being excited about it then we're never going to have kids. We feel
that we'd like to live one way, and that the changes that children might

make would be interfering.'' Notice the frequency of negative statements, e.g., "I don't want it to be something we're not excited about." She continues, "And I'm just trying to be realistic. I guess that's where my priorities are right now and I'm pretty clear on that. I won't give up my career . . . I think I would resent my child. I also feel that I am just about ready to decide. I want to be prepared. That's really what I need . . . I would like to be in a position where I would feel like I deserved the time and that I could take the time off to be comfortable and prepare. One of the reasons I've been in a hurry all these years is that I always felt there was a deadline. OK, you quit doing this and you start doing that . . . the mother bit. I just keep pushing the deadline. If all conditions are right, yes definitely, I will have a baby. If not, I'll adopt a baby. I've never really been infatuated with babies anyway. I suppose though, that I'll 'accidently on purpose' become pregnant." (How similar this last statement is to Dr. A. whom we met in the introduction.)

Louise's comment is especially revealing since we know how important control is for her. She's got to be in control in her decision to have a baby; yet she can't resist the allusion to "accidently" becoming pregnant, as if she really did not run the show.

SUMMARY

In trying to understand the nature of Louise's ambivalence, the following elements emerge:

1. Relationship to Father—Louise has fond memories of her special relationship to father. In psychodynamic terms, we assume that she has successfully resolved the oedipal issues that enabled early affirmation of self as female. As the oedipal daughter, she tells us that femininity means being sexually female, being physically attractive. Nurturant behaviors are associated with the less successful identification with mother, and are not connected in her mind with the self as feminine.
2. Relationship to Mother—As we have seen, Louise is fairly confident cf mother's love, although she always worried that somehow sister's place vis a vis mother was more secure than her own. Louise perceived her mother's orientation to femininity as nurturing. Louise, however, is highly conflicted in terms of identification with this mode. Her mother's current experiences remind her that children do not ensure life-long self-worth; that you can't depend on children; and that mothering somehow makes one second—less equal.

   Apparently too, there's also a lingering, negative maternal message in terms of the physical components of pregnancy, childbirth, and early nurturing, that Louise is only somewhat conscious of. She equates pregnancy with sickness and wishes to avoid the whole process. At this point Louise seems unable to integrate nurturance into her feminine self-concept.

3. Relationship to Spouse—Although Louise's relationship to her husband is terribly important to her, she deals with him in primarily intellectual ways. She is not satisfied with her spouse's affective support. He's described as jealous, competitive, and needing to be "managed carefully," i.e., by manipulative "feminine wiles." Given this feeling toward him, she questions what will happen to their marriage system if her attention focuses on baby and is deflected from him. Unlike women who are not secure financially, and whose concern is that they'd have no help with the physical aspects of child raising, Louise's concern is that her husband would not assume an equal emotional share of the burden of child raising. On another level, she may also feel some jealousy toward the anticipated father/baby relationship.

Louise and Bob have talked "endlessly" about whether or when to have kids, but have never reached a clear decision. Their discussions about child care, life-style changes, career changes, and physical changes are heavily intellectualized. They seem unable to confront the basic realities of the unavoidable changes, especially the fact that her life is apt to change the most. Nowhere in our meetings (except in her adoption fantasy) did Louise refer to children other than as infants. This preoccupation with the years of infancy illustrates how the decision is focused largely on self-image and on practical management issues. Feelings that were voiced by some other women in Group A and all the women in Group B, regarding the excitement of seeing a child grow up, issues of legacy, the anticipated love for a child, changes in relationships, are not allowed to come to consciousness for Louise.

4. Career—Louise, valuing her identity as an achiever, cherishes her career success and visibility, and remains in conflict as to whether the time out for a baby wouldn't interfere with her career track. She has dreams of building a professional consultation service, which come to mind each time she tries to envision having a baby. However, for Louise, having established a long, successful pattern, career pressures seem almost minimum, compared with other over-riding issues of self-concept.

Louise sees herself as "set in her ways." She likes control and a clearly regulated, carefully structured life. She knows this is not a realistic expectation of life with young babies, and she worries that she may not be flexible enough to alter her lifestyle.

5. Self-Concept as Different—Because she sees herself as not an ordinary woman, from time to time Louise has wondered if this represents a mas-

culine identification. She has a strong external orientation, and views herself as dominant, aggressive, and powerful. Louise's self-concept as different, apparently feels discordant with her fantasy of motherhood. She struggles but, at this point, does not seem to be able to integrate a nurturant aspect of self into her "different" self-concept. She feels very uncomfortable as she tries to anticipate the role of motherhood. She guards against allowing any affective material to come into her considerations, and struggles to keep things at an intellectual level. For Louise, the question of difference still seems unsettled. Does different mean more male than female? Does different mean more externalizing than nurturing? Louise has not resolved these questions.

6. Ambivalence Regarding Children—Louise's ambivalence seems to stem from the following conscious elements: (a) feminine identification as sexual and externally oriented, but questioning the nurturing component. Negative feelings toward physical aspects of pregnancy and childbirth; (b) marriage relationship has some elements of insecurity. No confidence that parenting would be shared responsibility; (c) very high value given to achievement. Professional self-concept is highly satisfactory; (d) doubts about ability or interest in becoming sufficiently flexible in terms of altering career investment and/or lifestyle.

In the chapters that follow, we will explore both conscious and unconscious elements which may be related to Louise's sense of ambivalence in terms of her decision to have children.

7
PERSONALITY

In investigating the significant personality characteristics found in ambivalent women, we must first try to position her socially, to see her public image, to see her the way the world sees her. Then we hope to deepen our understanding of her in order to see her the way she sees herself.

In many ways, of course, the ambivalent woman is very much like other dual-career women. She appears attractive, articulate, successful, well-educated, and confident. She's generally poised, outgoing, and extremely accomplished. Extroverted and competitive, she's accustomed to achievement and has a history of success, both as a child and as an adult. Conditioned to hard work and to getting what she wants, she's demonstrated that she can set goals, and stay on course until they are reached. Her persistence has served her well. For example, persistence is often found to be characteristic of people who receive advanced degrees.[1] The ambivalent group had the highest number of women with Ph.D.'s and other advanced professional degrees.

Typically, our subject had a relatively easy time getting started professionally. Somehow she was able to be in the right place at the right time. Now, having worked in her field for an average of eight years, she considers herself as having "almost arrived" in the sense of being well beyond the entry position in salary and responsibility.

She has experience with leadership and seems comfortable with it. She gets along with others, appears interested in them, and very often is seen as a motivator and a model for others.

She's able to form an intimate relationship, demonstrated by the fact that she's been married an average of four years. We recall that many subjects stated that their spouse was the single most important person in their lives.

Given this general picture, it would seem that, if judged by many of the standards set by our society, this individual has "got it made," and "ought" to be satisfied. Obviously, this notion has occurred to our subjects as well. Therefore, at those times when she is feeling dissatisfied (e.g., when an ambivalent woman is anxious about her inability to make decisions), she is

117

made very uncomfortable by the discrepancy between the way she "should" feel and her actual feelings.

What we are concerned with in this chapter, in contrast to the objective view that the world has of her, is her inner view—her subjective experience. We want to understand how she feels and reacts; what she loves/ what she hates; what she's afraid of; what she understands/ what she doesn't; how she experiences the multiple elements of her complex life. We want to know the part of her that is not displayed to those she works with, or to those who touch her life only superficially. We want to know the part of her that is private, internalized, and represented more by affect than by behavior. We want to focus on her internal experience, both conscious and unconscious.

As we explore the personality of the woman who is ambivalent about having children, we will see that she is often insecure and dissatisfied. She characteristically displays a high need for dominance and control, and is somewhat inflexible. Though continuously seeking the endorsement of an external authority, she is frequently uncomfortable in such a relationship and is unable to accept a dependent position. Rather than allowing herself to become dependent on those around her and thus risk closeness, she tends to hold herself apart from others. This leads to an unsatisfying pattern of interpersonal relationships, based on superficiality rather than intimacy.

As we might expect, ambivalent dual-career women have problems with many decisions; they seemed to have had a harder time (than other dual-career women) with the decision about career focus, with the decision to marry, with decisions about where and how to live, with decisions about use of leisure time, about relationships to extended family, and obviously, about children. As you will recall from the chart on page 100, ambivalent dual-career women appear to vascillate between primary orientation to career vs. primary orientation to relationship and/or self.

In terms of her defensive structure, we will see that the typical ambivalent woman employs denial, intellectualization, and a form of acting out. She also seems to use a splitting mechanism which reflects the split self-concept.

NARCISSISTIC PERSONALITY ORIENTATION

In many ways, the ambivalent woman suggests a narcissistic personality configuration. As we begin this discussion, it's important to distinguish this personality description from the clinical description of a narcissistic personality disorder. In no way am I suggesting the existence of a characterological disorder. It's clear, that up to this point in her life, this individual has functioned very well and has given no evidence of being psychiatrically

disabled. Nevertheless, as I probed more deeply into the psychological position of the ambivalent woman, it became apparent that she displays many
narcissistic characteristics. By seeing her in this light, I believe that we will
get a clearer picture of the areas of neurotic conflict and of her defensive
structure, both adaptive and maladaptive. Furthermore, the description of
the ambivalent woman as narcissistic also provides an approach to treatment issues, which will be discussed in Part III.

In Chapter 2 it was mentioned that Deutsch and other early psychodynamic theorists describe women as oriented to narcissism, masochism, and
passivity.[2] From my perspective, however, these descriptors *do not* give us
a useful or accurate view of the ambivalent dual-career woman. Although
I am using the narcissistic personality orientation as a general perspective
on ambivalence, I want to make it very clear that I do not see this as inevitably linked to masochism and passivity. Indeed, as I said earlier, I have
not found evidence of masochistic or passive processes as a dominant organizing focus of the personality. Nevertheless, I have found characteristics
that I believe can be more fully understood as developmentally similar to
what we have come to know as the narcissistic personality.

Unfortunately, the term narcissistic has a negative connotation for both
the non-clinical and clinical population. In the popular psychological literature, narcissism has come to be equated with the "me" generation and
with an exclusive emphasis on self over others. But we do the women in
question an injustice, and limit our pursuit of understanding, if we allow
this superficial, pejorative label to keep us from looking more deeply into
what we know about the dynamic basis for the development of the narcissistic personality.

The theoretical analysis of the narcissistic personality that I have found
most helpful in considering the subject under investigation, is the Kohutian
analysis.[3] Narcissism, according to Kohut, is defined " . . . not by the target
of the instinctual investment (i.e., whether it is the subject himself or other
people) but by the nature and quality of the instinctual charge."[4] That is,
rather than grounding the description of the narcissistic personality exclusively in the direction of the focus (i.e., toward either self or others), Kohut
turns our attention to the nature and quality of that focus, and asks, what
does that focus represent and what factors determine (influence) its content? He states, " . . . the expected control over such (self-object) others
is then closer to the concept of the control which a grown-up expects to
have over his own body than to the concept of the control which he expects
to have over others."[5]

As we know, the narcissistic personality is marked by a general failure
at managing object relations. Kohut reminds us that the narcissistic individual's object relations are governed throughout life by the nature and

quality of the earliest, unsatisfactory object relationships. Object relations theorists have described the life long pattern of unsatisfactory relationships as a repetition of the experience of failure at the earliest object relations task, i.e., the primitive relationship to mother.[6] An infantile inability to tolerate and ultimately integrate both the good and bad internal representation of the mother, damages the adult's capacity to integrate both good and bad aspects of the mature self-configuration.

The cathexis of self-objects arising from an individual's deficit position (in terms of the self) is thus qualitatively different from a cathexis based on an adequate, individuated foundation. Marlis's words illustrate this orientation: " . . . she loved me as long as I was perfect." She continued, " . . . she needed me to be perfect . . . and now I seem to need that for myself . . . " For this woman, the imperfect part of herself (that is, the imperfect part which was the *origin*—the *cause*—of the projected maternal rejection) was intolerable as part of the self, and was split off. The only self allowed by mother, and thus allowable to self through the process of projective identification, was the perfect one. Stated differently, in the mirroring of self vis a vis mother, the only possible source of self-esteem then, was that arising from the perfect self.[7] The development and functioning of such an ego, in all subsequent relationships, is colored by this flawed and fragile self-concept. For example, as the maturation process proceeds, the task of maintaining close relationships with its accompanying intimate demands and rewards, becomes overwhelming since it depends on an ability to tolerate the conflict of dealing with the imperfect self and other. Thus, adult relationships trigger these earliest fears and revive the infantile trauma.

The narcissistic personality seems unable to regulate self-esteem in a satisfying manner. This inability becomes the primary source of psychic discomfort. Also characteristic of the narcissistic personality is a grandiosity which serves as defense against the emergence of more primitive and chaotic borderline characteristics.[8]*

Clinically, we see the narcissistic personality as aloof, exhibiting a superior air; lacking humor; either projecting arrogance or shyness. These positions serve as a shield to the narcissist—a defense against the fears of rejection and abandonment—and of an uncontrollable primitive regression. Kohut states, " . . . the preconscious center from which these characterological disturbances emanate is the sense of an incomplete reality of the self, and secondarily, of the external world."[10]

Taking the narcissistic descriptors given thus far, let us measure them

---

*Kohut makes a distinction between the narcissistic and borderline personality, whereas Kernberg sees narcissism as a particular manifestation of the borderline structure.[9]

against what I have discovered about the ambivalent woman under consideration. We have said that narcissistic persons:

1. Are unable to regulate self-esteem in a satisfying manner, reflecting their inability to integrate good and bad aspects of the self.
2. Exhibit an omnipotence, a certain grandiosity.
3. Are characteristically either arrogant or shy.
4. Have learned to distance themselves from others.

In discussing the evidence which has led me to formulate the general conclusion that the ambivalent position is basically narcissistic, I will again draw on both conscious and pre/unconscious material provided by these subjects.

Inability to Regulate Self-Esteem

I have found that the ambivalent woman displays an inability to regulate self-esteem, by which I mean that she cannot maintain a satisfying balance between the contents of the good and bad self. However, it is important to remember that she *is* capable of experiencing a cohesive sense of self. Although the ambivalent woman's sense of self is vulnerable and fragile, and threatened at times (which, as we know, is vastly disruptive to the individual), she is not subject to the wide mood swings and pathological defenses characteristic of the borderline personality. This cohesive ability is critical to her maintenance of an acceptable level of functioning, as well as to her ability to make use of the therapeutic transference relationship.

As stated earlier, all the dual-career women I studied experienced what I have termed the "fear of being found out" (see Chapter 2). That is, regardless of an external projection of self-confidence, they were subject to continuous fears and doubts about their competence, their control (of self and others) and, ultimately, about the love from significant others. They routinely discounted what was obvious to others. That is, they were unable to test certain realities about themselves in an appropriate fashion. Therefore, academic achievements, career success, and relationships were apparently devalued. Fear of being found out is the fear that once another person is allowed to see the inner self, the "perfect" cover will vanish, and the truth about the damaged and inadequate self will be revealed.

Although the women in all of the groups studied expressed this "fear of being found out," the underlying content of this fear differed for each group. For example the baby group (who described the same fear of being found out), found that the experience was not paralyzing. Developmentally, the baby group has progressed through a positive early experience with both mother and father. As adults, a portion of their self-concept is grounded in an indentification with these early, satisfactory aspects of self. Their fear of being found out was a more or less realistic response to their position in a new and untested place in terms of adult feminine tasks. They were frequently a minority in their work setting; they lacked mentors; they felt the challenge of charting a unique path. Of course, they also had no model for their grand plan; that is, not many before them had demonstrated that women could actually combine career and parenthood in a satisfying manner. Therefore, the fears that they reported were grounded in their lack of experience, lack of support groups, and lack of models.*

Of course, since all the dual-career women were in a similarly new role we can assume that the socio-cultural pressures were similar for all of them. For the childless group, Group C, the fear of being found out is closer to the experience of the ambivalent group. Group C women all struggled with intimacy and with fear of rejection. From what we have learned about their infantile experience, this adult position should come as no surprise. We know that these women have internalized a sense of rejection stemming from both parents. They reported that they never felt accepted by either mother or father. However, in spite of these deficits, the adult self-concept—the externalized aspects of self at any rate—appears to be cohesive, integrated, and certainly functioning. Apparently, these women (Group C) were able to deal with, and integrate, the knowledge of parental rejection without damage to their adult ability to project confidence. Group C differs from Group A in that the women who have decided to remain childless have apparently made peace (either through denial or integration) with the reality of their early parental rejection. For Group A, the struggle continues. Yet the Group C ego has learned caution. This ego fears intimacy based on these early experiences. Denise (C) illustrates this caution. She recalls, "Before I met my husband, I used to think that no man, if he really knew me, would accept me."

The fear of being found out is a fear of being known. The fear in the ambivalent group is grounded in the split between the damaged self (reflective of the mother's conditional love, experienced as withheld) and the omnipotent, or perfect self (reflective of the father's total acceptance as revealed in the "chosen one" self-concept). For the ambivalent group, the fear of being found out can best be understood in terms of the underlying narcissistic position. The omnipotence so characteristic of the narcissistic personality is defense against any threat to the "perfect," but fragile self.

---

*Since I became interested in this phenomenon ("fear of being found out") I have heard many reports that suggest that this fear is not exclusively feminine. However, in our society, it is not acceptable for the dominant person (either male or female) to acknowledge this fear.

This external, perfect self must be protected and separated, and must remain untainted by the contents of the bad self. As we have said this process is a repetition—a consequence of the primitive distancing (split) from the maternal bad object. This is extended into a denial and rejection of any negative threat to the self. Therefore, for these women, the overt denigration of the value of the self, for example, as reflected in academic accomplishments, career success, lifestyle, and relationships, is actually a defense against the unconscious, fantasized overvalutation and overestimate of one's perfection. (Here we have identified a conflict of clinical importance, since it is likely to produce stress in the individual which may bring her into treatment.)

However, in trying to maintain this view of perfection (requiring a denial of reality), the ambivalent individual runs into trouble. The reality of imperfection is all too evident. Therefore, inevitable disappointments intrude on the primitive, grandiose position, and serve as an unbearable challenge to the "perfect" self structure. This again is a repetition of the infantile position.

A continuous denial (rejection) of split-off, bad self-objects represents a solution that is too extreme for this subject (that would describe a pathological consequence). Therefore, the ambivalent ego, relatively intact, refrains from such a radical course on a routine basis. However, the partial acknowledgment, but failure to integrate, negative-self objects into a cohesive frame becomes extremely conflictual. It's a question of degree here, between the neurotic and pathological management of such conflict. The ambivalent subject I am discussing evolves into a neurotic position which sets the stage for the pervasive ambivalence which is her badge.

Let's look at some case material for support of what I have said. Louise, whose history we read in Chapter 6 tells us that, "I'm used to being the little princess." Yet, we have some data which suggest that though she may have wished to be the little princess, that position was not really hers.* Louise says, "I feel as though I guess I'm really paranoid about being second. It's a conflict . . . Why do I have to be second? Why should I be second? Why is he better than I am? Then I start feeling guilty about it . . . " Here Louise is talking about the competitive relationship with her spouse. However, when we remember that she is the second daughter and that she grew up thinking her sister knew how to please mother, but that she did not, we can read the above statement in a different light. This reading allows us to see that she feels she is second in the sense of receiving mother's love. She suggests that she has failed somehow in the task of pleas-

---

*From time to time I will be repeating some of the case material quoted earlier. My purpose is to offer a different view, to try to deepen the meaning of the same words.

ing mother, thus making identification with mother conflicted and subsequent adoption of the mothering (nurturant) role dissonant.

For further evidence of a narcissistic orientation, consider Louise's following comments, which focus on body image and sacrifice: "I'm ready to be a father. I would love it if he could be the one to get pregnant, have the kid, have morning sickness, and get fat—the whole bit . . . " Later she said, "I look at it this way . . . I'm a busy woman. I have lots of things I want to do, so I don't really have time to be sick. Believe me, I would have morning sickness . . . because I can't even take the Pill without having morning sickness."

Louise has a pervasive uneasiness with the physical aspects of pregnancy. Children for her are equated with being sick and looking bad ("getting fat . . . the whole bit . . . "). The little princess must always "look good."

There is other evidence that Louise's self-image is predominantly focused on external physical characteristics, on the way she looks to others: "No. You can't do it all. You have to sacrifice. You have to make choices. I have missed a lot along the way. Like wasting time. When I go shopping it's always rush, rush, rush. I'd like to go have my hair done more often. I realize that I don't look as good as I could. I don't spend time on myself. I don't get enough sleep. I read far too many hours a day. I don't set my hair as often as I should. I don't feel pretty sometimes. That's one of the sacrifices." Louise's "sacrifices" revolve primarily around traditional feminine external characteristics ("looking good"). She says she sacrificed being pretty (feminine) in order to have her career. We might expect her to look somewhat plain, maybe dowdy, from her self-description. However, that is not the case at all. As described in Chapter 6, she was very attractive, well dressed, and perfectly groomed; hair elegantly coiffed, wardrobe ideal for her professional position, and accessories fashionable and proper. Hardly the drab sacrifice she talked of.

Her preoccupation with physical appearance surfaced in five MTAT responses (total series is 12).

MTAT #1: (woman looking at blank wall) "She feels totally competent, and she feels as though she's as good as anybody else, perhaps better than some of them . . . quite confident . . . Only she really wishes she had worn a business suit . . ."

MTAT #5: (woman looking out of window) "She wants to be somewhere else—not where she is . . . she wants to be just looking absolutely terrific . . ."

MTAT #6: (office scene; handshake between woman and man) " . . . she is a little bit young and looks like she is not 100% experienced . . . first of all, she seems to have a dress on again. She really should have on a business suit."

MTAT #8: (office scene: woman standing behind seated male) "Lady boss definitely . . . doing her periodic motivation trip . . . because she's an attractive lady and she's seeking him out . . . so he's feeling pretty good about that."

Louise was not the only ambivalent woman who attributed importance to the way others see you, and to external appearance in general. For example, to MTAT #1 (woman looking at blank wall) Jane (A) said, " . . . the clothes and the watch throw me off . . ." And later on she added ". . . the clothes aren't very business like, so maybe she's picking out a picture for her boss . . . " (Earlier in the story the office was hers.) When Jane began to feel (identify with) a loss in self-confidence, she no longer felt she deserved an office like the one she gave her boss.

I found further evidence of the inability to regulate self-esteem in the expression—by many subjects—that "they could never do enough." By this they mean that no matter how their accomplishments appear to others, they still feel that there must be something more to do; what they're doing may be a good start, but it isn't enough—it never seems to be enough. As adults, this pressure is manifested in the need for achievement. We trace this to the experience vis a vis mother, and to the conditional basis on which her love was given. (Remember, this is the daughter's perspective and may or may not accurately reflect the early reality.) Marlis says, " . . . but my mother's love felt contingent . . . there was the enormous pressure from my mother to just do a little better. She didn't know I felt so unworthy all the time. I couldn't be good enough. As she saw it, she was encouraging me. As I saw it, no matter how hard I tried, I was a disaster in her eyes. She was always pushing for achievement. If I didn't achieve, I didn't exist. When I did something wrong like breaking some plates or something, my mother used to pretend I wasn't there . . . I would disappear. I had no self . . . If I was accomplishing and doing well, nobody loved me more than my mother. That's still true. If I failed at something, I had to express just enormous pain; I had to fall apart; so then she would love me again. It had to hurt so bad that it transcended the failure." Marlis implies that she had to return to infantile helplessness: "I couldn't handle it (failure)—just brushing it off. There were two things to do: be perfect; and if imperfection were to strike (this is always in achievement things), then I had to fall apart so that she would still love me; in other kinds of areas, like having friends or dancing school (I had all the lessons), then I could be mediocre. That didn't matter to her." Note that she chooses to achieve only those things that mother valued.

Omnipotence

The second narcissistic characteristic we have identified is a pervasive omnipotence, which reflects the grandiose, infantile self-concept. I found that the ambivalent woman simultaneously displays an air of grandiosity as well as a fear of loss of love. In Kohut's terms, this would be a fear of losing the idealized parental imago.[11] The ambivalent woman's grandiosity is evidenced by her extroversion and her somewhat hypomanic, artificial stimulation of the environment; her overintellectualization; her insatiable search for external affirmation. Her fear of loss of love is manifested in her competitive nature, conflict with authority figures, inflexibility, insecurity, and distancing tendency. Yet this person fears losing love more powerfully than she fears punishment, shame, and guilt.[12]

The ambivalent women reported that omnipotence sometimes took the form of a view of oneself as unique and different and other times as superior. For example, Alyssa (A) said that both as a child and a teenager she felt like she "was the only one"—very unique and very special: "But all during my growing up years I felt that our age was the only one that existed—like when I was 16 they had this song "Sweet Sixteen," and these candles came out—and of course everyone else was 16; it never occurred to me that everyone wasn't 16. When I graduated from college the *Graduate* was the movie . . . I always felt we were the only ones." In another example, Jane (A) demonstrates her feelings of superiority vis a vis her male colleagues. She said, " . . . well . . . I was coming into a department without the right degree and there were some here with that degree and I got the job . . . They (the men) probably saw me as a threat. 'What does she have that I don't have and why are they bringing her in? She doesn't even have the right degree.' . . . Hired as their boss . . . yeah, higher than them (they seemed to be saying) how could I possibly know more than them with that degree . . . "

Jane's response to MTAT #6 (office scene: handshake between woman and man) also reflects her feelings of superiority: "Here's the manager of the office congratulating her employee on his new promotion. That's the way I look at it . . . He reports to her . . . she's got the skills, she knows how to do it . . . she called him into her office and said I'd like to talk to you . . . she's feeling good. She helps him along and that makes her look good. She wants to help the people who report to her."

Louise's MTAT's portray males as weak and females as dominant. Her identification with the female character is strong and consistent. She *is* the woman in all the male/female stories. But her superiority and wish for control extends to other women (mother) as well, representing a maternal transference response. Consider her response to MTAT #4 (older couple sitting facing a younger woman): Louise begins by ignoring the woman. Her first words are, " . . . Young girl with her father . . . " She goes on to describe the daughter's decision to follow a masculine career. After she introduces the mother into the scene, she talks about her realization, " . . . that she's not going to look for very much support . . . they're losing control." Why does Louise ignore the woman, who is as visually dominant in the picture as the man? Her omission suggests the possibility of an underlying oedipal wish to eliminate mother from the picture in order to have father all to herself. As her story progresses, when the mother is introduced, the content focuses on loss of support, loss of control, and disappointment. The sequence suggests the following: she and father do well together until mother appears, at which point she loses his support and her control over the situation. His support is apparently linked to an exclusive relationship, which falls apart with mother's appearance. The oedipal rivalry continues to rage.

Self as Different

Earlier (Chapter 2) we talked about the fact that the dual-career women in this study generally felt that they were somehow "different" from other women. One aspect of this self-concept as different focuses on issues of gender and role as expressed by the question, Am I more masculine than feminine since I value achievement, assertive behavior and competition (stereotypic male description)? In Chapter 8 we return to the gender issue, but at this point we recognize that self as different for some women is equated with self as different from, and superior to, mother. For example, Louise (A): "There aren't many women who can do what I do . . . " Lisa (A): "I was not content to follow the pattern my mother had in mind . . . that is to get married and stay put." In another sequence Lisa said, "I do all the bookkeeping . . . I took it over . . . once a year we budget . . . I let him do that . . . he introduces all this fancy footwork instead of just doing it like I would . . . I can't stand that . . . "

Jane (A) (about another woman in her organization): " . . . she's slipping into her old games of Miss Little Girl. When that happens I don't want anything to do with her. I feel like she's using me. I'm not going to put up with it at all . . . I don't mind understanding but I do mind being used. I know I can do all these things so much better than she does . . . or most anyone for that matter. I need a chance to show it . . . " Jane recognizes, at least in part, that the origin for these competitive pressures and conflicts can be traced back to her early family position. Jane remembers vying with her sister for mother's attention and feeling she needed to fight for her place. She uses the word "battle." Jane: " . . . I probably didn't like her (sister) because she was probably in my way. With five kids, you are battling for your territory. The way she got along with my mother bothered me at various times. My relationship was not anything with my mother. It was a battle." Throughout our discussion, Jane's thinking reflects an overt belief in her superiority and an impatience with having to deal with others' incompetence. Whether this is a defense against an underlying insecurity is not clear.

As Arrogant or Shy

Another characteristic of a narcissistic orientation is the projection of either arrogance or shyness. Two women in the ambivalent group frankly described themselves as shy, three as arrogant, and three (the most sophisticated of the group) used intellectualization as a veneer for an arrogant self-concept. Lisa and Alyssa, the overtly shy women, generally thought of themselves as uncomfortable in interpersonal situations. Alyssa frequently stated that as a child she had been beset with feelings of inadequacy and self-doubt. She says, " . . . our parents thought John and I were just wonderful . . . but somehow I didn't have a lot of self-confidence anyway . . . , though he did." Growing up she had girl friends, but was not really close to them. She worried about her lack of dates, her height (she was tall for her age), her inability to make small talk, and most importantly, about not knowing how to please mother. To MTAT X (the mentor card), Alyssa says, " . . . mother comes in and kind of looks over what she has been doing but is not that interested . . . " (Later on) " . . . daughter pretty well knows what she wants to do, but would appreciate comments from the mother . . . but mother says nothing . . . "

Lisa told us that she grew up learning " . . . not to make waves . . . " She was safest (from mother) when she didn't speak up, when she " . . . went along . . . " Barbara, who describes herself as arrogant and generally sure of herself, also talked about childhood issues of shyness and feelings of inferiority. But she compensated by always being "perfect"—a "goody two shoes." (This phrase was used by so many as a self label!)

Diane also remembers being somewhat shy in school as a young child. She said she was able to achieve some social success only because she followed an older sister, who was much more social. Diane, however, always "knew she was more capable than the others." She adopted a shy demeanor as a safe position from which to achieve her goals. On the other hand, Louise says, "I always knew the right answers and loved to answer all the questions." She was self-conscious because of her small stature, and her dark hair and complexion, but thought she compensated by being the first, the smartest, the most outspoken, the "princess." Louise's arrogant position is revealed in two of her MTAT stories—the first, in which she talks about "lady boss doing her periodic motivation trip . . . " and again, as the friend who visits the mother and baby upstairs in order to do some special research, " . . . I have some time so I decided I should practice my human interaction and see how she's doing . . . but . . . we're not talking about (the baby) we're talking about business . . . " (i.e., herself).

Distancing

The final characteristic that suggests a narcissistic position, is an apparently unconscious need to remain distant—to keep others away. This orientation reflects an underlying fear of dependence, a fear of intimacy, which is the representation of an unconscious fear of the power of an uncontrolled regressive tendency.[13] As I have come to understand it, the characteristic distancing that I observed in the ambivalent woman, is the antithesis of an interdependent orientation, which is so critical to a successful dual-career relationship. I have defined interdependence as the ability to be both dependent and independent within the structure of a relationship. This ability is very evident in those couples who are able to establish a mutually satisfying marital system. In such an interdependent system, the couple derives mutual support for both their dependence on each other and their autonomous functioning.

I also believe that there is a relationship between an interdependent capacity and the wish to have a child. A mother must be able to tolerate the infant's absolute early dependence without reacting as if this reliance constitutes a threat to the mother's cohesive self. The ability to give freely to another and to enter into this kind of symbiotic state is basic to the definition of nurturance, which the reader will recall from Chapter 1. To repeat: I have defined nurturance as those attitudes and behaviors that are oriented toward fulfilling both the psychic and physical needs of the other.

In this context we are reminded of the message the ambivalent woman received from her mother. Mother's message was, "I love you only if you meet my needs." This represents a reversal of the nurturant model as I see it. Little wonder our subject is unable to adopt a nurturant self-concept. She herself feels as if she cannot give what she has yet to receive. We get a clear picture of this characteristic both from the way in which our subjects see their spouse and the way in which they relate to others in their work organization.

RELATIONSHIP TO OTHERS

The Parental Model for Intimacy

To understand how our subject deals with intimate relationships, we must inquire first about her parents' relationship. What is her model for intimacy? The data on mother's attitude toward father is valuable here. Comparing the three groups we noted that in the baby group, all but one mother had a positive attitude toward spouse and toward men in general. In the childless group, all but one mother had a negative attitude toward men in general and spouse in particular. In the ambivalent group there were three mothers who projected a negative feeling toward their spouse (as interpreted by daughter). Yet, when we look more closely at the data regarding the daughter's perception of parental intimacy, regardless of how she described her mother's attitude toward men, we find that ambivalent daughters saw parents as distant, somewhat afraid of sexual intimacy, and somewhat cold toward each other. Whether this "cold" perception is an extension of daughter's feeling that maternal love for her was conditioned on her (unattainable) perfection, rather than a realistic observation of the way the parents actually related to each other, is really not important here. What is important is that to the daughter, the parents seemed distant from each other and unable to demonstrate comfortable intimacy. How does this model of intimacy affect the adult daughter's relationship to her spouse?

Relationship to Spouse

The responses to the sentence completion test illustrate some aspects of the relationship to spouse, as well as some of the differences between the ambivalent woman and the other two groups. For example, all the baby group completed the phrase, *"My spouse . . . "** with statements such as " . . . is wonderful . . . ," " . . . understands and supports . . . ," " . . . loving wonderful person . . . ," "he is . . . the beloved other . . . " In contrast, the ambivalent group said, " . . . has changed since we were married . . . " (no further elaboration), " . . . one of the most interesting people I know . . . ," " . . . helps me with problems at work . . . ," " . . . my main source of entertainment . . . ," " . . . would have a difficult time with changes . . . ," " . . . have to be careful or I'll be engulfed . . . " Nowhere in the ambivalent responses do we hear words that indicate a loving, shared intimacy. The words "interesting" and "entertaining" reflect an intellectual relationship, and we are reminded of the relationship this woman had with her father. Although she felt she was the "chosen one," the father/daughter relationship was based on a verbal (distanced) interaction, rather than an emotional (intimate) one.

The affective relationship suggested by Marlis' words, " . . . have to be careful or I'll be engulfed . . . ," is a reflection of a primitive fear—an infantile fear of engulfment, stemming from a fear of the totality of the

---

*This was #7 in the Sentence Completion Test. See Appendix C for Complete Test Sequence.

maternal power. Object relations theorists[14] have analyzed this process as follows: Briefly, the infant fears the danger of regression, which in this primitive stage, would mean a return to the pure (prenatal) symbiotic state (engulfment). Such a regression is synonymous with death. Thus the fight against engulfment can be seen to represent the fight for life. At the same time, however, the infant is totally dependent on maternal resources for its very life. Thus she must depend on that very power which is so terrifying. This situation sets the stage for later conflicts, since at this stage of her development, the expected and inevitable disappointments (which object relations theorists conceptualize as the good breast/bad breast split) arise.

As we suggested earlier, the task for the infant is to tolerate the experience of rejection (bad breast), and to integrate the maternal object (self representation) into a container for both good and bad. Unless this is accomplished to a satisfactory degree, the emerging self develops within a split, rather than a cohesive and integrated framework. This split, which in the clinical setting is readily observed in the borderline personality disorder, is not as apparent in the ambivalent woman we are discussing. As we have suggested, the ego of the ambivalent woman is somewhat, though imperfectly, integrated, and the defensive structure predominantly functional.

Returning to the question of the ambivalent disposition toward distancing, we conclude that the tentativeness, reluctance, and insecurity relative to relationships, reflects this deeper, more generalized failure in terms of having achieved a solid, early self-concept. The self is not experienced as a constant and dependable object. This self is unbearably threatened in any situation that demands closeness and requires giving. The only known position is the dependent one, which takes everything from the other and demands nothing from self. But that posture brings us full circle, to the fear of the disasterous consequences of the dependent state. Such a developmental deficit was manifested in many ways in the women studied here. For example, some subjects translated their fear of intimacy into a fear of being labeled selfish. For them the internal dialogue might be as follows: "I am afraid to allow myself to become attached to another, because to do so would represent a loss of self." This also becomes one of the sources of ambivalence regarding children; that is, "I am afraid of the mother/infant attachment." The unconscious fear is that "with this attachment, I will lose my own dependent position (symbiotic state vis a vis mother/spouse), and I will have to become the one on whom another is dependent." The conscious conclusion is as follows: "I will be seen as selfish."

The fear of external disapproval is a mirror of the internal pressure which, at this point, is great indeed. Lisa expresses these feelings, as she describes her fear that not wanting to have children will be seen as an inability to give to another: "I wonder if I am so selfish that I can't give myself to another person . . . to a child . . . " Lisa labels herself as selfish. In contrast, some Group C women said that the selfish label was imposed on them. For example, Larla (C) said, " . . . He in fact does feel that I am selfish not to want children . . . now that bothers me, but gradually I realized that this is his idea, not mine . . . He's really worried about his own selfishness . . . "

It appears from this that Larla is able to distinguish between an emotion that stems from her own intrapsychic structure and the pressure put on her by her spouse. Feeling conflicted, however, she recognizes that she is still dealing with this issue. Several investigators have pointed out that women who are " . . . childfree by choice, report considerable social pressure . . . (they are) considered selfish, abnormal, immature, or unhappy."[15] Childlessness was also labeled a sign of irresponsibility, emotional instability, and/or marital unhappiness.[16] Lisa's "selfish" worries reflect her identification with these negative stereotypes.

When we consider the way in which our ambivalent subjects relate to others in their work environment, we find other incidences of distancing. For example, Marlis works for a large organization as Director of a special program. As such, she employs several people and must maintain a close relationship to top management. Talking about her relationship to her colleagues, she said that she had problems getting beyond a superficial closeness. In thinking about her early development, she was able to see her current behavior as part of a lifelong orientation: "I remember a couple of kids, before 5th grade, who were sort of marginally my friends. But I didn't get invited to birthday parties. I guess I was lonely, but the teachers liked me . . . On the playground, I was the last one—I wasn't included. I was living in a kind of separate world. The consequences are that I still have a good case of distance."

Mentors

Finally, considerations of intimacy bring us to the question of mentors (also see Chapter 2 above). The mentoring relationship frequently is an intimate one, one which depends on the younger person being able to establish and maintain a dependency relationship with the mentor, who in turn must be able to support, teach, guide, and ultimately relinquish the younger colleague. Therefore, it is useful to examine the nature of the mentoring relationship for the ambivalent group and compare their relationships with those of the other two groups.

Whereas there were four women in the baby group and four in the childless group who reported a fairly positive mentoring relationship, only one

(Louise) in the ambivalent group really felt positive about her mentor. Two others who had received mentoring (Jane and Marlis) were conflicted about that relationship and the other five had not had a mentor. Louise said she had had a good experience in terms of mentoring: "John was my mentor. He gave me all the freedom I needed to do this job. But when I got into trouble, he was there so I could run and hide behind him. He wouldn't yell at me. He'd say OK tell me what you did; and I would always go in and confess first. I'd say John I just did this really terrible thing. I would tell him very much like a father . . . "

Louise talked about her continuing search for a female professional relationship: "So female relationships, as far as Ph.D.s in my field, have not been totally successful. I want a female companion who is fairly normal. Not someone who is freaky. I want somebody who doesn't know anything about life." (Does she want to be that other woman's mentor?) "I want somebody who is attractive. Somebody who is interested in the things I am. That's hard to find. She doesn't have to be a mathematician. I think it would be good for me, I think I would enjoy it a lot. I'm used to being the little princess. I think I'd be delighted. I wouldn't mind an association with an older woman, who had accomplished more than I had—a mentor. Then it would be absolutely. . . . I think I'd be jealous and threatened but I'm willing to try it."

Other Group A women talked about a significant teacher in their developing years, but not a mentor in the sense of a professional protector and guide. From studies of the mentor/mentee relationship, we know that the younger person has to be able to accept the authority of the more experienced colleague, and to use it positively without becoming defensive. This raises another question: How do our subjects fare in authority relationships? To answer this question we must look to the primary authority relationship—that is, the relationship to mother—for some guidance toward understanding the adult capacity. Knowing that the issue of maternal acceptance felt unsettled (these women thought of themselves as engaged in a continual effort to try to figure out how to please mother, how to "meet her needs," and how to finally "get it right") we assume that it might affect their adult relationship to authority figures.

The pattern I discovered can be labeled "rebellion with guilt." The dominant, competitive, and assertive nature of our subject serves as a defense against anyone who challenges her autonomy. This is a counter-dependent position. She strives for independence, for freedom to achieve her goals. Yet, she can't seem to keep on course without sooner or later succumbing to the old fear that she has not done enough; has not done what she needed to please the authority figure. Feeling guilty, assuming that she is responsible for the other's displeasure (projection), she may wish to make reparation—to make amends—to approach the authority without a defensive position. Yet, because she is inexperienced with intimacy, and is terrified of dependency, she is unable to reach out to the other, and instead, remains somewhat apart, guilty, but externally cool. Two cards in the projective series, Cards X and XII, provide some support for these statements, and illustrate some differences between the women.

In Card X, (the mentor card) an obviously older woman is standing next to a younger woman, who is seated. During the period of development for this card, I referred to it as the "mentor" card, since it was intended to stimulate feelings about authority issues in the relationship between older and younger women. Jane describes a scene in which the older woman is losing out on the basic age competition: "This older woman is trying to look younger, but can't." For Jane, younger = better, more powerful. Alyssa's response to the same card is as follows: " . . . the daughter is competent, maybe more so than mother—their relationship is good, but the mother loves the daughter more than the daughter loves the mother . . . " Here, daughter withholds love from mother, in deliberate punishment for her mother's authority role, rather than for her behavior vis a vis daughter at this point. Louise's response to this card reveals not only her wish to reverse roles with the mother (to control and dominate the mother), but also illustrates her unfulfilled need for nurturance: " . . . she's trying to teach me something . . . I will just keep feeding her questions and gain as much as I can from her . . . I would have exhausted her . . . " (Note the oral nature of the focus.) Diane stated, to Card X: "The older one is the boss and the younger one . . . is listening to what the older one has to say . . . the older one has worked all her life in this field and she wants very much to help the younger person whom she sees as being a very hypertension (sic) type of person . . . And the younger one is glad she is getting the help although she doesn't agree all the time . . . the younger woman is reflecting on the experiences she had in college and the certain risk in willingness to be creative. There is a conflict here that is a bit hidden, but is not a problem at this time . . . they are getting something out of helping each other. The younger woman is in fact giving the older woman a reason for spending the time; there is a benefit to both in this relationship . . . "

Let's examine Diane's response. We first ask, what is the meaning behind her statement that the younger woman (with whom she has identified) is " . . . very hypertension type . . . " Why is this thought introduced? One possible interpretation is that the situation (older vs. younger female) creates a serious problem for the younger person. What is the problem about? Diane tells us that intimate relationships contain an element of risk: " . . . glad she's getting the help, but doesn't agree all the time . . . " We wonder about the reference to the risk in willingness to be creative. Does "creative" equate here with noncompliance, rebellion, and unwillingness to follow? This seems to be the case, since in the very next association, the subject sees a "conflict here that is a bit hidden . . . " Intimacy is related to risk and conflict. Her association between risk and conflict in relationships emerges as the story concludes, and culminates in statements implying that one ultimately gets what they need from apparent submissiveness.

To understand Marlis' difficulties with authority figures, we must go back to her response to Card IX (two seated women, one obviously pregnant) to fully understand Card X: " . . . the older woman has stopped by . . . to ask for help from the one who is pregnant. The woman who is pregnant is about 30 and she works and has come home and not changed . . . they are talking about 'this is your first child' and you are still working, and the other woman has two children 10 and 12 and she hasn't worked since they were born and she is kind of curious about the younger woman because it is a different kind of life. They are having a real direct conversation about her pregnancy . . . she (young one) feels superior . . . proud that she can do all these things; real nervous (does this mean not willing to take advice?) . . . about the child, but trying to be real together . . . she has the air of competence . . . but it's clear things are going to get harder . . . she's not going to admit the truth about how she feels . . . the older one is envious . . . " Marlis' mood here is surface compliance and order. There is a denial of the existence of underlying feelings. Marlis seems to identify with aspects of both women. She is the younger one trying to cover her fears and look calm; she is also the older one giving advice and having it rejected. The theme is external projection of competence, rejection of maternal assistance, and internalized fear.

Marlis' response to Card X continues with the theme of envy, although she attempts to deny it. Three times in this story she says how much the women really like each other: "These two women work in an advertising agency or public relations . . . very chic . . . the older woman runs the place, she gets things done, directs . . . not competitive with the other one . . . they really like each other . . . older one is real calm and together . . . younger one may have some bright ideas . . . but not always accepted . . . they really care about each other . . . They don't see much of each other outside . . . younger one is not married . . . really care about each other. The older one doesn't envy the younger one . . . I really like them . . . " Why is Marlis so concerned with how they feel about each other? Three expressions of good feelings toward each other are suspicious. The envy, which she sees as a problem, is denied. Why does she bring up their relationship outside the work setting? I would guess that this stems from her need to put the two women into a family setting, similar to the setting in which she experienced this same conflict before.

Let's follow Marlis's associations. Going on to Card XII, we find a picture of a male figure with his back to the viewer, gazing out of the window, which frames a female figure seen walking away. Responses to this card frequently evoked images of abandonment, loss, resentment, and conflict toward the maternal figure. Marlis first says the two people don't know each other; then she switches the story to one of a broken relationship: " . . . Interesting . . . I am having trouble with this one . . . These two people don't know each other. He is a partner . . . late on a Saturday afternoon in the winter . . . and the woman . . . (long pause) . . . they weren't living together, but they were having a relationship . . . but they have broken up and he is gazing out the window . . . and she is walking by and curious about new relationships. He feels down and guilty and bad—not angry, just down . . . old jeans and sweatshirt to hang around on a late Saturday afternoon; it looks as if he needs a little straightening up and that's sad too . . . it's cold and gray . . . doesn't know what to do . . . " Notice that Marlis established the fact that the rejecting female feels no pain: " . . . she is curious about new relationships." She is ready to replace him immediately. This is the projection of the continuous fear of the ambivalent woman. That is, failure to please is inevitable and enduring, and the maternal object is capable of forgetting her completely. On the other hand, the male figure, left behind and rejected, feels sadness, as well as guilt: "He feels down and guilty and bad . . . " What significance does she find in describing his as a "partner"? What is the meaning of her emphasis on the fact that he is "not angry"? Again, it seems that he is not permitted to express anger at rejection, but internalizes it as due to his failure and inadequacy. Here again, as in Card IX, Marlis' identification is with both figures in the story. She is the rejecting female in symbiotic identification with her mother; she is also the rejected one, identifying with her own fears of abandonment.

Let's consider one other ambivalent response to Card XII. Lisa: "I don't want to make this a divorce story, but it looks so typical . . . This is the husband and the wife. She is going off to her profession—something she is very happy with. He, on the other hand, is unemployed and cannot find a job that he is happy with . . . He's changed fields three times and he is having a really hard time, and now he has decided to go back to school again. He is standing there watching her leave and feeling a great sense of aloneness, that somehow she is not sharing his problem. Because she is happy with herself . . . so he is almost resentful. He envies her and at the same time is angry because he wants to be the happy one, because tradition says that he should be going off, but he can't seem to get it together . . . "

" . . . She feels bad for him and has tried to help. He won't accept her advice. He is shutting her out . . . She feels she is reaching the end. She has been very good about it up till this point, and she is saying that she is going to go her own way . . . He is bringing her down. She has a lot going for her, and yet her husband does not seem to be able to be happy for anyone else . . . He does not find his way back to school. And she is feeling very tired of it all because she has been the full support and she has had to deal with his emotional problems as well and nothing is reciprocated. It seems she has done all the giving. So she leaves him . . . she feels very guilty . . . and she feels very bad for him, but she leaves him.''

Again, we see that the consequence for successful autonomy is the loss of the relationship.

Group C responses to MTAT XII also focused on themes of rejection and loss. In comparison, the Group B stories frequently described the love between these two people in spite of the fact that she had to leave for some purpose.

Having presented my view, that the ambivalent position can also be described as basically narcissistic, we now proceed to discuss a few personality dimensions, which are characteristic of the ambivalent subjects.

AMBITION/ NEED
FOR ACHIEVEMENT / COMPETITION

As described in Part I, all the dual-career women in this study, including the ambivalent group, displayed a high need for achievement. The question under consideration here, is whether and in what ways, need for achievement is associated with ambivalence regarding children. We will ask how these women differ from the other groups of childless dual career women, in terms of their ambition, achievement drive and competitive motivation.

As indicated earlier, external markers of achievement are not experienced as satisfying for the ambivalent woman. In the following material, I will illustrate some of the achievement expectations expressed by Group A, and try to understand their development and the unconscious purposes (origins) of the devaluation process.

We will see that throughout the ambivalent protocols, the thrust toward achievement was very often associated with the conflict about children. Achievement in some ways always feels like a threat to the nurturant aspect of self and the fantasies about maternal functioning.

Lisa's words, which follow, illustrate the association between achievement and ambivalence regarding children. She also stresses her identification with father, and her conflict with mother. It is interesting to follow Lisa's associations through a sequence of responses. She proceeds from a statement of ambition, to a memory of father's encouragement, then to mother's lack of interest, and finally to mother's failure to support her development into mature femininity, which for her, is symbolic of motherhood. She begins with a recollection of childhood: "My brother delivered papers—and I would get up with him at 6 A.M. on Saturdays and walk or bicycle all over the countryside in Kentucky. I babysat when I was 10 years old because I wanted the money. I guess I felt some satisfaction from earning money way back then. Being around my brother who was six years older than me . . . he was very ambitious always plotting and scheming for money . . . I guess having those older ones in the family talking about making money encouraged me to do the same." She paused for a moment, then continued the association between development of ambition and the relationship to significant male figures, which reflected a period of positive self-concept: "I may have picked that up from my father because he encouraged me . . . " However, the memory of the good paternal object cannot overcome what was for her, more significant—the lack of maternal love, caring, and guidance. She says, "I don't think she (mother) cared, because it got me out of the way. My mother never had a job in her life—she was a real home person. She never took me in the kitchen and said, 'OK I am going to teach you how to bake,' or anything like that—she never took me aside—she said nothing about dressing or anything. In fact, when I did start to menstruate—I was so upset—I didn't know what it was about. I knew my sisters did but I didn't know what it was about—and when I went to my mother . . . she said go into the bathroom and change and I will send in your sister to talk to you—and that is what she did—and I remember the next day my father came around and said, how are you feeling—do you understand what is going on and everything—and I was embarrassed to talk to him at that point—and I was embarrassed because I really didn't understand it." This series of associations is so important, it's worth reemphasizing. Lisa's thoughts proceed from self-esteem (in the ambitious, achieving young self), to positive feelings about father (men in general), which quickly lead her to focus on the lack of maternal interest she sensed (deprivation) and an emerging self-doubt, which is connected to conflict regarding early adolescent feminine development and puberty.

In another sequence, Lisa repeats her feeling that ambition leads to conflict in terms of femininity (children): "I know one thing I wanted to do at that time—I wanted to be involved with some kind of business of my own—and I remember discussions with Bob, my boyfriend." Here, her ambition is again set within the context of a male relationship. She continues, "I never thought I would stay in an organization like X—to this day I think I must get out. I still have very definite goals of being in my own business—I really do want to have my own business after I have finished graduate school." Yet, she continues, " . . . I suppose I have to reevaluate that goal, reevaluate my work, have a family, you know . . . The lifestyle that you become accustomed to with two people working . . . with no one to worry about except yourselves . . . it's quite different from a situation with kids. I wonder about how I'll feel if I have to give up my goals. I wonder if I am so selfish . . . " (see above, page 132). Again, Lisa spells out her conflict. For her, the child is associated with a sacrifice of self. In particular, a sacrifice of those ambitions that formulate so much of her self-concept—the positive aspects of the self.

Lisa's association of ambition with a sacrifice of self is so dominant that she returns to this theme in still another frame of reference. This time the conflict emerges over the wish to continue her education. She says, "We were having this discussion just yesterday—I guess it was the house and all the bedrooms—and our friends are taking it for granted because we are moving out to the suburbs—that it is now time for a family. I don't say anything to them—we just want to try the suburbs . . . the question came up—well when is the baby due, and I said, well there isn't going to be one— so later John and I talked about it. I told John that it isn't that I don't want children—but it's just a matter of I haven't been able to achieve a lot of other things that I want to do. And we were talking about school and I have to make some decisions about that very soon . . . I have to decide. On top of making those decisions, I just can't fit into that your wanting me to have a child—it just can't happen in the next 2 or 3 years. His comment to me was 'well you know I want them.' I told him I knew that, but that doesn't mean that I can have them right now. We talked about the fact that I am going to be 30 in another 2 1/2 years. I told John that he has that '30' in his mind—that is the last point I can have a child. But some of our friends have children, 31, 32, 34—it can be done—it might not be the easiest thing—but in our case . . . "

Father's Response to Achievement

Returning to our discussion of developmental factors that led to the characteristic high achievement need, as we have noted, father was often perceived as encouraging ambition and accomplishments. For the developing infant and the very young child, the father traditionally represents external resources. He is the one who models orientation to external domains, as compared to mother who supplies the stimulus for internal development. In our situation, father is seen as one who rewards autonomous functioning and responds to the executive aspects of the child, whereas mother is seen primarily as reflective of affective development.[17] Many subjects remember that, as a child, father was especially proud of them when they brought home success. Louise: "With father it didn't get all emotional . . . he would talk to me . . . '' Diane: ''I asked him about careers . . . we would have conversations all the time . . . '' Barbara: ''My father seemed to think what I did and thought was OK . . . ''

Mother's Response to Achievement

What are the maternal responses to daughter's achievement? According to my analysis, seven out of the eight mothers either covertly criticized daughter's ambition in the sense that the unstated message was, ''Why not be like me—be satisfied with wife/mother and forget a career'' or whose own inadequacy served as a point of departure and became a stimulus for daughter's decision never to live mother's life. For example, Louise saw her mother as bright, capable, but unfulfilled. And as ''lost'' as soon as her children grew up and left home. She talked about the development of her identification with achievement: ''Well, the fact that I saw a lot of women with unrealized potential—and also, I think maybe it was more than just the fact that I was always interested in things and enjoyed being a part of things— I felt that if I didn't pursue a career, somehow I'd be cut off.''

Marlis knew that father accepted whatever she did even though she was not perfect. On the other hand, mother was the source of some heavy pressure to achieve. Marlis has a vivid memory of an early scene: (note the difference in the way mother and father react) ''So when my report card came in the mail, the bastard had given me a B. I just fell apart. I couldn't talk. I was just hysterically crying. My father just held me and let me cry. . . . He helped me. My mother was distant and hurt and shaking, but he held me. When I got over the crying I was so mad. I was old enough and self-confident enough to be angry . . . From there on I started fighting back . . . This business where I have to achieve is still an enormous problem . . . I am more like my mother than my father . . . there are things about me that are like my father, but they're not associated with achievement. When my mother said you have to finish school first, she meant a Ph.D. My mother wanted me to have a profession so I'd be independent. My father was—oh wonderful, gold star. My kid, you know the doctor? Nobody ever mentioned career. They didn't talk about was I going to get married. With my friends we just presumed that we would grow up and get married and have children . . . when I was little. In college, it started to fade a bit. Nobody quite knew . . . and since then the career has kept me from . . . it has been my primary concern—it has kept me from putting much energy into finding the right person to marry and having children— that always seems to be secondary.''

Some women associated high achievement goals with their wish to be different from ''ordinary women'' (mother). Diane: ''Yes I wanted to be a doctor—When I was in the 8th grade I had to prepare a little booklet . . . what you want to be when you grow up . . . most of the women said airline stewardesses, teachers, nurses, and I wanted to be a doctor. I took biology and did quite well . . . "

Question: How did your family feel about your wanting to be a doctor? "My parents were encouraging me to do this. After college all of my friends were going on for some kind of advanced degree—I remember having conversations with my father as to what kinds of jobs I could get—and he indicated that most women went into secretarial positions—and I knew I didn't want that. As it turned out, when I went back for an academic degree and when I completed my master's—there was one woman who got her master's and decided to go to a business school. She was one of three at that time, so there were not a lot of them—a lot of role models. I did not want to be a grammar or high school teacher—I knew that. I don't think I ever thought about not getting married and I don't think I ever thought about not having kids. It was just that they were not top priority—the priority was being a doctor, and that has been true throughout. I think I developed that view partially because it was not imperative from the point of view of my mother—she didn't say 'you had to get married' or she didn't even indicate that that was the desired outcome. She didn't give me a direct negative—I guess what I am saying is that it was much more by analogy."

COMPETITION

Self as Second

So far, we have described the ambivalent subject's self-concept as competitive; as never feeling a sense of lasting satisfaction with accomplishments; as never quite "getting it right"—never doing enough to please mother; as being afraid that the "real" (i.e., the inadequate) self will be exposed and automatically rejected based on its obvious failures. One way to begin to understand the origin, development, and adult content of this self-concept is by analyzing very early developmental phases.

We begin with the competitive relationship inherent in the oedipal triangle. In the traditional understanding of this situation, the infant daughter changes her primary cathexis from mother to father based on an erotically derived impulse, which Freud and his followers describe as follows: The infant girl recognizes that she lacks a penis; the envy of those who have the desired penis is transformed into a wish for a penis, which is equated with having a baby; this develops into a desire to capture the father as giver of baby to mother. In so doing, the daughter's fantasy is to replace mother. This oedipal conflict is referred to as the primary triangle.

Since we have said that all but two women in the ambivalent group felt that they were either rejected by mother, or loved only on the condition that they met mother's needs, we recognize that the daughter's oedipal idealization of father (seeing herself as the "chosen one") also contains a reflection of her feelings of rejection by mother.

In a recent discussion of the role of the father in child development, emphasis on the oedipal triangle, in terms of the early competitive struggle, has been positioned as second to an earlier triangular situation in which a rival baby is the competitive object rather than the mother.[18] There is a conflict between the narcissistic wish to believe in the self as first, vs. the need to acknowledge the reality of self as second. What does this conflict mean for the individual? How does it become activated? What is the content and what are the consequences?

When I considered whether or not sibling competition had an impact on the ambivalent subjects, I found that in most cases where there were either older or younger siblings, the ambivalent woman felt that the other(s) knew how to please mother, knew the "right" thing to do, knew how to meet mother's needs, etc. The ambivalent woman felt "second best" regarding siblings. The following chart indicates birth order and relationship to mother.*

	Birth Order	Mother's Love			Older Sister
		Yes	Only If	No	
Marlis	Only		X		
Jane	4th			X	
Paula	2nd	X			
Alyssa	2nd		X		
Lisa	12th			X	X
Louise	2nd		X		X
Diane	2nd	X			X
Barbara	2nd		X		X

---

*For those curious about whether there was a relationship between ambivalence and number of siblings or birth order, although I noted that in Group C six subjects had more than two siblings, in contrast to three in Groups A and B who had more than two siblings, I do not believe the data are sufficient to draw any conclusions. I do not mean to imply that these elements don't impact on the individual woman's decision, but rather, in terms of what we can generalize about and formulate hypotheses to test in further work, that the information available on these variables (as well as on religious and socio-economic background) is too scanty to be useful at this point.

Some women were very aware of their anger at being second. For example, Louise said, "I guess I'm really paranoid about being second . . . Why do I always have to be second . . . "? Diane: " . . . My oldest sister suffers from asthma, and she would go off and spend time with my grandparents . . . I think she was always treated a little bit more delicately than the rest of us . . . I had a difficult time understanding that . . . My grandfather was a physician, and he favored my sister, and I think that affected me more than any single thing . . . I spent a great deal of time trying to win his favor because of his seeming clear preference for her . . . " The competitive orientation of the child who has siblings is evident in these subjects. However, how do we explain the competitive, rivalrous orientation of the women who had no sibling—no one to set the standard of perfection against which to measure oneself and the responses of one's parents. I discovered that it was not necessary that a comparison be made to an actual rival. Even more significant, in many instances, was a comparison made to the idealized self—the perfect self—the one mother "really loved" and whose image was held as the model. Compared to this perfection, which mother's response had made clear was the only acceptable one, the daughter's actual self was doomed to come in second. Moreover, I believe that this comparative process takes place whether or not there is an actual sibling.

We are well aware that the power of an unconsciously held position is much more resistant to change than an attitude, belief, or behavior that reflects deliberate and conscious awareness. Similarly, the unconsciously held belief in the self as second is firmly rooted and resistant to consciousness. Here again, we identify a treatment formulation. With this clarification, we deepen our understanding of why these highly successful adults are somehow unable to derive any satisfaction from the reality of their success. From her internal perspective, no matter what the ambivalent woman does, she can never do it as perfectly as the idealized fantasy of her perfect self. No matter what accomplishments she gathers, they are never enough. Therefore, as I see it, it did not matter whether or not there was an actual rival; the developing ego grew into adulthood bent by the weight of the quest for the ideal, but unobtainable self.

What evidence do I have for the above conclusion that the fantasied self as rival is significant as a source of the developing, competitive personality characteristic? Consider the following examples. Marlis: "No matter what I did, it just wasn't good enough . . . I felt I could never do anything right." When Marlis did something wrong, mother ignored her—gave her the silent treatment. She recalls, "I would disappear, I would have no self." Loss of self is equated with mother's withdrawal—with her failure to please. Since she knew she could not attain the desired perfection, (the idealized self) the self remaining—the self mother could not tolerate—was "lost" in the context of this dilemma. Jane: "We (mother and I) had no relationship at all . . . she didn't recognize me, I suppose." What does Jane mean by the word recognize? Is it to accept? to love? What is the consequence of not being recognized? Lisa: "It was always clear to me that mother didn't want me around. After 11 kids, who would? The others were so much older, too . . . it was almost as if I was just there growing up on my own . . . She just didn't want to deal with me at all . . . (The phrase "growing up on my own" suggests that the self is the sole competitor.) Alyssa MTAT VII: (two women with baby crawling between them): " . . . I am placing the child as an insignificant thing . . . because the child is on the floor . . . the child is pretty insignificant . . . that baby is down there without a face . . . the mother does not want to say I am not happy with what I am doing . . . " What is the meaning of the baby with no face—the baby who is "insignificant?" Throughout her projectives, Alyssa offers themes of loss and abandonment and of a fruitless search for approval. Alyssa's baby with no face, in my view, is illustrative of the notion that the baby (who is Alyssa), who is incapable of satisfying the mother, ceases to exist. The baby with no face, may be considered the self with no personna—the empty shell. This is very similar to Marlis' statement, " . . . I would disappear . . . I would have no self . . . "

DOMINANCE

Along with a competitive orientation, ambivalent subjects also exhibit a high need for dominance, power, and control. They share this characteristic with the other highly career-oriented subjects we have been discussing. What makes them different, however, (and what is also of therapeutic significance), is their conflicted sense of guilt regarding their need for control. For example, Louise states, "I don't want to lose control. That's the basis for everything is that I don't like to lose control. I like to be in control . . . others have to accept that . . . " (Does this mean that she feels others do not accept that?) Marlis talking about her relationship: "We fight all the time about everything—money, issues of control—the good thing is that I finally found someone I cannot dominate . . . But he consistently—despite my best efforts—will try to make me feel inadequate. I have all the qualities he is proud of, yet he wants to control me." How easily we can substitute "mother" for lover here! Later on, Marlis separates those areas of her life over which she has control, from other aspects: " . . . there are some important things that I feel I don't control. I don't know, everything else seems to come first—whether I want it or not—Everything like work and school—all the things I can control—they all seem very important—they have to be settled immediately. I have to get from one day to the next. I have to do the best I can. That's the stuff you have to deal with. That's what I can control . . . but relationships with men and children seem like the things that just happened. I have managed them but I don't control them. I feel that fate has not been kind to me and I don't know why I feel that way—I could just say yes or no . . . but I don't seem to . . . ''

According to Marlis, relationships with men and children are not things she can control. In her words, "fate has not been kind to me . . . '' What does she mean by fate? Is fate supposed to make her childbearing decision? Does fate reflect a sense of powerlessness—a wish to be governed by external events? How contradictory this sounds, knowing as we do Marlis's strong, dominant, independent, willful nature. This brings to mind the statement by the pediatrician, Dr. A., who said that she got pregnant by accident.

Marlis continued: "It feels depressing—it feels like I have never thought of it before until this moment . . . I knew I felt that all men I have had in relationships seemed to have been accidental—the person who came along at the right moment—the way I feel about this accidental quality of my relationships is exactly the same way I feel about this business about children . . . it's in the same category of life—it is just fate and whatever happens.'' I proceeded to ask Marlis the following questions to which she responded as follows:

Question: It's whatever happens?
"Yes."
Question: Are you telling me that you are not actively going to decide either to have children or not to have children?
"I guess so—if things happen, or if he (whoever that is) would come home tomorrow and say, 'well I have been thinking about it—children seem to be important to you—let's have a baby.' I would say yes—I would go along with it . . . but I guess I don't want to decide . . . ''

Is Motherhood Seen as a Way to Gain or Lose Power?

As we recall, many subjects saw their mother as sacrificing her own goals (power?) in the service of the child. This held true for many dual-career women—not just ambivalent women. For example, Diane talked about her mother's sacrifice of sexuality as well as career. " . . . I saw her more of a mother than a wife . . . (later on) . . . she gave up her earlier work as an artist and seemed bound into this endless domestic routine . . . '' Others also spoke of the sacrifice of career. Barbara never got over the feeling that mother was dissatisfied with her role as wife/mother. Before her children were born, mother had pride in herself. Although she clearly chose her role, she always hinted (Barbara's perception) that she paid a great price for that choice. Barbara's perception contributes to the sense of guilt she feels regarding mother.

Louise's mother also gloried in her motherhood role, but was left empty and purposeless after the girls grew up and left home. Louise also talked of feeling guilty for somehow failing in mother's eyes, in the sense of rejecting a traditional female lifeplan. Yet remember how intentional this so called failure is. We see the conflict. Wishing to please mother ("do as I did") yet needing to follow the pressure to be powerful, dominant, and unburdened seemed irreconcilable to Louise.

Think about Alyssa who said in her projective responses that "when you have children, you lose yourself." She says that having a child will jeopardize her control of things: "Right now I am in my own business . . . I am pretty much in control of how I do things—and if I don't get things done I am the one who will have to worry. But I am finding that here are these new creatures in our lives—or new creature—that here would be something that in a way you would have no control over that would be putting demands on my life. That would be demanding from both of us—that we may thoroughly enjoy—but at the same time, I wouldn't be able to be comfortably in control of things."

Dominance in Relationships

In what way is the choice of spouse related to the struggle with the parental figures, and in what way is the relationship a mirror of the struggle for dominance and power? What kind of men did these ambivalent women marry? What is the general nature of their relationships with men?

Paula married a passive man, thus modeling her parental situation. Marlis, on the other hand, said that she did not want a man like father, whom she recognized as passive, emotional, and giving, but weak. She has chosen someone strong, whom she can't dominate. Yet, she is beset by the fear that somehow since he is outside of her control he will drop out of the picture. (Such a male was not in the parental picture.) When she fantasized about the future, she could not see any male in her future; when she tried to see herself with a child, she could not develop that fantasy either.

Two other women sought out domineering men, who would serve as the continuation of either father's or grandfather's role. Jane's situation is interesting. She lives with a dominant spouse and maintains a surface of submission. This facade conflicts with her psychological position (she feels very superior). This imbalance creates a constant power struggle. She apparently has a need not to win, but a compulsion to try. Marlis refers to the constant power struggle. Diane, does not use these words but nevertheless, is in continuous competition with her spouse.

Louise, speaking about her husband: " . . . He thinks I dominate him . . . in certain ways he tries to be very protective . . . by making me feel guilty about certain things I do on my own . . . " A bit later she says, "I think that a lot of it has to do with the fact that he met me when I was a little girl. He thinks of me—wants me to be—very naive . . . For me it comes down to wanting control—wanting structure. It's got to be my structure, and then I'll be happy. I can't have that sort of success if it's somebody else's structure."

Paula, who feels competitive with spouse, worries about issues of marital dominance. Throughout the MTAT series, she sees women as dominant and controlling; males as weak and passive; motherhood as making women "feel superficial . . . " Paula, in MTAT V (woman looking out the window) describes a conflict between the father and the daughter, in which the daughter wins and then subsequently feels a great sense of guilt. She makes the connection between oedipal rivalry and guilt regarding the fantasy of control. Paula always sees mother as controlling and father as feeling. For her, the two aspects of personality are kept apart.

Paula had an interesting response to MTAT XII (male looking out the window at departing female figure). She tells a story about a small boy whose mother goes off to work and leaves him behind. The dominant female (mother) seems threatening in her story. The child feels lost and abandoned and fears that she is not coming back. Paula identified with both figures with a resulting sense of dissatisfaction and sadness.

The mentoring situation is another male/female relationship in which our subjects dealt with issues of dominance and control. As indicated above, only one reported a successful mentoring relationship with a male (Louise). The others either had no mentor, or felt a conflict with their mentor. In comparison, four women in Group B and four in Group C had a mentor. Seven of these mentors were males.

Finally, in discussing issues of dominance and control, we can look at the relationship between the need for control and the narcissistic orientation toward control over self. In this sense, the ambivalent woman is conflicted about exerting the necessary control, power, and dominance over others (e.g., at work) since she is also constantly in quest of acceptance, perfection, and love. She is in the kind of bind that the Group B and C women do not encounter.

Group C women have no conflict about what comes first, as was evidenced from their very first response, in which they clearly stated that their career was first. They also demonstrated their comfort with power. Group B, however, stating that relationships come first, implied that a need for control, especially control over professional development and relationships, did not determine either their feelings or their actions. But Group A could not decide—they could not focus unequivocally on either career or relationship. They were caught. (We return to this split in orientation in Chapter 9.)

There is further evidence of conflict regarding control in the ambivalent woman's inability to feel comfortable with a position of power. Accomplishments did not increase feelings of control. We will recall that more women in the ambivalent group had Ph.Ds and other professional degrees than any other group. Thus we suspect that, in all likelihood, those in the ambivalent group had opportunities for more advanced professional positions than women with fewer credentials. But despite their professional standing, the ambivalent women did not feel powerful, nor did their professional standing satisfy their need for control, or produce what had been sought—that is, a sense of "perfection."

CONFORMITY

I think it is important to mention briefly, my view of the way in which the need to conform contributes to the stress and conflict of the ambivalent position.

In contrast to Group C women, who saw their choice to depart from the traditional female (maternal) role as ego-sytonic and enhancing their dreams, the ambivalent group did not feel entirely comfortable with their new roles, and the new-found responsibility to determine and follow their own adult path. Ambivalent women are not rebels; they are not pioneers; they are not intent on upsetting the "establishment" (though in their younger days, as flower children, or would-be flower children, they may have thought of themselves in this way). They are basically conformers who find themselves caught in the tide of a revolution, some aspects of which they feel are beyond their control. I want to make it clear that I do not mean that these women do not choose the dual-career lifestyle with keen awareness of the difficulties that this new family pattern implies. However, having chosen this lifestyle, with its equal emphasis on the relationship as well as on individual achievement, they feel somehow caught up in a rejection of parental patterns, and in social expectations, which have somehow gotten away from them.

Thoroughly nontraditional in the sense of rejecting the stereotypic restraints on feminine professional goals, and in their insistence on individual rather than social control over their sexual behavior, ambivalent women nevertheless accepted the parental pressure to "grow up and get married," to stay in school (they went far beyond even the parent's dreams), and to strive for the good life, both socially and financially.

In terms of professional goals, our subjects chose very "establishment" fields. Physician, professor, MBA business woman, computer salesperson, pre-school teacher—all careers marked by traditional socio-cultural boundaries and expectations. Not iconoclasts at all.

Ambivalent women believe that marriage is a valuable and worthwhile commitment. (Once again they follow tradition.) The way they live, as well as the way they plan to live in the future—in comfortable, somewhat affluent surroundings—again suggests that they see themselves as like their parents. Middle-class, upwardly mobile, their environment seems compatible with traditional cultural norms. Even the complex dual-career lifestyle feels socially acceptable to ambivalent women since they mirror their peers. These women often form reference groups which help make their lifestyle seem ordinary. It is only in their ambivalence regarding children that they depart from their own and from society's expectations, in a way that feels uncomfortable and conflictual.

DEFENSIVE STRUCTURE

A very useful way to come to know an individual, is through an examination of that person's defensive structure. Therefore, in this section, we will try to understand the ambivalent woman, in terms of her characteristic defenses.

An individual's defensive structure is a unique, unconscious system which serves as protection from certain internal and external pressures. Initially outlined by Freud, our understanding of these processes was greatly expanded through the work of Anna Freud.[19]

Defenses screen the ego from confrontation with whatever is perceived as a threat. The ego invokes the defense as a cloak, a guard, a way of avoiding the necessity of dealing with the issue. The defense serves as a mechanism that relieves the tension associated with highly charged affective material (usually sexual and/or aggressive), which threatens to invade the consciousness. Defenses maintain an equilibrium, even though that state may be pathological.

Most individuals have a wide range of defensive mechanisms, which are unconsciously employed as needed. Defenses range from primitive to mature and from maladaptive to adaptive. Patterns characteristically utilized by an individual serve as a measure of maturity, as well as a guide in the diagnosis of pathology.

We have come to recognize that certain maladaptive and primitive defenses are characteristic of specific personality disorders. For example, in diagnosing a borderline personality disorder[20] we have learned that borderlines frequently utilize a splitting mechanism, reflecting an infantile, primitive position.*

At the same time that we state that defenses may be an indication of pathology, it's also important to realize that many aspects of our defensive structure are highly adaptive and ego-enhancing. Humor and altruistic behavior are good examples of this type of defense. Vaillant, in his longitudinal analysis of the life cycle of men, provides a helpful framework for thinking about defenses.[21] Vaillant developed a scale, which he labeled "Maturity of Defenses Scale."[22] In this scale, his subjects were rated according to the maturity and the adaptive nature of their defensive style. He divided defenses into three major categories, which he labeled as follows: immature defenses (fantasy, projection, passive aggression, hypochondriasis, acting out); neurotic defenses (intellectualization, repression, reaction formation, displacement, dissociation); and mature defenses (altruism, suppression, humor, anticipation, sublimation). Among Vaillant's conclusions regarding the characteristics that dominated the lives of those men he called "successful," is that one achieves maturity through a successful adaptation to stress (use of defenses). He states, "It is effective adaptation to stress that permits us to live."[23]

Although we will not discuss all the defenses outlined above, the reader has already discovered the ways in which our dual-career women used a mature defensive style, for example through the mechanisms of sublimation (academic achievement) and altruism (many were active in community or family "helping" activities). Furthermore, the reader is also aware that I do not consider any of these subjects to be dysfunctional, in the sense of displaying generalized and pervasive maladaptive responses to their environment (either internal or external). Therefore, although I have found evidence of immature and neurotic defenses (using the categories outlined above), I do not imply that such defenses represent any pathology.

I will discuss the ambivalent women's use of the following defenses: repression and denial; passive aggressive behavior; intellectualization; acting out and reaction formation.

Repression and Denial

One way to deal with stressful events is to push them away from consciousness. This is done through the process of *repression and denial.*

---

*To illustrate how this defense is manifested, when a borderline patient is hospitalized on a psychiatric unit, the staff—psychologists, psychiatrists, social workers, and nurses—may initially reproduce the patient's defense (splitting) by feeling angry at each other and divided among themselves as to treatment issues, unit behavior, patient motivation, etc.

I use the term repression to describe a mechanism attached to affects, thoughts, associations, and memories, which are conflictual and are blocked from consciousness. Denial, as used here, refers to the process by which an individual somehow alters her or his perception of reality, or buries that perception in an idiosyncratic distortion, which serves the needs of the ego at the moment. In other words, when an individual represses a feeling, she or he has already made some kind of contact with that feeling, but finds it intolerable; when an individual denies a feeling, in all probability it is beyond her or his conscious awareness.

Probably the most significant expression of denial is the statement we heard Dr. A. make in the introduction to Part II; that she "just got careless" about birth control. In these words, she is denying the real decision that this "carelessness" represents; that is, she is trying to call the unconscious choice an act of conscious carelessness. Louise, our compulsive planner, our scientist, the individual who prizes control, echoed this denial: " . . . I've never really been infatuated with babies anyway. I suppose though, that I'll accidently on purpose get pregnant." Another example of denial was given by Lisa: "Given our situation what if I should become pregnant and we have this humongous mortgage staring at us . . . Well that concerns me, but I also look at it and assume that nothing is going to happen . . . I am an optimist." This is clearly in contradiction of many of Lisa's projective responses which, as we saw, reveal the depths of her fear of pregnancy and the threat to the ego that this conflict reflects.

Marlis denies that she has control over " . . . things like relationships and children . . . " She tells herself these things are "fate" which "has been unkind." She denies the reality of her negative feelings regarding men and children. Alyssa talked about denial as a family characteristic. She was remembering her father: "He died in 1971 but had been very sick for 6 months, and for a year before that . . . really hadn't been well for 4 years. He never admitted that he had cancer . . . and this is a family trait and today we would talk about it differently . . . we talk about my brother . . . we all talk about him because it was opened up and he had surgery . . . he hardly ever talks about it now . . . but my Dad didn't talk about . . . he denied that there was anything wrong with him and he was an intelligent man . . . even when he was in the nursing home and I would go to visit him . . . he would say to another colleague . . . I just don't know what is wrong with me. I suppose in a way I'm like him."

Passive Aggressive Behavior

The person who "forgets" to keep an appointment, the person who is always late, the person who "accidentally" burns the toast or spills the coffee, or consistently mails the check late, is displaying *passive aggressive behavior*.

Lisa and Alyssa, who had described themselves as shy, present another aspect of passive aggressive behavior (as shy persons do quite often). In other words, shyness may cover a rage—a wish to attack and destroy—and serves as a manipulation—a manner of control. Lisa offered an example of passive aggression in relation to her husband's management of finances: "I let him do it" (referring to their budget). Actually she maintains control by her denigration of his ability, her arrogant certainty about her own greater skill, and her ultimate veto power. Lisa also complains about the housework, but refuses to hire someone to help. (How many dual-career subjects fell into this one!) It seems to me that by refusing any help, the woman is preserving her power, while claiming to be overworked and overwhelmed. For some, the objective seemed to be a wish that the spouse would feel guilty. In other cases, the refusal to hire household help was a joint one, thus suggesting some unconscious collusion in denial of the conflict created by the breakdown of the traditional female acceptance of domestic responsibility.

When we think about the external projection of conformity that these subjects exhibit, we are brought to the question of whether this conformity is a manifestation of a passive-aggressive mechanism which is denied by the individual. In other words, the woman says to herself, "Look, I am acting just like them (parents). I am married, I am working, I am successful . . . why should they . . . or she (mother) pressure me about kids? I do everything she did and more . . . what does she want from me?" The obvious answer: daughter does everything *except* identify with mother.

Jane shows still another kind of passive aggressive behavior. She says she was "feisty" and as a child admired "this feisty lady." By feisty Jane means that she considered herself highly assertive—not easily pushed around—that she can hold her own in any situation. However, Jane is actually extremely afraid of confrontation and avoids it, even though she realizes she is angry and a bit out of control. We heard Jane talk about how enraged she is because of the unfair treatment she received at the hands of some of her clients, who are "sexist and sly," or by some of her colleagues who are fooled by the pranks of her competitor (the woman who "used her . . . little Miss Innocent tricks"). In contrast, Jane is sure she is always straightforward, direct, and honest. Yet, when she describes her schemes to outwit the games she sees around her, she reveals her own pattern, which is a passive aggressive one—a highly indirect attack. She is certain she seems compliant, however, she is always on guard and ready for betrayal; belligerent, almost paranoid in her defensive posture.

Louise has recognized her passive aggressive behavior. She has labeled herself as devious. In reminiscing about herself as an adolescent she said, "The only regret I have is that maybe I should have been less devious, more straightforward . . . Playing on people in the sense that I do . . . "

Intellectualization

We have already seen the ways in which ambivalent women avoid making a decision by using *intellectualization*. Intellectualization, as we said before, is a verbal way to avoid confrontation with the emotional aspects of dealing with a person or situation. Intellectualization, as a defense, is frequently an adjunct to denial and may be highly adaptive. By this I mean that it may permit the psyche to "buy time" in response to a shock or trauma. However, it may also be maladaptive. For example, the individual verbalizes to excess and cloaks the reaction (to person, event, affect) with a rationalization, frequently a barrage of words—an adroit sophistry, which sounds on the surface as if it is a response, but actually is a meaningless avoidance charade.

Diane gives us a perfect example of the use of intellectualization to avoid talking about her feelings about having to make a childbearing decision. Notice how she uses the pronoun "you" rather than talking about herself. We were talking about her childbearing decision process: "I was thinking of something when you were asking me . . . a class that I took in business which was a one year programming . . . you look at all the restraints that exist in a variable . . . use the maximum of the output and then you have all these restraints and you have to maximize them as much as possible . . . that's what I mean . . . with the restraints that exist in your job in what is important to you ranking those constraints . . . What is most important to you . . . what is second most important to you . . . those get the largest share . . . Recognizing that you can't have maximum family . . . maximum job without excluding some of the other things . . . yes . . . Again it depends on the level you are shooting for. If you want to be president . . . if you want to be a senior V.P. . . . that may involve . . . something else . . . " Notice how Diane winds down, and can't seem to keep her feelings in place (hidden) although she seems to want to. What do we understand from her repeated use of the word restraint? What is she thinking when she says " . . . something else . . . " My guess is that the reference is to personal sacrifice—to the baby/career conflict. Later in the interview Diane seemed to recognize her own defense: "I had dinner last night with a friend of mine who had lost a child and was pregnant again, and she talked about what she was going through. I told her I thought the biggest obstacle was logistics and she said I wonder if that is a cover for emotional feelings that you don't want to deal with.''

When I first met Barbara, she gave a textbook example of intellectualization about the childbearing decision. All her statements were framed around theories of childraising, and involved an erudite analysis of alternate authoritative statements about the problems of raising children in a working parent environment. In addition, she never talked about baby as baby, or about herself as mother, but rather focused on whether she could arrange for a child-care person who would teach the appropriate socio-cultural values that she and Jim shared. Now, I must add that all of the Group B women also had thoughts about child-care arrangements, about what would happen to their careers, and about how their relationship to spouse would change. However, they were able to confront the affective component throughout, and did not feel compelled to flee—to hide behind their equally well-developed verbal capacity.

The following is an example of intellectualization. Note how Marlis switches from words like ''reasonable,'' ''rational,'' and ''natural'' to ''impractical,'' ''indulgence,'' ''a gift,'' and ''only appropriate when . . . if everything else was taken care of . . . '' She said, ''When I was younger it just seemed reasonable . . . I am not sure what I felt when I was 23 years old . . . in school . . . it just seemed rational . . . everyone would have thought that was natural . . . it was impractical . . . which has always seemed to be true . . . it's always seemed to be impractical . . . it seemed to be an enormous indulgence; a gift that you can give to yourself if the time was just right . . . and if you could afford it and if everything else was taken care of . . . then you could have a child.''

One final comment on intellectualization. It is possible that the pervasive sense of being ''different,'' which almost every subject was aware of, was actually a form of intellectualization; a defense against the unconscious fear that part of their concept of self as professional served to authenticate the self-concept of self as non-female.

In presenting these examples of intellectualization, I am suggesting that the ambivalence about nurturance—the incomplete identification with the maternal object (mother)—is reflected in the lifelong view of oneself as different. As I analyzed the very thoughtful way that these women talked about their differences, I realized that during the actual interview process, I failed to discover how much these ''differences'' were an intellectualized cover for questions related to sexual identity. Only on analysis of all the data, following the interview sequence, did I recognize the process which may have been underway, and the possible counter-transference implications of my own focus on their words instead of on the underlying meaning. I'll return to this question of counter-transference in Chapter 12.

Acting Out

Certainly, from all that has been said about women in the ambivalent group, it is clear that their behavior is hardly *acting out* in the clinical sense by which we refer to self-destructive behavior such as school-related defiance, running away, substance abuse, or suicidal gestures. However, you will recall that I have described a hypomanic quality—a superficial over-exuberance—which seemed characteristic of this group. I have noted that this woman tends to stir up her environment and maintains a superficial quality in her relationships, either by thinking about or actually pursuing a continuous reshuffling of the people in her life. Actually, the results of her somewhat hypomanic pace have an adaptive outcome, as well as a potentially maladaptive one; that is, she has been able to accomplish a lot and is functioning well in many facets of life. Of great significance is the fact that she has maintained a relationship with her spouse for an average of four years. Moreover, she appears psychologically mature on many measures.

Looking at prior relationships, in terms of the number of serious relationships before she "settled in" with a spouse, I found that four women in the group had had many partners prior to marrying, and four had had very few. In Group C, all but two women had had several prior relationships before meeting their spouse. The baby group seemed to have selected a spouse earlier in life and were more apt to have made fewer changes in their intimate relationship. From these data, however, I can draw no conclusions about whether the stability of relationships is related to the quality I am describing as hypomanic.

Reaction Formation

Once again, I refer to Vaillant's work on defenses for a useful definition. He says, "reaction formation is behavior in a fashion diametrically opposed to an unacceptable instinctual impulse . . . This mechanism includes overtly caring for someone else when one wishes to be cared for oneself, 'hating' someone or something one really likes, or 'loving' a hated rival or unpleasant duty."[24]

I would like to suggest that the same behavior which I have just described as hypomanic, can also be viewed as *reaction formation*. In this case, it is possible that the unacceptable instinctual pressure is the guilt surrounding the hesitation to identify with mother—that is, to become a mother. The ambivalence regarding children, as well as the relentless quest for professional success and the pursuit of a never-ending trail of "perfection" can be conceptualized as reactions to the overpowering unconscious impulse to reject and disappoint mother. In this sense Group A is quite different from the baby group, since in the latter case, the desire to become a mother arises from a basic, unconflicted identification with the maternal object.

The ambivalent daughter's inability to give up her search for maternal approval is also a reaction formation. As I see it, the aggressive impulse toward the rejecting mother compels daughter to turn away, attack, harm, and disappoint—to reflect her sense of rejection. However, to withdraw from mother, is paralyzingly frightening for this individual. Instead, daughter reacts in the opposite way, focusing unwaiveringly on mother, never able to let go, never confident enough of the autonomous self. The failure to trust one's ability to turn from mother, then leads to failure at every subsequent developmental opportunity for individuation.

When we consider the power of the relationship between father and daughter, we can also suggest that the strength of this bond may reflect a reaction formation to an unconscious envy and hatred of father, who seems to have won maternal favor. The image of father is invested with all the positive qualities that daughter actually craves from mother.

With these comments on the ambivalent defensive structure, we have completed a review of some personality characteristics of this group of women. Taking into consideration what we now know about how ambivalent women appear to the world, as well as how they respond internally, we will probe more deeply into the question of how some of their personality characteristics developed.

In Chapter 8, we present some thoughts about the psychodynamic origins of the positions discussed so far.

REFERENCES

1. Campbell, D. P. *Manual for the Strong-Campbell Interest Inventory.* Stanford, CA: Stanford University Press, 1974.
2. Deutsch, H. *The Psychology of Women.* New York: Grune & Stratton, 1944.
3. Kohut, H. *The Analysis of the Self.* New York: International Universities Press, 1971.
4. Ibid., p. 26.
5. Ibid., p. 27.
6. See Klein, M. *Love, Hate and Reparation.* New York: Dell Publishing, 1975.
   Winnicott, D. W. Transitional Objects and Transitional Phenomena. *International Journal of Psycho-Analysis.* 34:89–97.
   Kernberg, *Object Relations Theory and Clinical Psychoanalysis.* New York: Jason Aronson, Inc., 1976.
7. Kohut, *The Analysis of Self.*
8. Ibid., p. 20.
9. Ibid.
   also see Kernberg, *Object Relations Theory.*
   Jacobson, E. *The Self and Object World.* New York: International Universities Press, 1974.

10. Kohut, *Analysis of the Self.* p. 20.
11. Ibid., p. 21–26.
12. Ibid.
13. Ibid. Also see Kernberg, *Object Relations Theory.*
14. See Kernberg, *Object Relations Theory.*
    Mahler, M. S. *On Human Symbiosis and the Vicissitudes of Individuation.* New York: International Universities Press, 1968.
15. Bardwick, J. *In Transition.* New York: Holt, Rinehart & Winston, 1979. p. 173.
16. Ibid., p. 61.
17. Blum, E. H., ed. *Female Psychology.* New York: International Universities Press, 1977.
    Rapoport, R., and R. *Dual Career Families.* Harmondsworth, England, Penguin Books, 1971.
18. Machtlinger, V. J. The Father in Psychoanalytic Theory. In, Lamb, M. (ed.) *The Role of the Father in Child Development.* New York: John Wiley & Sons, 1981, p. 126.
19. Freud, A. *The Ego and the Mechanisms of Defense.* New York: International Universities Press, 1946.
20. American Psychiatric Association. *Diagnostic and Statistical Manual of Mental Disorders (Third Edition).* Washington, D. C.: 1980. (301.83 Borderline Personality Disorder)
21. Vaillant, G. *Adaptation to Life.* Boston: Little Brown & Co., 1977.
22. Ibid., p. 393.
23. Ibid., p. 374.
24. Ibid., p. 385.

8
PSYCHODYNAMIC DEVELOPMENT

We begin this discussion of the psychodynamic origins of the ambivalence toward childbearing with an analysis of the issues arising from the pre-oedipal period and the early mother/daughter struggle with the problems of separation and dependency. Ambivalent women have yet to resolve this critical developmental transition. Most of them describe a lifelong, ongoing feeling of insecurity re mother. Their adult attitude toward mother, especially the lack of a fully satisfying identification with her, reflects an aura of guilt which infuses all aspects of the ambivalent daughter's relationship to her mother. This guilt stems as much from her conscious impulse to question and/or reject the maternal role (to be different from mother) as it does from unconscious, intrapsychic pressures.

Following the natural developmental sequence, in the second part of this chapter, we analyze the oedipal constellation and the origins of the self-concept as the "chosen one" vis a vis father. As we said above, all the ambivalent women have very positive memories of their early relationship to father, as well as of the subsequent support, encouragement, and guidance he provided as they were growing up. The last section of this chapter concludes with a brief comment on some aspects of the development of femininity as it appears for the ambivalent group, with some thoughts on the differences in the content of the feminine self-concept between the baby group, the ambivalent group, and the childless group.

PRE-OEDIPAL ISSUES

Nancy Chodorow, in her study of the mothering process writes, " . . . the basic stance for parenting is founded during this period" (earliest infantile development).[1] Deutsch states that in order to wish to become a parent, the daughter must have a strong, nonaggressive identification with her mother[2] (see above Chapter 4).

We know that the ambivalent dual-career woman is uncomfortable with the notion that she is like mother, uncertain about her place in mother's life, uneasy about her identification with mother. We also know that she feels compelled to keep up the struggle to finally "get it right." In searching for an understanding of the lack of a fully satisfying adult identification with mother, a closer examination of the developmental history of many of the ambivalent women revealed that daughter recalls that mother's love was available only on a conditional basis.

Let us have another look at the chart first presented on page 53 (Chart I—Relationship to Father and Mother). Here we see that the relationship to mother was described as loving, conditional love, (i.e., "I love you only on condition that you meet my needs"), or rejection. We found that only two women in Group A felt as if they were loved by mother; four felt only conditionally loved; and two felt rejected. Thus we have six out of the eight women, who did not feel fully accepted by their mother.

An analysis of conscious and pre/unconscious data indicated that daughter believed that only "if" she was "perfect" and did the "right" thing, could she be certain of mother's love. Thus the daughter never felt an unconditional, spontaneous, and guaranteed sense of acceptability in her mother's eyes. Three-quarters of the ambivalent group described this feeling of conditional love and/or rejection. Marlis understood that mother's love was contingent on her performance. If she was achieving—if she was "being perfect"—she had mother's love. Let's listen to her words once again: "There was no question about my father's love. But my mother's love felt contingent . . . She was always pushing for achievement. If I didn't achieve, I didn't exist. When I did something wrong, like breaking some plates or something, my mother used to pretend I wasn't there. She used to get so mad, but she didn't like to express her anger. She would only deal with me in the absolute essentials. She would only address a few words to me. I would disappear. I had no self. I'd go up to my room and cry, but not in front of her if I could help it. You see she needed for me to be perfect . . . and now I seem to need that for myself." Marlis's words, " . . . I didn't exist . . . I would disappear . . . I had no self," are critical because they suggest a sense of undifferentiation—a lack of separateness between mother and daughter. Marlis's words indicate that certain aspects of the earliest, primitive, symbiotic, boundary-less state, continue to exist.

Research on infant and child development has taught us that this lack of differentiation occurs briefly as a natural and expected phase of infantile development.[3] During the primitive phase there is a blending of the "me" and "not me," a confusion between self and other. In most cases, in due course, the infant develops the capacity for differentiation. This capacity is critical, for without it, subsequent ego-developmental tasks are jeopardized.

As Marlis fears she will "disappear" she describes a return to this undifferentiated, and terrifying condition. The experience of this fear as an adult suggests the possibility of the existence of a structural, intrapsychic deficit.

The lack of differentiation that daughter experienced may be traced to an inadequate resolution of two developmental tasks, which have been identified in the literature as particularly significant.[4] Kohut has stated that failures in these early processes are pathognomonic for later emergence of a narcissistic personality disorder. These two critical tasks are: first, the need for mirroring (enjoyment) of infantile grandiosity; and second, the need for idealizing of parents.[5] Lack of success at these tasks may result in blockage of narcissistic maturation (the self love task) which in turn affects later developmental outcomes re self-esteem and self-worth.[6] I found that these developments are related to the wish to bear children.

To understand why the failure of these two developmental tasks is critical to the later childbearing decision, we need to examine the earliest phases of separation/individuation and dependence/independence. Mahler teaches us that during the infantile phase of separation/individuation, the child must experience a dependability in the maternal object, against whom she reflects herself.[7] During this early symbiotic phase, according to Mahler, " . . . the primary method of identity formation consists of mutual reflection . . . "[8] In this process, (which Kohut called mirroring), the infant develops a grandiose sense of herself.[9] That is, as mirrored by mother, she is the whole world, she controls the satisfaction of all needs; she is omnipotent.

The mirroring process, at this most primitive stage, facilitates the beginning of a sense of satisfaction with self. However, as soon as the infant recognizes that other aspects of self (that is, the mother) may not indeed by satisfying—as soon as the first inevitable disappointments arise—she begins to split the world into good and bad, into satisfying her and not satisfying her, and into good breast/bad breast.[10] Gradually, the power of the other—the power to withdraw and reject—fills the infant with terror at the dawning of the reality of the actual distinction between self and other. Only when the self is distinguished as separate, and, in continuation of the early mirroring process, is experienced as acceptable to the powerful other, can the individual begin to engage in the task of identification with mother (parents). To the infant, the parents are the powerful other. In the clinical setting, through a mirroring transference, the therapist is the powerful other. When there has been a failure to resolve this early phase, the infant (later the patient) remains undifferentiated and dependent. The goal of treatment is to help the patient begin to view the self as autonomous and acceptable.

As the infant moves to separate, the availability of the mother (therapist) enables the child to tolerate the anxiety of experiencing and testing herself as disconnected. Mahler has identified this as the rapproachment phase of separation.[11] Successful establishment of the autonomous self as a dependable object requires that a balance be struck between the regressive pull, which is experienced as engulfment fears (fears of disappearing into total symbiotic dependence and to the undifferentiated "I"/ "not I"), and the alternate fear that separation and ultimate autonomy will lead to abandonment and isolation.

The Dependent Position

The dependent position is both feared and desired. Dependency, which is desired as a return to safety—as a reunion with the maternal object—also holds an element of terror, since it is equated with engulfment, and loss of self. Repeatedly as ambivalent women talk about their relationships to mother, they use words like "smother" and "suffocate." Jane, comparing her boyfriend's mother to her own, gives an example of the split between good mother vs. bad mother and the fear that she will be smothered by her mother: " . . . his mother . . . yeah it was good, but it wasn't mothering smothering . . . " Marlis, having transferred her dependency fears from mother to her lover, states, "I have to fight against him all the time to have my space . . . he's like a big white whale taking up space . . . it's a struggle for survival all the time . . . I think he will smother me . . . I am always fighting against him engulfing me . . . "

Other words, however, give us a picture of the high level of dependency needs, which exist along with this fear of dependency. Dependency fears, as we said, are fears of loss of self—of engulfment. Dependency needs were frequently expressed as fear of abandonment. For example, Jane says, " . . . that's another thing . . . don't walk out on me . . . If we have a fight, don't slam, don't walk out on me. I can't stand that. And that's when R and I started talking about that. Well, why do I get a little bit irrational about some of these things?" Projecting her abandonment fears into a fantasy of a child's separation process Alyssa stated, " . . . at the same time I have the fear that the child isn't going to need me . . . they are going to go off and have their friends and their own life. And then . . . ?" She does not complete this question. We guess though, the thought has triggered feelings associated with her own separation experience. Others expressed their fear of abandonment in different ways. For some, the fear that the other would withdraw and not be available reflects the primitive rage and guilt stemming from a belief that they were not acceptable to the other (usually mother). The ambivalent woman's rejection of mother, thus can be seen as a reaction formation (see Chapter 7).

Some women expressed their sense of not pleasing the other as a feeling of not being "special," not being the best, not being first. We hear this fear in Louise's words: "I'm really paranoid about being second." Barbara (in reaction to her fear) says, "I guess I'm just used to expecting to be first and I get really wild and mad if I'm not." We remember that both Louise and Barbara are the second daughter in their respective families. Others said that they had the sense that they could not assert their independence out of fear that they would jeopardize their relationship to their spouse.

Lisa (the youngest of twelve children) says, " . . . deep down inside, I am used to accommodating, rather than upsetting the apple cart." She says accommodating, rather than fighting. However, this is not the way she behaves. Behaviorally, she certainly does not accommodate her mother. She fights continuously to be accepted. As she talked about the pull toward separation (her need for separation) we note that she equates separation with abandonment: " . . . yet to this day she (mother) will sometimes say that I was in large part the cause of her nervous breakdown . . . I left her alone. Now that doesn't have the effect on me she would like it to have because I knew that if I was ever to become the person I want to be I had to leave . . . but she still tries that stuff . . . "

Guilt

Lisa now brings us to the most pervasive affect related to this particular mother/daughter relationship, i.e., guilt. Menaker has pointed out that the adult woman's decision to be different from mother, that is, her decision not to become a mother, activates the guilt which daughter feels as a consequence of early separation.[12] Lisa's underlying guilt vis a vis mother is apparent in her projective responses. These also provide another example for us, of the discrepancy between the conscious and unconscious content of the ambivalent responses. To MTAT XII (male watching female figure walking away) Lisa says, " . . . nothing is reciprocated . . . she is doing all the giving. She leaves him, she feels guilt, and she feels very bad for him . . . but she leaves him." Here, her response reflects the unsatisfying separation. She attempts mastery by reversing roles (i.e., she leaves him), but finds she's left feeling guilty. We will recall how different these words are from her interview responses, in which she said that she didn't succumb to mother's manipulation, and did not feel guilty. The contradiction is very evident since in her projectives, guilt is the most powerful affect. In MTAT XII, guilt is the price she pays for autonomy.

We will see that for the ambivalent daughter, guilt also effects the energy invested in the daughter's pull toward the father, representing as it does, the turn away from mother. Chodorow states, "The special nature of the pre-oedipal mother/daughter relationship . . . its intensity, length and ambivalence—creates the psychological basis for the girl's turn to her father.''[13] Chodorow says that the turn to father reflects both an expression of hostility toward mother, as well as a response to father's heterosexual preoccupation with daughter. She says, ''every step of the way (through the oedipus complex) . . . a girl develops her relationship to her father while looking back at her mother . . . to see if her mother is envious, to make sure she is in fact separate, to see if she can in this way, win her mother, to see if she is really independent.''[14]

Roy Schafer notes that Freud was mostly concerned with the girl's turning away from mother to father. In contrast, Schafer states, ''A psychological approach to the pre-phallic period must center on the girl's primary, mind-formative, certainly . . . physical and ultimately indestructible relationship with her mother.''[15]

Thus pre-oedipal ambivalence is seen as an expression of desperate need to separate from mother, along with a simultaneous need to remain attached. In this way, the stage is set for the ''continuing oscillation between attachment to mother and father.''[16]

According to the present analysis, the ambivalent daughter's turn to father, developmentally determined, is colored by an unsatisfactory resolution of pre-oedipal issues, and is therefore inherently different in quality from the feminine position which builds on a satisfactory resolution of the earliest separation/individuation phase (found in Group B.). Regardless of later paternal validation in the oedipal resolution, which was freeing in nature, the ambivalent daughter remains bound, dependently, to mother, in perpetual search for rapproachment.[17]

According to one object relations theorist, ''Defects in the rapproachment subphase . . . lead to an inability to tolerate ambivalent experiences and see an object as whole and constant.''[18]

In contrast to those who felt openly rejected by mother, (Group C) the conditionally-loved daughter—subject to the more subtle, more devastating, and more permanently binding tentative withholding of love—found herself doomed to a never ending search for love. The terms of the separation from mother—that is, the conditions for even partial freedom—give us a clue to the lasting nature of the conflict. This individual is forced to keep up the search in hopes of one day, finally getting it right.

We are reminded of what the behaviorists report about the greater power of the intermittent reinforcement schedule as compared to regular, expectable reinforcement. We see the ambivalent daughter's never ending search for affirmation as the consequence of the power of this sporadic and undependable state of maternal affirmation.

A further consequence of the daughter's experience of mother as withholding can be seen in the adult tendency to remain somewhat apart from others, to avoid situations that demand intimacy. As discussed in Chapter

7, Kohut points out that the narcissistic personality displays a characteristic distancing tendency, i.e., an inclination to hold back, to separate self from other. He states that such persons have learned to distance themselves out of fear of an uncontrollable regressive pull,[19] which is traced back to this pre-oedipal stage. This ambivalent tendency to pull back—to stay apart—reflects not only the ongoing dependency conflict vis a vis mother, but also leads to an inability to accept an interdependent role which is a critical aspect of mothering.

Interdependence

We have said that mothering (nurturance) requires an ability to tolerate an interdependent position. To be able to tolerate the total symbiotic dependency of the infant/mother relationship requires that the mother wish for and be able to join with the infant in a temporarily boundaryless state. To illustrate the ambivalent woman's conflicted reaction to this demand we will recall Marlis's stated need to remain distant, her terror at the selflessness of a symbiotic experience, which coexists with her continuous search for intimacy and the dependent position.

The difficulty that the ambivalent woman has in establishing and maintaining close relationships with others, exemplifies her inability to be interdependent. Aside from the idealized early relationship to father, who is seen throughout by these women as dependable and constant—presenting no conflict— there were very few really comfortable, mutually satisfying, nonoppositional relationships with other important persons, either male or female. For example, remember how Lisa commented, " . . . I'm not as dependent on him as he is on me . . . " Later on, she says, " . . . and finally . . . after so much pain . . . you learn to keep the good to yourself as well as the bad." This expression of pain and withdrawal undermines her ability to relate spontaneously to her spouse. Clinical issues surrounding these feelings will be discussed below.

To recapitulate, although the ambivalent woman evidences a high level of dependency needs, she also appears to have a fear of dependency. The woman in this position is unable to fully identify with mother, in the sense of accepting mother as a model for nurturance. At the same time she cannot give up the quest for identification with mother. Unsatisfied with mother's response to her (remember that 3/4 of the ambivalent women reported that they were either totally unacceptable to mother or that her love was offered only on condition that they would be "perfect"), daughter constantly searches for the unknown (and of course unknowable) "perfect self" which would be loved. Again, it is Marlis who states this position. Mother's love is idealized, not mother herself: "I know one of the reasons that I try to do so much in this job . . . killing myself . . . why I don't quit and take a normal job . . . reason is . . . my mother . . . I can't quit and be the dutiful daughter . . . and she is not going to appreciate it . . . I can't do enough to please . . . and I blame my mother for that." However, regardless of where she places the blame, daughter has internalized a damaged, imperfect, unloved self object. She feels that she can never be acceptable to significant others, can never quite "get it right," can never do enough. In a sense, we can say that her ambivalence at this point is not only vis a vis mother, but is also a reflection of her damaged self-image, which we have traced developmentally to the earliest unsuccessful mirroring experience. Believing that she is unable to function separately, she feels a desperate sense of needing mother. Yet, she has a parallel, developmentally critical need to believe that she has the power to turn away, to be free, to become autonomous, to separate from mother. However, as Marlis tells us, she believes that she is flawed and unable to complete these tasks.

Further evidence that the ambivalent woman's self-representation reflects a flawed inner core, which lacks the requisite ego resources, is given by those dual-career women who report that they feel as if they had "tricked" the world with their external success (see Chapter 2).

Dissonance between an externally projected state of confidence and satisfaction, acccmpanied by an inner state of self-doubt, fear, and confusion (which we identified above) has been observed in many individuals, and not just dual-career women in the childbearing decision phase. Yet the psychological mechanism that accounts for this experience now becomes clear through an analysis of ambivalence vis a vis the childbearing decision. The incongruence between the external position, which looks "as if" she is independent and autonomous, and the internal representation, which reflects an incomplete, undifferentiated self, can be traced to two origins:

1. This individual achieved what may be called a *premature autonomy* in the earliest phase of separation/individuation. By premature autonomy, I refer to an artificial and unsatisfactory resolution of the earliest separation/individuation process. In this case, both mother and infant separate prematurely, in faulty reflection of the other. Mother withdraws too soon, in a mistaken response to the infant's struggle to become separate. Infant believes too soon in the strength of her newly discovered autonomy. Even the most confident mother when watching daughter's practicing separation—her initial autonomous behavior—feels somewhat unsure of herself. This uncertainty reflects her conflict about what she "should" do as a "good" mother as well as the pressure from her own internal, probably unconscious needs. How easy to misread the signals, especially from a bright, assertive, inquisitive baby. The task of the moment, which is both

to let go and still be available, is naturally influenced by the mother's own developmental history, her current psychological position, and the conscious and unconscious elements of her relationships to significant others. The mother's situation in this phase is reminiscent of her earlier struggle, just prior to the birth of her baby. At that point she also separates the "me" from the "not me" and allows the infant to be born. Later, the infant will repeat the me/not me separation.

Returning to the developmental dilemma, with each new indication that the baby was competent (or looked competent), either mother pulled away, or daughter feared she would, or both. Whatever the case, the result was the same. In Winnicott's terms, the "false self" emerged and became dominant in the child; this self seemed to take over the ego functions heretofore supplied by mother.[20] The "true self," which is able to accept dependence as well as independence, separation as well as interconnection, lies undeveloped—pushed aside. Yet, although daughter acts on the assumed power of this false self, on the unconscious level, she continues to doubt the strength of this false self and to know that it is inadequate and shallow. On the unconscious level, the flaw is recognized. The adult sense of " fear of being found out," is the fear that this internal flaw will be recognized by others.

2. The origin of the second aspect of development of the adult incongruence between the internal and external self-concept is found to occur at a later stage of development. The adult female appearance of confidence, reflects her solid and satisfying identification with father. The father, labeled the externalizing resource, was not bound by the symbiotic and suffocating ties that daughter experienced with mother. Daughter, idealizing father, encouraged, loved, and admired by him, was able to "look like" she too, was confident and free—not bound—able to act as though the paternal confirmation was sufficient. We have said, however, that on the unconscious level, the paternal confirmation, founded on a "false self" is experienced as inconclusive.

The following response from Alyssa illustrates the theme of mother's pattern of withholding and shows us once again, that maternal rejection overshadows paternal affirmation. In her interview, Alyssa said, " . . . I saw her more of a mother than a wife . . . " This sounds like oedipal jealousy, which is followed in a later response (to MTAT IV (women sitting down facing older couple)) " . . . they are all unhappy . . . uncomfortable with each other . . . the daughter is asking for their approval, but that is withheld by the mother . . . " Daughter asks both of them for approval, but the mother's response (denial of love) dominates the resulting sense of

disappointment and sadness, and overshadows what has already been identified as paternal approval.

Although not enough to fill the gap left by the sense of maternal rejection, the young daughter continued to bask in her identification with father
and thus established the process of expecting approval (reward) for external
orientation and for physical characteristics (e.g., emerging feminine sexuality) and autonomous (not maternally bound) behavior. This analysis may
help explain the apparently continuous, never satisfied pursuit of external
approval through further accomplishments. Early external approval, i.e.,
admiration and love from father, though sought after and welcomed, was
insufficient. Though obviously satisfying to the child, it was never enough
as an adult. It was not enough to counter the primary, overriding response
to the withholding, isolation, and incompleteness left by the experience of
maternal rejection.

Comparison of the Three Groups

My investigation of some aspects of pre-oedipal development shows that
the outcome of the ambivalent woman's pre-oedipal struggle is different
from that of either the baby group or those who elect to remain childless.
Group B women enter the oedipal situation feeling the strength of a satisfactory, preliminary experience with autonomy. They have, through their
own processes as well as mother's natural responses, begun the turn from
mother. This does not imply that they do so without constantly looking
over their shoulder, without continuing the dependence on the maternal
object, without using mother as a measure against which their relationship
to father will be formulated. However, they differ from ambivalent women
in the sense that their experience of mother as the powerful rival, develops
in partial reflection of their own emerging sense of power and independence. This is qualitatively different from the ambivalent view of mother as
withholding, vengeful, destructive, dangerous, unpredictable, and undependable. In contrast to the baby group at this stage, the ambivalent self
representation is dependent, relatively powerless, and insecure.

Six of the eight women in Group C reported unsatisfactory relationships
with mother. In addition, seven out of the eight mothers of these women,
had a negative attitude regarding spouse and men in general. In my view,
these two factors contributed to Group C's conflicted entry into the oedipal
phase. I have described these women as similar to Group A in terms of not
successfully accomplishing early separation tasks. Fearing mother's antagonism (according to their history this is an accurate representation of reality), daughter nevertheless, at least on a conscious level, seems to have

accepted and incorporated the relational rejection as part of the reality of her environment. Whether conflictual intrapsychically or not, the developmental outcome is one of apparent integration. They seem to have given up the struggle. Here they differ dramatically from the ambivalent women, whose struggle goes on endlessly. Since we do not have clinical evidence to the contrary, we assume that the resolution is satisfying to the Group C subjects. We accept this evaluation of themselves and marvel that they have been able to establish a loving relationship with their spouse, and to develop friendship patterns, work relationships, etc. Group C, at least at the conscious level, claims to have given up the quest for parental approval. Although the parents are the optimal resource for the developing infant, the individual may be able to utilize compensatory mechanisms.* Judy, in Group B is such a case. Her natural father and mother were divorced when she was an infant; step-father was harsh and rejecting; mother became unavailable to her; mother failed to rescue the child at every opportunity that presented itself along the way. Yet, Judy managed to preserve a sense of herself as able, autonomous, loved, and developed a totally satisfying ability to relate to self and others. We can speculate that since father left her at such an early age, she was able, through the idealization process, to preserve whatever view of him she needed and thus was able to overcome the actual lack of "good enough" mothering and fathering.

Returning to the women in Group A, we have indicated that due to a premature autonomy in the early separation/individuation phase, a "false self" developed. This led to an early self-image as inadequate. Mother's perceived inconsistency was transformed into a fear of rejection. However, since mother's rejection (withholding) is sometimes followed by approval (giving), daughter remains insecure and unsatisfied; certain neither of her position vis a vis mother, nor of her own power and autonomy. Given these conditions, identification with mother continues to be tinged with aggression and guilt. In terms of her ambivalence regarding childbearing, she cannot fully identify with the wish to become a mother herself, for to do so would require her to give up and accept the fact that she is no longer the child herself. The underlying significance of this is that to do this she must allow herself to separate from her own mother—to give up her own dependent position. As we have said, she has not yet been able to make this transition.[21]

Guilt, developing out of pre-oedipal rage and hostility regarding mother,

---

*We are reminded of the way in which the child of a schizophrenic parent is sometimes able to utilize another significant adult in order to avoid following the pathological path of the parent.

sets the foundation for the ambivalence and for the never ending search for approval and affirmation. As she develops, this search takes the form of the oedipal wish to become mother's substitute in father's life. Lisa says, "My mother admits that it's true that she did very little for me when I was an infant—she literally had too much to do . . . I was very close to my father . . . I was my father's pride and joy . . . By the time I was born my mother just had had it as far as children are concerned . . . and she finally said 'I just don't want any more.' I have two sisters; one is 10 years older than I and the other is 12 years older, and they swear that they did all the mothering and things for me that had to be done . . . which gave me this guilt thing . . . but of course it was so different with my father . . . " Yet she still compares herself to mother: "I have this nasty habit from my mother of keeping everything clean . . something inside me wants that . . . I feel I am somehow failing because my house is not clean. My mother somehow managed with all those kids to keep the house really clean."

Jane: "My relationship was not anything with my mother . . . She had a miscarriage after I was born . . . a lot of physical problems . . . I didn't know all of it. It was more or less a war . . . but I didn't relate much to her. I don't remember hating her . . . but I couldn't relate to her like my father."

With this review of some aspects of the ambivalent pre-oedipal situation we see that, as the ambivalent daughter turns to father in the oedipal constellation, she is ill-prepared to fully incorporate the feminine affirmation she is about to receive. In the discussion that follows, we will also see how the split between mother's rejection and father's acceptance makes adult interdependence feel like betrayal of mother.

OEDIPAL DAUGHTERS—THE "CHOSEN ONE"

In dramatic contrast to women who elected to remain voluntarily childless, none of whom experienced a positive early relationship with father, the ambivalent women and those who wish to have children describe themselves as father's "chosen one." In psychodynamic terms we label them *oedipal daughters*. Early memories reflect warm, loving, positive experiences with father, resulting in close identification. What was the basis for this identification? How did it develop? What are the adult consequences? What (if any) price did daughter pay for this approval? Finally, what is the relationship between this early paternal approval and the adult childbearing decision?

As noted above, often the self-concept as the "chosen one" was arrived at through a comparison to mother and siblings. Some women said that being the youngest child made them special. (Four out of the eight were the youngest in the family.) Marlis, an only child, thought that this was the reason why she was Daddy's girl.

In Chapter 7 we discussed the fact that, in every case where there was an older sister, the subject felt that sister and mother had a special relationship, but that she was father's "chosen one". We can speculate that the second daughter, responding to feelings of maternal rejection, feels impelled to develop another primary identification. For example, Jane said, "My mother and my sister seemed to get along better, and I got along with my dad. I was his . . . or at least, I thought I was, sort of chosen . . . and I loved it . . . "

The following words, typical of the ambivalent group, are worth repeating. Lisa said, "I was my father's pride and joy. For example, he took me to school and I would walk home, and when I came home I spent time with my brothers and sisters, not with my mom. But when my father came home he would spend at least two hours with me. My homework . . . I was a smart child, and he enjoyed that, and I could learn very easily, and he enjoyed helping me learn. And I would tag along with him on Saturdays; if he went to his office I went with him . . . if he went to the hardware store I would go with him . . . I would literally follow him everywhere . . . " Several important elements of the oedipal constellation are illustrated here.

Rejection of Mother. Lisa states that, though she may have "spent time with siblings" (biding time until father was available), she deliberately avoided mother. These words reflect the infantile sexual rivalry, as well as her perception of her competitive position vis a vis her siblings. We recall how she denigrated the work her mother did, describing her derisively as the "laundress." This description allows her to devalue mother, and diminish mother's power as a sexual rival. This split—father as good, loving, and accepting vs. mother as withholding, critical, and competitive—reflects a continuation of the primitive splitting mechanism which was initiated in infantile object relations. This daughter relates only on an either/or basis; that is, feeling either accepted or rejected by the parent in question. She also believed that to choose father, was to reject mother.

Father as Externally Oriented. As she remembers her father, Lisa says, " . . . we would wait for him (father) . . . he came home from work . . . he went every day to his office . . . he would go to the hardware store . . . he would be so busy . . . " Father's domain was largely outside the family circle. Although he came in and out of the daughter's life, his primary orientation was toward the external environment (or so it seemed to daughter). Two consequences can be inferred from this view of father. First, as the less constant, less available figure (as compared to mother), father is more easily idealized.[22] Second, in contrast to the internalized, subjective nature of the identification with mother, at this point, father represents growth and development, reflecting his identification with external resources. Mother, on the other hand, represents regression to the earlier, more primitive, less boundaried environment, reflecting her identification with internal resources. Thus the struggle to separate from mother is associated with the appreciation of external rewards and functions, and the depreciation of maternal rewards and functions (nurturance).

Father is viewed as independent; able to survive autonomously (i.e., without mother). Not only did daughter wish to identify with this orientation, but father's attention also supported her resolve. One author found that the father/daughter relationship was such that " . . . the girl's ego expanded sufficiently to enable her to sacrifice a measure of dependency and submission".[23] The more father became an ego resource, and his ability to leave mother and then return became a safe behavior model, the more easily daughter's separation anxieties were managed. Father's verbal behavior provides a clue to this process. To understand the significance of father/daughter verbal interaction it's important to remember that the development of language is part of the search for mastery, and serves as a vehicle that assists in the establishment of autonomy.[24]

Identification with Father. We hear Lisa's reference to herself as special to father e.g., his "pride and joy". From Lisa's comments it is clear that father's attention was focused on the fact that she was smart, learned easily, and accepted his help. Her memory is that they shared a mutual pride in her activities (note: not in her feelings). She was smart, for him; she learned easily, for him. He was always watching, and always encouraging. He selected her to follow in his footsteps; and she did so, both literally and figuratively. In early childhood it was to "follow him everywhere." Developmentally, the implication is that she would follow his example—would try to be like him. The identification was intense.

In choosing an identification with father, the ambivalent daughter models the independent (paternal) vs. the dependent (maternal) position; the dominant vs. the passive role. She chooses to be the achiever; the externally rewarded, following the (stereotypic) masculine model.

Many studies of dual-career women, commenting on the father/daughter relationship, report that dual-career women felt pressured by father to become independent, competitive, to achieve, and succeed.[25] Evidence of this pressure can be heard in the following statement, as Louise, whose father had no sons, looked to her to be his follower, to achieve as he did, in nonfamily events. Note that the relationship to father was verbal " . . . we could always talk . . . " not emotional. Especially hear Louise's statement that " . . . he and I were really alike. . . . "

"But . . . with my Dad . . . you see, he didn't have any sons and he used to take me with him; down to the shop where he worked. He and I were really alike, and we did special things together. He treated me, I think, the way girls ought to be treated . . . as someone who is feminine and someone who should look pretty and who was a pretty little girl, and he was proud of that . . . As I grew up my father treated me more as a person than my mother did. We could always talk. It didn't get emotional like with my mother . . . I'm probably more like my father than my mother. I spent more time with my mother, but I think there was something in me that always wanted to be a controlled person, and I saw my father as being less emotional—the quieter type. I was drawn to that personality. My mother was always expressing herself about everything. My sister's more like my mother." Here Louise reveals both the sexually stimulating evaluation by her father, " . . . he treated me as a pretty little girl . . . ," as well as her belief that their closeness was based on verbal, intellectual skills.

An important element of this early period is the fact that for both Groups A and B, the special relationship with father was an exclusive one. Mother was not part of it; siblings were clearly out. All of these women saw themselves and father as occupying a private, unique, exclusive world, which allowed the daughter to develop a sense of specialness, safety, and separateness. Although women in A and B are similar in that they both developed this special relationship to father and both became oedipal daughters, they entered this phase with a critically different developmental history. Group B women had successfully begun the separation from mother and were therefore launched into the oedipal process with a firmer and more unified self-concept. For Group A, the separation process was much more complicated, conflictual, and ongoing.

To recap, ambivalent women have conscious memories that their special relationship with father focused on a verbal, unemotional partnership, an admiration for control, autonomy, independence, externalization. This conclusion is based on their interview responses. At the same time, projective data reveal that these memories serve as a cover for other, more chaotic, eroticized feelings. These emerge as the daughter's oedipal wish to win father, and in so doing, replace mother and the rivalrous siblings.

Father's approval, and admiration of her physical "prettiness," allowed daughter to experience herself as sexually triumphant over mother (at least temporarily), and served as the basis for the development of her sense of herself as sexually female (see page 174). In addition, father's approval allowed her to identify with him in terms of the externalized and powerful role he played in the family. However, on the unconscious level, her victory vis a vis father is accompanied by the ongoing conflict with mother. The latter pressure becomes dominant as the daughter develops into adolescence and adulthood.

Father's attentions may actually have contributed to the conflicted developing self-concept. The implicit message from father was: be like me in terms of independence and autonomy. It's possible that the ambivalent daughter extended this "be like me" directive to a rejection of maternity, since in daughter's eyes, in order for her to be chosen, mother had to be rejected. As I said earlier, through the process of projective identification, in her fantasy father has rejected mother; therefore, she must do so as well.

Returning to the questions posed at the outset of this section, I believe that the basis for identification with father was both sexual and social. Father offered approval for erotic as well as intellectual and autonomous impulses. Daughter was thus permitted and encouraged to develop these aspects of self without conflict, with a sense of specialness, and significantly, with a sense of separateness. This separateness is, as we have seen, in sharp contrast to her situation vis a vis mother. The boundaries with mother are confused, vague, and insecure; the boundaries with father are clear. Father is separate from mother; daughter, then, can also be separate from father.

Among the consequences of the ambivalent daughter's identification with father are two factors which apply here:

1. Father's approval led to the establishment of an early sense of affirmation of female sexuality. We have seen that this aspect of self has been satisfactorily developed in these subjects' adult sexual identity.

The oedipal victory also results in an internalization of the belief that achievement (intellectual, external, sexual) leads to acceptance and love.

2. The pre-oedipal impulse to question and/or reject identification with mother is reinforced by daughter's identification with father. This is the price the ambivalent woman pays for her "chosen one" position. In contrast, women in the baby group were able to accept father's love without destruction of the maternal identification and nurturant self-concept.

Given the ambivalent propensity for splitting in object relations, as early sexuality was rewarded (i.e., daughter's provacative, erotic position won the father), nurturance (the mother) was rejected. Identification with the maternal object felt disloyal to father, and represented a conflict, for at least some oedipal daughters. This leads to an adult feminine self-concept that is sexual but questions an identification with nurturance. For other oedipal daughters (Group B), the nurturant self-concept was compatible with the emerging sexual self-concept.

To repeat, the oedipal relationship does not appear to differ in women who are ambivalent regarding children vs. those who decided to have children. Therefore, although this early affirmation of femininity by father seems a *necessary* prior condition to the wish to become a mother (remember none of the child-free women were oedipal daughters), it is apparently necessary, but *not sufficient*. The difference in response between Groups A and B to oedipal affirmation is a consequence of the prior pre-oedipal resolution. Here we see that although sexuality seems to be affirmed at the oedipal stage, the identification with maternal functioning, which I have labeled nurturance, is not as available to those who are developmentally arrested at a pre-oedipal level. Without the successful resolution of the earliest separation/individuation efforts, the individual is hampered in the development of a separate and adequate sense of self, and consequently unable to trust in the stability of self and/or object. Therefore, it is my conclusion that a satisfactory resolution of both pre-oedipal and oedipal processes contributes to the adult ability to maintain the delicate but critical balance between autonomous functioning, in which sexuality is a dominant aspect, and the capacity for nurturance, in which the ability to relate to another is dominant. Both nurturance and sexuality are considered essential to the development of the self-concept as maternal.

DEVELOPMENT OF THE FEMININE SELF-CONCEPT IN AMBIVALENT DUAL-CAREER WOMEN

Traditionally, the definition of femininity included, but did not separate, aspects of both sexuality and nurturance. I believe that the definition becomes more useful if we distinguish between sexual and nurturant functioning. I have stated that there is a difference in the nature of the female self-concept as "feminine," between those women who are ambivalent vs. either the baby group or those who plan to remain childless. Women who describe themselves as wishing to become mothers, include aspects of both sexuality and nurturance in the content of the feminine self-concept. Women who do not want to have children see themselves as sexually female, but not nurturant. On the other hand, ambivalent women, confident of their sexuality, remain uncertain and conflicted regarding a nurturant self-concept.

In this section, I hope to advance the understanding of some of the dynamics of the ambivalent position, through a discussion of the way in which feminine self-concept develops for this group. I want to make it clear that this is not a general discussion of the development of sexual identity. The interested reader is referred to any number of good discussions on that topic.[26] Rather, this discussion is confined to the development of a feminine self-concept in this specific group of dual-career women who feel conflicted about their inability to reach a satisfying childbearing decision. Some comparisons are made between the three groups of dual-career women.

In Chapter 4 the terms sexuality, nurturance, and gender identity were defined as follows: *Sexuality* refers to attributes of a biological (e.g., chromosomal), physiological (e.g., hormonal and reproductive secondary sex characteristics), and functional (e.g., genital impulses and activities, behaviors, feelings, attitudes) nature.[27] Sexuality for these dual-career subjects is equated with heterosexual behaviors, both physiological and social. For this group, sexuality does not describe maturity, nurturance, or parenting. *Nurturance* is defined as those attitudes and behaviors that organize one's psychic and physical energies in the service of satisfying the needs of another individual. These women make a distinction between their sexual orientation and the orientation toward nurturance. *Gender identity* refers to the social, cultural label of female or male, which is attached to the individual first by others and then by the self.[28] Gender identity is firmly established by the time the child has developed sufficient cognitive capacities[29] and has learned to talk. The label, the gender self-concept, begins with an indentification via external, physical characteristics, such as hair and body size and shape, and later becomes associated with psychosexual characteristics. Research has shown that by the age of two the child is absolutely certain of her gender as well as that of others.[30]

The significance of gender identity is obvious to all of us; it's the first issue at birth; in the family and in the larger social structure, gender is the primary identifying and organizing principle. The term *gender role* refers to the total range of behaviors that label (for oneself and others) the self as masculine, feminine, or ambivalent.[31]

This section discusses the development of femininity as a self-concept: first, in reference to the relationship to mother; then, to the relationship to father; and, finally, in light of individual developmental processes.

Impact of the Relationship to Mother

Thus far, I have identified three ways in which developmental aspects of the relationship to mother differ for these three groups of women. These differences are found in: a) pre-oedipal issues of separation/individuation; b) maternal attitude toward spouse and toward men in general; c) the degree of maternal externalization.

Separation/ Individuation—the Early Dependency Conflict. The ambivalent daughter grows into adulthood without having resolved the primary separation struggle vis a vis mother. This woman, who behaves as if she is independent, autonomous, assertive, and self-confident, reveals through the unconscious data, that she is bound dependently to mother, in a never-ending, fruitless search for maternal approval and release. She believes that if only she persists, she will one day win mother's love. In contrast to the childless group, who believe that there is no hope of victory, the ambivalent daughter cannot give up.

The ambivalent woman does not experience the self as a dependable object. Utilizing a splitting mechanism, she attributes to mother the power to set her free, not recognizing that she herself must accomplish this task. We have observed that the ambivalent woman, as an adult, continues to feel dependent on mother's response. As indicated, although there has been a false sense of autonomy, which I labeled a *premature autonomy*, the unconscious recognizes the fragile nature of this early autonomy, and denies it any true power.

Apparently, the strength of the attachment to mother interferes with the infant's capacity to distance herself enough to see mother as separate. Without this separation, mother cannot serve as model, for she is equated with the self. Therefore, it seems that from this early fault in development, that is, from the point at which the child is unable to establish the necessary separation—daughter also begins to inhibit her ability to accept herself as nurturant—as maternal.[32] She cannot be maternal until she is separate from mother herself. In contrast, women in the baby group appear to have been able to tolerate the pressure of the early separation/individuation phase, and have experienced some satisfaction with a practicing independence. The maternal response to self and to others (father) has provided a "good enough," stable environment.[33] Within this successful pre-oedipal position, the individual has developed the beginning structure—the framework for the development of self-confidence, as well as for the identification with the maternal model and with nurturance as a self-concept.

The childless group tells us that the outcome of the maternal/infant early struggle was not satisfactory, in the sense that daughter does not recall the pleasure of ever being fully accepted. She can never find a time, a memory, a feeling of the self as acceptable to the mother. She remains bitter, feeling deprived and cheated. Typical of Group C responses is the following: Kay (C): " . . . my mother's message was . . . her large message was . . . don't be . . . just don't be . . . life could have been easier if you hadn't been here . . . " How then, does this woman develop a feminine (sexual) sense of self? Apparently, it does not depend on maternal affirmation. Over and over, Group C women repeat this theme: "I am not acceptable to mother. I have never been acceptable, and I never will be." As I said before, this daughter has given up the struggle. Whatever intrapsychic residue there is from this early rejection, it is apparently not incorporated into a rejection of sexuality. Even in projective responses, we never hear any indication that mother's relationship with daughter has affected daughter's sexuality; rather it affects maternal functioning, as reflected in the Group C rejection of the self as mother. Nurturance is ruled out as part of her self-concept.

Both Group B and Group C reveal a sense of confidence in their independence and autonomy. Although there may be differences in their capacity for relationships, this does not emerge into a conscious position (i.e., they all have satisfactory relationships with spouse). We do not know whether the conflict for the childless women is so repressed that it is hidden from the projective measures utilized here, or whether the issues regarding mother are actually resolved.

Since all subjects were able to arrive at a satisfying adult sexual self-concept, we conclude that sexuality, as an aspect of femininity, apparently does not depend on optimal preoedipal resolution. Nurturance apparently does. Only Group B women were able to establish an unconflicted identification with nurturance. For these women, satisfactory early experiences with mother led to the adult capacity for nurturance. A lack of autonomy and early individuation and a less than satisfying resolution of pre-oedipal tasks was observed in the other two groups. As adults, Group A women, unable to accept nurturance, still try to identify with this self-concept, though the effort feels interminable. On the other hand, Group C women apparently accept the fact that for them, being feminine is not being nurturant. They reject, without overt conflict, any link between sexuality and nurturance.

There were no differences found between groups in terms of the content of their unconscious or conscious attitudes or responses regarding heterosexual identification. This finding contradicts the writings of authors such as Freud and Deutsch, who believed that sexual self-concept was bound up in the ability to establish an unconflicted identification with mother.[34] However, I want to make it clear that, although these dual-career women arrived at an adult position that was clearly heterosexual, the development of adult sexuality was not without conflict. For example, Becky's (B) fears of sexuality were revealed in both interview and projective responses. She said, " . . . as a kid of course I know that other girls did that, but I was convinced that it was wrong . . . I would have nightmares . . . I wondered if I would scream and fall apart . . . I'd have fantasies about all the things that could happen . . . " Lee (C): " . . . for me, there was always a lot of guilt . . . and fear . . . the terrible, terrible guilt and fear . . . what a terrible person I was to have those erotic feelings . . . I was afraid that sex was something I was going to have to put up with, just as my mother had told me . . . " Marlis (A): " . . . I didn't want to talk about this (sexuality) . . . sexuality makes me anxious . . . it's a whole new rock to be turned over and those little crawlies . . . I don't want to talk about it . . . '' Marlis uses sexual imagery to describe her conflict. She's afraid of both herself and the phantom male. Her anxiety can be seen in her associations, e.g., her use of "rock" (the rigid self) and "crawlies" (the invading male).

Maternal Attitude Toward Spouse and Men in General.   From Chart I (Relationship to Father and Mother, page 53) we note that five women in Group A, seven in Group B, and only one in Group C recall that mother had a positive attitude regarding spouse and men in general. Since we have found that the dual-career woman's relationship to spouse was equally good (or bad) for subjects across groups, these data about mother do not imply that daughter will follow suit and feel negatively toward men.

As previously suggested, I believe that much more study is needed to understand the implications of this material. One interesting question concerns the puzzle of how the Group C woman, rejected by both mother and father, and observing mother's rejection of men (sexuality), is able to develop an adult sexual self-concept. We know that daughter's conscious memories are that mother rejected her. This rejection extends beyond the self (i.e., nurturance), however, with the disclosure of mother's negative attitude toward men, to include father (sexuality). Apparently, mother's rejection of father may have been internalized by daughter as an aspect of mother's rejection of nurturant functioning. Mother refuses to nurture the daughter and won't satisfy father either. Whether this (projection) is actually the case, it permitted daughter to believe herself to be without a sexual competitor—without a rival—the fantasized resolution of every oedipal constellation. In the adult memory, and from the pre/unconscious material, daughter believes she was free to conquer.

How much more terrible, then, that in spite of this fantasy of having him all to herself, father remained distant, unaccepting, negative, harsh, withholding, rejecting. This, on the conscious level, is the outcome. Denial of love. Yet knowing of the power of the earliest libidinal energy, as well as the unconscious erotic stimulation that father inevitably projects, the struggle continues intrapsychically. We'll come back to a discussion of the impact of father's attitude in the material that follows.

We know that the Group C daughter, like all the other women studied, has developed a sexually feminine sense of self. Therefore, it is reasonable to assume that the maternal rejection of father, and later the rejection of all men, did not interfere with the emergence of sexuality for any of these subjects.

Impact of Maternal Externalization.   We'll mention one other way in which the relationship to mother affects the development of femininity as a self-concept. It was discovered that mother's love, unconflicted for two women in Group A and five in Group B, and conflicted for all the other women in these groups, was formulated around a relational position. That is, regardless of what mother did outside the family (and we have noted that most of these mothers were employed outside the home), Group A and B mothers and daughters related to each other from the point of view of each person's primary needs. In infancy, in the primitive situation, the ability of each to respond to the other comes from the internal pressure of each participant—from the individual pressure of mother and infant—rather than from the demands imposed by the other. Soon, however, the internal needs and pressure from the other balance each other out, and are mutually satisfying and become mutually reinforcing. This is the optimal resolution.

The relational nature of this mother/daughter position is interesting in view of recent discussions about the differences in the development of superego morality structures between men and women.[35] According to this author, women develop a sense of moral functioning in response to their relational development, whereas men develop a moral position out of a sense of law, order, and external structure.

In contrast to the relational nature of the mother/daughter interaction in Groups A and B, the two Group C women, who identified strongly and positively with mother, emphasized mother's career identity, independence, and external orientation. Karen (C): "My mother ran a grocery store until I was about five . . . It was a situation that if you needed her you could run into the store and get her." Merryl (C): "Well, my mother, I saw her as a woman who was . . . She also had a profession . . . a nursing profession. I clearly understood that women worked . . . my aunt worked. She was a professional woman. The women all around me worked. No one just stayed home with kids."

I believe that the impact of the internal vs. the external orientation affects the ability to identify with nurturance as an aspect of the feminine self-concept. The women in Groups A and B, who were the recipients of maternal love which was based on a relational foundation, were able to accept a nurturant self-concept because it too is based on the consciousness of the needs of the other. Nurturance by definition is relational. Group C's positive relationship with mother reflects identification with mother's executive, externalized functioning. It does not require modification of self according to the needs of the other.

We have found that those women in both Group A and C, who felt either rejection or only conditional acceptance, also described their position regarding mother in relational terms. The struggle with mother reflected, in part, the envy that daughter felt toward mother's apparent acceptance of other persons and other relationships.

Impact of the Relationship to Father

We have learned first from Freud, and then from the work of subsequent psychoanalytic writers, that the struggle between infant, mother, and father—the oedipal triangle—is a universal developmental process. We know that for the female child, father is the sought-after prize, who must be captured; mother must be replaced—removed from father's attentions. This process has both sexual and relational significance.

As we know, Freud's theory of female development is based on the female's lack of a penis. According to Freud, when the small girl realizes that she lacks a penis, she first blames herself as inadequate. Later she realizes that mother too is "castrated" and thus she comes to "know" that all females are "less" than males, lacking as they do this most powerful and satisfying organ. Thus, according to Freud, the oedipal struggle for the female child is an attempt to redress this loss, to obtain a penis by capturing father, and ultimately, to obtain a penis through the birth of a male child. Freud also related the process of super-ego development (for males, at any rate) to the resolution of the oedipal complex.

I believe that a more useful way to understand the power of the oedipal phase, especially its developmental significance, is found in the analysis of recent authors such as Chodorow and Bardwick.[36] Their writings, a contemporary interpretation of traditional psychoanalytic conceptualizations, suggest that our focus ought to be on the psychosocial as well as the psychosexual processes. That is, the psychological resources and energies of each parent, including both libidinal and socializing energies, and the relational system of the family, impact more significantly on the nature and outcome of the infant's developmental processes than the simple awareness (or lack thereof) of anatomical differences. This perspective does not deny the importance of the infant's development at varying psychosexual stages, but broadens our basis for understanding the overall development of the infant.

Returning to the ambivalent daughter, she enters the oedipal phase without having reached a fully satisfying pre-oedipal resolution. Though the ambivalent daughter is not sure of herself as separate, we have noted in our discussion of her personality that she is characterologically dominant, assertive, and strong-willed. Therefore, we attribute her ability to accept father's attentions as a result of her own unique strength, as well as the intermittent acceptance she experienced from mother.

In previous sections we have heard the words " . . . I was . . . sort of special," " . . . I was the chosen one," "I would follow him everywhere . . . ," "I felt real close to him . . . ," and " . . . he looks at her with these dark adoring eyes, and sort of laps after her everywhere she goes . . . " These statements, offered by ambivalent women in response to questions in the interviews and to the projectives, indicate that as far as they were concerned, father was theirs. The content of this approval becomes sexualized in several ways. First, father chooses them (the ambivalent woman) and discards the other siblings. Recall how often the ambivalent women said that the older sister and mother were close, but she was special to father. Then, father chooses to love them instead of mother. The fantasy of oedipal victory is made clear in some of the ambivalent woman's responses. For example, Marlis contrasts her own sexualized relationship with father, with the unsexual relationship between father and mother, in the following association: " . . . My father hugged me, and when he hugged me, I bit him on the arm . . . not hard . . . He didn't seem to notice—he was too busy hugging me . . . (Question: What significance did that have?) . . . I don't think my parents were sleeping together by then . . . my mother hated it. No touching, no hugging. My mother would recoil if my father even patted her . . . " In another example, Louise associates her own success vis a vis father, with mother's rejection. She says, to MTAT IV: (older couple sitting facing younger woman)), " . . . the man is absolutely enthralled with her and worries about her constantly . . . but the mother is reserved . . . something bad has happened . . . and they don't really talk about it . . . " Louise suggests that the bad happening may be that father has chosen her. Guilt at her own success with father is associated with mother's reserved (witholding?) reaction.

The sexual nature of paternal affirmation, which is similar for women in Groups A and B, served to facilitate the growing girl's identification of self as sexual. This most critical identification, a key to future psychosexual processes, also allows the child to enlarge the confidence in self as a dependable object. From the point of view of this discussion, paternal affirmation of sexuality at the oedipal stage is also critical to the decision later in life to have a child.

For women in both the ambivalent group and the baby group, father's attentions, recalled with universal pleasure, arise from memories and associations which were of a conscious nature. Furthermore, I found a high level of congruence between conscious and pre/unconscious references to father. The growing sense of self as acceptable, begins to include self as sexually female (thus, as opposite, but complimentary to father).

In searching for an understanding of how the Group C women were able to develop a sexual sense of self, we stated that regardless of a father's overt rejection, which was found to be the case for every women in Group C, the covert message (the unconscious stimulation) was apparently forceful enough not to interfere with the development of sexuality. That is, in spite of paternal overt rejection, daughter's own sexual development proceeded without significant interference. To fight for that which is denied often becomes the most enduring and compelling struggle.

How do we understand the differences in response to maternal vs. paternal rejection? That is, why should Group C daughters keep up the struggle to become sexually female, and thus relate to father, and yet give up their efforts to identify with nurturance (relate to mother)? I have concluded that apparently, one aspect of femininity is not tied to the other. Group C women define themselves as sexual and non-nurturant. This development seems quite reasonable, when we consider the opposite process. Recent midlife studies tell of the ways in which nurturance is distinguished from female sexuality. For example, men as well as women have the capacity for nurturance. [37] Other findings illustrate the fact that women can wish to mother without wishing to be heterosexually female.

For Group C we found that although father is remembered as negative, he is also referred to as "a . . . shadowy figure . . . he would . . . come and go . . . "; " . . . he was never there . . . "; "I was afraid of him . . . " These responses suggest that father, though not available, may still be idealized, still sought after, still the object of oedipal longings.

Mother was the more constant, more available, more real figure. Her rejection became undeniable, even on the unconscious level. However, the sexualized contact with father (the fantasized, intangible, undependable, male object) may have provided the developing daughter with sufficient erotic stimulation.

Some Comments on Latency and Adolescent Development

Our discussion of the development of femininity as a self concept has thus far focused on the intrapsychic processes associated with the early psychosexual stages of development. Although I have made it clear that this is not intended to be an analysis of the development of sexual identity, a very brief comment on a few aspects of latency and adolescent development will help us understand how the adult feminine self-concept evolved.

Although there seem to have been the expected childhood difficulties and traumas, as I reviewed the data on the childhood of these subjects it became clear that for the most part, their experiences were relatively average. No unmanageable events, crises, or traumas were recalled. This is not to say that there were not problems, but rather that the subjects believed they were able to respond without feeling destroyed or chaotic, without too great a threat to the developing ego.

Although childhood memories continue to point to the significance of the early sense of rejection by either (Group A) or both (Group C) parents, in some way, perhaps due in part to the influence of other significant persons (who did not appear in the protocols), all the women in this study proceeded successfully through early childhood, latency, and adolescence. There were no major school problems, no instances of running away, no substance abuse, no antisocial behavior, nor any indication of emotional disorder. None of these girls was hospitalized for psychiatric reasons, and none was brought to the attention of either school or court authorities because of any behavioral problems. Whatever developmental hazards and/ or intrapsychic traumas they may have suffered, the results did not produce overt acting out or apparent psychic distress.

By the time these women reached their latency years, they had already been identified as bright and academically successful. As all children do during these years our subjects indicated that they worried about how they could become acceptable to their peers.

Shy Girls.   As I mentioned earlier, six of the eight ambivalent women had thought of themselves as shy children, and as having to overcome some kind of problem in order to be accepted by their peers. For example, we heard Louise talk so many times of how her small size was a problem. Marlis felt that she was the outsider on the playground. Jane compensated for her insecurity by becoming somewhat of a bully, and by defending herself and her younger sister. Diane thought she was too quiet and only made friends because she had an older, more social sister who led the way. Lisa felt out of it, because she was so much younger than all the others in her family. Paula recalls becoming an amateur radio celebrity at the age of six. But rather than securing acceptance, her "stardom" created some problems with her friends. She was made to feel "different"—special in a way, but not like the others. Barbara and Alyssa tried very hard to be like all the others, but continued to feel that they were really not accepted for what they were. However, there is no evidence from what I learned that the self-label "shy" or "different" was related to a maladaptive psychosexual developmental pattern.

Tom Boys.   As children, and in their beginning latency period, our subjects thought of themselves as tom boys, preferring boys' toys, boys' games, and boys' companionship. In this respect, ambivalent women were no different from the other dual-career subjects.

Earlier we mentioned the snapshot taken by Barbara's family at Christmas, in which the older sister is all dressed up in a frilly dress, and Barbara is wearing jeans and sneakers, frowning because she received a doll for Christmas instead of a truck. Similarly, Paula has an early memory of a doll, which was a disappointment to her, and became acceptable only when she realized that it was mechanical.

Subjects in all three groups recalled a period in their lives when they sought identification with masculine activities. Paula (A): " . . . my peer group was male dominated. I became very much the tom boy. I could play games with the roughest of them. When I moved and had to go to school, I did not really know how little girls acted." Louise (A): "Of course we played with dolls, but really would have preferred the mechanical toys . . . " Kay (C): "One of my biggest trips as a kid was being able to play tag with the boys and beat them. I never played with the girls. Boys did all the good things."

During this phase of development into womanhood, which Deutsch calls the "flight from childhood . . . ,"[38] our subjects told of having secrets, especially from mother and father, mostly concerning sexuality. It is well known that the sharing of secrets is an integral part of the friendship patterns that latency age girls establish. For those who were the second daughter, the older sister's development and passage into adolescence provided ready-made material for developing such secrets. Once again, all groups of women shared this phase.

Several subjects recall playing with paper dolls, and working through their secret sexual fantasies via the doll's life. Louise remembers that her favorite paper doll game included a very sophisticated career woman, who lived in a big city (Louise comes from a small town) and who had no children. Louise said, "I always used to project myself into that imaginary character. That character was a female living in a big city, was independent and didn't have kids. She was always beautiful . . . " From what we already know about Louise, we understand how important it is to be beautiful and how strong the connection is for her that, to be beautiful one does not have kids.

Other secrets that emerged from the data focused on pregnancy fantasies which began in latency. Most fantasies were negative and revived feelings of anxiety and fear. Once again, we note that there were no differences in Groups A, B, or C memories of pregnancy fantasies. Frequently the secrets were about menstruation, especially in those cases where mother did not talk easily with daughter. Beginning menstruation stirs up both aggressive and erotic feelings. Therefore, mother's attitude toward sexuality and her handling of daughter's sexual development are important for us to consider.

Mother's Attitude Toward Development of Sexuality

Most of the women in all three groups felt that their mother had a naive or negative attitude towards sexuality, and preferred not to deal with either her own feelings or daughter's developing femaleness. These observations are illustrated in the following comments: Jane (A): "My mother was busy teaching me that sex is this unfortunate business, because children are good . . . but there is something wrong with you if you kind of like it." Barbara (A): " . . . sexuality was scary to her . . . it was verboten . . . " Lisa (A): "Well I was taught that you didn't give in to these feelings until you were married . . . that sex was dirty . . . " Marlis (A): "She told me early enough, but she had a dreadful memory. She started menstruating and she didn't know what it was; it scared the shit out of her. She thought she was dying. She didn't tell me anything about sex . . . .But I guess my mother was teaching me that sex is not good, although I knew she thought that women should want children . . . " Alyssa (A): "Mother did not talk much about menstruation, she had given me some books—and we had seen the movie so we knew. I remember it was the trip to Nebraska . . . that was the time I got my period . . . talked with my girl friends . . . but my mother and I never talked about it." Paula (A): "I remember going home and telling my mother about . . . me . . . buying Kotex . . . and my mother and my father were so happy now to have a young woman in the house. I talked to my father, too. We talked about everything." In an interesting association which followed these comments about menstruation, Paula switched to a negative memory about children: "I had my first encounter at age 12 with a woman who didn't really care about her children and that left a lasting impression on me because . . . she asked me to babysit on a Friday night and her husband was not in town . . . and she went out to a bar and left me with the four kids . . . I called my mother . . . the woman did not say when she would be back . . . when she did come back I was upstairs with the kids . . . they were napping and I was sitting up there reading . . . I remember her coming in and she was quite drunk . . . and she was with a man . . . and I remember being really appalled." Judy (B) remembers her mother telling her that "Menstruation is a curse . . . that God gave to Eve . . . I still can't discuss sex with my friends . . . or anything about my feelings of being a woman . . . I just don't do that."

Whereas a few women in Group A and B remembered feeling either extremely negative or frightened at the onset of menstruation, all women in Group C were extremely upset by the experience. This group also had extremely adverse reactions to fantasies of pregnancy and childbirth. Lee (C) says, "Getting my period was a terrible thing . . . I was scared . . . came home from school and told my mother and unfortunately there was someone else there, and she said 'you don't talk about that in front of other people . . . I will talk to you later' . . . but she never did.'' Karen (C) says, ''When I got my period for the first time I was beside myself. I could not bear the thought of it . . . I remembered hoping and praying that it was an accident, that it wouldn't happen again. I hated that first physical characteristic of womanhood very much.'' Kay (C) says, ''I hated it, I always felt terrible . . . and I always hated what it meant. I just couldn't handle any of those physical things well . . . my mother avoided me too, which didn't help.'' These examples from Group C subjects clearly illustrate that the beginning of menstruation was uniformly experienced as difficult and conflicted. As mentioned, this seems to be in contrast to the way in which the other subjects responded to this first, major physiological marker of adult female development. At this stage of the research, not enough data have been accumulated from which we can draw any conclusions about this contrast, although it does seem to dramatically divide the women who wish to remain childless from the other women studied here.

Adolescence

Although this is not the place for a discussion of the complicated developmental processes that we lump together under the label ''adolescence,'' it is useful to take a look at one significant relationship which changes so dramatically during adolescence—daughter's relationship to father. Helene Deutsch writes, ''The task of adolescence . . . is to master the Oedipus complex . . . also to continue work begun in pre-puberty and puberty, i.e., to give adult forms to the old, much deeper and much more primitive ties with the mother, and to end all bisexual waverings in favor of a definite heterosexual orientation.''[39]

As the task of latency was to confront (once again) and attempt to loosen the dependency ties with mother, so one of the tasks of feminine adolescent development is to rework the ties to father; to give up the earlier attachment to him, in order to be ready to find a substitute. It's already been noted that as part of her ''chosen one'' position, the young girl knew she would be applauded for intellectual achievement. All the dual-career women were high achievers in their adolescent years. But in spite their high achievement, the dominant memory of adolescence is a negative one, which the subjects attributed to their feelings about high school. Diane (A) says, ''I didn't hate high school but I wouldn't want to repeat it. My sister had a large group of friends while I tended to have fewer, but close friends. I didn't date a lot in high school . . . the kind of dates I had were for the major dances, etc.—not the casual dates . . . my mother did not want us to go out on

dates all that much . . . I think she did not want us to grow up too fast
. . . and also I think the sexual thing was of concern . . . '' Diane's comments are typical. Though none of the dual-career women had any academic problems, social pressures made high school very difficult. However,
there were exceptions in each group. In Group A, Louise was the exception.
She was editor of her high school paper, senior class officer, etc.; in Group
B, Julie was the high school star; in Group C, it was Kay, Denise, and
Francine. All the other subjects said that high school years were filled with
one struggle after another.

In spite of the expected teenage stresses, all subjects (Groups A, B and
C) felt that they had started to date in an acceptable way, and that they
were "average" in terms of feeling successful with boys. In general, they
were a fairly conservative group; they dated in high school mostly as part
of a large group of kids; parents were fairly strict regarding curfew; and
the daughters were not rebels (at least not when they were in high school).

In terms of the development of sexuality, the early heterosexual relationships for these ambivalent women were apparently "good enough" (to bor-
row Winnicot's term). During their adolescence, they began to feel sexually
female and began to see themselves as growing up sexually. In the data
available to me, I found no evidence of abnormalities in resolution of the
adolescent task of letting go of father.

The case material on latency and adolescence reveals that there were no
major differences in the development of femininity as a self concept between the groups. One exception that we have seen, however, was the response to the onset of menstruation. Whereas some of the women in the
ambivalent and baby groups had negative first experiences, for the most
part, they passed through this phase of development with relative ease. All
the women in Group C, however, recalled that they were appalled to find
that they had begun to menstruate, hated this first encounter with their
adult female hormones, and felt disgust and shame. They clearly rejected
this identification with female maturation.

These comments on the psychodynamic origins of the emerging sense of
self as female, serve as an introduction to the next topic we will consider.
In chapter 9, we turn to an analysis of other developmental issues which
will increase our understanding of how the ambivalent dual-career woman
approaches the childbearing decision.

REFERENCES

1. Chodorow, N. *The Reproduction of Mothering: Psychoanalysis and the Sociology of Gender.* Berkeley, CA.: University of California Press, 1978. p. 57.
2. Deutsch, H. *The Psychology of Women.* New York: Grune & Stratton, 1944.

3. Chodorow. *Reproduction of Mothering*. p. 61.
   Mahler, M. S. et al. *The Psychological Birth of the Human Infant*. New York: Basic Books, 1975.
4. Jacobson, E. *The Self and Object World*. New York: International Universities Press, 1964.
   Kohut, H. *The Analysis of the Self*. New York: International Universities Press, 1971.
5. Ibid.
   Also see Bernstein, S. B. "Some Psychoanalytic Contributions to the Understanding and Treatment of Patients with Primitive Personalities". In *Psychoanalysis: Critical Explorations in Contemporary Theory and Practice*. Edited by Jacobson, A. M. and Parmlee, D. X. New York: Bruner/ Mazel, 1982, p. 74–118.
6. Ibid., p. 94.
7. Mahler, et al. *The Psychological Birth of the Human Infant*. p. 75.
8. Ibid., p. 19.
   Also see Winnicott, D. "Transitional Objects and Transitional Phenomena" (1953) in *Playing and Reality*. New York: Basic Books, 1971
9. Mahler, et al. *The Psychological Birth of the Human Infant*.
10. Klein, M. *New Directions in Psychoanalysis*. New York: Basic Books, 1965.
11. Mahler, et al. *The Psychological Birth of the Human Infant*.
12. Menaker, E. "Some Inner Conflicts of Women in a Changing Society." In *Career and Motherhood,* edited by A. Roland and B. Harris. New York: Human Sciences Press, 1979.
13. Chodorow, N. *Reproduction of Mothering*. p. 121.
14. Ibid., p. 126.
15. Shafer, R. "Problems in Freud's Psychology of Women." In *Female Psychology,* edited by H. Blum. New York: International Universities Press, 1977, p. 351
16. Chodorow. *Reproduction of Mothering*. p. 129.
17. Mahler, et al. *The Psychological Birth of the Human Infant*.
18. Bernstein, S. B. "Patients with Primitive Personalities." p. 81.
19. Kohut. H. *The Analysis of the Self*. p. 12.
20. Winnicott, D. "Ego Distortion in term of True and False Self." In *The Maturational Processes and the Facilitating Environment*. New York: International Universities Press, 1960.
21. Gutmann, D. "Parenthood: A Key to the Comparative Study of the Life Cycle." In *Life-Span Developmental Psychology,* edited by P. Datan and L. Ginsberg. New York: Academic Press, 1975.
   Johnson, R. "Post-Menopausal Childless Women: A Life Cycle Perspective." Personal discussion with author.
22. Chodorow, *The Reproduction of Mothering*.
   Shafer, "Problems in Freud's Psychology of Women."
23. Bernstein, D. "Female Identity Synthesis." In *Careers and Motherhood,* edited by A. Roland and B. Harris. p. 138.
24. Piaget, J. *The Language and Thought of the Child*. New York: World Publishing Co., 1957.
25. Rapoport, R. and R. *Dual-Career Families*. Harmondsworth, England: Penguin Books, 1967.
26. For example, see: Bardwick, J. *Psychology of Women*. New York: Harper & Row, 1971.
   Bardwick J. *In Transition*. New York: Holt, Reinhart and Winston, 1976.
   Rubin, L. *Women of a Certain Age*. New York: Harper & Row, 1979.
   Deutsch, H. *The Psychology of Women*.
   Rohrbauch, J. B. *Women: Psychology's Puzzle*. New York: Basic Books, Inc., 1979.

Contratto, S. W. "Maternal Sexuality and Asexual Motherhood" in *Women, Sex and Sexuality* edited by Stimpson, C., and Person, E., Chicago: University of Chicago Press, 1980. p. 224–240.

27. Person, E. S. "Sexuality as the Mainstay of Identity: Psychoanalytic Perspectives" in *Women, Sex and Sexuality* edited by Stimpson, C. and Person, E. p. 36–61.

28. Sherif, C. W. "Self System." *Psychology of Women Quarterly.* Volume 6 (4) Summer 1982. p. 379.

29. Kohlberg, L. "Development of Moral Character and Moral Ideology." In *Review of Child Development Research,* edited by M. and L.W. Hoffman. New York: Russel Sage Foundation, 1964.

30. Kagan, J. and Moss, H. *Birth to Maturity: A Study in Psychological Development.* New York: John Wiley, 1962. (Fels Institute Study)

31. Spence J. and Helmreich, R. *Masculinity and Femininity: Their Psychological Dimensions, Correlates and Antecedents.* Austin: University of Texas Press, 1978.

32. Mahler, M. S. *On Human Symbiosis and the Vicissitudes of Individuation.* New York: International Universities Press, 1968.

33. Winnicott, "Ego Distortion in terms of True and False Self."

34. Freud, S. "Female Sexuality." *The Complete Psychological Works.* Standard Edition, Vol. 21 p. 223–243 London: Hogarth Press, 1931.
Deutsch, *The Psychology of Women.*

35. Gilligan C. *In a Different Voice.* Cambridge MA: Harvard University Press, 1982.

36. Chodorow, *Reproduction of Mothering.*
Bardwick, *Psychology of Women.*

37. Gutmann, D. and Neugarten B. "Age-Sex Roles and Personality in Middle Age: A Thematic Apperception Study." In *Middle Age and Aging,* edited by B. Neugarten. Chicago: University of Chicago Press, 1968.

38. Deutsch, *The Psychology of Women.* p. 5.

39. Ibid., p. 116.

9
DEVELOPMENTAL ISSUES AND CHILDBEARING AMBIVALENCE

In this chapter we'll consider the way in which ambivalent women respond to a few critical adult developmental issues.* First, we'll examine developmental changes in the self-concept, and focus on the way childbearing and childraising are internalized by ambivalent women as a threat to the formation of the adult self. These threats are anticipated as losses of the childhood aspects of self; losses to the sexual aspects of self; losses to the adult and/or professional aspects of self.

In the next section we'll discuss aspects of the adult Dream which surround the childbearing decision. Ambivalent women appear caught up in a conflict between opposite adult Dreams—in Stewart's terms, between the choice of a *Relational* vs. an *Individualistic* Dream.[2] Stewart's framework seems particularly relevant here, since we have one group of women (Group B) stating that relationships come first in their lives; another group (Group C) stating that careers come first; and still a third group (Group A) who seem caught between choices.[3]

Following these comments on the adult Dream, we'll look at parenthood as part of the aging process. Here we'll review issues related to physiological aspects of pregnancy, and to the view of parenthood as a developmental stage. We'll consider issues related to the need for a legacy and finally, we'll discuss modifications of early aspects of grandiosity.

CHANGES IN THE SELF-CONCEPT

One's view of oneself changes continuously throughout a lifetime. Although there are certain aspects of the self that reflect the very earliest events and relationships of infancy and childhood, superimposed on these prim-

---

*Although most studies of adult development have focused on men (e.g., Levinson et al.; Vaillant; Gould) a few authors have considered female aspects of adult development. Reader should see Bardwick; Neugarten; Gutmann; Stewart; Rubin.)[1]

itive elements are many layers of intrapsychic, physiological, and social experiences. Theories of adult development take these factors into account. Erikson's theory, describing development as dynamic and epigenetic, helps clarify this perspective.[4] An analogy that's frequently given describes a pebble tossed into a pond. Each expanding ripple comes from the center. The center changes, but does not disappear as the circle becomes larger and larger. Thus, one's self-concept is reflective of the way in which one has internalized, utilized, and responded to the people, the events, and the pressures encountered as part of the growth process. The self grows from the earliest primitive experiences with mother to the adult stage, always adding layers on top of the original experience. In addition, external events, historic, social, and economic factors, continuously impact on the individual's intrapsychic drama.

When subjects talked about the ways they would change if they became a mother, they were reflecting the adult self as determined by all the separate elements just described. They presented an age-thirty self-concept, which contained the infant self, the self as young child, the adolescent, the college girl, the daughter, the wife, the political activist, the competent professional woman, the self-confident, secure woman, the frightened, insecure woman, etc. I mention this now because, although we focus throughout this book on the self as mother-or-not (as nurturer-or-not), it's important to remember that this represents only one aspect of the conscious self and only one part of the content of the unconscious self—not the whole self.

When ambivalent women talked about the ways they would change if they became a mother, what emerged was a pattern of anticipated losses to certain aspects of their self-concept. In examining the language throughout the protocols, I found that ambivalent women perceived childbearing and childraising as somewhat of a threat to the self as child, to the self as sexual person, and to the self as professional person. We'll consider each of these.

Loss of Self as Child

All of us retain aspects of the self as child. As adults, the capacity for intimacy depends, in part, on the ability of the individual to react in some of the old child-like ways. For example, the ability to allow another person to take care of you; to relinquish some of the defensive barriers in order to feel safe; to approach a person with full confidence of acceptance; to accept love and nurturance without conflict—these are child-like responses. At the same time, however, all of us retain other, less benevolent aspects of the self as child. These emerge as the petulant, grandiose, demanding, sulking, selfish, totally narcissistic self. The self as child is the dependent self—the omnipotent self. It allows for no other needs, no other priorities, and no other individual.

For the woman to consider herself as mother, to wish to become a mother, she has to be able to give up her claim on being the omnipotent child. She must give up her self as child. As we said in Chapter 6, in order to do this, she must be willing to consider changing the nature of her primary relationship to mother.

In contrast to their public (adult) image, the subjects in all groups talked about the ways they allowed themselves to be childish. At home, for example, they said they could act foolish, irresponsible, silly, use childish language, even sulk, become petulant, and uninhibited. They allowed themselves to be taken care of, to be pampered, in a sense to regress to a dependent, infantile mode. In turn, they wanted to (expected to) be able to take care of their spouse in the same way, and to permit similar regressive behaviors in him. It's as if the self as child can emerge within the privacy and safety of the marriage, and can be separated from the self as adult, the self as autonomous, and the self as professional. The self as child—the irrational, selfish, omnipotent, narcissistic, demanding self—continues to be partially tolerated, and does not need to be put aside in service of the needs of the other. But if the other is the anticipated child, then self as child must be put away. This is the conflict which presents itself as the couple begins to consider having children.

Here we come to one of the central issues in the dual-career childbearing decision process. All the dual-career women—all these couples—have had a child-free lifestyle for many years (average 4 years). As a couple, they are accustomed to making decisions based on mutual needs, without a third person (baby) to account for. This is not to say that they have not encountered stress, and have not argued, fought, been miserable, reconciled, fought again, and once again found each other. But they have done these things as a couple. The balance, the intimacy centers around just the two of them. They have allowed themselves to become dependent and to become the one on whom the other can depend. This mature, dependable significant other, who can offer support, love, and stability, is a sharp contrast to a baby, who is conceptualized as selfish and totally demanding.

As I have stated before, all the couples had talked about children before they married. For many, the question was also answered before marriage; that is, they *knew* because they both had agreed to either have a child, or not have a child. Others, talked endlessly about the subject, but deferred their decision. But with time, most of the subjects in this study felt the need to re-encounter the question of children; and once again they went through the decision process.

As we know, Group A women still appear trapped in an intellectual exercise; they sort out all their theories of childraising, and dwell on the child-as-infant (see below). They do not see child as a developing person, which seems reflective of their own position of self as child (i.e., the child cannot mother).

Group B progress, though not without stress, through an intellectualizing stage, to a point where they bring a sense of reality and compromise to their discussion. They reach a stage where they realize they probably will never reach the "perfect" time to have children. It won't be perfect from a career point of view, it won't be perfect from a financial point of view, and it won't be perfect from a lifestyle point of view. Somehow they tolerate this sense of imperfection, and are able to consider the more critical issue— self as mother. At this point, they begin to relinquish their primarily narcissistic stance, in favor of a more relational, interpersonal position.

Group C women engage in much of the same intellectualizing as Groups A and B women, but manage to avoid the stress which is characteristic of Group A. That is, in spite of the pro-natalist pressures they feel from parents, other women, and even colleagues, they become comfortable with their decision to remain childless. I do not see this as the decision to remain childish. It became apparent throughout the protocols that Group C women have integrated their fantasy of staying as a child, into a manageable part of the adult self. Although it's quite possible that certain aspects of this situation are repressed, and that the Group C woman will have to deal with the consequences of this repression later in life, at this point in their development they offer no evidence to suggest that they are still pursuing maternal affirmation. In fact, as we saw in Chapter 8, they appear to have integrated the maternal rejection without hindering their ability to form an intimate relationship with their spouse. (In the discussion below, we'll consider some data on later life pathology among childless women. However, at this phase of their lives, none of the three groups of dual-career women present evidence of clinically significant neurotic tendencies.)

Unlike the Group C woman, the ambivalent woman is still caught up in the maternal net. To allow herself to become a mother, would necessitate a shift in her dependent position vis a vis her own mother.[5] The ambivalent woman's psychic energy is invested in gaining and maintaining a constant flow of externally derived (maternal) energy, connection, and approval, in an insatiable effort to stem the distress of a regressive and chaotic lack of internal (self) constancy. We have traced this outcome to an unsatisfactory resolution of the pre-oedipal separation/individuation process. Though unlike the Group C woman, in the sense that she is soon to become the recipient of father's "special" love (which in adult life is represented by external achievements), the ambivalent daughter is not free to identify fully with these achievements and with whatever gratification they might represent, since she is continuously pulled back toward mother—toward her struggle for permission to accept this derived validation of self. Thus her self-concept lacks a spontaneous and vigorous confidence. Her self-concept remains self-conscious and competitive. She cannot allow the self as child to shift into a subordinate role.

The projective responses once again provide some support for the above statements. Louise, for example, never thinks about children in any but their infantile state. In the following response, we hear that her orientation is first to herself, and then to the child as infant. Louise: "I'm a busy woman. I have lots of things to do and I don't really have time to be sick— like time for morning sickness . . . .My mother was really sick, and I know that's probably what's going to happen to me . . . " (Another response) "I have no real desire; the baby part doesn't appeal to me a whole lot . . . don't think I really need to go through that . . . yet at the same time I wonder . . . if I didn't have children I'd be passing up a part of life that I want to experience . . . " She continues in this vein, talking about her wish to experience as much as she can; she does not talk about the experience of the developing child. It's *her* experience that counts.

Although Group B women also focused on children as infants, they were able to consider the problems of the child's growth and development; about how it would be to have adult children; about how children would impact on their old age. For example, Joyce: "I'd like the experience of raising children and having them around. I'd like to see them grow up."*

The anticipation of motherhood, and the need to relinquish the infantile aspects of self—to move from the primary, dependent position—are similar to some aspects of the early rivalry with siblings. The older child, forced from glory and forced to step aside for the new baby, must encounter this developmental challenge. We will recall that five out of the eight women in the ambivalent group, were the youngest child (one was an only child). These daughters never had the experience of being pushed aside for a younger sibling. The ambivalent psyche has had no experience with this kind of a threat. However, it would be a mistake to conclude that youngest daughters or only daughters are thus bound into ambivalence re childbearing. As I have said before, this particular set of developmental circumstances, built upon an unsatisfactory primary effort to separate from the mother, contributed to the adult ambivalence we now observe.

It was interesting to find that this sense of rivalry was transformed, for some women, into a feeling that the child would compete with her for the

---

*Here we have another clinical issue: therapists can try to help ambivalent patients think through this stage and begin to deal with the child growing up, with adult benefits and losses, in order to help patients anticipate a relationship beyond the first few years.

husband's attention. This reminds us of the analysis offered by Rubin on the ways in which the husband reacted with jealousy to the birth of the child.[6] This adult (ambivalent) psyche, reflective of so many aspects that in the past were labeled masculine, now shows us one more contradiction. Rubin's point,[7] is that because women mother, sons have a more difficult time (than daughters) in surrendering their attachment to the first female (mother) and become frantic at the prospect of once again suffering a loss of the significant female, this time the wife.

The ambivalent woman's struggle to "finally get it right" may be seen as another manifestation of the struggle to work out the dependency position vis a vis mother. In other words, if she were confident of mother's approval (only possible for her when she "gets it right"), she would then gain the necessary autonomy and thus free up the energies now devoted to her unending search for approval. However, we know that daughter does not believe she is capable of fully autonomous functioning; that is, she does not trust herself. Therefore we can assume that on an unconscious level, she is making certain never to "get it right," for to do so would necessitate separation and subsequent guilt. To "get it right" means to separate; to separate means to be abandoned. The boundaries between freedom and rejection, abandonment and loss of self are unclear, as we will see in the subject's words which follow. Louise says to MTAT II (picture of woman looking at photos on desk of male and two children), " . . . this woman is not free; she has nothing for herself . . . "To MTAT V (woman looking out window) she says, " . . . she's saying, My God! How did I ever get myself into this . . . I want to be free and in charge of myself . . . " Louise is describing her fear that children threaten her "freedom", which we can interpret to mean her "self."

For Alyssa, the threat to self emerges in the following conflicted response to MTAT VII (two women seated, baby crawling on floor between them). She changed her mind three times in trying to identify which woman was the mother, then she said, " . . . the idea is that kids are restricting . . . and make you artificial . . . she isn't quite sure she likes being a mother, but is embarrassed to admit it . . . it's silly to have a child, you knew what you were getting into; notice the baby has no face . . . after you've had a baby you're not yourself . . . very ill at ease . . . miserable . . . ". Alyssa's response is so revealing that we need to take it apart and examine its elements. First, we start by recognizing that Alyssa's struggle to decide which woman is the mother is a reflection of her conflict and uncertainty about identifying with the stimulus. She is made uncomfortable by the presence of the baby. The need to decide which one is the mother stirs up her own indecision and anxiety. If she decides which woman is the mother, she must then decide on whether to identify with her or not. We notice that Alyssa talks about artificiality and restriction " . . . Kids make you artificial . . . " This suggests that she believes to act like a mother is not natural, but rather is artificial; to feel as she thinks the mother should feel would be artificial. This is a very unusual word, but perhaps it reflects her own ongoing issue regarding mother. That is, she wants genuine approval, but feels as if she gets only artificial (fake) praise. It is not clear here, but the word artificial suggests that Alyssa's association to the baby and her need to decide which woman is the mother, makes her feel pressured and phony. Alyssa's feeling that perhaps there is no real choice for her regarding whether or not to become a mother—that it's no longer an option—is revealed in her next words, as she states, " . . . she isn't sure she likes being a mother, but is embarrassed to admit it . . . " Consider for a moment the setting in which this response was given. She and I were engaged in a lengthy probe of the issue of childbearing decisions. Perhaps Alyssa's responses were meant to make her "look good" to the interviewer. Perhaps she is unable (embarrassed) to acknowledge her true feelings about children.

Notice how Alyssa changes the tense, from "she" to "you" in her response: " . . . you knew what you were getting into . . . " Then she says, "notice, the baby has no face . . . after you've had a baby you're not yourself." Again, she describes an artificial self, but not "yourself". The baby with no face is the critical clue to her feelings about what will happen should she have children. She dreads this situation, because she equates it with a loss of self. If you have no face, you are not a person; you cannot see or be seen. The face represents the person.* Alyssa actually states this as the conclusion: "After you have a baby, you're not yourself . . . "

I want to add another comment, which in this case applies just to Alyssa, but may be useful to help understand her response. When she and her husband were married, the issue of what name to use was terribly difficult for her. She decided not to adopt his name at all—neither hyphenated nor as an extra name—but instead to keep her maiden name as it was. This decision is not considered a particularly unusual practice, especially among career women. However, Alyssa's conflict about her name continued. For example, she said to me, "I've always been Alyssa B., as a child and growing up. Who would I be if I changed that? . . . I wouldn't know myself." This response reflects the self-as-child concept, which she cannot relinquish. She thought of herself as Alyssa B. To change would alter and threaten the self she had become accustomed to.

Change is threatening to Alyssa. Change is always a threat. Change in

---

*We are reminded of the oriental, "loss of face" concept. To lose face, is to become embarrassed, to become less than before, to become a non-person, so to speak.

the content of the self—from self as child to self as mother—requires major reshuffling on many levels. One of these levels is the self as sexual object.

Loss of Self as Sexual Object

Women (as well as men) have internalized the notion that maternity and sexuality are opposite aspects of adult female behavior. The ideal, the fantasy of the perfect mother, is associated with the good, pure, holy, loving, selfless object; the fantasy of the sexual woman is raw and instinctive; is erotic impulse; untamed, selfish, wild, greedy, seductive, and untrustworthy. Myths, based on this split in the feminine psyche persist even today, although their meaning is difficult to understand. Francine, in Group C, voices this split: "Femininity is being a sexual woman . . . not mothering . . . in fact, I think you become less sexual as you become maternal . . . "

The view of oneself as sexually female has its developmental origin in the young girl's seductive experience with father. In this phase, the rival, the competitor for father's attentions, is obviously the mother. In order to rule her out, daughter concludes: mothers are maternal; mothers are not sexual. This idea is generally accepted. That is, most women do not consider their mother as sexual. This is a defensive position, a projection established during the oedipal conflict, when mother was clearly identified as the sexual rival. For our purposes, when and how this identification began is less important than the fact that the concept was well in place by the time we met our subjects. To be mother is to be asexual.

Although this particular group of dual-career women—educated, emancipated, liberalized, and feminized—has become more comfortable than earlier generations with sexuality as a healthy, natural, appreciated aspect of self, they maintain the distinction either on the conscious level or unconscious level, between mothering and sexuality. Some subjects suggest that one must give up sexuality in order to become maternal. The either/or split is very clear for Group C women; they choose sexuality. Sexuality is positive, healthy, and desirable. Their language for mother (mothering) is filled with harsh imagery, criticism, negative affect, and sadness.

Group B women, who have a more relaxed attitude toward themselves in general, believe that they can allow the sexual aspects of themself to move aside temporarily for the maternal self. They apparently feel confident that they will continue to be sexual. For example, Julie (B) talked about how earlier in her life, she used her sexuality in order to outwit her male colleagues. "Now" she said, she "could be sexual, without having to threaten others, without having to manipulate, or be devious . . . ". "It's like, I know this part of myself is ok and I can try out other parts . . . "

To see how sexuality is split from maternity for women in Group A, we'll begin with several MTAT responses given by Marlis. For Card I (woman looking at blank wall) her story is of a woman who is happily pregnant. The affective tone is wishful; it sounds like a pleasant fantasy. Her response to Card II, however, tells us that there's little stability under the apparent casual reference to the pregnant woman. She reverses the mood completely; anxiety takes over as she is presented with the stimulus of a woman looking at pictures of a man and children, with a diploma on the wall. Marlis: "This is not a woman looking at her Ph.D diploma wondering why she isn't doing anything . . . it is not. Obviously a woman in someone else's office. It feels like a man's office, but that's not right because there is a photo of a man on the credenza here or desk, so it must be a woman's office; but it feels to me that she is coming to a man's office for some professional reason probably a doctor but it doesn't feel like a doctor's office. I am in trouble with this one. She has come into this office . . . been left alone . . . has to wait . . . and she is browsing around . . . feeling nervous not sure what is going to happen next. Whoever she is going to see is going to be a professional and is a possible solution to a difficult situation, and she is comforting herself by reading the credentials on the diploma. She needs a solution to something . . . I can't tell what the problem is or who it is or how it is going to be solved, and I keep feeling it is a man's office, although the sign before me is that it's a woman's office. I can't do more with that . . . I don't see a story . . . all I feel is her anxiety . . . The man will come in and sit behind his desk and she will sit in the visitor's chair, and she will tell her story and in her telling it she will keep it from sounding as scary as it really is. She will be professional—she will be a professional client—and the solutions will be proposed, but she will never show how scared she really is. She is now feeling it before he comes in; her hands are cold. When she starts talking to him she will get self-confidence and she will feel outside of herself . . . If it's a doctor I think there may be something really wrong with her, although she looks healthy, and she will pretend to be rational about it and will even feel rather rational about it but not really." The theme in Marlis' response is denial and conflict. Her response is indicative of her ambivalence regarding sexuality. Since she has just imagined a pregnant woman (in the previous card), we assume that this vision has set the conflict in motion. She's still responding to the former stimulus.

The scene in Card II stirs up Marlis' anxiety even more. The combination of the office setting with the diploma on the wall and the pictures of a man and two children throws her off balance completely. She can't reconcile the feeling that this is a man's office with the evidence before her that it is the woman's office. She cannot identify with the stimulus as given, so she changes it in order to account for the presence of the children in the picture; they are not hers. She denies the reality of what she sees. These words stand out: "trouble; tentative; alone; nervous; anxiety; problem; scary; cold; outside herself; something really wrong." Is having a child "really wrong"? Is having a child "really outside herself"?

Continuing with the projective sequence, Marlis sees the next card, Card III (group scene), as a cold impersonal dinner party with no intimacy between the "still awkward people." She draws back into isolation, still responding to the stress of the previous stimulus. In response to MTAT IV (older man and woman with younger woman), once again Marlis tells us what this picture is not: "A daughter and her parents . . . but I don't think so . . . I don't know who this is . . . she is not their daughter . . . " (she continues a bit) " . . . maybe something bad . . . " Later she talks about the father crying. To MTAT V (woman looking out of window), Marlis repeats the process: there's a sad outcome—a negative tone. She sees the woman in an " . . . institutional setting, not a home . . . " She mentions trying to decide what to do, " . . . coming to a turning point . . . feeling hopeless . . . "

So far, all responses, with the exception of the first response, have a negative outcome; the mood is sad, the language reflects conflict and dissonance. In contrast, in the next story, MTAT VI (woman and man in office setting), Marlis is comfortable with the stimulus. Her story is longer, her mood is confident, and her affect is almost superior, as she describes a woman executive who is interviewing a male job candidate. Her last comment confirms our hunch, " . . . this is an easier card for me." She feels safe again; this situation and its underlying competition between man and woman is easy for her.

One way to understand Marlis' responses is to think about how she views maternity. We know from the rest of her case material that Marlis is conflicted regarding children. We know that children are a threat to her sense of self. Children require a stepping back from the sexual sense she is confident about. Children represent a loss of some aspects of that sexual self. Therefore, the family pictures, the dinner party, and the relationship with parents, all tap into her anxiety about children. In contrast, the office allows her to return to an adult, professional, confident self-concept.

We have heard Marlis talk with confidence about her childhood and adolescence, her sexual development, her first marriage, and her competence in dealing with male colleagues. In her first marriage, she was the one who decided it wouldn't work; she said they simply grew apart. There were no sexual problems. She's always been sexually confident. But when she talks about children she loses this confidence. She is the subject who said, " . . . I can manage things like school and a career . . . how is it that I somehow allowed relationships and children to get away from me? . . . "

Lisa, another ambivalent woman, also reveals through her projective responses, the sense that maternity threatens her sexual sense of herself. Lisa is tentative, sad, unhappy, and fearful in all responses in which she refers to children. For example, to MTAT II (woman in office: pictures of male and children on desk; diploma on wall), she says, "housewife looking at this photograph . . . probably in an office . . . probably her degree on the wall and she is looking at the photo of her family and wondering . . . looking at her life right now and wondering if she should have done more . . . wondering if this is all there is . . . not happy . . . " In contrast, Lisa become positive, assertive, superior, and controlling when the stimulus is sexually stimulating, as in the male/female business setting of MTAT VI and VIII. To MTAT VI (office scene: handshake between woman and man), she tells about a woman who is on a sales call. The man, " . . . is not really taking her seriously, and he is just going through the mannerisms, flirting a bit . . . she's very accustomed to it . . . very determined to keep working . . . so that one day men will be more receptive to a woman coming in to sell computers . . . so she gives her sales pitch . . . and pretty soon she says something that catches his attention and he takes on a new interest . . . and he begins to really respond to her . . . so he is going to really start listening . . . listening to her as a sales person, rather than just a woman talking . . . she knows it and keeps up the contact and some time down the road she makes a big sale . . . " Again in Card VIII (office scene: woman standing behind seated male) Lisa responds, " . . . this particular man is threatened by her because she is a woman . . . he does a mediocre job and she has to deal with this; she tries to accept it for a while, but at this point she is having a hard time letting it go . . . what will happen is that he will probably leave . . . I would like to see this happen . . . she will say it has to be this way, and it has to be that way or they were going to have a serious talk . . . at which point she will fire him, because he has been giving her some bad vibrations . . . "

Lisa is confident in her dealings with men. When her sexual self is dominant, she emerges as the winner. She is confident as she says, "she knows it." Louise, whose view of femininity is predominantly sexual, is very competitive with men, and tells us that women manipulate men in order to feel superior. She talked about how their friends teased them, her husband particularly, about how it feels to " . . . have such a successful wife . . . they mean who's on top sexually . . . and otherwise . . . "

One further element has contributed to my conclusion that for most of the women in Groups A and C, anticipation of maternity is experienced as a threat to the sexual self. This is the discovery that so many of these women described themselves as "different." We saw that the self-concept that they were "different" was common to women in all three groups. Earlier I said that perhaps the difficulty of managing the dual-career system accounted for this feeling of not being like other women. It is certainly true that in many ways, these women are not like their traditional mothers or grandmothers. First, dual-career women take themselves seriously as career women. Their adult identity is based partially on a sense of themselves as professionals. They are not content, as their mothers were, with a vicarious identity based on the achievement of their spouse.[8] Furthermore, dual-career women and their partner share the understanding that each individual is as committed to her or his work as they are to the relationship.

Perhaps, another part of the sense of being different from other women grows out of the fear that maternity will threaten their sense of themselves as sexually female. If such is the case, then they *must* be different from other women. Obviously they know women are both sexual and maternal—look at mother and grandmother. Even as the conscious denies mother a sexual identity, the unconscious knows otherwise. The denial is necessary as the developing ego evolves a sexual identity.

As we have stated before, the sense of being different is, of course, different from mother. Mother was both sexual and maternal. In questioning motherhood, they declare their difference. But once this process is set in motion, it does not stop with being different maternally. The question for many subjects was that by ruling out maternity, were they somehow not quite female? If all women before them have chosen to mother, how will they change by choosing to remain childless? The unspoken fear is that somehow, this choice may make them less female—less sexually female.

The subjects managed to work their way through these issues in various ways. For the most part, Group C women come to a point where they see the separation of sexuality and maternity as ego-syntonic. They feel no unmanageable threat to themselves sexually. However, Group A still feels a sense of turmoil, a sense of internal disruption when they try on a self-concept that is totally non-maternal. This is their dilemma, and it feels impossible to resolve. The overt separation of nurturance and sexuality, which was so easy for Group C and so conflictual for Group A, reflects the way that maternity is perceived as a threat to the sexual sense of self.

Loss to the Professional Self

In many ways, the fear that maternity is a threat professionally is a very appropriate response to reality. In today's competitive professional climate, women are not made to feel that they can be sure of their job, be sure of their promotability, or be sure that they're taken seriously as a professional, once they have a family. There is no way to avoid the truth that taking time out for children violates the rules, according to the traditional (male) career model.[9] We are gradually beginning to identify some new mothers who manage to feel good about their professional development. But as we all know, most of the evidence comes from those who struggle with a continuous and unsettled pull between the professional and the maternal self.

It's not difficult to understand the sense of foreboding that the childbearing decision stirs up in women who have spent so many years developing and cultivating their professional identity. Formulated first in reflection of father's positive appraisal of them (especially their verbal skills and intellectual competence), the sense of themselves as professionally able is very precious indeed. They have grown up defending this sense of professional confidence by competing with the men in their family, their schools, and their workplace. Maintaining a sense of being equal/superior to men professionally is part of a lifetime effort. But listen to Diane, as she describes what is a very familiar situation: " . . . the kid begins to fight with your ability to do the job, and even though you are able to put out the same amount of work . . . It's acceptable for men, for instance, to leave work and go off golfing because an army buddy is in town; but it's not acceptable for a woman to go home because the kid is sick." There are several interesting aspects to Diane's comment. She tells us that it's fine for the man to take off, not that he feels fine. By that we see she means that from the organization's point of view, it's an accepted policy. But then she also tells that the woman *feels* guilty when she takes time off: " . . . kids fight with your ability to do the job . . . " This has nothing to do with policy (though that also may be the case), but rather with the way she has internalized the problem. She says that she can't be taken seriously as a professional once she allows herself to respond to her needs as a mother. Diane also suggests that she will change her orientation, will become less professionally dedicated, and will deflect some of her energies. Of course, she will—that's her dilemma.

Louise, who told us so convincingly about herself as professionally competent, described the fantasy that disturbs her whenever she thinks about being pregnant. She sees herself, in her role as consultant to a group of male colleagues, trying to be credible, trying to be appreciated: "The other thing is I'm not going to be a really dynamic speaker if I'm eight months pregnant. You don't go to an electrical engineering sort of thing, with seven hundred men that are in the army's department of defense—with crewcuts—and get your point across easily if you're pregnant." Because we know Louise, we know how important body image (being beautiful) is to her. It's the way she defines herself. Beautiful and smart. How can she change this self-image in order to become pregnant, which she has told us in definitely not beautiful, but is "fat and ugly"? She apparently feels it can't be done. There's another element in Louise's fantasy. Louise sees herself in what could be a victorious situation vis a vis a large group of strong (defense department) men. Her sexual self, competitive and confident, can handle this situation easily. But at eight months pregnant, she's no longer the same. Her anticipated maternal self feels the conflict.

One last example of how I have come to see how maternity is a threat to the adult, professional self-concept is as follows. Many women seem to seek out one professional challenge after another, in what looks very much like an avoidance behavior; that is, the time is never "right," they are not at the "right" place in their career, they need one more promotion, one more degree, before it is safe to take time off, need to make one more career move, etc. Moreover, they believe this as sincerely as their male colleagues do. That's the problem. Once again, the male career pattern is the measure. It's both a convenient facade (for some this was apparent) and a recognition of the requirements and sacrifices demanded of people who reach significant career success.

To summarize, we have stated that the decision to have children is experienced as a threat to three separate aspects of the self-concept: first to the self as child, second, to the self as sexual object, and third, to the self as professional. Discussion of the professional self-concept leads us into the next part of this analysis of developmental issues.

When we talk about the self as professional, we refer to the externalized, executive functions of the public self. This is the self that the individual has cultivated to meet the needs of the Individualistic Dream.

CHANGES IN THE DREAM

Developmentalists have told us that one of the tasks of adulthood is to come to grips with those aspects of oneself that were denied earlier in life. This is a critical phase in the process of establishing a fully cohesive adult self-concept.[10] Research has found that somewhere around midlife there is a major shift in orientation. Previously denied aspects of one's sexual identity appear in the consciousness with a new and relentless force. It has been observed that midlife men become more passive, nurturant, affiliative, and interdependent; midlife women seem to become more outgoing, dominant, assertive, and independent. Gutmann and Neugarten refer to this as a shift in the dominance/submission polarities.[11]

Although the literature on adult development sees the confrontation with denied aspects of self as part of midlife development, I have found that non-traditional age-thirty women, who are at the decision point regarding childbearing, apparently experience a similar process. That is, they have attended thus far in life to the externalizing, intellectualized, competitive, aggressive, dominant, unemotional aspects of self. These descriptors are, of course, all traditionally used to refer to masculinity. They also form an apt description of the person whose psychic energy is invested in an *Individualistic Dream.*[12] However, in the process of confronting their feelings about having children, at about age 30, our subjects are forced to deal with other, previously suppressed aspects of the psyche. The other aspects are reminiscent of what Stewart calls the *Relational Dream.*

Expanding Levinson's work, Stuart suggests that there are two distinct early life Dreams*—the *Relational Dream,* which is formed primarily around relationships with others especially through marriage and motherhood; and the *Individualistic Dream,* which reflects the need to " . . . become a certain kind of individual, most typically through forming a career identity."[13] The latter represents the culturally validated male position; the former, the traditional female position.

Some of the women interviewed in the present study made it clear that an either/or dichotomy on this Individualistic/Relational scale is too simplistic. Instead, as the developmental process evolves, one moves up and back between the two positions. What occurs is a struggle toward integration of both the masculine and feminine positions.

In another study[15] which focused on midlife dual-career couples, I hypothesized that dual-career women who married and had children at the traditional age, found themselves at about age forty in a dilemma very similar to male midlife crisis.[16] One such case is illustrated in the diagram that follows, and focuses on the swings in behavior between the extreme individualistic/independent position, and the relational/interdependent one. This particular case involves a midlife woman who has had a continuous career path. That is, she did not stop working when her children were born. Although for purposes of illustration the process of development seems to flow in a steady line, in reality there is actually a constant ebb and flow—regressive as well as progressive pulls—moving in the general direction as indicated.

On the chart, the solid line represents the traditional woman, who had an Individualistic Dream prior to age 20. As a girl growing up, she was rewarded for independent achievement, primarily related to school achievement. Gradually there is a shift from satisfaction with achievements, to the wish to be needed and to nurture. Bardwick[17] argues that as girls reach adolescence, their sources of approval are based on affiliation and a sense of interdependence, as opposed to earlier stages when they received approval for individual achievement as well as affiliative behaviors. By age 20, the traditional woman has reached an interdependent position, similar

---

*"Dream" is well defined by Gaston as " . . . more than a fantasy and less than a detailed plan; it is a crucial agent and source of purpose . . . an evanescent image of one's evolving identity projected into the world."[14]

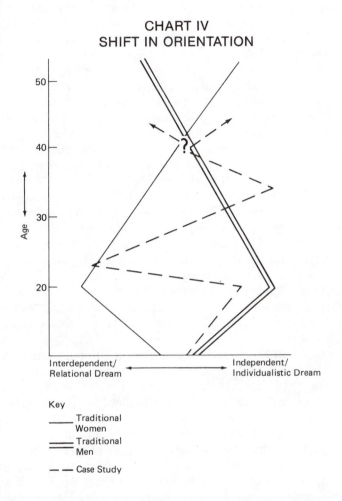

CHART IV
SHIFT IN ORIENTATION

to what Stuart labels a Relational Dream. However, as seen on the chart, as our subject matured, she moved toward greater independence.

The double line on the chart represents the traditional male position. Starting at an early age in the externalized, achieving, independent, individualistic position, traditional men move toward a more nurturant, affiliative, interdependent, relational sense of self as they approach midlife.

The curved line represents a 40 year old dual-career woman (case study, Kay S), who has been working full-time for the past eleven years. As we can see on the chart, she moves up and back between independence and interdependence, struggling to balance the pulls between her needs for achievement, power, autonomy, and separation vs. her needs for nurturance, affiliation, dependence, and fusion. We can see that at about age 24, with two children, she is far to the extreme interdependent pole. At least this is the way she appears behaviorally. When I probed more deeply, however, I found that she was never psychologically invested in this behavior. Her basic self-configuration remained fixed at the independent pole. Very soon after her two children were born she began to recognize that her frustration and dissatisfaction stemmed from the fact that her relational/interdependent behavior was not consistent with her primary sense of self (with the way she really saw herself), with her dominant pattern of self identification.[18] Responding to this internal pressure, she moves quickly to the extreme opposite pole, so that by the time she's in her early 30's, once again she's highly independent, living out the Individualistic Dream. By about age 40, however, she seems to be swinging back to an interdependent position; only this time, she is caught in the middle and really doesn't know which way she'll go. This sense of fluctuation through progressive stages in ways of experiencing oneself in relation to others, is described by Karpel as the process of movement to individuation from fusion.[19] Karpel describes the middle stage as ambivalence, which is experienced as acute emotional swings between two fears, i.e., of either being swallowed through fusion, or being isolated through separation. Kay S. seems to be caught in this dilemma.

The language that Kay S. uses to describe her current position, which is represented by the question mark on the chart, is reminiscent of the way the male midlife crisis has been described, i.e., as a questioning of the meaning and value of one's life, with the implied need for restructuring of the basic elements before life can continue.[20] Kay describes herself: "I feel as if I'm in the middle of a huge colorless desert . . . an existential crisis . . . not really sure that it makes one damn bit of difference what I do anymore . . . my work doesn't take on the meaning that it used to." Although she is at a career decision point where growth demands a reinvestment of her time and energy, she says, "I'm not as mesmerized by the concept of achievement anymore . . . "

An accumulation of recent traumatic family events—the death of her mother, the serious illness of a daughter, and the shaky state of her marriage—compound the present crisis for Kay, and illustrate the very complex intermingling of intrapsychic, marital, and career issues that dual-career couples may face.

Another midlife dual-career woman, Helen J., exemplifies the continuous nature of the efforts to integrate different aspects of self, and the persistent need to work toward incorporating these opposing forces. Unlike Kay S., Helen J., age 37, is just starting her career. Having completed professional training, she is in the process of applying for her first job. Responding to a MTAT II (woman in office, with pictures of male and two children): Helen says, " . . . opening up an office . . . the first client is waiting to come in . . . and she goes over to the desk and she says (to the picture) . . . I've made it . . . here I am . . . give me your blessing . . . you're going to be a little watching me, too." Through this response, Helen lets us hear the struggle she's experiencing in trying to create a balance between the press for independence and professional growth and achievement ("I've made it, here I am") vs. the relational self as wife/mother; wanting, asking their blessing (i.e., their permission to start her new life). Some of her ambivalence and insecurity is displayed, as she says, almost fearfully: "you're going to be a little watching me, too."

These two cases, Kay and Helen, differ from the ambivalent women discussed here because they already are mothers. How do women in the childbearing decision stage appear in reference to the Individualistic vs. the Relational Dream.

In response to the very first question in each subject's interview process, we heard the Dream that was currently relevant. That is, they responded to the question "Tell me about your life right now" as follows:

	GROUP A	GROUP B	GROUP C
Career Focus	4	1	8
Relationship and/or Self-Focus	4	7	0

We can see that Group B is apparently invested in a Relational Dream. Their focus throughout the interview was on the way their relationship was effected by other pressures, by their ambition, their decision to work, their relationship to the extended family, the dual-career system, and their decision regarding children. Their conversations about children were framed within the context of the way children would change their relationship to each other, and how as individuals they would be changed in the process of relating to their child. Their Dream is to be involved psychologically with another. The Dream for these women is consonant with their present and/or specifically planned future behavior. Joyce is very certain of this as she comments, "I think probably the relationship has to come first. I would not sacrifice the relationship because I think in some ways they are harder to come by than a career."

With apparently just as firm and unconflicted a view, Group C women focused on their career, and presented all subsequent data from this perspective. Although their relationship was of critical importance, it did not come before career. Their struggle was to establish a family system that allowed each to continue with the primary career focus, without causing too great a disruption to the relationship. By and large, they said that they had developed a successful dual-career formula, which made their career-first orientation work out well. For example, Alice said, to the first question, "Right now I have two, maybe three careers that I'm trying to balance. I'm a conference planner and designer for XYZ . . . but the other half of my life and training is music . . . I'm a professional cellist . . . and teaching is my third career . . . "

The ambivalent women were evenly divided in response to the first question, in terms of their current life. Half talked about their work; half talked about their relationship and/or themselves.

Career Focus

Jane: "State of utter confusion right now, work and school. I'm really trying right now to finish up . . . trying to get through the end of the semester . . . After 82,000 years of going to school, I'll be done." Louise: "Well, what I do . . . all the things I'm involved in right now . . . I guess I'm in somewhat of a transitional phase right now. And I go through a transitional phase about once every three years on the average. Normally I change my professional environment . . . " Paula: "Right now—I'm the busiest I have ever been . . . not enough hours in the day to do all I am asked to do and a few weeks ago I felt that I must control that . . . I worked for the past ten years to get to this point to be a much sought after consultant . . . " Barbara: "I'm working during the day, and trying to finish up my MBA in Hospital Administration in the evenings . . . "

Relationship and/or Self

Marlis: "We've had a couple of disasters lately . . . my feelings are curiously dichotomous . . . I think . . . mainly because of my family circumstances . . . " Diane: "We're living in X right now for about two and a half years . . . moved here from downtown and before that we lived on the south side . . . " Lisa: "Right now it is very structured and yet doesn't seem structured . . . we are both working in careers and I also go to school in the evenings . . . " Alyssa, "At this point I have been married for five years and involved with this job for five years." Jane, Louise, Paula, and Barbara focus first on their work, although they refer to spouse as well. Marlis, Diane, Lisa, and Alyssa talk about "we" and "I" as they focus on relationship or self.

We can use Kay's story (she was the 40 year old presented above) to understand something more about the differences between groups. In Kay's case I found that although as a young woman she may have been behaving as if she was in pursuit of the Relational Dream, she was psychologically invested in quite the opposite Dream. This dissonance was the source of her distress. When she became aware of what the pain was about, she was able to arrange her life in a much more satisfactory way.

Perhaps Kay's experience is a clue to understanding the dissonance in Group A's case material. Group A's interview statements were frequently inconsistent, and contradicted by their projective responses. In their conscious reports they appear fairly unemotional, sure of themselves, able to separate, talking about independence, and talking about autonomy. In the projectives they show themselves to be conflicted, insecure, highly dependent on spouse, fearful of the future, and holding on to mother psychologically in an unending battle for separation.

They are ambivalent, in part, because they behave as if they know what their Dream is. However, based on the data reflective of their internal distress, we have come to recognize that they are developmentally unprepared to formulate an adult Dream.

Once Kay recognized her Dream, she was able to change her orientation, and become less conflicted. The ambivalent group is not yet ready psychologically, to articulate the framework of an adult Dream. They are still caught in the powerful drama of the earliest individuation efforts. Listen to Alyssa's tortured analysis of her goals: "I wish I could lead two lives . . . I want . . . I like this career development and I enjoy this aspect of my life and then the other life is that of being a mother . . . I do feel strongly . . . though I said I would stay working . . . I also would like to have another life that I would be a mother, but I am not sure that that's this life . . . and I think in five years I would be accepting of it . . . because hopefully I will continue to do the things I am doing now . . . it's challenging and really interesting . . . I can't see myself looking back and saying . . . Gee, I wish I had had kids . . . I hope I am not that type of person . . . once you sit and make a decision you either don't look back and you don't dwell on a decision that was made or that you . . . you spend all this time talking and then you make a decision and you live with that decision." Her reference to the two lives, are to the Relational vs. the Individualistic Dream. She uses tentative statements, e.g., "would like," "I hope I am not that type of person," "I think in five years I would be accepting of it . . . " Accepting seems a strange word to use, and suggests that she has to accept what she really does not want. Note also, how she changes from "I" to "you" when she begins to talk about making a decision. "I" cannot make the decision; "you" (someone else) can.

Response to an Abortion

One other, very dramatic indication of the way in which the Dream is internalized in quite different ways by dual-career women, was in their response to their decision to have an abortion. These data are presented without any claim that they are generalizable. There were only a few women in each group who had been pregnant and who had had an abortion, although several had had pregnancy "scares." Although their response to that experience seems very revealing, it would be a mistake to make too much of these few cases. On the other hand, this information should not be ignored.

Marlis in Group A, Joyce in Group B, and Lee in Group C had had an abortion. Let's consider their reactions to this experience. For all three women, the actual pregnancy forced them into a new position. They had to make a decision, rather than talk about making a decision. As we've said so often here, they are all experts at intellectualization, so talking about childbearing, though stressful, was part of what they knew how to do. On the other hand, realizing that they were pregnant, actually experiencing the early physiological signs of pregnancy, forced them into a confrontation with all they had talked about for so long, with their current life structure, and most significantly, with their Dream.

Let's begin with Lee (Group C), because the decision was easiest for her. There was no choice. She felt strongly that it was not appropriate for her to have a child. She thought about both herself and the future child, and knew that she could not be the kind of mother that she thought children should have. She said, "It's not that I'm against children. I'm not. But, I know that I would resent the way the kid was changing me and taking me away from what I really want to do. And, taking me away from my husband." Lee is the second daughter in a family that had what seemed like two sets of children. When she was 11 a brother was born; two years later there was another brother. Lee felt that mother preferred the boys over her sister and herself. Lee remembers that her mother was always tired, always angry at something (or someone); never satisfied with the kids, her house, her husband, or her life. The parents argued constantly, mostly about the children and about money. There never seemed to be enough money for what the mother wanted. Lee is now 30, and has been married for seven years. She works in the sales department of a very large publishing house, and says she's been tagged in her organization as a winner. She loves her job and anticipates a big salary boost shortly.

Lee and her husband own a condominium in the city, as well as a few other pieces of income property. They spend several weeks a year on ski trips and other vacations. They move in a circle of dual-career couples, some of whom have children, others do not. They feel pretty comfortable with their current relationships, their extended families, and their friends. Lee says, "Maybe it's selfish, maybe it's basically selfish. What do I have to give up to have a child? . . . and I have to give up everything, and I am not willing to give up anything . . . everything is beautiful right now. I don't have the problems of kids sassing me back, diapers, babysitters, and people pointing a finger about raising children . . . nobody can be the perfect mother, there is always something wrong . . . I have heard people say that until you have children you don't know what joy is in life. I look at all the hurt and I say what little joy you get out of it . . . all the hurt you get. I see this with everyone who has children . . . kids disrupt your household, disrupt your marriage. Many of the fights my parents had were over us kids . . . my mother pressures me . . . it revolves around the fact that when you reach an older age and don't move as fast and all the joy seems to have gone . . . what do you have left except the kids . . . and I argue that I do have a family, I have a husband . . . we have a good life together . . . we have our arguments, but we do so much more than anybody else.

"I had an abortion 3 1/2 years after we were married. At that time there was no conceivable way I could be pregnant. I had a Catholic doctor who did not believe in birth control . . . and I thought I was following everything to the letter and did not find out about the doctor until it was too late. He did not agree with me that I did not want to have children! I was having problems with birth control pills (they were since taken off the market), and he switched me to another brand which was the problem. He took me off the pills completely for a while and gave me foam, and I was not aware that foam is not a good birth control method. It was like the day that I went off birth control pills that I became pregnant. I waited a couple of weeks and went to the doctor. He said when you go off birth control pills there is often a delay with the period, so don't worry about it . . . and a month later I said I still haven't gotten my period and he said he would give me pills that would bring it on in five days . . . and after that I would have been about two months pregnant, but don't worry, baloney . . . Then I went to another doctor had a pregnancy test and was pregnant . . . At that stage abortions were not legal so I had to fly to X. Got an appointment there and they confirmed the pregnancy. I was 16 weeks pregnant so he made an appointment for two weeks later when I aborted. At the time I became pregnant I didn't think about symptoms. I didn't think I had any symptoms. I knew what I was going to do without even having to talk to my husband . . . and it was not a matter of thinking at all . . . I just knew that I was not going to have this baby, and when I told my husband that I wanted an abortion, he asked me how I felt about it and said it was my body and he didn't want me to make a decision that might affect me for the rest of my life. I asked him how he felt about it and he said that after I had given it some real thought whatever I decided would be alright with him. When we were going together . . . (we went together for 7 1/2 years before we got married) we had a meeting of the minds. It was not really a discussion. The only thing we discussed was whether or not we were going to do anything permanent. We made the decision to get married at 23. It would have been difficult as a newly married couple to get a doctor who was reputable to either perform a tubal on me or a vasectomy on my husband. I firmly believe at that time that I did not want children . . . I am not a changeable person, but like to leave myself options . . . at 23 I didn't know if at 26 or 28 I wouldn't change my mind. And so when my husband turned 30 we decided we are not going to change our minds, and that is why my husband had a vasectomy—mainly because the vasectomy was much easier, being an outpatient . . . I was afraid of the abortion. I didn't know what to expect. I would have liked to have had someone to talk about it, a friend or my mother. I don't know how my mom would react to the fact that I had an abortion. I would say that after all these years she would not be so upset by it . . . but my husband's family, if they are not priests or nuns they are pretty close to it . . . and it would have meant being totally alienated from the family . . . my very close girl friend is a very religious person . . . although she never voiced her opinions about abortion, I always knew she felt it was killing a life . . . The decision for me was not a mental one as much as it was physical. I had never been educated in sex education, and when I got my first period I was 14 years old. My mother never told us anything. I panicked and my girl friend explained everything to me . . . it was very traumatic . . . and at 17, my girl friend was pregnant and she didn't know how she got pregnant . . . and didn't know how the baby came out . . . and she came to me for information because she was ashamed to ask her doctor. The two of us were pretty ignorant . . . I remember as a child I thought that the belly expanded and burst and that was how the baby came out . . . believe it or not . . . My mother-in-law sat me down and taught me the facts of life before we were married."

To MTAT II (woman in office: pictures of male and children on desk; diploma on wall), Lee says, "I don't like all the clutter . . . I would think of all the things I would have to dust. Looks like a diploma, which probably would be gone immediately. Because it would be of no interest to anyone but myself and it is something you wouldn't want to brag about so it should not be in a prominent spot . . . I would say that woman has her precious things around her so she probably has these things around for a while; and she is reminiscing about the good old days, and I am not that kind of a person who would sit back and say. 'Now in the good old days.' Thinking back to her school days and to the time when her kids were small and what it was like when she was first married. Probably sits there and thinks . . . she is probably depressed about how things are now. People get unsettled and dissatisfied with their lives . . . humdrum and drab . . . things become so routine with no excitement in their lives. It becomes a struggle. You are not free temporarily and looking forward to the future when maybe the kids will be gone and you can have that freedom again. It seems to me that when you have the kids it's something that you have to attend to. It's not something you can give your attention part-time; you have to give this your attention all the time and therefore you have nothing left for yourself. After the kids are gone you are free to do what I would have done if I had not had children. By the time your kids are through college and married, you are almost too old to do anything . . . and if you are lucky you won't have children coming back with marital problems and divorce and children's problems. All of a sudden going skiing isn't fun anymore . . . you are too old to have a hobby like that, and you feel foolish going rink skating at 45-50 years old . . . you don't belong anywhere anymore. Isn't that a terrible thing to be saying . . . that is terrible.''

To MTAT VII (two women and baby crawling between them), Lee says, "This goes back to the time when I was over at my girl friend's house that one night and it was the most miserable night I spent, because you are trying to talk about whatever and the kid . . . all the conversation revolves around her pregnancy and how she delivered and the labor and how many nights she had to spend up . . . how exhausted she is . . . how she can never get away from the house . . . and the kid's crying . . . there is no peace . . . uncomfortable situation . . . it would be nice if she could get away for a few hours. You feel her tension as much as you can feel yours . . . as she knows she has to attend to the kid and watch him and she is trying to carry on a conversation and yet that can't be since she has to give so much attention to the baby. And after this I almost feel a little sorry that when you are going to have a little time to get together with someone else that you can't at least steal that hour away from the kid. I think everyone should have the right to have an hour away.''

A portion (perhaps the conscious element) of Lee's decision to have the abortion was based on discomfort with anticipation of the physical process of pregnancy. Having her period was traumatic; early notions of childbearing were terrifying. " . . . I thought the belly expanded and burst . . . " She felt tricked by the doctor, and angry that he did not honor her wish to avoid a pregnancy. Her husband was supportive of her decision, and apparently felt very strongly on his own about not wanting children. This is evident from his words before they were married as well as his opting to have a vasectomy. He also did not bully her into the decision, asked her to take the time she needed, went with her to see the doctor, and went back again at the time of the abortion. Very supportive, very thoughtful of her feelings.

Their lifestyle also played a big part in the decision to remain child-free. She tells us about not being able to "have fun" anymore if you have kids. In the MTAT VII, her friend can't even take an "hour off" . . . You feel her tension as much as you can feel you own . . . " And in MTAT II, " . . . by the time your kids are through college and married, you are almost too old to do anything . . . all of a sudden going skiing isn't fun anymore, you are too old . . . you don't belong anywhere anymore . . . " The words in the beginning of this projective are revealing. Thinking about the children in the picture, she says " . . . Depressed, unsettled, dissatisfied . . . humdrum and drab . . . so routine, no excitement . . . not free . . . "

Now let's turn to Joyce (Group B) who intends to have a child in the next year or so. Joyce is just as convinced about the correctness of her decision as Lee was about hers: "I like children, I think I would like to experience raising children . . . I would like to have them around . . . see them grow up . . . It could be a really basic feeling . . . I have always wanted children at some point . . . and I have come to the point where I have to make a decision . . . do I really want children or don't I . . . and I do want to have children . . . I would be disappointed if I didn't have children to the point where I would probably adopt . . . I think the biological part . . . that would satisfy a basic need I have . . . I would be disappointed if I didn't have children . . . and if I couldn't have my own, I would adopt. During my twenties I decided having children was something I really wanted to do, but not then . . . something to do around my thirties . . . but I didn't want them then. I was enjoying my life with Tom . . . it was more exciting, we were doing a lot of traveling. I thought that by 30 I would have done things that I wanted to do—traveling, school—really working in a place where I had always wanted to work. So that had been accomplished. Then I found that I was pregnant. I think it began to hit me that I didn't want Tom as the father. It would just complicate things for us and would not be good for the child. I knew it would not be good for me. My reaction surprised me—that I felt so strongly. And was so unhappy. I knew I would have the abortion, but I was not happy about it and would not do it again . . . We talked about it . . . both of our immediate decision was that we could not have the baby, but I think he was more flippant about it. I knew that was not the way I felt. My relationship now is quite the opposite. He is more mature, stable—much more secure and self-sufficient. He's patient and does not have a temper. And I feel he will be very good with children. We have a relationship that is calm and confident. We both feel the same about children. We plan to start a family in the next year. We have some property, some land up in New York, and we have been thinking about building a house there . . . I would like to have two or three children. I don't have any hesitancy that this responsibility wouldn't be shared. He feels confident with children.''

Joyce's response to some of the projectives provides another perspective regarding her attitude toward children. To CARD VII (two women with a baby crawling on the floor between them), she says, ''They are enjoying the visit . . . they are both self-sufficient. They are both in careers and the baby doesn't encumber either one. I don't see the baby as a burden . . . she wouldn't consider letting the baby hold her back from what she wants to do . . . '' As we noted before, in her protest that the baby is not a burden, Joyce seems to be denying some underlying fears she may have about the unknown aspects of mothering and the difficulty of achieving her complicated goal of having a family and a career.

In other responses, Joyce's reveals her conflicted feelings about family and career, and also indicates the way she has integrated them into a decision to have a child: To MTAT II, (office with family pictures), Joyce says, '' . . . this is part of her life . . . these two things, and she is thinking about her family right now while she is in her office, and she feels great contentment.'' To MTAT III (group scene): '' . . . the female is probably more high-powered than the male . . . '' (Females can do what males cannot . . . that is can have children *and* career.) In Joyce's response to Card IV (older couple sitting facing younger woman), we hear her indecision: '' . . . she's not married and does not have children, and she doesn't know what way she is going . . . '' To Card V (woman looking out of window), she said, '' . . . she decides to go on with her career and put off her family for a while . . . (As we know, this is a reflection of what actually happened in her case.) To card VI (two women sitting together, one is obviously pregnant), she says, '' . . . two friends, one is pregnant and the one on the right is the mother . . . they are talking about pregnancies and about families . . . woman on the right is concerned . . . woman on the left seems confident . . . '' Joyce identifies with the pregnant woman, since she is not already a mother. She is confused as to whether or not this is her mother (at first, she saw the picture as two friends). By seeing the pregnant woman as confident, she is telling us that although others may be concerned (as is the mother here), she will be able to handle it well.

Let's review the elements in Joyce's case. She divorced her first husband, partly because of her feelings about children. She said her first husband would not be a good father, and would not share the responsibility of parenting. (We know, of course, that there are other factors underlying her divorce, but the feelings about him as father were certainly important.) She seems to be fairly comfortable with the idea of changing her work. She has told us that she wanted to wait until she had gotten a foothold in her field.

Now that she's accomplished that career objective she's ready for the next phase of her own development.

Joyce has a healthy curiosity about being pregnant. She told us in the interview that she thought it would be an "interesting" experience. This response may reflect her intellectualizing position, but nevertheless, it allows her to remain neutral, not negative. She has fairly positive feelings about her own physical maturation, recalling that her older sister helped her feel comfortable about her developing femininity. She had her first period without trauma. She expresses a healthy curiosity about being pregnant, about the birthing process, about nursing, about all aspects of the infant/mother bonding process—in other words, she is not afraid of the physiological elements of childbearing.

One point must be repeated to really understand Joyce's decision about the abortion. She knew this was not the time to have children. She knew this was not the right relationship. She knew she felt very strongly against having to abort, but that it was the best decision at the time. But, she said to herself, never again.

Finally, we turn to Marlis in Group A, and see how she responded to having an abortion. Marlis said that in her first marriage, when she was about age 23, she had a pregnancy scare. She said then, that it would have been inconvenient, not the right time, really tough, but that well maybe . . . they'd see. She was not pregnant. However, a few years later, she said she thought with sadness, that if she had been pregnant at that time, it would have solved her problem. She would have had the baby and that decision would have been made: "No . . . it seemed not an entirely bad idea . . . well we are going to do it eventually, prefer to wait, but the plan was when we finished graduate school. Maybe when I was writing my dissertation would be the time . . . I would be home. We expected to have a child or two. I don't know if we decided one or two. In retrospect . . . even with the divorce I wish I had been pregnant and had gone through with it . . . ten years ago. Kid would be 10 now, and I would like to have a ten year old. Because I would be through with all the baby business and solved most of the problems. But my life would be entirely different . . . In a way I am kind of sorry. It seems such a shame, if I had been pregnant, not to have gone through and had it. We were so naive, we didn't recognize the problem . . . didn't recognize it as a choice. But now the longer you let it go the more difficult it is. How complex it is and it really is a choice. At 22 or 23 we would have gotten through it and we would have managed . . . That was the only time it came up in the marriage. We were clearly postponing it and after a while, when things started to get rocky, we didn't talk about it anymore. We sneered at people who talked about having a child to bring them together. Well now (in this relationship) the question is what are we going to do about children. We know a lot more now than we used to, because last November I got pregnant. It started the summer when I was in New York . . . I got a bad pelvic disease. And I didn't have an available doctor. Finally had to go to the hospital, penicillin, I.V., the whole thing. Then the question arose about my tubes. Now there is a test to find out for sure but it requires an X-ray; all they could do was guess. The best guess when I left N.Y. was that I had probably scarred my right side because of the infection. The left was fine. From that time on I became convinced in my head that I probably couldn't get pregnant, and I started getting sloppier and sloppier, postponing using the diaphragm . . . I had had a bladder infection in October and had gone to the Dr. and got medicine; I was still infected and they started giving me sulpha drugs. I was to take that for ten days, and went back for a check, and still had it. I was going out of town for a meeting. When I got a new prescription and started taking it at the meetings, it turned out that I was violently allergic and ran a terrifically high fever. I was delirious. Got home the next day and called the Dr. He wanted to run an X-ray series to see if there was an obstruction; 16 X-rays. My period was due, but with the fever . . . On Monday morning I woke up sick to my stomach. I knew I was pregnant. I took the pregnancy test. Just had the X-ray series and I was in my fourth week of pregnancy. I told the Dr. about the fever and the X-rays. It was obvious that they felt an abortion was in order. I told John. I was shaken. It took exactly a day. He said it first. We were enormously lucky . . . the decision had been made for us. The fetus could have been damaged. But I found out I could get pregnant. And now we could think about it rationally. That we didn't have to choose right then. I went through the abortion and because I had had an infection they wanted me to wait until I was 7 or 8 weeks in so that they knew for sure it was in my uterus and not in the tube. So I walked around pregnant for a few weeks, and had the abortion after Christmas. I felt crummy. Swollen and crummy. I desperately wanted to have the abortion over with. Then I learned that because I was not going to have this baby, I didn't get the support from people you usually get. The physical discomfort would be short lived. It was just something to get through and then there would be the baby. But that was not the case here. I had the abortion in the Dr's office. And it really hurt. I felt really good when it was over. Partly psychological, I'm sure.

"But it surely is not over. We had a fight last night . . . and it came out again . . . . I left the room and then came out again . . . and got madder and madder at him. I was thinking about the abortion business . . . and I was thinking that he was impossible, that our relationship was impossible— maybe all this happened because I knew we were going to come to that. I somehow felt it was his fault that I got the abortion, which is absolutely irrational . . . I sort of felt that if he were going to be cruel like that I couldn't stand it . . . The costs were higher than the rewards, and the only thing to do was to leave . . . why didn't I leave . . . and the feeling under that . . . the trauma of that is children . . . in five years I will be 38. I always think he doesn't take this as seriously as I do. He is younger than I am for one thing, not much, but younger. Maybe he's more realistic than I am when he says there's plenty of time . . . in a way he's right, but I feel that there isn't a lot of time. I don't know . . . how much time is there left to have children? A time in my life that I am ticking off. There is still a lot of time to do anything I want . . . but with children that is not so . . . I don't know. If I were 23 instead of 33 . . . well then the relationship would be just interesting and we would have that and it would be OK. But I am past that. Now, I'm past that. The other thing I was mad at . . . he was talking about children as if having children was an irrational thing to do; as though there were no reasons for having children . . . except pathological. I heard that and it enraged me. I wanted to say that people have children for very good reasons . . . The difficulty is that I really love him. If I didn't, the minor things would be a pain in the ass but that would be it, and I could leave. Now I obviously don't want to leave . . . But . . . I feel that I don't control these things. I don't know. Things that are so important . . . I don't know. Everything else seems to come first, whether I want it to or not. Everything like work and school, all the things I can control. They all seem very important . . . have to be settled immediately. That's the stuff I can deal with. Relationships with men and children seem like things that just happen. I have managed them, but I don't control them. I feel that fate has not been kind to me and I don't know why I feel that way. It feels depressing. It feels like I have never thought of it before until this moment. I feel that the relationships I have had have been accidental. I have never controlled or planned them. It's not so awful, but I guess I'm not in control. It feels that way. I feel there is an accidental quality in my relationship and it's exactly the same way I feel about this business about children. It's in the same category of life. As if it is just fate and whatever happens. I guess if he would come home tomorrow and say, Well, I have been thinking about children. Children seem important to you, let's have a baby . . . I would say yes—I would go along with it." (Later) "So what I suppose I'm saying is I don't want to decide."

Let's consider Marlis's dilemma. She took the first pregnancy "scare" very lightly. It seems she thought that if she was, she was, and then they'd go from there. But the abortion was another matter.

She knew the abortion was the thing to do . . . the fetus might have been damaged. She said the decision took only a day. She remembers physical pain, and psychological relief. But the psychological position is apparently not simply relief. For the issue of the abortion (which she refers to as the abortion "business") still stirs up very irrational (how many times she uses the work irrational), very painful feelings. Marlis blames John for the abortion. When they argue, she thinks about the abortion, and blames him. She says that's totally irrational, but somehow she holds him responsible.

We can hear Marlis floundering. This woman, who is so rational, who is the totally competent professional person, who is in control of a large, complex organization, who can make decisions about budgets, personnel, and planning, finds herself unable to think rationally about "things like men and children." And when she recalls the actual pregnancy she becomes depressed, very sad. She did not have the joy of expecting that the discomfort would pass and she would have the baby. She did not get support from others. (We know that it was Christmas, a very highly charged, emotional time for her . . . she spent the time with her mother and did not tell her that she was pregnant.)

Marlis sees her age as a threat. She says if she were 23 instead of 33, the decision about children would still be possible. But now, time is running out. She feels unsure; unsure about her self, her relationship, her ability to decide, and her future. She finally comes to the conclusion that she does not want to decide.

Marlis's decision leaves us with a sense of sadness and loss. Marlis would like to be able to have a child. She would like to be able to say yes, I will have a child. She even says she would agree if John would suggest it. But she can't bring herself to make that decision. Marlis says it's fate that prevents her from making a decision to have a child; it's fate that has intervened in a cruel and unjust manner. She does not appear able to take any responsibility for her part in the decision. She labels it fate, feels mistreated by life, and feels surprised (recall how she said, "it feels that I have never thought of it before this moment.")

When we review what we know about the unconscious aspects of Marlis's position (especially the reigning ambivalence re mother) we can better understand the pain that Marlis is experiencing. For, as I said earlier (and as other ambivalent subjects said to me so often), Marlis is not against children. Here she differs dramatically from Group C women, who are not "against" children either. They told me so in very clear terms. What they are against is that the children should be theirs. Marlis, on the contrary, is very much in favor of children, although in many ways the wish seems to be that she be allowed to be the child in relation to the mother. We heard some of Marlis's projections referring to pregnancy. Though she first sees a happy pregnant women, the mood shifts to confusion and sadness, to " . . . something really wrong . . . " Marlis concludes: "I would like to be able to say next year at this time I'll be pregnant. But I really think what we're going to do is not decide . . . for a year or so . . . then maybe break up . . . I'd be 36 . . . and then try to meet the ideal person to have a child with . . . I'm afraid I have stalled for so long . . . time . . . person . . . never right at the right time . . . '' Marlis feels a loss that's clearly recognizable. But there's also an element of relief. She says, '' . . . It would be an enormous disruption . . . I'd have to change so many things.'' ''Yet,'' she adds, ''It's not how I think it's how I act. I feel the loss . . . how did this happen to me . . . how have I put children in the category of things that cannot be controlled?''

In discussing these three different responses to an abortion, it is clear that for each individual, a different Dream was dominant. Lee, fully identified with the Individualistic Dream, felt very strongly that the abortion was the correct and the only decision to make. She would make the same decision if it became necessary.

Joyce felt that, given the nature of her relationship, the decision to abort was the correct one. But we recall how strongly she felt that she would not do that again, and that she would have the child should she become pregnant. She is clearly and solidly identifying with a Relational Dream. On the other hand, Marlis remains unable to take any guidance from her abortion experience. Although it was several years ago, she feels very conflicted about it to this day, regrets what might have been, regrets that she couldn't go through with the pregnancy (although she accepted the medical conclusion that it was too risky), and regrets that she can't say now that she'd never have another abortion. She still feels that the decision to have a child is not within her control. She is unable to either reject or accept the Relational Dream. Yet she feels sadness and loss at the prospect of an exclusive identification with the Individualistic Dream.

ISSUES OF AGING

''Kids make you old . . . you lose yourself . . . '' We heard Alyssa say this. What does she mean—kids make you old? In this section we look at the childbearing decision as a developmental issue related to aging.

We said earlier, that having a child forced one to give up the claim to be a child. In the process of giving up on childhood, one is forced into confrontation with one's own developmental cycle. Ultimately, to no longer be the child, is to confront one's own death.[21] We are suggesting that childbearing ambivalence reflects a resistance to growing up; a resistance to giving up one's self as child; a resistance to giving up one's youth; a resistance to giving up freedom in favor of responsibility; finally, a resistance to the pressure of having to deal with one's own finite life cycle.

We know the struggle with developmental issues takes on increased dominance with the occurrence of trauma, such as a life threatening disease, or the death of a parent. No matter the age, given such events, the individual is forced to face his or her own death.[22] Once again, it is Marlis whose words are relevant. Marlis talked about a legacy, which developmental research has told us is one of the important tasks of midlife. That is, the way of ensuring one's immortality is to leave a mark on the world, either in the form of children to carry on one's name, or significant work to carry on one's professional life. Those who serve as mentors see this as a way of ensuring a legacy. Obviously, for most of the world the next generation ensures the legacy. Marlis said, "Children are neat . . . and for the rest of your life you have children. You really love them and are close to them . . . and who will love you forever. My mother is the only person on whom I can absolutely depend . . . obviously can't depend on (men) . . . sometimes I feel kind of alone. What will happen to me when my mother dies and there is nobody . . . ?" Marlis is confronting both the legacy issue and her old age. She anticipates isolation, her lack of familial ties, her separateness. Whereas others, in Group C especially, talk about their old age in community-oriented terms—that is, they will become the wise old woman serving the needs of society—Marlis, and the women in the ambivalent group, talk about old age in a private, personal sense. They do not identify with the larger social picture. They see themselves either alone or with a mate. When they envision the future, they do not fill out the picture with children and grandchildren the way the baby group does. They can't identify who the others are. Ambivalence regarding childbearing stirs up these fears, because the mature aspect of self (which is well developed in all our subjects) acknowledges the developmental changes that parenting brings about. Simultaneously, however, infantile aspects of self constantly press for denial of this truth. This is the conflict that we hear so poignantly from our ambivalent women.

What emerges from the ambivalent women's inability to reach a childbearing decision is their wish to remain in the early, formative, unsettled stages of life. Remember, they are still working on "getting it right." This is the meaning of "kids make you old." Alyssa said that she is very happy to be taken for a much younger woman, and she added, this is so because she does not have children.* We assume that the "old" self in Alyssa's image is the internalization of the actual mother, who is obviously, older than daughter.

---

*Ask any mother who compares herself to a friend her age who does not have children, and she will tell you that somehow the friend "looks much younger."

Denial of Biological Aging

Many ambivalent women thought about how they would change physically—would age—by becoming a mother. It was not only physiological changes they were thinking about, but also the way in which they would be seen by others.

Remember how Louise talked about physical appearance; how important it is to her to "look good." We know she means physically beautiful and physically sexual—not maternal. Alyssa said that she could envision herself with a child in a store; the child would be screaming and others would look at her, criticize her as a mother, and think of her as old. There is a certain element of grandiosity in what Alyssa says. She believes that the world is looking at her. She is both self-conscious and grandiose. The grandiose self, the narcissistic self, is the characterological picture we used earlier to describe many ambivalent women.

Gutmann has written about parenting in a way that is instructive here. He says that, in the service of meeting the needs of the child, " . . . both parents routinely give up the claim to omnipotentiality, and concede it to the child."[23] Although I do not totally agree with Gutmann's theory of parental imperative (whereby each parent cedes to the other properties which could conceivably harm the child), the notion that parenthood requires a retreat from omnipotence is important to us.

We know that the requirements of motherhood are anticipated as a change in the self-concept. We have stated that one of the important changes is a shift from a focus on the past, to a focus on the future. One cannot anticipate (the very word is future directed) the birth of a child without envisioning a nine month growth interval, followed by the actual birth and the beginning of life—the life of another. With this shift, the individual moves away from the omnipotence of being the only one, to a more individuated position in which one relates to another. We have suggested that in order to accomplish this shift from a self-conscious, narcissistic, dependent status, to one that is able to manage the threats inherent in individuation, the individual must have a sense of separation and a sense of confidence in the self as a dependable object. The ambivalent woman has not yet reached this stage of individuation. Therefore, the contemplation of being in the parental position calls up unconsciously held fears of chaos and destruction.

As we have come to know more about the aging process, we have seen aging as a developmental stage. Whereas in the past there was a temptation to look upon aging as a decline, this theory is no longer regarded as useful or accurate.[24] Parenting has also been seen as a developmental process. The parenting process requires that the individual learn new feelings, new behaviors, new ways to experience the self, and learn to accept a changed circle of significant objects. If this learning is anticipated with dread or fear (the affective tone of the ambivalent group), then parenthood is equated with decline.

It has been noted in mythology and in the folk lore of primitive societies, that childbirth is sometimes feared because the woman is afraid she will die in the process.[25] I have observed this phenomenon in my clinical practice. The patient, a pregnant woman, was recovering from a psychotic episode. Her dreams were filled with fears of dying. The dream images reflected the fantasy that in order to give birth, in order to allow the child to have life, she would need to give up her own life. On an unconscious level she felt pressure to choose between herself and the unborn child. The closer she came to delivery—the more she became willing to separate self from fetus—the less pressure she felt from these fears of dying.

Think about how Alyssa said, "I'd like to have another life." In an interesting study of older, childless women, who were admitted to a psychiatric hospital for the first time in their late 60's, Gutmann stated that " . . . non-parental women appear to be particularly susceptible to late onset depressions and transient psychoses, particularly following the death of an aging mother, or the onset of a potentially lethal disease."[26] Both of these events—the death of a parent, and the development of a life threatening disease—force one to confront one's own death. Gutmann continues: " . . . significant psychological development around issues of separation and individuation continue long after childhood and adolescence . . . maturation . . . which takes place in adulthood, has vital and independent consequences for the psychological functioning and mental health of the older woman."*[27] What Gutmann (and others) have found about the ongoing nature of the separation/individuation process is important here.

The point we have made about the ambivalent woman is that she is unprepared for the adult developmental aspects of the individuation process, because she is still working on the earlier tasks. We have related this to the basically narcissistic orientation that she presents. The early unsatisfactory separation from mother, as well as her ongoing resistance to change and maturation, prevent her from fully accepting a spontaneous attachment to another. Even in the marriage relationship, we have seen that she is unable to freely enjoy the merged aspects of marriage. The early deficit position interferes with her ability to manage the intimate, relational aspects of parenthood, maturity, and aging.

In summary, this discussion of some developmental issues related to the ambivalence about childbearing indicates that ambivalent women appear to

---

*The reader is cautioned not to interpret these findings as implying that childlessness leads to later life pathology. This pattern was found in this particular group of psychiatric patients.

be somewhat arrested psychologically, having only marginally encountered some critical adult developmental tasks. The literature on adulthood tells us that certain aspects of individuation continue as adults. However, unless there is an adequate foundation for growth as an adult, some of the major adult tasks (such as childbearing) will be experienced as overwhelming and conflictual. In this chapter, we have said that the women in the ambivalent group present many unresolved developmental issues relating to separation/individuation, which they must address before they can appropriately deal with their decision about children. In the next part of this book, we consider the ways in which ambivalent women (and couples) can be helped to work through these critical developmental stages, and explore some clinical issues and treatment strategies which might be employed in this process.

REFERENCES

1. Levinson D. et al. *The Seasons of a Man's Life.* New York: Alfred A. Knopf, 1978. Vaillant, G. *Adaptation to Life.* Boston: Little Brown & Co., 1977.
   Also see: Bardwick, J. *In Transition.* New York: Hold, Rinehart & Winston, 1979.
   Newgarten B., (ed.) *Middle Age and Aging.* Chicago: University of Chicago Press, 1968.
   Rubin, L. B. *Women of A Certain Age: The Midlife Search for Self.* New York: Harper & Row, 1979.
2. Stewart, W. *A Psychological Study of the Formation of the early Adult Life in Women.* Ph.D. Diss., Columbia University, 1977.
3. Also see: Levinson, *The Seasons of a Man's Life.*
   Gaston, C. *Women, Age 30 and The Dream.* Unpublished paper, 1978.
4. Erikson, E. *Identity, Youth and Crisis.* New York: W. W. Norton, 1968.
   Erikson, E. "Inner and Outer Space: Reflections on Womanhood." In *The Woman in America,* edited by Lifton, R. J. Boston: Houghton Mifflin, 1964.
5. Gutmann, D. "Parenthood: A key to the Comparative Study of the Life Cycle." In *Life Span Developmental Psychology,* edited by Datan and Ginsberg. New York: Academic Press, 1975.
6. Rubin, L. *Intimate Strangers.* New York: Harper & Row, 1983.
7. Ibid.
   Also see Chodorow, N. *The Reproduction of Mothering: Psychoanalysis and the Sociology of Gender.* Berkeley, CA: University of California Press, 1979.
8. Lipman-Bluman, J. "How Ideology Shapes Women's Lives." *Scientific America.* 1972, 226 (1) 34–42.
9. Kanter, R. M. *Men and Women of the Corporation.* New York: Basic Books, 1977.
10. Jung, C. G. "The Stages of Life." *Structure and Dynamics of the Psyche.* (Translated by R. F. C. Hull) Princeton, NJ: Princeton University Press, 1969. V. 8, Chapter 5.
    Levinson, et al. *Seasons of a Man's Life.*
    Cytrynbaum, S. et al. "Gender and Adult Midlife Development: A Critical Appraisal." Paper Presented at American Psychological Association Annual Convention, Toronto, Canada, 1978.
11. Neugarten, B. and Datan, N. Sociological Perspectives on the Life Cycle. In *Life Span Developmental Psychology,* edited by Baltes and Shaie. New York: Academic Press, 1973.
    Gutmann, D. "Parenthood: A Key to the Comparative Study of the Life Cycle."

12. Stewart, *The Formation of the Early Adult Life in Women.*
13. Stewart, *The Formation of Early Adult Life in Women.* Page 79.
    Levinson et al., *The Seasons of a Man's Life.*
14. Gaston, *Women, Age 30 and the Dream.* p. 2.
15. Wilk, C. "Coping and Adaptation in Midlife Dual-Career Families." In Cytrynbaum S. (Chair) Symposium: *Midlife Development: Influence of Gender, Personality and Social Systems.* Presented to the American Psychological Association Annual Convention, New York, 1979.
16. Jaques, E. "Death and the Mid-life Crisis." *The International Journal of Psychoanalysis.* 46 (part 4) 502–512, 1965.
17. Bardwick, J. *In Transition.* New York: Holt, Rinehart & Winston, 1979.
18. Stein, J. "Gender and Midlife Developmental Processes." In Cytrynbaum, S. et al. Paper presented to the American Psychological Association Annual Convention, Toronto, 1978.
19. Karpel, M. "Individuation: From Fusion to Dialogue." *Family Process.* March, 1976, 65–82.
20. Levinson, et al., *Seasons of a Man's Life.*
21. Cytrynbaum, S. et al. "Midlife Development: A Personality and Social Systems Perspective." In *Aging in the 1980's,* edited by L. Poon. Washington, DC: American Psychological Association, 1980.
    Jaques, *Death and the Midlife Crisis.*
22. Blum, L. In Cytrynbaum et al., "Midlife Development: A Personality and Social Systems Perspective."
23. Gutmann, D. *Psychoanalysis and Aging: A Developmental View.* p. 20. Manuscript discussed with the author.
    Gutmann, D. "Parenthood: A Key to the Comparative Study of the Life Cycle."
24. Newgarten, *Middle Age and Aging.*
25. Williams, J. *Psychology of Women—Behavior in a Biosocial Context.* New York: W. W. Norton, 1977.
    Also see, Blum, E. H. ed. *Female Psychology.* New York: International Universities Press, 1977.
26. Gutmann, D. et al., *The Clinical Psychology of Later Life: Developmental Paradigms.* Presented at the Meetings of the American Gerontological Society, Washington, D. C., 1979. p. 54.
27. Ibid., p. 54.

Part III
Clinical Issues: Psychotherapy with Ambivalent Dual-Career Individuals and Couples

Part III outlines the treatment issues and strategies that I consider important for dual-career individuals and/or couples looking for some help in resolving their childbearing dilemma. For some, the resolution of the struggle will be the decision to have a child. For others, it will be the decision not to have a child. In either case, the satisfaction of having acknowledged and considered some of the underlying components of the decision will reduce the anxiety that has engulfed their struggle.

We have focused on the individual woman who is part of the dual-career couple. Now as we begin to discuss clinical issues and treatment strategies that address some of the identified problems, we must start with the question of who is the patient? Is it the individual woman, or the ambivalent couple? Do we treat the woman alone, or treat the couple in marital counseling? I have come to believe that a combination of both individual and marital therapy is the optimal modality. A word about the risks inherent in this recommendation. In terms of maximizing the sense of marital satisfaction and equity (see Chapter 11) and creating an ideal environment for future interaction between parents and child; I am convinced that the couple must share responsibility for the childbearing decision. Therefore, when we treat just one member of the couple, we must be careful to avoid allowing either patient or spouse to assume that we have identified the "sick" one, or that the ambivalence about children is her or his "fault." The goal of treatment is to help the couple reach a psychological position in which a decision becomes possible. In order to do this, each member of the couple must be able to participate freely and fully in the process. The task of individual treatment is to help the conflicted person (or persons) arrive at a sufficiently stable situation, intrapsychically, to fully engage in the childbearing decision. The task of conjoint marital treatment is to help the couple develop an interpersonal system that permits a relatively unconflicted consideration of the childbearing issue.

In the first phase, the treatment of the individual, I suggest that an analytically oriented psychotherapy be used. As we know, this woman is functioning well in her work and in her marriage. At the same time, she is experiencing conflict and consequently, may experience symptoms of anxiety and/or depression. However, these symptoms are not debilitating; she is able to tolerate disruptive feelings without interruption of her ordinary routine activities. Therefore, I believe that this particular individual is a good candidate for dynamically oriented individual psychotherapy.*

The second phase of treatment—that is, the treatment of the dual-career couple—is described in a systems framework, since in my experience, a systems approach to the treatment of marital conflict is optimal.[2] The decision model, which was developed in order to understand the interaction of the different elements of the dual career system, will serve as a guide for the discussion of marital treatment issues.

It is not the decision about whether or not to have children that I regard as the most clinically important issue, although it is probably what the individual has in mind. Rather, it is the way in which this decision is experienced; the conflict, or lack thereof; the dissonance in terms of other aspects of the dual-career system, which will be the focus of the present discussion. As we proceed, we first examine issues relating to treatment of the individual, and then to treatment of the couple. Consistent with the earlier chapters, the primary focus is on the individual woman. Work with the couple is discussed much more briefly.

There may very well be some women who have decided not to have children, but who continue to feel conflicted abut this decision; they might benefit from treatment. Obviously, there may also be some women who plan to have children, and who are still trying to work their way through

---

*We should mention that psychoanalysis has been recommended for the treatment of the more pervasively disruptive narcissistic personality disorder.[1]

the varying phases of that decision. They, too, may benefit from treatment. However, based on what I have found, we can anticipate that the ambivalent group will experience ongoing conflict, will feel needy and dissatisfied. As I stated in the first part of this book, I believe that the ambivalent woman is more apt than other dual-career women to seek professional therapeutic help. She has appeared throughout this analysis to be the most anxious and the most dissatisfied with herself, her spouse, her work, and her lifestyle. Therefore, although the other women present important clinical issues, this discussion focuses exclusively on ambivalent women, and on their dilemma.

In Chapter 10, we concentrate on the individual, and on the intrapsychic conflicts that impede her ability to reach a satisfying decision. We examine the theoretical conclusions outlined in Chapters 7, 8, and 9, and extract the clinical issues. Treatment strategies based on these issues are outlined. The purpose here is to outline some of the major issues and conflicts, and some of the characteristic defenses we have come to recognize, in order to develop the clinical understanding necessary for effective treatment. For example, it was mentioned in Chapter 3, that the women in this study regarded the childbearing decision as mostly their responsibility. They told me that their spouse had "veto" power. This was true for woman in all three groups, although the baby group shared the decision with spouse in a much more balanced way Is this a treatment issue? Do the ambivalent women take responsibility for the childbearing decision as defense against establishing a system of equity[3] or as defense against some unconscious pressures? These questions are addressed in the discussion that follows.

Chapter 11 considers the ambivalent dual-career couple, focusing particularly on a series of separate elements in their childbearing decision process. From my analysis of this process, I have learned that there are two distinct phases in the childbearing decision. First, the couple seems stuck in an endless intellectualizing exercise. The clinician will have to be able to help them confront the underlying issues in order to progress to the second phase of the decision process, in which they more or less realistically encounter their conflictual position.

Based on my work with dual-career couples, both in the childbearing decision stage and at later developmental stages, I have developed some understanding of the characteristics of couples who are satisfied with their lives. The basic elements of the stress management system that these couples have evolved is presented.

Finally, in Chapter 12, we turn to the clinician and to the issues of countertransference. In discussions with other therapists, I have found that the subject of childbearing decisions is always a difficult one. One's own decision about children, and one's own relationship with mother, father, spouse, children, and colleagues, all intrude upon the therapeutic interactions with the patients, as they work their way through the underlying conflicts and defensive layers.

REFERENCES

1. Kernberg, O. *Borderline Conditions and Pathological Narcissism.* New York: Jason Aronson, 1975.
   Kohut, H. *The Analysis of the Self.* New York: International Universities Press, 1971.
   Masterson, J. *Treatment of the Borderline Adolescent: A Developmental Approach.* New York: Wiley-Interscience, 1972.
2. Neill, J., and Kniskern, D. (eds.) *From Psyche to System: The Evolving Therapy of Carl Whitaker.* New York: Guilford Press, 1982.
3. Rice, D. *Dual-Career Marriage.* New York: Free Press, 1979.

10
INDIVIDUALS IN TREATMENT

We know that many (probably most) childbearing decisions are made without conscious awareness of the intrapsychic position. Why is this particular decision different? To answer this question we look to the dual-career situation and to the personality of the dual-career individual. As clinicians, we need to understand as much as possible about who the dual-career woman is and what she is dealing with, in terms of the underlying intrapsychic issues and psychosocial stressors, in order to provide the arena for her psychological growth.

The dual-career individual is different in many ways from her traditional counterparts; that is, different from women in a traditional decision phase regarding children. We have noted that she is older than her traditional predecessors (the average age is thirty). She has postponed making a decision about children until she has been able to launch both her career and her marriage. She is accustomed (as is spouse) to a family system that accommodates two autonomous adults, both terribly busy, both thoroughly invested in their relationship and their work. Therefore, she may be unlike other women who face the decision about children in the sense that she has developed an adult identity that is satisfying and feels complete.

Furthermore, as we said earlier, she has already created an adult, child-free lifestyle. Her identity as part of a dual-career couple is well established. She feels free to plan her schedule around herself and her spouse. She has gotten used to the complex dual-career marital system, with all its inherent stresses and bonuses. In Chapter 1 we described the characteristics of the childless dual-career lifestyle, and saw that it enabled the couple to spend what limited free time they had on an exclusive relationship with each other. We also noted that the ambivalent dual-career woman described her spouse as the single most important person in her life. We have come to recognize, however, that the ambivalent woman is extremely conflicted about her inability to reach a satisfying childbearing decision. I believe that, given the importance she attaches to this question, and because she is sophisticated, well educated, verbal, and relatively stable psychologically, she will be able to ask for help. She will come into treatment, and will hope to work her way through her inability to reach a decision. On the other hand, she may realize that she is anxious and dissatisfied, but may not be able to identify the childbearing issue as the underlying issue. She may come in with complaints relating to her marriage, her job, her relationships, her feelings of emptiness, or her inability to respond emotionally.

I do not think it will be simple for his woman to enter into a treatment situation, since several aspects of her intrapsychic dilemma will affect her ability to tolerate the patient/therapist relationship. We know that one of her significant characterological positions is a fear of intimacy, and a habitual distancing tendency. She has a great difficulty believing that an important other person will accept her. Yet, she craves intimacy and wishes to replace her feelings of emptiness with the security of a confident relationship to another. Kernberg has said, " . . . the more a person wishes to overcome feelings of emptiness, difficulties in empathizing with others, and his internal coldness, the better the prognosis."[1] Therefore, we can hope that the motivation for treatment, based on her relatively intact sense of self, will overcome the resistance based on her fears.

The ambivalent woman fears dependency, although we have noted repeatedly that she craves the dependent position. Furthermore, she is conflicted in situations where she deals with anyone she perceives as an authority figure. As much as she tries to maintain a distance from such a figure (who is probably the representation of the maternal object), she feels herself compelled to seek out the authority, whom she perceives as the source of power. Once the individual submits to such an authority, once such an interaction is accepted by the individual, it becomes very difficult to relinquish the dependency. Therefore, separating from such a figure presents difficulties for the ambivalent woman.

These elements—intimacy, dependency, autonomy, authority, and separation issues—are inherent in the therapeutic relationship. It is an intimate relationship, in which the patient gradually allows herself to become known (dependent)—to become real (autonomous)—through her relationship to the therapist (authority), in order to become separate and autonomous. Ideally, in the treatment situation, the individual who initially fears such an intimate relationship out of fear of rejection, is able to work through this position. However, it is not an easy beginning for the patient, and we must be sensitive to her anticipatory fears, and to what is apt to emerge early in the therapeutic process. We must be particularly sensitive to the underlying dynamics of her ambivalence toward dependency. There is a double threat here, in terms of her ability to tolerate the treatment situation. On the one hand, there is the danger that, out of fear of becoming too dependent, the patient will never allow herself to invest her psychic energies into the treatment situation. This is countered by the opposite danger she feels that her wish for dependency will overcome her resistance, and she will be "lost" and overpowered by the important therapeutic figure.

Finally, we recognize the tremendous power and authority invested in the therapist by the patient. Therefore, we know how difficult it will be for this woman to retain her autonomous sense of self within the intimate, dependent relationship with this authoritative figure.

TREATMENT ISSUES

Narcissistic Orientation

In Chapter 7, I presented a description of the ambivalent woman, as evidencing a narcissistic personality orientation. Now we can take this description, and see if it helps us formulate a clinical evaluation and treatment strategy. The nature of the transference will be diagnostic. That is, the narcissistic personality forms a transference reflective of her primitive grandiosity, her need for mirroring, and her need for idealizing.[2] According to Kohut, the narcissistic personality can be more successfully treated than the borderline personality, since the narcissistic individual retains the more cohesive sense of self, which permits the establishment of a stable narcissistic transference.[3]

Kohut sees the transference relationship as an opportunity to complete some critical infantile developmental processes.[4] In contrast to the more primitive borderline personality, the narcissistic "self" is not as vulnerable to fragmentation, and not as threatened by fears of regression or disintegration. Given this relatively stable and cohesive self, we can anticipate a constructive transference. The focus of the transference, whether based on the need for mirroring (the need to be admired) or on the need for idealizing (the need to admire) will help clarify the stage of developmental (structural) arrest [5] and will help the therapist develop an appropriate treatment strategy.

I have stated that our subject appears omnipotent, and seems to project a grandiose and arrogant self-concept. However, this was found to be a superficial position, lacking a solid ground, or sufficient stability. When we probed more deeply, we found, with great consistency, that under the superficial arrogance and external projection of self-confidence, the individual was actually terrified of being "found out." The arrogance served as a defense against fears of retaliation in response to underlying rage and aggressive wishes. The fear of being found out also suggests that the self is split as follows: one aspect is modeled on the externalized, accepting paternal figure; the other aspect of the self is modeled on the internalized, rejecting maternal figure. We'll return to this idea later.

Related to the split in the self-concept, I found that the ambivalent woman has difficulty in regulating her self-esteem. That is, she is unable to integrate the good and bad aspects of self in a way that feels confident and loved. The earliest formation of self-esteem develops, in part, from the infant's ability to tolerate separation and to maintain an aspect of self as good. In treatment, this process is repeated in the mirroring transference. In the case of the ambivalent woman, the confidence in the self waivered because it was grounded in a premature autonomy and false sense of stability. Issues of self-esteem, particularly failures arising from the early separation/individuation phase, which were later cemented in the split between maternal and paternal identification, will need to be addressed clinically. As they emerge in the transference, the original inability to tolerate the aspects of self (mother), which felt threatening, can be re-examined. Both the infantile splitting mechanism and the later repetition, can be understood as defensive and destructive. When the opportunity for reappraisal is available, care must be taken not to repeat the original incorrect evaluation and response to what appears to be autonomous functioning.

What the ambivalent woman fears, perhaps on both a conscious and unconscious level, is that she will be abandoned. She will probably test this fear in her relationship with the clinician. She may try many different manipulative maneuvers, in a somewhat compulsive effort to repeat the early disappointment. In this respect, she resembles the borderline personality. The difference—and this is important diagnostically—is that her testing is *not* pathological. She is able to give it up after a period of trial. Only when, is spite of her efforts, she is still accepted (only when the therapist can continually tolerate the pressure of her challenges), will she relinquish some of her defensive fears.

As just mentioned, ambivalent women have difficulty with intimacy. Although they have been married for an average of four years and state that spouse is the most important person in their lives, they routinely test him in the same way we have just described, and seem to distance themselves from him and from significant others. We stated above that this fear of intimacy was a representation of an unconscious fear of the power of the uncontrolled regressive tendency. Tracing this tendency back once again to the earliest unsuccessful resolution of pre-oedipal issues of separation/individuation, I hypothesized that ambivalent women seem to be structurally arrested at the pre-oedipal level.

If we are correct in the conclusion that a developmental arrest occurred at the pre-oedipal stage, we have some insight into why this woman seems to be able to think about children only as infants. That is, she apparently never felt intrapsychic validation beyond this infantile stage. She therefore, cannot conceptualize a relationship between child and mother at any later stage of development. Evidence of this pre-oedipal developmental arrest may come up in various ways throughout the treatment process. It will, of course, be apparent in the transference, in the patient's need to assume the dependent and symbiotic role. In this phase of the transference, which Kohut labels the mirroring transference, the individual repeats the primitive situation, in which she looked for total, unequivocal admiration and acceptance.[6] In the initial efforts she was disappointed. The treatment situation gives her a second chance. Kohut describes three distinct forms of the mirroring transference, which he sees as a progression from the most primitive form of merger to individuation, and then gradually to separation. As the self grows and progresses in its capacity to sustain an internalized aspect of positive, good, dependable reflections, it gradually is able to tolerate the withdrawal from the maternal object, which this progression implies.

I believe that the pre-oedipal developmental arrest will also be apparent in a much more overt fashion, that is, in the individual's intellectualization in regard to child development. I found that the ambivalent woman finds comfort in the avoidance that this defensive position permits. In fact, she is a pro at this exercise. It takes great vigilance on the therapist's part, not to be taken in by this diversionary tactic; we must try to keep her on task, try to help her focus on why she needs to indulge in excess verbalizations about infant and child development, about child-care facilities, about colleagues who have infants, etc. This intellectualization is a retreat from affective contact with the issues, as well as a way of avoiding confrontation with the concept of children who grow up, and who are no longer infants.

The tendency to intellectualize about children was apparent in sessions with both members of the couple, not just the woman alone. In fact, here may be a clue to why the ambivalent woman continues to claim that she has the major responsibility for the childbearing decision, and that spouse has only veto power. Although she talks (endlessly) as if the decision is hers, by allocating the ultimate decision to spouse (in effect, of course, that is what the veto is), she is actually saying, "I really will not decide. I will talk about it, but defer the actual decision to spouse."

In treatment, as the woman begins to drop her need to intellectualize, she may recognize that to defer to husband—that is, to say he has veto power—is tantamount to deciding not to decide. When both members of the couple engage in this kind of avoidance, we recognize that there is a collusion in their wish not to decide. The literature on those who elect to remain childless describes this as a stage which is common in those who ultimately decide to remain childless.[7] The couple seems to progress through a series of postponements until they begin to feel that it's "too late." However, the woman who comes into treatment, recognizes (perhaps only un-consciously) that she can become active; that she can grow and put herself back into the decision. She does not have to remain the helpless bystander.

The treatment goal is to help her understand the decision process as it actually is. That is, if she wishes to defer the decision, it should become apparent to her. To allow it to go unexamined, is to risk the emergence of anger directed toward the spouse for making the "wrong" decision and, on some level, anger directed at herself for engineering the "wrong" de-cision. In treatment, she may or may not decide that a joint decision is appropriate. For instance, some situations might demand that she make the decision for both partners. Regardless of the dangers which I see as inherent when one member of a couple is the sole decision maker, the individual woman must be free to consider such an option. I believe that the oppor-tunity to consider this question is important in terms of relieving the conflict she is experiencing.

As the ambivalent woman begins to address the question of responsibility for the childbearing decision, she must deal with the nature of her rela-tionship to spouse. She will then confront the issues of intimacy. We are aware of how difficult it is for the narcissistically oriented person to develop an intimate relationship with another. She fears intimacy out of the prim-itive fear that to get too close is to risk rejection; to become too intimate is to risk losing oneself to the power of the other. Intimacy is equated with rejection and regression. However, given the safety of the therapeutic re-lationship, the fear of intimacy and the fear of regression may gradually diminish.

Related to the issue of intimacy are problems in relationships with au-thority figures. More specifically, ambivalent women seem to adopt a counter-dependent position, which reflects their fear of intimacy. However, this position interferes with their successful functioning, both personally and professionally. They are resistant to the dependency inherent in a re-lationship to an authority figure. Yet, we found that they are forced, due to some pressures that are probably unconscious, to constantly seek out a relationship with a dominant authority. As we said, they are caught between their wish and their fear of intimacy. The counter-dependent position is a reaction formation, a defense against the fantasy of rejection. To state this dynamically, the sought after, idealized, infantile dependency, which was not acceptable to mother, becomes unacceptable to self.

We noted that ambivalent women defensively employ denial, intellec-tualization, passive-aggression, and a externalized, hypomanic and artificial stimulation of their environment. These defenses must be explored as they become apparent within the clinical situation.

In the next section, we analyze issues arising from pre-oedipal and oedipal outcomes. I also suggest a few of the symptoms which I believe we are likely to see in the ambivalent patient. She may enter treatment feeling an unbearable pressure stemming from her anxiety about her inability to reach a decision. At the same time, she may also be depressed, feeling weighed down by the conflict that the childbearing decision uncovers. Of course, as I said earlier, she may have displaced these conflicts onto other aspects of her life, especially to issues of marital conflict, job stress, or family discord.

Pre-Oedipal and Oedipal Issues

The most important new finding in this research concerns the relationship between pre-oedipal and oedipal outcomes and the adult childbearing decision. I believe that the lack of a satisfying resolution of the pre-oedipal and oedipal constellations affects the adult woman's desire to have children. The ambivalent woman describes herself as having been "chosen" by father, but does not feel any sense of confidence in her mother's love. You will recall that six out of the eight women in the ambivalent group regard themselves as either rejected or loved only on condition that they met their mother's needs. This was related to the later ambivalent identification with nurturance as a self-concept. The women who felt they were not fully acceptable to mother were conflicted about their adult identification with nurturance. In dealing with these issues clinically, it is necessary first to establish whether or not the individual subject is actually arrested pre-oedipally. If so, the therapeutic task will be to try to go back with her to certain aspects of this level of development and proceed in a reconstructive fashion. Although this is viewed as a long term process, it is important to recall that some developmental tasks have already been satisfactorily accomplished. Therefore, although I believe that the difficulties are traced back to the early insufficiently individuated self, it is not a self without some cohesive strength. This self, as we said before, has some stability. Although there is a characteristic temptation to split off undesirable self objects (including ideal objects and actual self objects), the individual usually manages to contain these impulses. For example, we have seen the split of parental objects into the all good, idealized father vs. the all bad, mirrored mother. This split is followed by the self split into the all good, externalized self (modeled on a fantasy of interactions with father, in which the woman feels confidence) vs. the all bad, internalized model of the experience with mother, which leaves her feeling lost, helpless, and terrified. Most of the time, the external, confident self is supreme. It is only under certain kinds of stress that the splitting takes over and she becomes vulnerable. The situation we are considering—that is her felt need to reach a childbearing decision—obviously provides the kind of stress that sends her into a regressive freeze.

Let's retrace the major conclusions in terms of the outcome of the primitive situation vis a vis mother. I have noted that most of the ambivalent women report that they never felt acceptable to mother and never felt that she loved them unconditionally. All their lives they were engaged in a continuous struggle to "finally get it right." They wished to please mother; wished to do whatever they could to win her over. But they felt that it was a hopeless task, since their entire lives had been invested in this same struggle with no success. At various phases in her life, other people (e.g., the therapist) assume the mother's role. That is, in various life situations, the ambivalent woman attributes to others the powerful ability to render her helpless. This dilemma leaves her in a rage; or rather we should say, this dilemma begins with a sense of rage, followed by a sense of guilt at the emergence of the aggressive self. We have said that in the primitive position, there was apparently a less than optimal resolution of an early phase of the lifelong separation/individuation task. Consequently, the infant established what I termed a pre-mature autonomy. She appeared to mother, and perhaps experienced herself, *as if* she was capable, *as if* she had established a sufficient sense of stability, *as if* the self was ready to begin its path toward autonomy. However, we found that this self was not ready. This infant, who behaved *as if* she could manage the first terrors of separation, actually could not. She never completed the first separation between self and object. The expected trial with separation which is normally followed by the bliss of reunion, never took place, either because mother would not allow it due to her own (mother's) psychological impairment, or because the infant could not accomplish it. The result of this premature separation, premature autonomy, is that she never felt the joys of rapprochement.[8] She never felt safe in the required return to mother. She never experienced a certainty that her wish for reparation would be acceptable. The turning away from mother was too soon; she was not ready. This lack of a satisfactory period in which to consolidate the infantile narcissistic capacity for self love, inhibits the later capacity for self-esteem and self-confidence. The required period of grandiosity, of experiencing the world as entirely one's own, had come to an abrupt, and inappropriate end. In the clinical setting, the grandiosity emerges in the transference situation. The opportunity for growth then becomes available once again. This time, hopefully, the outcome will be different.

How do I substantiate my conclusions? You will recall that throughout the data presentation, I have used the words of the subjects to present both their conscious and, wherever possible, their pre/unconscious ideation. Their responses served as the basis for my notions regarding the formation of a premature autonomy, and the lack of a fully satisfying early period of stable experimentation with separation. How often did we hear the words

" . . . I keep trying to check it out with her . . . I always worry about pleasing her . . . all my life I wanted to please her, but I couldn't figure out what to do . . . I can never do enough . . . Even to this day, I hold my mother responsible for my needing to work this way, work too much . . . I guess I'm still trying to get it right." The ambivalent woman needs to be perfect, in order to be perfectly loved; to be totally, uncritically accepted. Her need is to have the "perfect" self represented, mirrored, by the object. In the clinical setting, the object is the therapist. The adult need for perfection is a continuation of the infantile grandiosity, reflective of the primitive undifferentiated (infant) self/mother dyad. Given the evidence at hand, we are in a position to know that this is the primary orientation of the ambivalent woman at the stage we are considering. We remember the words Marlis used: "She needed me to be perfect, and now I need that for myself . . . "

The ambivalent ego develops, we have said, without a fully integrated, fully cohesive structure. We saw that the ambivalent woman characteristically tends to split off the bad part object, thus disassociating herself from the aspect of self that felt dissonant. This splitting mechanism, which continues in adult life as the inability to regulate self-esteem, arises from the earliest inability to integrate both good and bad aspects of the infant's environment (internal and external). As a result, this ego is not able to maintain its equilibrium in relation to both good and bad objects. We see this individual continuously, almost compulsively, devaluing, splitting off, that aspect of herself that she regards as unacceptable to the significant other (representation of self at this point). Boundaries between self and other become blurred and undifferentiated. When she tries to consider childbearing, we know that the anxiety level is way up. I see the anxiety as evidence of the psychic tension, which reflects her need to simultaneously identify with and reject the split off, bad (maternal) self object. It is due to the blurring of a distinction between self and other that the anxiety feels so destructive. The anxiety also reflects the guilt that emerges at this point. She feels a pervasive sense of guilt toward her failure to be what mother needed her to be. She blames herself, but is also enraged that she has been rejected by mother. She is terrified (guilty) because of the power of her rage toward mother.

The anxiety that the ambivalent women experiences reflects another consequence of the splitting off of unacceptable aspects of self. I refer to the fact that the ambivalent woman is not able to test reality in an appropriate fashion. She appears to undermine the reality of her accomplishments, which we have described as a defense against the actual overvaluation of herself. It is employed unconsciously to fend off a challenge to the fantasy of perfection. This basic characteristic is evidence of her narcissistic orientation. She looks constantly for the perfect self, and needs to feel reassured by the existence of the perfect self. At this stage in her development, however, no one, not self, spouse, nor anyone who matters, can supply this reassurance. Kohut has described this situation in very explicit and helpful terms. Talking about pathological narcissism, he says, " . . . there is a fusion of ideal self, ideal object and actual self images as a defense against an intolerable reality in the interpersonal realm . . . In their fantasies, the patients identity themselves with their own ideal self images in order to deny normal dependency on external objects and on the internalized representation of the external objects."[9] This situation will emerge in the transference and may be the first major treatment crisis. That is, after the expected entry phase (because she is accustomed to being the "goody two shoes" we expect her to try very hard to be the "good patient" and act in a superficially compliant fashion at the outset of her relationship with the therapist), she will seek to continue her pattern of denial of dependency, continue the devaluation of a perceived powerful other, try to fend off fears of rage and aggression against the rejecting other, and will again encounter the unsatisfying resolution of the pre-oedipal situation. In a repetition construction, through the mirroring transference reaction, she will look to the therapist to recreate the "perfect" self object, which is the representation of the (infantile) self at this point. Although acceptance by the therapist is critical, the wish for perfection represents a repetition of the primitive split and must be guarded against. When this wish is frustrated, the ensuing rage, if properly handled, will allow her to begin to work on the underlying developmental deficits.

Masterson has said, " . . . in my experience, the mother's defective mirroring springs from a specific emotional withdrawal, because this specific child is expressing his/her own unique self or grandiose exhibitionistic self. This expression interrupts or frustrates his/her resonating with the projections the mother has placed on the child in order to shape him or her for use as an object essential to maintain her own intrapsychic equilibrium."[10] Here Masterson indicates the way in which mother has rewarded the infant's regression. The need to be unconditionally loved takes precedence over the individual's need for growth. The task in treatment is to rework this situation in order to prevent a repetition of the destructive regression. (Remember, such a regression is the pathological outcome, which we use as a frame of reference. It is unlikely that the ambivalent woman will regress to this extreme position.) We can recognize how very difficult it will be to change this pattern, since the patient has already indicated that she will do anything and everything to win mother's love. If the condition for love is regression, it is little wonder the developmental process has been arrested.

For this reason, I have recommended that the woman be seen in individual treatment first, followed by conjoint marital therapy. She will not be able to utilize marital treatment until she has worked through the depressive position, which has been the consequence of the failure in the early relationship with mother. In marriage counseling, some progress might appear on the surface in terms of, for example, a better understanding of the unspoken marital contract, etc. However, unless she has developed the structural stability, unless the fractured and faulty self-concept has been repaired, it seems unlikely that any long term gains can be accomplished. Furthermore, if she states that her objective in treatment is to reach a decision about children, then I believe nothing can be settled until the underlying structural deficit is encountered. For this individual the self-structure is at risk. The self-concept is frail and vulnerable, searching constantly for external verification. On the surface, however, she is functioning quite well, is successful and achieving, and is satisfied with herself most of the time. But, as we said before, this external self is experienced as a shell; as empty, lonely, and isolated. The ambivalent woman is afraid that it will be discovered for what is really is (i.e., afraid that it will be "found out").

As we begin to appreciate the pain that the "empty shell" self-concept implies, we have a partial explanation of the reason why relationships are experienced as superficial rather than intimate. We know the ambivalent woman fears that the inside of the shell is empty, void, and meaningless (equated with death). As one subject said, "I was afraid that no one (here this can be read as mother) would accept me if they really knew me." The shell image, protection for the external, sophisticated, successful partial self, protects against intimacy. To permit intimacy is to risk being known. To be known is to risk rejection; better to be superficially accepted than to chance rejection.

In treatment, the "fear of being found out" is excruciating. Although the patient needs to be known, she fears it. She may recognize that without such knowledge and without the empathy she craves, she will be unable to resolve her conflicted dependency struggle. Yet she is terrified of allowing another to penetrate the shell of isolation. This emptiness is a narcissistic defense, a false position, which allows her to devalue both external and internal objects. She needs to devalue such objects to reduce the pain and anguish she feels in envy of the fantasied, perfect other.[11]

As we said before, we can assume that she will devalue treatment and will resist each turn toward intimacy. Careful interpretations, directed toward helping her understand the underlying dynamic objective of the devaluation of the therapist, will gradually enable her to tolerate the emergence of the dependency relationship. Kernberg has said, " . . . this resistance to treatment illustrates the intensity of the narcissistic patient's need to deny any dependent relationship . . . "[12] As the patient begins to relinquish her omnipotence, we can anticipate that depressive symptoms will emerge. However, by this time, the therapeutic alliance will have been solidified, and so even if she temporarily feels the impulse to leave treatment (act out) in order to avoid the depressive experience, I doubt this will happen.

I believe that what we will see in treatment is that the patient assumes both her own and mother's position. Mother expected the patient to continually meet her needs. In turn, the patient felt constantly frustrated in that mother did not meet *her* needs (for perfect, unequivocal acceptance). Now, in treatment, the patient will reenact these demands with the therapist. The patient will look for perfect mirroring, in order to re-experience infantile grandiosity and omnipotence. Only in frustration of this (transference) wish/fear for merger (which may precipitate some acting out) will the therapist be able to begin the process of helping her to differentiate self from object. Perfect mirroring will not be available, as of course it wasn't originally. However, we hope that this time the individual will tolerate the fear and frustration, rather than regress into the earlier depressive position. On the other hand, if such regression becomes apparent in treatment, the opportunity is now available to rework the previous, unsatisfactory outcome. This depressive position, which represents the infantile fear of abandonment, threatens to reoccur with each developmental opportunity for separation and individuation. Let's consider, for a moment, parenthood as a developmental stage. We have said that the inability to tolerate self as separate, prevents the ambivalent woman from wishing to identify herself as mother. Now we have established a dynamic basis for this unconscious ambivalence. One aspect of the fear of motherhood is the fear of a return to the abandonment depression. I speculated before that, if carried to the extreme, this fear of abandonment represents the fear of death. The literature on the psychology of pregnancy, and on the intrapsychic changes that take place during pregnancy, also refers to the fear that childbirth is equated with death.[13]

The ambivalence regarding the need to be dependent vs. the fear of dependency, also relates to the conflict surrounding the adoption of a nurturant self-concept. Nurturance requires that the individual be able to respond, without conflict (both psychologically and behaviorally), to the dependency needs of another. Earlier I suggested that the mother of this ambivalent woman was unable to provide such a model for nurturance. It has been observed[14] that parents of narcissistic personalities often appear to have been cold, rejecting figures, whose marginal tolerance of the infant was based on the infant's ability to satisfy some aspect of mother's own deficient intrapsychic structure. The infant, who, at this stage is totally omnipotent, totally invested in self, and unable to distinguish between self and other, comes to internalize this rejecting object as rejecting self. It is rage against this previously denied rejection (repressed and avoided at all costs) that now, as an adult, emerges in the effort to confront one's self as would-be nurturer. The question again is, how can one nurture, when one is still thrashing about intrapsychically in pursuit of nurturance?

In the therapeutic situation, the individual must re-experience her rage and must begin to allow the aggressive impulses, which had been repressed, to emerge. This will happen within the transference relationship. This does not imply that she will evolve into a nurturant position. I have concluded that, for this individual, there is a confusion between "perfection" and nurturance. We know that she felt she could only receive mother's love (nurturance) on the condition that she was "perfect." It was clear to her that "perfect" meant meeting mother's needs—mother's dependency needs. How confusing. Once again, there was a merger between self and other (mother). This time, merger issues constellate around dependency needs. We can expect to see confusion between "me" and "not me". Although perfection is associated more with the "not me," than it is with the narcissistic "me," it remains blended into the concept of nurturance. We hope to enable her to distinguish between this idealized "perfection" (which Kohut described as the fusion of ideal self, ideal object, and actual self) and nurturance.

I want to make it clear that we do not have, as a treatment goal, the objective of converting her energies into nurturant services. Rather our goal is to create the environment in which she can resolve the internal dilemma regarding identification with nurturance. Our goal is to help her replace the omnipotent and destructive fantasies, with ego-syntonic goals and purposes.[15] For some women, this will allow the subsequent identification with nurturance as a self concept; for others, the outcome will be satisfaction with rejection of nurturance.

This confrontation with issues of nurturance will permit another aspect of the ambivalent conflict to emerge. Underlying issues relating to sexual identity frequently infuse the conflict re nurturance. Let us take up these issues here.

Sexual Identity

This brief discussion of sexual identity issues relates only to the dual-career women whom I have described in this book. This is not a discussion of the wide range of issues relating to sexual identity, which are brought into the treatment situation by patients.

In Part II I described the development of a feminine identity which contained two separate aspects: sexuality and nurturance. I found that women who were planning to have children were comfortable with both the sexual and the nurturant elements of their self-concept. I also found that women who intended to remain childless, identified themselves as sexually female, but rejected identification with nurturance. Finally, we said that women who were ambivalent about having children, were ambivalent about nurturance, but identified with sexual femininity.

I found that ambivalent women never felt an unconflicted acceptance in the earliest phases of their sexual development. That is, that did not feel acceptable to mother, the model for female sexuality. Therefore, even though I found that all ambivalent women idealized father, identified with him, and felt that they were his "chosen one," thus receiving oedipal validation of self as sexual, this did not result in an adult unconflicted identification with the maternal model of femininity. They continued to question identification with nurturance (the aspect of femininity identified with mother) although they did accept sexuality (the aspect of femininity identified with father). We remember that the ambivalent woman's identification with father felt tantamount to betrayal of mother. The oedipal nature of this conflict has been discussed. Beyond that, however, the "betrayal" may have been in some way confused with, equated with, rejection of sexuality. This is not the usual oedipal outcome, which seems to be related (for some women at least) to the development of a feminine self-concept which includes both sexuality and nurturance. My belief is that confusion developed in this case because daughter remained invested pre-oedipally, and could not fully incorporate the sexual affirmation offered by father's acceptance.

We heard the ambivalent women talk about themselves as "different." By "different" they meant, in part, not the same as other women, and perhaps, not quite female. In their stories, we hear examples of the way that the self as different suggests to our subjects a self that is non-female, implying that somehow to be female was less desired. Many women reported that as children they were tom boys. They said that at a very young age they discovered that boy's games were more fun and boy's toys more challenging. (Remember the picture of Barbara who wanted a mechanical truck for Christmas and was disappointed because mother gave her a doll?) Even as young girls, they discovered that men held the power in society. Given the climate of the late 50's and early 60's it's not hard to imagine that for these girls growing up, to be female may have seemed secondary.

As our ambivalent subjects were growing up, father served as the model. It was father they wished to emulate. They learned, became verbal, and tried to separate from mother, all in observation of father's behavior. On some level, it seems quite possible that they may have wondered if their identification with father meant they were assuming a masculine identity. The expected childhood experimentation with bisexuality may have become confused with a masculine identity. Especially for women whose ambivalence cannot be resolved, the underlying issue may be a questioning of female sexuality, female identity. Although indications of predominantly masculine orientation were not apparent in any of the subjects in this study, in treatment, a further opportunity to examine the meaning attached to sexual identification might be useful.

The adult ambivalence toward childbearing may tap into this early, denied identification with aspects of one's masculine self. Childhood ambiguities about sexual identity raise guilt feelings in the child, which we can assume remain untroublesome and untouched in the average adult female. In treatment, however, the guilt will reemerge, as the individual comes closer to the sources of her ambivalence. She is vulnerable to her own doubts concerning her sexual identity. She confuses her questioning of maternity with a rejection of femininity, because she, like most of us, has not separated nurturance from sexuality. As I said before, it is fundamentally important for us to recognize that nurturance and sexuality are in fact, two distinct functions, neither one dependent on the other. In therapy, the individual will have the opportunity to examine the fear that she will become less sexually female if she rejects maternity. This fear is accompanied by guilt, because those aspects of self that she finds the most rewarding, which as a child she fantasized as making her like father (her dominant, achieving, successful, independent self), are precisely those which we know are labeled masculine. She feels guilt in the pleasure she takes from being masculine. She feels guilt in the pleasure she takes from not being like mother.

Early in the development of sexual identity, one feels internal (and external) pressure to reject the contrasexual opposite aspect of one's evolving sexual self. The young girl's developmental task is to reject (temporarily) the masculine aspects of self in order to develop as feminine. In treatment, the objective is to allow the ambivalent patient to become comfortable with both masculine and feminine aspects of self; to recognize that she does not "give up" her externalized, achieving self in order to become nurturant. Neither does she give up her sexually feminine self if her decision is not to have children. Since the original emergence of these sexual identifications was engulfed in guilt, we know that when they come up again in treatment, once again they will be infused with guilt.

In working through feelings of guilt related to sexuality, the treatment process focuses on aspects of the early relationship to mother and father. I have found that ambivalent women are very much in touch with some of their feelings of guilt re mother, but are much less so re father. For example, they expressed concern that even their delay of childbearing would be interpreted by mother as rejection.

The nature and extent of the underlying rage and guilt vis a vis mother, will emerge as the individual gradually begins to deal with her conflict with mother. In other words, once she can relinquish some defensive manifestations of the pre-oedipal conflict, once she has stopped intellectualizing about the pros and cons of becoming a mother and actually begins to identify with the issues, she will face a series of critical questions. For example, on the conscious level, she will wonder if mother will become more loving, more accepting, if she, too, is a mother? We saw an example of this wish in the projective response that Lisa gave to the MTAT portrayal of two women and a baby. Lisa saw in this situation a possibility of rapprochement. However, she concluded that such an outcome was not possible. On the other hand, if she decides to reject maternity, how will mother react? Will mother assume that daughter is rejecting her as mother? Rejecting her as model? Although we recognize that on an unconscious level such rejection may support her wish for revenge against maternal conditional acceptance, in all likelihood such wishes will be vigorously repressed. On the overt level, any manifestation of these wishes will feel very frightening for our subject.

A goal of treatment is to enhance the ambivalent woman's capacity to acknowledge and deal with her ambivalence toward mother. If this can be accomplished she will be in a stronger position to confront her feelings about children. However, as long as she continues the battle vis a vis mother, the childbearing decision will feel like a part of the same issue.

Toward the final phase of the oedipal period, there is a stage in which the daughter, having "won" father, would be expected to assume an identification with feminine sexuality in pursuit of her fantasy of taking over mother's functions. In order to replace mother, she has to become more like mother. To become more like mother, she must come to know mother and to identify with mother's femininity. Once again, her task is to confront the maternal object. Knowing her capacity for splitting, for projection of the negative content, we assume that as she approaches mother, she will experience rejection and once again, will be disappointed. By now we know what she does. She blames herself for not being "perfect." If she had been, mother would be accepting.

The clinical task will be to allow the early sexual fantasies to emerge and be integrated into the newly consolidated self structure. In the original phase of sexual development, we suspect that the sexual self may have felt as inadequate, as much an "empty shell", as the other aspects of self. As an adult, this patient may experience her ambivalence regarding childbearing, and her questions regarding her nurturant identity, as a threat to her fragile sexual self-concept. Insecurity about the sexual self may lead to a generalized and chaotic uncertainty about the stability of the larger self-concept, which has evolved over her thirty year lifespan. It will be important for her to explore the parameters of this uncertainty, in order to form an integrated sexual identity. Her sexual identity, like the self-concept of which it is a part, cannot generate the vitality it needs in its current, "fragile shell" state. It will be as if the sexual self must be allowed to reemerge, and to be reworked in the adult. When this individual, who has acted as if she was autonomous, finally becomes aware of her dependency, she may begin to question all aspects of her persona. We know that her sexual identity will be on her agenda.

As she comes to grips with her ambivalence regarding nurturance, as she clarifies her struggle with identification with the maternal model, and confronts her ambivalence re mother, we suspect that she may become anxious and quite possibly, depressed. She is challenging very fundamental aspects of herself when she asks, can I be sexual and non-nurturant? We have addressed the theoretical aspects of this issue previously. Thus, when it appears in the clinical setting we will be aware of the nature of the challenge it presents to the sense of self, and allow the patient to work through her conflicted feelings in a carefully supportive, but neutral environment.

Defenses

The diagnostic question early in treatment is whether or not the structural deficits I have outlined are apparent in the patient. If so, the treatment is difficult, probably long term in nature, and demanding scrupulous attention to the narcissistic vulnerability. Although she is hardly disabled, in the sense of exhibiting a narcissistic personality disorder, she does manifest narcissistic symptoms. By treating the underlying narcissistic orientation, and continually interpreting the narcissistic vulnerability, we will gradually help her uncover the earliest deficits in the self. As I mentioned, the critical therapeutic posture will be to maintain an awareness of the ambivalent woman's extraordinary sensitivity.

To recapitulate, the goals of treatment are to help this individual develop the capacity to separate self from object. In treatment, we will help her confront her need to be perfect and her need to split off those objects (self, ideal, and other) that threaten her fantasy of perfection. Masterson has written an extensive case history of a patient who said, "perfection was my protection."[16] We hope to help this woman let go of her protective shield. In the process, the fear of the destructive power of the other will gradually decrease and the ability to trust both self and other will increase. Slowly she will be able to tolerate both good and bad aspects of the self and to consolidate them into an integrated unit. We hope to help her develop the ability to give up her overwhelming conviction that her self value can be authenticated only through the mirroring (validation) by an external object in whom she invests this power. She must replace the fantasies of omnipotence with an ability to test reality with some degree of accuracy. In relinquishing her grandiosity, her infantile omnipotence, she will set the stage for the development of self that is experienced as more than the current "empty shell." This emptiness represents a false cover and is a way of maintaining the devaluation of objects and object representations. Once the shell is given up, once she no longer is subject to the destructive fear of being found out, the individual becomes more real, and becomes capable of loving another more fully.

We can anticipate that, as developments occur, the individual may experience an increase in depression and anxiety. The defenses she typically invokes—intellectualization, denial, and a hypomanic acting out—can be expected to emerge as she struggles to come to grips with issues of intimacy, dependency, and autonomy. The ambivalent woman's hypomanic stirring up of the environment can be viewed as a way to defend against intimacy. She maintains center stage and feels the stimulation of being noticed, admired, and acclaimed for her achievements, yet she does not have to risk exposing her inner self. She is able to maintain the "shell." She stirs up events, as I noted in Chapter 7, out of her need to maintain a degree of superficiality. She engenders a continuous reshuffling of peripheral relationships. Yet, fortunately, we remember that she does not do this with her primary relationship. With spouse there is apparently no longer the need to keep up the manic type superficiality. When we have come to the point in treatment where the ambivalent client is no longer defending against assuming an intimate or dependent position, she will have developed a more comfortable, less conflicted intrapsychic environment in which she may consider the decision about childbearing. The underlying fear of intimacy and the conflict re dependency seem to be very closely related to the fear of the infant/mother attachment. When she is no longer totally enmeshed in her own struggle with her relationship to mother she will be in a stronger position to deal directly with the reality of the decision process.

Initially, the ambivalent woman was unable to tolerate depression, and interpreted anxiety as stemming from her failure to be "perfect." With the increasing stability and cohesiveness of the self, however, the depressive reality will become tolerable and perfection will be recognized as unavailable.

When the ego has begun to manage separation/individuation without the overwhelming fears of regression, which had been so pervasive for this individual, it becomes possible to feel a confidence in one's ability to tolerate separation. The boundary between self and other becomes more explicit. I believe that the experience of separation must be established prior to a realistic contemplation of nurturance as a self-concept. I also believe that without the ability to think of oneself as nurturant, childbearing will be extremely conflictual. As the ambivalent woman begins to relinquish these destructive defenses, she will then be able to allow her spouse to assume a more realistic share of the decision process. If they do not develop a shared decision, I believe that the chances are good that the relationship between the couple will deteriorate.

Let us assume that the dual-career couple decides to have a baby. This child is not going to be born to a single parent. It is the couple's child. They will jointly raise the child. The changes she anticipates in her work life, in her career development, and in herself, are going to be inherently different than those of her spouse. Yet the psychological environment of becoming parents, and the attitude toward the sharing of parenthood are formed at the very moment the decision process is seriously begun. It seems to me that if a woman excludes her spouse from this decision it will have a disastrous impact on their basic marital system. Although, it is true that her life will change the most, this is not at issue here. At issue is her response to these changes, her attitude toward self and spouse, the fears she may have as she anticipates the changes in their life which childbearing necessitates.

As we begin to consider the ambivalent woman's feelings about spouse and about the balance of their relationship, we must shift the focus of treatment from the individual to the couple. I believe at this point it is advisable to move into conjoint marital therapy. In Chapter 11 we look into treatment issues and clinical strategies for dual-career couples who are conflicted about whether or not to have children.

REFERENCES

1. Kernberg, O. *Borderline Conditions and Pathological Narcissism*. New York: Jason Aronson, 1975. p. 257.
2. Kohut, H. *The Analysis of the Self*. New York: International Universities Press, 1971. Masterson, J. *Treatment of the Borderline Adolescent: A Developmental Approach*. New York: Wiley-Interscience, 1972.
3. Kohut, *The Analysis of the Self*.
4. Ibid. Bernstein, D. Female Identity Synthesis. In *Career and Motherhood*, edited by A. Roland and B. Harris. New York: Human Sciences Press, 1979.
5. Ibid., p. 95.
6. Kohut, *The Analysis of Self*.
7. Veevers, J. E. Life Style of Voluntary Childlessness. In *The Canadian Family in Comparative Prospective*, edited by L. Larson. Toronto: Prentice Hall, 1976.
8. Mahler, M. S. *On Human Symbiosis and the Vicissitudes of Individuation*. New York: International Universities Press, 1968.
9. Kohut, *The Analysis of the Self*. p. 231.
10. Masterson, J. *Treatment of the Borderline Adolescent*. p. 22.
11. Kernberg, O. *Borderline Conditions*.

12. Ibid., p. 245.
13. Williams, J. *Psychology of Women*. New York: W. W. Norton and Co., 1977.
    Also see:
    Bibring, G. et al. "Considerations of the Psychological Processes in Pregnancy." *Psychoanalytic Study of the Child*. 15 (1959) p. 113–121.
    De Beauvoir, S. *The Second Sex*. New York: Bantam Books, 1952.
    Slater, P. *Footholds*. New York: E. P. Dutton, 1977.
14. Kohut, *The Analysis of the Self*. p. 254.
15. Ibid, p. 107.
16. Masterson, J. *Psychotherapy of the Borderline Adult*. New York: Bruner/Mazel, 1976. p. 75.

11
TREATMENT ISSUES
FOR AMBIVALENT COUPLES

In Chapter 10, I stated that the woman who is ambivalent about her decision regarding children would benefit from an opportunity to explore some of the intrapsychic aspects of her ambivalence in individual psychotherapy. I believe that she will be unable to reach a truly satisfying decision as long as she remains trapped in the conflicts stemming from early developmental deficits. However, as she increases her ability to drop some of the defensive maneuvers that have clouded her childbearing decision thus far, she will be able to enter into a more genuine evaluation of her feelings about having children. At this point (as indicated in the last chapter) the therapy should move into a conjoint marital modality.

I approach the treatment of marital issues from a systems orientation. In marital therapy we have three patients: the wife, the husband, and the marriage, or, as I am labeling it, the system.[1] We have said that dual-career marriages that feel most satisfying to the participants reflect the belief, strongly held by each partner, that the synergism created by the interaction between the two individuals allows each of them to be more powerful, more effective, happier, more loving, more creative, more energetic, more thoughtful, etc., than either one of them could be alone.

As we think about a marriage as a system, we become aware of the way in which pathological outcomes, as well as those just described, are also reflective of the interlocking forces created by the system. Therefore, we must keep in mind that so often in treatment of couples, although one person is identified as the patient—the one who carries the symptoms, the "sick" one—this is an inaccurate and misleading description. If we undertake therapy with the individual woman (or man) as the first phase of treatment, caution needs to be taken not to buy into a splitting phenomena, where one member of the couple is labeled the good healthy one, and the other the sick one. The system is maintained, or disintegrates at times, in reflection of how these roles and tasks are assigned and managed by the couple. As we proceed, we will explore the way the dual-career marriage allocates resources, strengths, symptoms, defenses, and responsibility for growth. Our task is to help the couple recognize when, and hopefully why, this allocation has become rigid, stuck—not growing, not developing—and help them create the environment in which change can take place.

In my research with dual-career couples, which included those who were deciding about children as well as those at later family stages, I found, as have other clinicians[2], that although they do not describe themselves as deliberately setting out to establish a new norm, these couples most certainly encounter a host of new marital issues. Perhaps, a better way to state this is that along with all the very complex tasks involved in making a marriage work, the dual-career couple adds a new set of issues. The system they create is inherently different from their parents'. Unless these differences are understood, and confronted if they are disruptive, it is my firm belief that the marriage system will suffer.

As throughout this book, the focus in this Chapter continues to be on the dissonance associated with the inability to reach a satisfying childbearing decision. What I have discovered in getting to know the people presented in this book is that the stress connected with indecision about children, that is, the difficulty experienced by those in the ambivalent group, was different from the stress experienced by other married couples, and different from the other dual-career subjects. For those in the baby group, anxiety was associated with their need to evolve from an autonomous couple—very protective of their boundaries, very invested in their own and each other's work, and in the interaction between them—into a system that was flexible enough to respond positively to the introduction of a child.

Stress for those in the group who did not plan to have children seemed to be related to the newness of their decision—that is, their break with tradition—and to the conflictual demands and pressures related to balancing career vs. relationship. As can be imagined, the decision to remain childless, to depart intentionally from the socially sanctioned pro-natalist orientation of our culture, adds a heavy layer of stress for Group C. Pressure comes from all sides: from parents who frequently interpret the decision not to have children as an indictment on themselves as parents; from family members who may want the family name to continue; from friends who have children (who may want others to validate their decision); from colleagues who may be responding—perhaps jealously—to the competitive edge that they themselves relinquish as they take time out to have children. Many issues make the lives of those who decide not to have children difficult, and make therapeutic intervention useful at times. However, as we have said so often, it is the ambivalent couple who have exhibited the greatest anxiety, and who are dissatisfied with the conflict they experience, although they may or may not relate this conflict to their inability to reach a decision about children. They are the subject of this discussion of treatment issues.[3]

The primary goal of the treatment which I will discuss is to bring the ambivalent couple to the place where they are satisfied with their childbearing decision. It is not to help them (or persuade them) either to decide to have children or not to have children. (That may be a significant countertransference issue, however, which we will address in Chapter 12). In order to do this, we must deal with the conscious and unconscious system that the couple has in operation. As we begin to work toward a fuller resolution of intrapsychic conflicts on the part of each individual member of the couple, we will also hope that the systemic conflicts can be addressed. In the process, we will help them identify the blocks which have thus far worked against their stated desire to settle the childbearing dilemma. The task is to assist them in being able to tolerate the anticipated challenges to the intrapsychic and interpersonal structure.

The reader will recall the childbearing decision model (see Chapter 4) that I developed in order to understand the complexity of the process of trying to reach a satisfying decision about whether or when to have a child. Now we return to this model, and explore treatment issues and intervention strategies which can be based on this framework. We will examine the four separate interacting determinants of the childbearing decision: intrapsychic determinants, marriage determinants, career determinants, and lifestyle determinants.

In my work with dual-career couples, I have found certain characteristics which seem to be present in couples who are satisfied with their marriage. These so called "successful" dual-career couples have developed a stress management system and a working interdependence which I think will be useful for the clinician to consider in planning the treatment with the ambivalent couple. Advice from dual-career individuals, including some in the ambivalent group, will be included in order to gain some insight into how those closest to the situation evaluate the critical elements for success.

We will focus on the hidden agendas, the unspoken issues, the unconscious elements that operate all the time in a marriage (and perhaps in other important relationships as well). In marriages that are growing and feel satisfying, these hidden elements often work toward the continuing stability and functioning of the system. On the other hand, in marriages that are conflictual, the hidden issues foster dissonance and quite possibly, destruction of the unit.

One final introductory comment deals with the advisability of co-therapists vs. a single therapist. Having worked with a co-therapist in conjoint marital therapy, both in treatment of individual couples and with a group of married couples, I believe co-therapy creates a constructive environment in which to help a couple deal with their difficulties. How often we have heard couples talk about their inability to get their partner to deal directly with them. How often the conflict seems to stem from misunderstandings which arise out of a faulty system of communication. They don't seem to be able to talk and/or listen. In treatment with two therapists, ideally a female/male team, the patients have a vehicle for working through their transferences (maternal and paternal) as well as for observing a working communication system. A team of co-therapists can provide a model that demonstrates how each partner can be an individual, who can at times disagree with the other, without destroying the relationship or their mutual respect.

DUAL-CAREER CHILDBEARING DECISION MODEL

I found that the dual-career childbearing decision evolved out of an interaction between the following elements:

1. Intrapsychic determinants, especially those arising out of the early relationships to mother and father, and certain personality and identity factors.
2. Marriage determinants, e.g., stability, level of satisfaction with emotional and domestic support.
3. Career determinants.
4. Lifestyle determinants.

I think it is helpful to use this model in planning the treatment of the childless dual-career couple who present themselves as being unable to reach a decision about children. Each of the determinants can be used to identify separate treatment issues.

Intrapsychic Determinants

We have already talked about the treatment of the individual woman, who may or may not have identified her ambivalence re children as the presenting problem. In some cases, it may also be useful to see the husband individually, to help him work through the defensive layers which may inhibit his ability to consider the childbearing issue. (Obviously, a full understanding of the issues related to his treatment are equally important, although we cannot take them up here.)

At this point, let us assume that the couple comes in together and we begin conjoint marital therapy. I believe that at the very least, the couple must develop an increased sensitivity and understanding of their patterns of intimacy, dependency, autonomy, and separation. Regardless of whether they are able to develop insight into the dynamic origins of their adult positions, they must confront their current psychological situation, their current responses. However, the more understanding of early processes and outcomes, the better our current chances of conflict resolution. The therapist's ability to formulate a psychodynamic analysis of the etiology of their position is critical at this point, since it is my belief that the adult child-bearing decision is directly affected by the outcome of early intrapsychic processes affecting intimacy, dependency, autonomy, and separation.

The defensive structure of each partner, the way they manage stress, their idiosyncratic approach to perceived threats to the psyche as well as to the marital system, and the way they respond to intimate demands by the other, will affect the couple's management of the decision process. The interaction between the couple—in effect, the transferences between them—will illustrate individual defenses, strengths, and vulnerabilities. Observation of these processes will help the therapist understand the characterological positions and developmental problems of each individual, and aid in the formulation of a treatment approach. For example, I have said that the ambivalent woman displays a vulnerability, an instability, in reflection of the fragile nature of the self. You will recall that I traced the origin of this vulnerability to the unsatisfactory resolution of the primitive relationship with mother. How does this get acted out vis a vis a spouse? Does she become overbearing and dominant as defense against her fears? Does she act in a passive-aggressive, manipulative fashion, reflecting the same underlying deficit? Is her (or his) vulnerability going to be transformed into a competitive syndrome; into a depressive position? Does her wish and/or fear re children mask her struggle for intimacy, for emotional support from spouse? In other words, does she look to spouse to resolve the ongoing struggle with mother? Does she assume the symptoms associated with ambivalence as her unconscious acceptance of herself as the "problem"? Why does she, why do they, tolerate the disruptive elements in their system? What needs does it serve? As we work toward clarification and understanding of these questions, especially in terms of how they affect the interaction between the wife and husband, we are in effect, dealing with the second category of the decision model, marriage issues.

Marriage Determinants

The data from this study indicate that unless there was confidence in the long term, ongoing stability of the marriage, the issue of children would be put aside. Lisa said, " . . . If I could be confident that ten years from now we'd still be married, I might feel differently. But I can't say that for sure.

I don't know . . . and I feel so terrible saying this . . . '' Therefore, as I see it, in the early stages of treatment for this couple, we must focus on the marriage system itself rather than on whether or not they will have children. Consciously or unconsciously, couples may use their ambivalence or disagreements about having children as a defense against confrontation with underlying issues basic to the marital relationship. We must guard against missing (colluding with?) the more primitive forces at work.

At the outset, as the couple begins to clarify the conflict issues, treatment often focuses on the marriage contract, which probably has been unspoken and hidden. Whether explicit or not, however, it is this contract that determines the balance of power in a marriage, regulates the couple's sexual relationship, determines the management of support systems, and ultimately results in feelings of equity or inequity. Rice, who has written about treatment for dual-career couples has stated, '' . . . the goal in marital therapy with dual-career couples is the restoration of a sense of equity in the relationship . . . ''[4] He describes equity as more a concept of fairness than of equality. We know, of course, that fairness is a highly individual concept. What matters is that the partners agree on what is equitable. The definition of what is fair can't be a unilateral notion. The treatment task is to work with the dual-career couple to enable them to identify the unspoken elements of the contract. Hidden agendas, sometimes known to both partners on an implicit, but unacknowledged level, will emerge during the course of treatment. As they are exposed, they will need to be managed gently, so that neither partner bolts. We'll come to a case that illustrates a hidden agenda shortly.

As the marriage contract becomes clear it may need to be renegotiated. Obviously, the ongoing, four-year marriage is not the same as the initial, perhaps unrealistic fantasy. The support—emotional and practical—that each partner needs and expects from the other may very well have to be reworked after the honeymoon is over. As Jane said, '' . . . I finally realized it's crazy to think that if he "really" loved me. he'd know what I'm thinking, he'd know what I want. I found out it's much better to say what I mean. I've got to use the words, rather than build up these walls.'' Every clinician who has ever worked with couples can recognize the truth of Jane's insight. But in treatment it becomes painfully clear how difficult it is to "say what I mean." First, of course, the individual must be able to identify the affect, need, idea. If she's had some individual therapy, she'll have a head start here. She also has to be able to share her understanding with her spouse. These two elements—to know what you mean and to feel safe enough to share it—require first, that defensive maneuvers be kept at a minimum, and second, that the couple shares a confidence that intimate, private, even painful feelings are acceptable and will be respected, even if they depart far from one's own feelings.

As the couple begins to consider how their relationship will change with the introduction of a child, they try to anticipate how they will react toward each other when the other is not the exclusive love object. The initial marriage contract assumed only one intimate relationship. Contemplating the addition of a child forces the couple to relinquish this exclusive relationship to each other and to alter their intimate boundaries. This alteration was often very difficult to envision, and for some couples, felt absolutely impossible. Others, however, felt an almost irrational resistance to the notion of having to give up what they called "playing house." That is, in spite of the complexity and pressure of having to adjust their lives and careers to each other, the couples displayed (or wished for) a certain playful quality in their relationship to each other. But they were afraid that having children would challenge the possibility of playfulness. Having children would force them to accept responsibility and would change them into adult mirrors of their parents. Very rarely do children think of their parents' marriage as playful. You will also remember that we heard Alyssa say that having children made one old. It is reasonable to expect that this transition—from young to old, from playful to serious and responsible, from exclusive concentration on each other, to sharing the other with a demanding third person—will come up in the course of treatment. In fact, I found that these issues often provided material for the excessive intellectualization characteristic of the first stage of the decision process. I believe that these are important issues, but we must be careful not to allow the decision process to be sabotaged by an inappropriate concentration on these transitional questions.

From the research on dual-career couples we know that issues of competition and power and control are to be anticipated. Little wonder—we have two high achievers, two strong personalities, two success types, two superstars. Feelings related to professional competition may well affect the woman's childbearing decision, especially if she feels that by taking time out she has to "give up" her career dreams. We know from her case history, that she and spouse started out on a similar success track. If she feels that she's to be the only one to make significant changes, she may well feel angry and conflicted toward spouse. Even though on an intellectual level she deals with the issues directly, we have to help her manage the underlying competitive feelings vis a vis spouse as well as toward colleagues, other women (mother) at the childbearing stage, siblings, and of course, the therapist.

Another issue we can anticipate relates to the power that the individual attaches to her or his ability to generate an income. The need to relinquish this income (and its implied power), which many women anticipate as part of their childbearing "time out," feels like a threat to the balance between partners and to their lifestyle.

In treatment we need to help the couple identify and articulate their Dream. We must keep in mind the differences between primary orientation to the Relational vs. the Individualistic Dream. (This was discussed at length in Chapter 9.) In therapy it will become possible for each or both partners to confront their Dream, to understand it, and even to alter it, if that seems appropriate.The way this is handled by each person is instructive. Do they each have a hidden Dream—a fantasy of self which the *other* partner was intended to make possible? In traditional marriages this expectation, described as the vicarious identity syndrome,[5] referred to the situation wherein the wife's sense of self was determined by the husband's achievement and status. As the couple considers having children, the need to encounter the Dream, hidden or explicit, becomes critical since the child will dramatically alter the conditions of their relationship. In the dual-career, non-traditional marital system we would expect that each spouse's Dream might very well differ from traditional adult masculine and feminine Dreams.

Interestingly, it has been found that dual-career women frequently revert to traditional roles at home, regardless of how non-traditional they are professionally.[6] They seem to want to preserve some aspects of the traditional female role. Sometimes it appears that this is an unconscious wish, since many dual-career women consciously complain about the perceived domestic inequities. The important issue here is not how they share domestic tasks, but how they feel about their system. I remember one woman telling me that she knew her spouse would never share the ordinary child care responsibilities, since he wouldn't even share responsibility for the dog. Whether or not this was a good predictor of his parenting behavior, by dealing with this in therapy his actual intentions could be made clear. It became apparent that this one outburst reflected her general feeling of anger at his irresponsibility and represented her reason (justification?) why they should not have children.

In Chapter 9, I presented an illustration of the way in which an individual swings between polarities of the Individualistic and the Relational Dream. As I said, in marriage counseling there are three patients: the woman, the man, and the system; thus, there could very well be many separate Dreams. In treatment, we need to help the couple sort out their Dream priorities and help them confront the need to balance their Dreams. I have come to recognize that frequently, underlying resentment festers around the fear that one's private Dream will have to be sacrificed to the Dream of the system. If the anticipated child represents the Dream of the system, and the career represents the Dream of the individual, unless there seems to be a way to manage these Dream priorities in sequence, one Dream will feel like a threat to the other and will result in conflict, fear, and resentment. When this fear is dominant in the psyche it is little wonder that dissonance erupts.

I use the term Dream to represent the ideal self in the future, as well as a way of organizing one's view of oneself at the moment.[7] These orientations fluctuate throughout the course of an individual's life. In treatment, we help the patients clarify whether or not their energies are focused in a direction that is consistent with their Dream. It may be that they are actually sabotaging themselves. For reasons of which they are possibly unaware, they may be working to undermine their Dream. If they come to understand that the anxiety they are experiencing reflects an unconscious attempt to thwart their overt Dream, we have begun to get to the origin of the ambivalence. It is possible that the experience of anxiety is the symptom that can lead us to the dynamic source of the conflict.

For some patients, treatment provides a safe setting in which to explore the fit between their current persona and their Dream. Some will test out the new persona that they must create in the course of developing an altered Dream. This is what the ambivalent task is. It is to examine the ways in which they will change as they alter their Dream, their self-concept. Their present Dream, which is probably a career Dream or, as we have labeled it, the Individualistic Dream, will have to make way for the Relational Dream if they are to be satisfied with the decision to have a child. Is this possible? Is this consistent with their intrapsychic position? Is this apt to lead to dissonance, or will it allow them to grow and to develop the way they would like? These are the issues to be confronted in treatment.

The couples who plan to have children seemed more flexible than the ambivalent couples. In addition, you will recall that I found that the Group B women saw themselves as more flexible than their spouses. It may be that in treatment, some of the rigidly held positions can make way for this apparently critical flexible self-concept.

The way in which each partner experiences her or his own Dream must be consistent with the way she or he envisions the marital Dream. If these are not consistent, there will be dissonance as the individuals apparently move in an autonomous direction, regardless of the needs of the marriage.[8] This is not to say that one Dream or another may not take precedence at different times in the course of the marriage. Rather that the couple has worked out what they regard as a system of equity, which allows each to pursue his or her own Dream without violating the goals of the marriage. In order to do this they must have developed a sense of interdependence.

Interdependence.   I have referred many times throughout this book to the need for the dual-career couple to develop an interdependent structure.

Interdependence allows each person to be both dependent and independent without fearing that intimacy, closeness, and dependence on each other will lead to a loss of autonomy, loss of self, loss of individuation, and ultimate engulfment. The dual-career couples I described in Chapter 1, who seem to have developed a satisfying balance between their own needs and the needs of the marriage, demonstrated this kind of interdependence. I found, in these so called "success" couples, a kind of synergy which enabled each individual to become more as a member of the couple than they could if they were separate. However, as long as either partner remains unable to relinquish some aspects of their autonomy in the service of the marriage, to attach some psychic energy to the needs of the other, it seems to me that they will have a very hard time in managing the temporarily selfless state required in the early stages of parenthood. Therefore, another treatment goal is to help facilitate whatever level of interdependence is appropriate for that particular couple. Again, the goal is not to help them elect to become parents or to remain childless. I believe that the correct goal is to bring them to the point where they have the capacity to make such a decision. Unless they have an interdependent system, I do not believe the necessary capacity is in place. The data on which I base these beliefs have been given throughout this book. Again, let's hear what the dual-career subjects regard as critical for success. Lisa: "At the beginning, have some clear understandings and honesty and communicate about it . . . that is, really talk honestly, even before the wedding. Discuss where you are going in your career. Then keep communicating about it on a regular basis. That is something that we failed to do, and that hurt us. You have to know what you expect from marriage, and we never talked about that. We assumed it . . . but we should have said it. That still is taking a lot of time, a lot of time . . . I don't know. I tell myself if we got divorced that I would not remarry. That doesn't mean that I haven't enjoyed it. It's just that some people shouldn't be married, and I think I am one of those people. I catch myself being very mad sometimes, about what I need and am not getting . . . and about what he takes away from me . . . I don't like to be so dependent on him, and I don't like him to be dependent on me for all these things either . . . " Having had a chance to know something about Lisa, we recognize that her dependency issues stem from her ongoing separation fears. We remember Lisa's fear that she could never trust mother, although she craved the stability of maternal acceptance. Now she repeats this situation with her spouse. She fears his dependency as well as her own. How can she realistically consider assuming a mothering role given this basic fear? She believes she is stuck. Her ambivalence reflects the developmental incompleteness, the lack of successful individuation.

Diane had a list of requirements for dual-career success. She said first that you need to be "enormously supportive of each other . . . You need to decide to communicate and keep communicating. You need to coordinate everything . . . This is very important because there is no one to do the back up things, like the cleaners, etc. It's not automatic, you have to plan and decide who does what, or you will become angry over unimportant things. You have to train yourself not to let things bother you, or if they do, you have to talk them over. Mainly, I think, you have to have a sense of commitment to the marriage first. But I have found that I want to be able to depend on him. I want him to depend on me, too. I like that sometimes, I just don't want the feeling that I can't stand alone if I wanted to or that he can't." Diane's statement that "You have to have a sense of commitment to the marriage first" is very important. The marriage has to come first. This was the orientation of every couple who described their dual-career marriage as satisfactory. We have identified another treatment goal. The couple needs to examine their commitment to each other and to the balance in their relationship, before they can seriously engage in the decision about children. Diane's words reflect not only the priority she attaches to their relationship, but also illustrates the kind of interdependence that I believe is critical to a satisfying dual-career system.

After the initial stages of treatment, when the spoken and unspoken marriage contract has been clarified, and if necessary, renegotiated, we will be in a better position to understand the defensive structure the couple has developed. Then we can identify the way the couple allocates their resources, their individual and combined strengths, as well as their regressive tendencies. The defensive structure, which can be adaptive as pointed out in the earlier discussion of defenses, also helps to illuminate the hidden agendas upon which the system is based.

Career Determinants

It's not hard to understand how difficult it is for dual-career types to think about making major career changes. So much of the formulation of their adult sense of self is based on their professional identity and economic independence. Now, as they begin to consider alterations in their identification with their work, they are confronting their basic self-concept.

Let's review a few of the many career elements that affect the couple's childbearing deliberations. Many women felt that unless they waited until they were at a sufficiently high level in their professional career, they would be unable to return to work after having a child without having to start all over again. However, I also heard from other women that it was because they were at such a responsible position, because they had so many people dependent on them, because they were in a critical position, that they could in no way consider taking much time off. Obviously, we need to understand the importance attached to this issue of career responsibility by the individual and by the spouse. It certainly seems possible that this kind of issue could serve as defense against some other less acceptable motivations.

The nature of the organization, the political climate, and the attitude toward women, especially professional women who elect to become mothers, all bear directly on the flexibility the individual feels she has in making a decision about career changes necessitated by having a child. Certain women, such as those in academic careers, who have a built-in system for sabbatical, found the scheduling of extended time out much simpler than others who worked in less flexible environments. However, regardless of the nature of their profession, I found that the women in the baby group seemed to be the most willing to consider making career changes, either changing positions in order to, for example, travel less, or changing their hours from full to part-time, or even changing fields entirely. The women in the baby group did not believe that such changes would dramatically alter their pursuit of professional goals. I found the difference between this somewhat relaxed career orientation and the more intense, inflexible orientation of those in the ambivalent group, to be quite dramatic.

Another career issue that the couple will need to confront has been referred to before as the general issue of competition. Women who resent the fact that their career must change but their spouse's will not, and who are angry at him because of their sense of losing the competitive race, have grounded their inability to make a decision more on the relationship between self and spouse than on the elements of change which accompany the arrival of a child. In treatment, they have a chance to confront their competitive feelings, and sort out what each partner is doing to maintain the conflict in terms of the focus on individual career growth.

A Series of Losses.   As I worked with these women who were struggling with their inability to feel comfortable with career changes, I recognized that the decision to have a child and to alter their career path was experienced as a complex series of losses. First, as we have said, there was a threat to loss of self since so much of the self-concept was developed around a professional identification. Remember Julie (B) who said that she didn't think she'd be an interesting person if she wasn't working. These women saw themselves as career women. They had established this self-concept long before they met and married their spouse. If this was to change, how would they know themselves? How would they feel about themselves? Who would they be? How would they relate to spouse and to the other important people without this career persona? These questions bring us to the next anticipated loss, the threat of loss of balance in the relationship. They had formulated their original partnership based on two equally dominant careers. The fear of many ambivalent women was that they would become less significant to their spouse, would lose out in terms of his respect (a projection?), if they stepped out of the professional world and into the domestic one. This fear may be a reaction to the mother who appeared dissatisfied with her own life and with her own choices.

We also know that the loss of income is important to dual-career women on many levels. Obviously, the couple needs the money in order to live the way they do. In addition, we have seen that the ability to generate a significant income has been equated with the assumption of power and with the ability to share or, in some cases, control important marital decisions. Therefore, the woman who believes that she "sacrifices" her chances of earning a significant amount of money if she takes time out for a baby, may begin to blame the spouse for this loss of power.

Finally, the decision to take a professional leave of absence may be experienced as a loss of friendships and colleagues. Although we have noted that the number of significant mentoring relationships was very limited, and that intimate relationships were difficult to form, we nevertheless found that our subjects valued their interactions with colleagues and worried about the loss of shared experiences and professional stimulation. These losses, which subjects feared as threats to self, to the marriage, to power (income) and to relationships with colleagues, will emerge as career changes are contemplated. They need to be considered honestly and directly by both members of the couple.

Lifestyle Determinants

You will remember the picture we drew of the lifestyle of the dual-career couple. Because their income was based on two good salaries they had already acquired a relatively high level of material stability. These couples had, for the most part, become accustomed to living in a fashion very similar to the one they recalled from their childhood. They were used to taking vacations, to free weekends, to going out to dinner whenever they chose. They enjoyed their spontaneity and their ability to make last minute social plans. At the same time, because they were so dedicated to their work, professional tasks often took up what otherwise might have been personal time. But this use of free time fit in with their scheme of a satisfying lifestyle. As they looked at friends who were having children and recognized the stress their friends were experiencing, their own free lifestyle felt very precious. The research on new parents confirms what they saw; new parents report the highest degree of personal and marital stress when compared to any other married group.[9]

As dual-career couples begin to evaluate their feelings about having children, in terms of the changes they will have to make in their lives, they seem to go through two distinct and different phases.

Two Phases in the Decision Process.   In another study of dual-career issues[10] I found that couples seemed to progress through two distinct stages in their decision about whether or not to have a child. The first stage was a highly intellectualized discussion, for example, of alternate methods of child-care, or of theories about what happened to the child's development when parents were professionally preoccupied. Some couples dwelled on the possibility that either she or he would have an irresistible career opportunity that would require a move to another city, and then what would they do? Sometimes the politics of their professional life took up so much of their energy and discussion time that questions relating to children never had time to come up. Almost anything, e.g., work, family, vacations, living arrangements, or money management, could be used in this kind of avoidance process. I found that the couple, or perhaps only one member of the couple, used this kind of intellectualization as a defense against confronting their fear of making any fundamental changes in their relationship. In the treatment of the couple who are at this stage of the decision process, it is critical to allow them to air their fears in the security of a non-threatening, neutral, non-decision framework. That is, they need to be able to confront these fears slowly and carefully without feeling any pressure to deal prematurely with anticipated realities. They need the time, they need the security, and they need to hear each other accept their individual and mutual fear. They may need help to tell each other how they anticipate their lifestyle and marriage will be altered, possibly destroyed, by the fantasized child. They need to talk about jealousy and about their competitive feelings re the unborn child. They need to confront their own, probably unconscious, need to remain the child. They may need time to work through their dread of loss of self and the fears they may have of the return of infantile terrors. These are primitive, possibly unconscious, and certainly vaguely formed fears, often hidden behind the intellectualization, submerged under the theoretical verbiage. However, since we know that this couple is so good at intellectualization, we are aware of the likelihood that they will attempt to sabotage treatment through this device. I am reminded of the way that Barbara and Jim, when I first met them, avoided confronting their feelings about children by talking endlessly, without direction, and certainly without reaching any increased awareness of the real nature of their ambivalence.

One of the advantages I see in dealing with the childbearing decision within the therapeutic setting is that given time and safety, and help in talking about what feels very threatening, it's likely that the couple will gradually manage the transition to the next stage of the decision process. It is important to help the couple work through the issues that serve as a core to the intellectualization. There are very real, very difficult situations to face, changes to make, shifts to allow. For example, there is no "ideal" day-care system; there aren't handy back-up relatives waiting to pitch in; the job really won't stand still; their relationship to each other will be changed by the presence of their child.

In treatment we can help them move into the second stage of the childbearing decision in which they actually begin to consider these ideas, deal with these fears, and begin to integrate the anticipated relationship to a child into their current affective system—into their private, seclusive, intimate world. In this stage, they start to deal with reality, or rather, with a host of separate realities; the reality of how they will change as individuals, change toward each other, and change toward their extended families; the reality of career changes; of lifestyle changes. They can then begin, more directly, to sort out their contradictory feelings and their conflicting images of the future self. At this stage, couples often feel the need to explore a future that does not include children. This lurks in the background of every case of ambivalence, and is useful to bring out in the open. The task is to help them experiment with a self-concept that is not parental. As we noted before, increasing numbers of women have stated their intention to remain childless. When they begin to explore this notion, all sorts of fears are set in motion, which they need to have the time to examine. The rebelliousness—the contradictory life course it represents (contradictory to parents, of course)—feels very threatening to most people. The basic question they ask themselves is: Are you really normal if you do not want children? They ask: What will we miss, if we don't have children? The old myths about requirements for maturity get stirred up as the couple begins to explore their feelings about this choice.

If the couple comes into treatment with true ambivalent feelings about their wish to become parents—that is, if the childbearing block is not invoked in order to avoid other underlying marital issues—they must have the freedom to fantasize about what their lives would be if they did not have children. Should they miss out on this phase of the decision process, a question will remain in the psyche (a kernel of resentment), which we have the opportunity to examine at this exact moment in the treatment process. This is also a good way of helping move the process from an intellectual exercise into a realistic confrontation. In order to know if a couple presents a case of true ambivalence, we need to focus as clearly as we can on the hidden agendas, on the secrets underneath the presenting problem, the secrets which are so difficult to discern.

In more ways than we can identify, smokescreens are erected by individuals and/or by couples in treatment as a way to avoid dealing directly with powerful, but unacceptable underlying impulses and issues. At times, as we've said, these hidden issues operate from an unconscious level. More often, I suspect, the individual has some awareness of what's really important, but uses a great deal of energy to suppress these feelings, thus acting as if other issues, behaviors, and/or symptoms, were more critical.

HIDDEN AGENDAS

The following are just a few of the issues we can anticipate as part of the dual-career hidden agenda list:

1. *Reluctance to Refute the Pro-natalist Bias.* Some women talked as if they believed that the social bias in favor of children did not influence their ambivalence about children. Yet, hidden under the layers of external self-confidence and the projection of independence, I heard the fear that somehow their reluctance to follow the so called "normal" adult path was a violation of what they "ought" to do. Although the new dual-career pattern and their career orientation was also somewhat different from the life of their mothers and grandmothers, so far, they were not departing significantly from mother's model of adulthood.

We heard some subjects say that they could quickly reach a decision regarding childbearing were it not for all the other things that kept cropping up in their lives. Marlis, we remember, offered a perfect example of this kind of thinking. Many times she said that her education, then her career, and then her lifestyle, were things she could manage as they came up, but not children. She then went on to talk about what the pressure to have children was like; the way those who do not have children seem to be outside the mainstream, to be missing something, etc. Marlis believed that this was her mother's message. Children are the critical issue (marriage was not). Marlis was caught up in the social pressure (which she labeled mother's message), which told her that women should want to have children, should want to complete this natural aspect of their development, etc. We have explored some of these issues in terms of the intrapsychic processes and outcomes they reflect. Unless clarified, they can form a barrier which inhibits the ability to formulate a satisfying decision. But Marlis is unable to confront these issues with any vitality. She poses under her confusion, and believes that children are "what she cannot manage." For Marlis, the hidden agenda is her inability to confront mother, to deal with mother's message, and to deal with the pro-natalist pressure.

2. *Wish to Retaliate Against Mother.* The temptation to retaliate against mother and to be different from mother are both related to the childbearing conflict. To choose to be different from mother, to tease self and mother with this possibility, can appear as a hidden, secret pleasure, which the individual may be unaware of. In therapy, when the underlying resistance has been even partially moved aside, the individual may be able to see that the retaliation actually impacts on her life to a much greater extent than it does on mother's. I have found that both husband and wife may share some of this secret wish—may collude in the way they act—out of their need to be different from the parent. If such is the case, it is important to work through this problem.

3. *Career or Parenthood? "You Can't Have Both!"* Commitment to one's career, the value attached to one's career identity, and a reluctance to alter a career path (a path which has led to external acclaim), often lurks as a hidden agenda. The career, which is the external representation of the self for so many of the women we studied, has also served the spouse as a way of defining himself. If this is given up (so the self talk goes), what will be left? The unspoken fear surrounds the unknown outcome of putting aside a tradition that says women can have *either* a career or parenthood, but not both. There are no ground rules, no experience to help evaluate the future, to know what might happen if the traditional pattern is changed. The individual is at a loss, feels incomplete. However, this feeling is not allowed to surface immediately. The individual fears that revelation of the importance of one's career identity will be labeled selfish. How often did we hear this fear. Yet, there is the accompanying fear that, as Louise said, " . . . maybe children are something I don't want to miss out on . . . maybe children are a part of life that I don't want to miss."

4. *Resistance to Change.* Though a marriage may appear chaotic to the therapists and to other outsiders, frequently such a system stays in place through one or both partner's resistance to change. In some way, possibly destructive, the needs of that individual or those individuals are met through the disruption. Such is the case with Katie and Dan. Their marriage was painful to both of them. But each, in her or his own way, participated in a continuation of the patterns that cemented the dissonance.

Katie and Dan: An Example of a Hidden Agenda

Katie and Dan are both 30 years old. They have been married five years and have no children. The following material is based on a series of assessment interviews, in which the couple were seen by a team of co-therapists.

Katie, an R.N. working at a large metropolitan hospital, is currently enrolled in a graduate program in nursing administration. She has worked for the last eight years, and says that she's finally beginning to feel confident about herself as a nurse. She says, " . . . I've always loved nursing, but I used to be scared all the time. I guess I think finally, this is something I can really do right." Katie is the second in a family of ten children. She said that although she tried to do what mother wanted, and idolized her father, she felt that neither parent ever had enough time for her. She recalls that as the oldest girl, she was given a great deal of responsibility for the younger children, and she thought of herself as very competent, very responsible, and very conscientious. Today, when she thinks about her childhood and youth, she is somewhat resentful about having to be so "good" all the time, but in general, remembers her early life as satisfactory.

Dan is currently unemployed. For the last five years he's been working in personnel, mostly on a commission basis. Gradually, his income dropped lower and lower until last month he decided (after much pressure from Katie) that he had to look for something else. He says that he hated to leave the field he was in. He had enjoyed the work and said that he regards himself as an extrovert and interested in all sorts of things; and those are the qualities you need for that business. He's finding it very difficult to start over again. Even though he had worked in the career search field, he said it was hard to apply his theories to himself. He was also reluctant to talk to his former colleagues about his problems. Dan's family background is quite different from Katie's. He is the second of two children, raised by a doting mother and aunt. His father died when he was about seven years old. He says he has few memories of his father. Aside from father's death, he says that he had a great childhood, was very active in sports, had lots of friends, and belonged to many clubs.

Katie and Dan's marriage has been stormy. They met while they were both in college, and it was an on-again off-again romance for several years. When they decided to marry, Dan was already employed in the personnel field, and Katie had been working at a hospital for a few years. Their combined income was quite good, and they both felt they had made a very good beginning. After two years in the city, they bought a house in the suburbs. Katie: " . . . I kept saying that the house was too big an investment for us, and that we were going to get in trouble making the payments. But Dan really wanted this, so we bought it. Now I know it's too hard. Now that Dan has lost his job, I know we won't make it."

About a year ago, Katie contacted a therapist, stating that she was thinking about getting a divorce. She had become more and more aware of her anger at Dan, and of her feeling that she was the only one who cared about paying the bills, keeping the lawn mowed, and keeping up with home repairs. She stated that Dan was always " . . . off playing on his baseball league, or bowling, or playing football. Lately, he's been staying out really late to drink with his friends.'' She said that she and Dan were arguing almost every day, their sex life was terrible, and Dan was drinking too much. Katie refused the therapist's suggestion that Dan come in with her. She stated that she didn't want to deal with him in a treatment situation, but only wanted to talk about how her life would be if she went ahead with the divorce. The only issue she appeared ready to deal with was her fear of losing the house, which she said was due to Dan's financial irresponsibility. She felt she was the only conscientious one. Katie decided to work out a system of separate bank accounts. Against the therapist's advice, she withdrew from treatment at that point, because she felt somewhat better. She agreed to contact the therapist again should problems arise. Six months later she called stating that things were coming apart in their marriage. This time she agreed to come in with Dan, and a series of assessment interviews with a team of co-therapists was arranged. (Note: original therapist was not one of the team.)

Katie and Dan are both tall, attractive, and well groomed. Katie has a rather serious, almost angry expression on her face most of the time. Dan maintains a pleasant, friendly demeanor. They are both articulate and above average in intellectual functioning. Neither one has a history of psychiatric problems. Katie started the session: "Dan was drunk last week, and got a DUI. They called me from the police station. It cost us a fortune, and I can't stand this any more." Dan, looking rather sheepish and watching Katie all the time, said that he knew he'd been wrong and knew he was drinking too much that night. He said, " . . . I was really feeling lousy . . . I'd been talking to my old friends, but I couldn't tell them abut my job problems. So we just kept drinking, and I guess I overdid it . . . ''

As their story unfolded, it appeared that Dan had had an affair about two years ago. Katie was unable to forgive him. She was angry at that, angry at his apparent inability to get a job, angry at him for convincing her to buy the big house, angry at him for playing baseball, angry at his drinking, angry at everything he did. At first, Dan said he was unable to understand why they were fighting and arguing. As he became more comfortable in treatment, he began to talk about his resentment that Katie had assumed the management of their lives. He began to recognize that he thought of her as a parental figure. She was his mother, his aunt, and all his school teachers. She was judgmental and angry. He said that he found it very difficult to believe that she loved him, since she was always in a rage at him. When he talked about his old affair, he said that he thought he was running away from Katie, not looking for another woman. However, he went on in a rather pressured manner to say that he now had a plan for a new job, and was working on an idea with a friend which would lead to a "really good spot," and that Katie should just give him a little time to get himself straightened out. He was sure he'd get back on his feet. Dan talked at great length about his plans, about his friend's reliability, and about how this time it would be different. This sent Katie into a rage. She said, in tears, "You've told me that so many other times, I don't believe you any more. I can't wait for you to grow up. You know how I feel about having kids. It's going to be too late, and I'll be too old."

There it was. The unspoken fear. The hidden agenda. Dan's reaction was interesting. He looked surprised, as if he'd never heard this before. He said, "I don't know why you say that."

In the course of further sessions, the childbearing theme was repeated many times, in different ways. Katie would only talk about children when she was feeling defenseless, and would act as if he was solely responsible for the fact that she didn't have children. Dan would never deal directly with this issue, but would either slip into an endless dialogue about how to raise children, or would act sullen and hurt. Each partner kept taking on different roles. Dan was alternately the helpless child, unwilling to take a back seat to another child; then he'd become the drunk, the irresponsible wild person, who wanted to tell the world where to get off; then he'd be the macho male, critical of Katie's bossiness, needing to be independent and free, and refusing to think about changes. His poor self-concept, and extreme vulnerability to criticism became more and more apparent. He revealed that he had been frightened of Katie when they first met, convinced that he could never be good enough for her. Now, he said that he knew his early fears were well founded. He could never please her; he could never be what she wanted.

Katie, too, assumed many different roles. At times it was apparent that she really enjoyed her feeling of superiority, her dominant role in the marriage. She was proud of her ability to be the only income producer, proud that she could pay the bills, and proud that she could do what he could not. She seemed to take pleasure in each reminder that she was powerful and he was weak. Her angry expression served as a constant reminder to him that he was on the wrong track. Then Katie would shift into the little girl. She pouted and cried; all the fluency in language left her, all her manipulative posturing disappeared, and she became helpless and lost.

As the issues became clarified, it was possible to see that Dan's apparent adolescent acting out (his affair, his increased drinking, his focus on sports and not work, etc.) served as a defense against a meaningful confrontation with his own adult developmental issues. As long as he was irresponsible and stirring up trouble, he didn't have to deal with the pressures inherent in an honest consideration of the childbearing decision. As long as he acted like the child, Katie could be the mother. She assumed the mother's role (or her memory of the mother's role) with ease and agility. She was able to help him feel safe, but dependent and on the defensive. She assumed responsibility for the adult functions in their marriage, and let him return to the carefree boy. Then she could become the angry mother, annoyed at his irresponsibility, annoyed at his unwillingness to grow up. Yet, he had no reason to alter his behavior, as long as she took on the mother's role. Remember, he had always been cared for by strong, competent women.

Katie was also trapped by their marital system, and by the apparent deadlock. She really didn't want to relinquish the dominant role. She really did not want to stop working, really enjoyed nursing, and really relished the power her income gave her. Although she said she wanted to have a child, she appeared to be using this as a threat; a way of intimidating Dan and keeping him off balance, rather than as a description of her genuine objective. She said she felt threatened by the thought that if she stopped working to have a child, they'd lose their house. But it was clear that there were secondary gains inherent in their apparent dilemma. They kept each other constantly on guard. She said she was the only responsible one; she thought she ran the show, yet knew she was miserable. He said he was confused, but appeared to enjoy his passive-aggressive power. As much as Katie attributed her unhappiness to Dan's behavior, and thought about ending the marriage, the system this couple had established was clearly the work of both partners. He was the baby, the child, the needy one, the irresponsible, careless youth. She was the strong, conscientious, dominant force, hardworking and responsible. She was already the parent. Neither one was really satisfied, yet neither knew how to break the cycle.

Katie and Dan both used the childbearing issue as the focus of their conflict, although that disguised the true unspoken agenda. She said that she really wanted to have a child, but couldn't risk the loss of income and couldn't take time out of her work. Yet it certainly is not clear that she was willing to alter any part of her current life. (Remember she said that nursing was finally something she could do right.) Dan believed that he'd lose her, lose his youth, and lose his identity if they changed the balance of power which was causing him such trouble. They were both colluding in keeping the issue of children out of the realm of the possible. Neither Katie nor Dan would have said that they were avoiding the issue; they said they couldn't think about it.

In planning the treatment for this couple, I think the childbearing decision model can be useful. Let's take a look at a few issues in this case and see if the model suggests a therapeutic framework.

Intrapsychic Issues. We need much more data on early developmental processes and outcomes, to know whether the hypotheses presented in this book have any relevance for this couple. However, some hints are apparent from the data we have thus far.

Katie felt she had to mother Dan. The marriage pattern is a repetition of her childhood. She told us that as a child she'd been too "good," too responsible, and too conscientious. This self-concept suggests the existence of a too harsh superego, reflecting also, an underlying reservoir of resentment against mother. This self-concept may also indicate that the individual resents children, other than herself as child, since she believes that she was never adequately mothered herself. Katie appears to be rigid, harsh, judgmental, and afraid of her own sexuality. What pre-oedipal and/or oedipal issues remain unresolved? We know, for example, that she always tried to please mother. Did she succeed intrapsychically? Did she ever feel as if mother was satisfied? We have come to recognize that unless this was the case, she probably never adequately separated from mother at the pre-oedipal stage. What about father? She idolized him, she said. We know that there was an older brother. Did the brother take the special, "chosen one" spot? Or was it hers? As many questions can be posed about Dan's early development. What was the impact of the loss of father at the start of his latency period? We are alerted by his statement that he has few memories of his father. Why not? This seems odd since he was seven years old when his father died. How did he respond to the over-mothering he received from both mother and aunt? Why does he seem to be stuck at an adolescent stage? What happened during his actual adolescence? What happened as he began to develop sexually? Did mother and aunt encourage his development or make him wish to return to an earlier, safer stage of life?

We must begin to gather some information about the development of self-confidence, sexual identity, and individuation for each member of the couple. We want to know the origins for the competitive and dominant role that Katie has assumed. And what does she gain from being so "good"? Is this a reflection of guilt about herself as child vis a vis mother? Why does Dan seem to be so afraid of her? What was the nature of their relationship before he had his affair? How do the rules of their system reflect their intrapsychic development? Obviously, we need a good psychological history, in order to develop an understanding and dynamic perspective on these individuals.

Marriage Determinants. As we begin to think about this marriage, we remember that their relationship started as an on-again off-again affair. We need to ask what made them finally decide to marry? What were some of the problems they had before they married? Why did they change their mind so often?

The initial marital contract (unspoken in this as in most cases) may have assumed that each partner would be equal. They both wanted to continue their work and both enjoyed the professional identity they were formulating. They also said that they both wanted the security of belonging to someone. (Remember, she felt herself to be lost in all those brothers and sisters.) He, because his father had died, felt the loss of a dependable male figure. Did they have the intrapsychic experience on which to form an intimate relationship?

When they first married, they both shared the same Dream; or at least they shared the words, the intellectual Dream. But we know that he wanted a continuation of the maternal dependency. She seemed too ready to fill that need.

When Katie talked about children she cried. As I mentioned before, she only brought up the subject of children when she felt defenseless, pushed to the wall, frustrated, and angry. Although they said that before they were married they had talked about having children sometime in the future, those conversations were vague. It sounded as if they had been talking abut someone else's future, not their own. Katie had said she wanted to have a family of her own. Having raised her younger sibs, she said she knew what it was really about. Yet, the language she used when she talked about children was revealing. She talked about the "burden" of children, of children as a "heavy responsibility," and of children as "something to deal with," to "manage." When Katie became tearful about children she really cried for herself as child, not for the child she wished to have. Never did she talk about children with any sense of joy or with any sense of future. When Katie cried about children, Dan felt terrible. He said that he knew it was his problem, his fault, that they didn't have the security they needed to start a family. They couldn't afford to give up her income; they were trapped. But, as with Katie, his guilt and his sadness were for himself, for the loss of self as child; sadness was associated with the anticipation of needing to give up Katie as exclusively his; sadness was associated with having to grow up.

Career Determinants.   Dan's inability to focus on a career change seemed symbolic. He didn't want anything to change. And, it seemed, neither did Katie. She told us that she finally had reached a point where she felt confident. Imagine the reluctance to "give up" this new sense of herself. For Katie, working (especially her anticipated administrative career) was an acceptable means to achieve a dominant role.

In the treatment setting we hope this couple will go beyond their apparent stalemate and begin to deal with career goals in a more realistic manner. What did he gain from staying out of work? What was the core of his resistance to using his job hunting skills in his own behalf? Katie would have to begin to envision a future in which she could combine working with parenting. Was she willing to make any changes? What would happen to her graduate study? Could she continue in her present position? Was part-time possible? How would she feel if she stopped nursing for a while? Could she consider any other kind of work? And, most significantly, could she give up her dominant role as primary income producer, at least tempo-rarily? If she did so, what would that do to the marital balance? Obviously, all these issues must be clarified and the couple must be helped to confront their feelings.

Lifestyle Determinants.   The lifestyle that Katie and Dan have created is clearly not satisfying to either one; at least that is what they say about it. They live in a state of perpetual conflict. In treatment, they have to be able to consider the ways that they each contribute to the continuation of those conflicts, and whether or not they can maintain their marital system once the conflicts are reduced. They will have to focus on marital goals, both their early fantasy and their current Dream. They need to be able to define a marital Dream that allows each to become whatever they can, with-out feeling trapped or forced into a pattern by the other. The issue here is not the house, or his job, or her anger. The issue is whether there is suf-ficient basis for a shared future. They can't confront the question of chil-dren until they believe they have a future. Until this happens, everything else is secondary.

We don't have a resolution for Katie and Dan. They are still working on it. The real question right now is whether they can tolerate the pressure of staying in treatment in order to develop the psychological climate that per-mits confrontation with the underlying, hidden agenda.

I stated earlier that I believe the critical issues to be dealt with are those of intimacy, dependency, autonomy, and separation. I believe that in con-joint marital therapy, these issues can be approached by the dual-career couple. Once that happens, they will have begun the process of creating a system that permits the development of a satisfying childbearing decision.

We have one last topic to consider in this brief discussion of treatment of the childbearing dilemma, the question of countertransference. I have found that whenever the question of having children comes up, everyone's psychic temperature rises. That includes the therapist, of course. It's im-portant to anticipate and recognize the impact of this reaction.

REFERENCES

1. See Neill, J. R., and Kniskern, D. P. *From Psyche to System: The Evolving Therapy of Carl Whitaker.* New York: The Guilford Press, 1982.
2. Rice, D. *Dual Career Marriage.* New York: Free Press, 1979.

Rapoport, R. and R., and Bumstead, J., (eds.) *Working Couples.* New York: Harper and Row, 1978.

3. For other discussions of treatment issues, see the following:
   Hall, D. T. and F. S. *The Two-Career Couple.* Reading, MA.: Addison Wesley, 1979.
   Rice, *Dual Career Marriage.*
   Epstein, C. *Women's Place.* Berkeley, CA.: University of California Press, 1970.
   Johnson, C. L. and F. A. "Attitudes Toward Parenting in Dual-Career Families." *American Journal of Psychiatry.* April, 1978, 134, (4) 391–395.

4. Rice, *Dual Career Marriage.* p. 104.

5. Lipman-Blumen, J. "How Ideology Shapes Women's Lives." *Scientific America.* 1972, 7, 107–115.

6. Rapoport, R. & R. and Bumstead, J., (eds.) *Working Couples.*

7. Gaston, C. *Women, Age 30, and the Dream.* Unpublished paper 1978. Northwestern University, Evanston, Il. Quoted with author's permission.

8. Hall, *The Two Career Couple.*

9. Dyer, E. "Parenthood as a Crisis: A Re-Study." In *Human Adaptation: Coping With Life Crisis,* edited by R. Moos. Lexington, MA.: D. C. Heath & Co., 1976.
   Cowan, P. and C. "The Volcanic Upheaval Called Baby." *Behavior Today.* November 28, 1977.

10. Wilk, C. "Midlife Dual-Career Families: Intervention Implications for Counseling Dual-Career Midlife Couples." In Cytrynbaum, S. (Chair) *Intervening in Relation to Midlife Families: Implications of Recent Developmental Theory and Research.* Symposium presented at the American Educational Research Association Annual Meeting, Boston, MA, April, 1980.

12
ISSUES OF COUNTERTRANSFERENCE

In this chapter, we focus on a few countertransference issues related to the childbearing decision, and to the possibility of an unconscious resistance that therapists may anticipate in their management of the issues presented by ambivalent dual-career women or couples. First we consider the pronatalist bias, and our own unconscious collusion with this attitude. Then we move to a discussion of the "fear of being found out," which you will recall was universally expressed by the subjects in this research and, which I have discovered, is also true of many therapists, as well. The concept of self as "different," which is related to the fear of being found out, also has implications as far as the development of one's sexual identity. The final portion of this brief discussion of countertransference issues deals with the willingness of the therapist to consider the issues related to her or his own sexual identity and with the therapist's unconscious fears of discovering more about herself or himself.

In discussing the hypotheses described in this book with other therapists, I have found that they often stirred up highly charged responses in the clinician. At first, I took responsibility for the problem. That is, I thought that perhaps I presented the material in too sketchy a fashion, or that there were not enough substantiating data, or that I appeared to be jumping to conclusions about the intrapsychic dynamics which my colleagues found unjustified. However, although I certainly agree with the need to continue to collect more data and refine the ideas I have developed, it has become apparent, in the course of more than six years of work on this topic, that some of the tension displayed by other clinicians was a reflection of their own psychological response to the material associated with the childbearing decision. Most clinicians agree that the ideal of absolute neutrality is impossible in psychotherapy. Instead, we seek to identify, clarify, and become conscious of the dynamic sources of our lack of neutrality. When we are willing to look at these countertransference issues, we can in fact become more sensitive to what the patient is probably experiencing.

Many patients who present themselves for psychotherapy, for one reason or another, do not seem appropriate for treatment by that particular clinician. When this is recognized, the standard practice is to refer that individual to another therapist or special clinic. Therapists who refer patients do so either because they feel they do not have the necessary expertise, or because they believe they will not be able to establish the necessary neutrality—the distance required to work constructively with the individual and the underlying dynamics of the case. Patients who are at the childbearing decision stage and whose anxiety arises from the conflictual nature of this position, present special problems in terms of ensuring the correct match between patient and therapist. Therapists understand this when accepting dual-career patients for treatment. The need for caution arises out of the therapist's recognition of the power of the unconscious aspects of the anticipated response to the material at the core of the patient's conflict. As we know, the countertransference reaction arises out of the unconscious identification with some element of the patient's situation. The task, as clinicians, is to increase our sensitivity to whatever unconscious processes are at work in our dealing with a particular patient. I have found, personally, that the times when I am most vulnerable to countertransference denial—that is, to an unwillingness to look at what is at hand; when I seem to allow the patient to continue in what may actually be a self-destructive vein—is when the patient is acting out my own shadow side, my own negative persona. When I find I am colluding with some behavior or affect which is actually destructive to the patient, and which allows the patient to remain blocked and fail to progress in treatment, it may very well be in reflection of my own hidden, unrealized, inarticulate wish to behave in that exact manner.

Since the issues involved in the ambivalent decision about children are apt to touch on so many critical aspects of the therapist's own development, we can anticipate countertransference-based resistance to direct confrontation of anxiety producing topics or aspects of the shadow self. Before we embark on the discussion of some specific countertransference issues, I want to repeat my conclusion that ambivalent dual-career women frequently exhibit a basically narcissistic personality orientation. We need to remind ourselves that narcissistic persons usually treat the therapist, as Kernberg tells us, " . . . as extensions of themselves . . . (therefore) the analyst's emotional experience reflects more closely than usual what the patient is struggling with internally, and thus the use of countertransference reactions is particularly revealing in treatment."[1] Therefore, the more knowledge we have about the treatment of narcissistic personalities, and the more sensitive we are to narcissistic transference and countertransference dilemmas, the better off we will be in managing the therapeutic relationship upon which this treatment will depend.

PRO-NATALIST BIAS

The more I analyze my work with women who are ambivalent about having children, the more I realize that there are two opposing biases which I probably exhibited at different times, with different women. I will describe my reactions to the women who took part in my research, in the hope that these reactions will be instructive for others who work with this group as patients. On the one hand, because I am the mother of three grown children, and regard my mothering experiences as very satisfying, my response to my subjects probably reflected this personal history. It's most likely, even though it certainly was not deliberate, that my own experiences influenced my interactions with the subjects. I do recall at times, thinking that it would be a shame if this particular person decided not to have children. I have to admit that my response may have reflected more than a sociological regret that the species would lose out if such a super-type failed to reproduce. What was I acting on? What did these thoughts represent? I believe this attitude reflected my bias in favor of having children, and was a somewhat defensive response. Regardless of the scientific interest I believe I have in studying women who elect to remain childless or who are ambivalent about having children, on some level their position is a threat to my own choice. On an unconscious level, I may very well feel challenged by them and by their rejection of my own experience. I may also be envious of some aspects of their lives, and at the same time guilty because of this envy. As a way of counteracting these pressures, of which I was probably unaware, it's possible that I moved to the opposite bias, one which appears to support childlessness. I was conscious of making an effort to be neutral. Yet, I recall taking a particular pleasure in the fact that, after all the research sessions were completed, women often told me they had no idea what my feelings were about having children. What part did my unconscious play in creating this effect? How much were they telling me what they knew I wanted to hear? In retrospect, I have to believe that I was inadvertently influencing their attitude. (You will remember that in order to counteract the possibility of bias, all protocols were analyzed by a blind reviewer.)

The therapist who does not have children, to me, seems as vulnerable to bias as I was. For example, the clinician who is around thirty years old, who has developed a self-concept highly dependent on her professional sense of self, who is working hard to create a satisfying intimate relationship, and who has not yet been able to decide whether or not she wishes to have children—in other words the clinician who is an ambivalent dual-career woman herself—will no doubt be very intrigued by the prospect of treating the ambivalent patient. Whether or not she feels she can handle the tensions inherent in such a situation depends on her own intrapsychic position, and probably on whether or not she herself has had an opportunity for treatment. Still another possibility is the therapist who may have wished to have a family (but did not do so for whatever reasons) who may be consciously or unconsciously enraged by the woman who apparently can make the choice that she or he (the therapist) was denied, but who vascillates, remains ambivalent. We can understand the clinician who, recognizing the conflict, decides to seek consultation and/or refer such a patient. A situation that I believe is actually more dangerous, however, is one in which the therapist does not recognize the need for referral. The clinician who is unaware of the degree of her or his own remaining conflict, may unconsciously try to work through this unresolved aggression in treatment with the patient. This would be unfortunate, in light of what the patient needs. Thus, I have found that there may be many elements, both conscious and unconscious, that impinge on the therapist's ability to bring a clear mind to the sessions with the ambivalent patient and avoid collusion with either a pro or antinatalist bias. The opportunity to examine oneself and one's treatment dilemmas is a critically important aspect of successful treatment with ambivalent dual-career patients.

If, as I have suggested, bias was possible in the relatively impersonal setting of the research interviews, I feel most certain that in the more intimate treatment situation, the same influences and the same possibility of prejudice exists. Therefore, the clinician has to be vigilant in monitoring her or his pro or antinatalist orientation. Obviously, the ideal is to present no personal bias at all. Since we can assume that such a position is unlikely, the next best case is to be conscious of the countertransference one brings to the treatment of the patient struggling with a childbearing decision. It's worth repeating that I do not see the goal of therapy as bringing the patients to a decision either to have a child or to remain childless, but rather to work with the patients until they feel satisfied with whatever decision they reach.

FEAR OF BEING FOUND OUT

You will recall the way I described the "fear of being found out." I discovered that many people who appeared to be so sure of themselves, so successful and satisfied, who projected an external attitude of self-confidence, actually felt as if they had to be constantly on guard, constantly looking over their shoulder in fear that someone would come along who could see them for what they actually were. That is, someone would see that they were scared to death; frightened that their inner, fragile, insecure, unworthy self would be "found out." In discussing the treatment of such an individual in Chapter 10, I considered this fear as evidence of an underlying narcissistic personality orientation. The individual has split the self-concept into those aspects of self which are good, positive, and acceptable, that is, the external aspects of self vs. those inner, unacceptable, bad aspects. The bad self which must remain hidden and which must never be allowed to emerge, contains the secret, flawed, unloved self objects.

As I stated, I have also come to recognize that many clinicians admit to having aspects of a similar fear of being found out. Although they have apparently managed to direct the energies attached to these fears into constructive avenues, at certain times, under certain kinds of stress, they too, admit to being afraid that their "cover" will be blown and that they will be seen for who they "really" are. When the fear on the patient's part begins to resonate with the fear of the therapist, what may happen is that the treatment will come to a halt. Progress in terms of confrontation with the underlying defensive structure will become impossible as long as both patient and therapist are caught up and blocked by the same experience. What might be a clue for the therapist is a recognition of having been trapped in an intellectual dialogue with the patient. When this occurs, it seems to me that a red light ought to go off, warning the clinician that some kind of collusive effort is underway which will corrupt the treatment.

We often identify with the struggle to make a decision that we ourselves have already made. I am reminded of the experience of one of my colleagues, a therapist of wide experience and excellent clinical skills. The therapist described her fury at a patient who was about to throw away an opportunity that she had worked many years for, out of her fear that she wouldn't be able to manage the pressures, that she "wasn't up to it," that she would be "found out." After we had had a chance to explore the countertransference issues underlying her response, my colleague recognized that she was bitterly resentful of the patient, because she herself had been pressured to accept similar challenges and had done so with great personal sacrifice. Part of the countertransference reaction, part of her anger, stemmed from her unfulfilled wish to have given up, to have folded, to have taken exactly the course of action the patient had chosen.

I recognize how difficult it will be for the therapist to come to grips with her/his own fear of being found out. A lifetime of effort has gone into the creation of a persona which looks secure, which appears confident, which reassures both patients and self that one can handle whatever trauma is about to be revealed. Very difficult to allow any self doubt to enter the treatment room. But, I believe, without the ability to acknowledge such an aspect of the self, the therapist who actually is afraid, who is vulnerable to the fear of being found out, remains unavailable to the person in treatment. On the other hand, the therapist who has had an opportunity to examine her/his underlying fears, and who is sensitive to the manipulation and avoidance reactions which such fears can produce, is in a position to be much more useful to the client.

SELF AS DIFFERENT—ISSUES OF SEXUAL IDENTITY

The concept of self as different allows the individual to maintain a certain aspect of grandiosity, a certain omnipotence, and a certain archaic fantasy of perfection. Furthermore, a self-concept as different allows you to believe that since you are not like most others, some of the ordinary expectations, as well as ordinary restraints, do not apply. The concept of self as different fits in well with our notion of the resemblance between a narcissistic personality orientation and the ambivalent woman.

What I found in the course of my research with dual-career women, was an almost universal acceptance of the concept of self as different. These women thought they were different from other girls growing up, different from other women their age, different from some colleagues, and from previous cohorts of women at the childbearing decision point. Most frightening, because it was accompanied by an additional fear of invoking rejection, was the ambivalent woman's concept of self as different from mother. Along with the sense of mother's lifelong unavailability (to her), if mother's life appears empty and incomplete to daughter and/or mother herself, if the daughter believes that mother's life could have been more than it was, and then if daughter determines not to repeat mother's pattern, the fears associated with being different from mother are apt to be significantly disruptive. The idea of being different from others of one's group usually reflects an idealized identification with what one wants to be instead of what one is. That is, if an individual rejects a certain pattern it may be because an alternate appears more desirable. However, part of the ambivalent sense of confusion and dissonance arises from the fact that she does not have a replacement identity that she wishes to assume. If she rejects mother, all other women, and prior patterns of adult femininity, but does not have an alternate self ideal, little wonder she is left feeling vacant and empty. Often, I heard this confusion stated in questions such as, "Why can't I be content just to be like other women?"

Some women, as I have said, also wondered if their sense of not being like other women meant that they were different in terms of their sexual identity. The questions were framed somewhat as follows: Can I be different from other women, and still be sexually female? Can I be dominant, assertive, successful, and still be sexually female? Can I be in doubt about my wish to be nurturant, and still be sexually female? Can I be ambivalent about children, and still be sexually female? And finally, can I be different from mother and still be sexually female? The ambivalent effort to sort out these questions in treatment demands a therapist sufficiently comfortable with her or his own sexual identity, so that the patient's self-examination can proceed. If the patient wants to experiment with a self-concept that rejects female sexual identification and incorporates a predominantly masculine orientation, will the therapist experience that as a personal threat? Will the therapist be able to tolerate the anxiety created by an exploration of what may contain aspects of one's own unexamined wishes or fears?

The therapist, as much as anyone else in our society, is likely to have equated external success, and an orientation toward competition, assertiveness, dominance, and power with masculinity; and to have associated sensitivity, gentleness, submission, and nurturance with femininity. Although a conscious effort to avoid such stereotypic labeling may well be made, it is certainly possible that these cultural biases persist in the therapist as well as the patient. If, for example, the therapist unconsciously attributes greater desirability to the masculine role, we could then understand the ways in which she or he might unconsciously reinforce the patient's attraction to the countrasexual opposite.[2] Thus, there might be a certain unconscious pressure from the therapist, an unconscious collusion with the patient, that encourages the individual to experiment with the countrasexual opposite aspect of self. The important question is one of timing. When is the patient psychologically ready to address these integrative pressures? Obviously, we know there is great value in enabling an individual to explore, and when appropriate, to integrate both masculine and feminine aspects of the self; to become comfortable with affects, behaviors, and attitudes that have previously been ruled out of the acceptable self-concept. The work on midlife development is instructive here.[3] We know that at midlife, the individual feels pressured to allow previously denied aspects of the self to emerge. Frequently, these internal pressures feel like they are in conflict with the culturally prescribed, age-appropriate, social roles. Thus men feel threatened, almost in danger of a kind of self-seduction, by their feminine self, and women by what they label as their unacceptable masculine tendencies.

As we discussed earlier in Chapter 9, I believe that contemporary dual-career women appear to be going through some of these integrative struggles at a much earlier age than had been previously described. It is quite possible that the ambivalent woman who comes into treatment conflicted about her motivations, her attitudes, her self-concept, and her sexuality, will be dealing with some of the pressures from opposing aspects of her sexual identity. The therapist will need to take great care to ensure that working through this conflict is of value to the patient, rather than to herself or himself. Otherwise we run the risk of what I indicated earlier; that is, that the experimentation with other aspects of one's sexuality—of one's gender orientation and of one's identity—will be undertaken vicariously through the patient. We need to be continuously sensitive to the possibility that the shadow side of self, the hidden, repressed, unacceptable side, will be encouraged to emerge in the patient.

As suggested before, one of these unacceptable elements may be the therapist's unconscious wish to experiment with either a maternal or a non-maternal self (non-paternal self), which for the therapist as well as the patient may be linked to sexual identification. This wish, unacceptable on a conscious level, may be activated by the patient's struggle. At whatever stage the therapist is in terms of her or his ongoing, perhaps unresolved, issues vis a vis mother and/or father, whatever residual issues persist in terms of intimacy, dependency, autonomy, and separation, whatever the actual or fantasized relationship between oneself and one's child—these could affect the interaction between patient and therapist. The wish to experiment with a symbiotic fantasy of total dependency, or with the opposing temptations of aggression and rejection, or to "finally get it right" (vis a vis mother or father or their contemporary representations), may be acted out in a countertransference reaction.

To summarize this brief discussion of some of the expected countertransference dilemmas that can be anticipated by those who treat ambivalent dual-career women or couples, we have suggested that it is precisely because the issue is so universal and so "normal" that the therapist must be sensitive to countertransference reactions. Unlike others who come in for treatment, whose pathology blatantly demands our attention, or whose neurotic symptoms appear so dramatically dysfunctional, and who are therefore so different from ourselves, we can expect to identify very closely with the ambivalent individuals discussed here. Because of the personal nature of this identification, and because we have conceptualized these patients as manifesting a narcissistic orientation, I believe that successful treatment of these individuals demands an acute sensitivity to our countertransference reactions. This discussion has identified only a few of the expected critical countertransference issues. We have mentioned the pressures to either accept or contradict the socially sanctioned pro-natalist bias; we have talked about some aspects of the therapist's "fear of being found out" and the ways in which this fear could contaminate treatment; and finally we discussed the concept of self as different, focusing especially on the fear that "different" suggests differences in sexual identity.

By recognizing a countertransference response, the clinician can enhance her or his understanding of the dynamic processes. I believe that as we encounter more and more patients who are dealing with the factors associated with childbearing ambivalence, we will undoubtedly discover more about the significant issues that we as clinicians need to recognize about ourselves in order to offer increasingly meaningful treatment.

REFERENCES

1. Kernberg, O. *Borderline Conditions and Pathological Narcissism.* New York: Jason Aronson, 1975. p. 247.
2. Jung, C. G. "The Stages of Life." In *Structure and Dynamics of the Psyche.* (Translated by R. F. C. Hull) Princeton, NJ: Princeton University Press, 1969. Vol. 8. Chapter 5.
3. Cytrybaum, S. et al. "Midlife Development: A Personality and Social Systems Perspective." In *Aging in the 1980's.* edited by L. Poon. Washington, D.C.: American Psychological Association, 1980.
   Levinson, D. et al. *The Seasons of a Man's Life.* New York: Alfred A. Knopf, 1978.

13
CLOSING THOUGHTS: SOME
CONCLUSIONS AND THOUGHTS
FOR FUTURE RESEARCH

As we have seen throughout this book, the dual-career marriage is complex and without precedent. Unintentionally, first generation dual-career women and men find themselves creating a new adult family norm. As we accumulate experience with couples who experiment with different combinations of family and work and different lifestyles, as they create innovative and individualistic timetables with alternate emphasis on career vs. family, patterns will be established, pitfalls recognized, and successful adaptations identified. In the future, it will be possible to evaluate the impact of this new family system not only on the dual-career women and men, but on their children, and on their professional life. At this point, however, there are no models, guidelines, standards, or prototypes against which the individuals themselves, or society as a whole, can measure their private decisions, their lifeplan, or their dreams. There is little history they can use to help them predict their future.

In this analysis, we have seen that dual-career couples start out their married lives with a different set of dreams than their parents did. In addition to their commitment to each other, they share a professional orientation grounded in many years of education and experience. The women and men we have met in this book are different from their parents in the sense that they each attribute equal value to the professional goals of the other. As we have said, although it was very likely that either one or both members of the dual-career couple came from a background in which both parents worked outside the home, the mother's work was not considered "serious" or important. Usually, when mother worked, it was a case of temporary economic necessity. In the traditional, middle-class family in which most contemporary dual-career individuals were raised, the "real" feminine work—the important adult female occupation—was expected to focus on bearing and raising children.

Throughout this book we have examined a group of women who, in re-flection of several major social revolutions (especially the women's revo-lution), have elected to question the traditional feminine role. In question-ing, in challenging the inevitability of traditional feminine life choices, they have elected to differ from mother in the sense of not following tradition, unless it also suited their unique needs. Although we all recognize the many ways in which contemporary women differ from women in earlier gener-ations, perhaps the most dramatic alteration of traditional adult femininity is a result of their elective childbearing capacity, which enables this non-traditional approach to the question of whether or when they have children. From our analysis of the lives and childbearing decisions of a few dual-career women we have formulated some ideas about the critical elements that affect their childbearing decision. At this point, I would like to call your attention to the major hypotheses I have developed, and suggest some di-rections we might consider in terms of testing these ideas in future research.

1. As you will recall, I have said that dual-career childbearing decisions are developed out of the interaction of a series of determinants, including intrapsychic elements, marital elements, career elements, and lifestyle elements. With the development of the dual-career childbearing decision model, which is in effect a diagram of the interaction of these four separate determinants, we are now in a position to use this model with dual-career couples and see if it can provide any help to those struggling with the child-bearing decision.

I have concluded that the adult decision to have children is profoundly affected by the outcome of a series of early intrapsychic events. Specifically, I have found that women who have not successfully managed the very ear-liest developmental tasks related to the establishment of autonomy, the ca-pacity for intimacy, and to the creation of a satisfactory relationship with both mother and father, and who have not developed an adult feminine self-concept that is both sexual and nurturant, find the childbearing deci-sion extremely conflictual.

From my analysis of the differences between dual-career women in terms of their ability to reach a satisfying decision about whether or when to have children, we know that certain psychological issues must be encountered. This can happen either spontaneously or in treatment. I believe that the woman who is still bound intrapsychically to mother, will not be able to enter freely into the symbiotic world of intimacy inherent in motherhood. Women who continue to struggle against identification with nurturance will find themselves conflicted in terms of their wish to become a mother. Women whose fear of dependency has interfered with their ability to form an interdependent marital system are apt to be terrified by the anticipated maternal/infant dependency. Women whose lives are dominated by their "fear of being found out" seem to need to continue the pursuit of external, rather than internal, satisfactions. In order to test these findings, and have confidence in the generalizability of my conclusions, I would hope that a study of a much larger pool of subjects will be undertaken.

According to what I have discovered, the group of women who appear to be the most conflicted about the childbearing decision exhibit psychological characteristics that I have compared to the narcissistic personality. We can use what we know about the narcissistic individual, about the adult manifestations as well as the dynamic origins of this characterological position, in order to discover whether or not this description provides us with a useful perspective.

2. One of the most interesting findings of this study focused on the relationship between mother's attitude toward men and the daughter's childbearing intentions. Mothers of women who decided to have children had a generally positive attitude toward spouse and to men in general; mothers of Group C women held a generally negative attitude toward spouse and men in general. The strength of this finding, that is, that seven out of eight Group B mothers were positive toward man and that seven out of eight Group C mothers were anti-male, is impressive. However, the mechanisms by which this maternal attitude affects the daughter's childbearing decision remain as very intriguing questions requiring future study.

For example, it would be important to investigate the mother's developmental history, especially her early relationship to mother and father. How did she progress in terms of early feminine identification? Having made clear some ideas I have about the significance of pre-oedipal and oedipal issues in terms of later relationships to children, we need to examine the mother's sense of autonomy, self-concept, and sexual identity. We need to understand the nature of her individuation, from the very earliest phases, through early adult and parental stages. How did she manage these processes? Was she able to establish an independent psychological position based on a stable, integrated, and well functioning ego? Or is she still tied herself to the earliest separation struggles?

The mother who is negative toward her spouse and men in general, in effect, is telling her daughter that she does not value, or has never experienced, is not capable of, cannot tolerate, a stable female/male interdependence. Daughter may extrapolate from this the notion that the interdependence required for parenting must first be experienced in the marital dyad.*

Marital interdependence assumes the combination of both the will and the capacity to be dependent, as well as the confidence to function autonomously. The interdependent couple can use each other as resources, and can allow themselves to merge into a single unit, without fear that they will lose their individuality. Those whose fear of dependence, whose counter-dependent position governs both their conscious behavior and the underlying unconscious content, would seem unable to achieve the interdependent state. The research question here would be framed in terms of the relationship between the mother's capacity for interdependence and the daughter's childbearing decision.

From a historical perspective, we recall that the mothers of these dual-career women bridge the gap in terms of being neither in nor out of the full impact of the women's revolution. Therefore, though they may combine work and family in a dual-career modality (and we saw that this was often the case), they have been socialized within a traditional (e.g., sex-gender) stereotypic frame of reference, which may create a conflicted orientation toward their own independence, ambition, and non-familial goals. This conflict may be reflected in the mother's rage at existing inequities, at males who hold the power roles in society, and at her husband who may hold the marital power. We would investigate whether daughter might also construe this anger as directed at herself, either at her failure to be "perfect" or at mother's response to the burden of parenthood.

3. In our analysis of career pressures, we identified two aspects of professional life which the women believed had a negative impact on their lives. First, and probably most universal, the women reported that they received contradictory messages in terms of the organizational attitude toward child-related time off. Organizations, like the rest of society, profess a pronatalist bias, which runs into conflict with their career-first policy. The double message, i.e., have children, and be a "real" woman, vs. stay in your career and be a "real" professional, is understandably confusing. Organizations will need to develop a consistent policy, one that is more flexible and more interested in helping women facilitate their willingness to combine their professional skills and experience with their family plans. However, according to those who have studied this dilemma,[1] it seems that any really

---

*This raises another question about the relationship between marriage and the decision to have children. Since we know that some women are electing to have children outside of marriage, it might be interesting to study the characteristics of these women as compared to the three groups of dual-career women under analysis here.

significant organizational changes are not likely to appear in the near future.

The second issue we found to be related to the degree of career satisfaction was a widespread lack of female mentors among these successful career women. In particular, there were no senior colleagues with sufficient experience combining work and children, who could offer guidance to those in the decision stage. The current interest in examining feminine mentoring relationships will give us some very important data about the impact of the experience of other successful female colleagues. I would urge those working in that area to consider the relationship between availability of a mentor, and dual-career childbearing decisions. At this stage, however, the lack of models points to the importance of providing those who find themselves caught up in the childbearing decision dilemma with an opportunity to work through these issues in treatment.

4. Since this study has concentrated on the feminine perspective, on female developmental issues, and on the new combination of wife/mother/career, it is obvious that we must now proceed to an equally intense study of the dynamics of the masculine position. As you may remember, in the present study I conducted a few interviews with men to see whether there seemed to be any consistency between the feminine and masculine orientation toward the childbearing decision. However, it is clear to me, that we require a very careful, equally unbiased approach to the study of the how men formulate a decision to have a child.

As evidenced by the dual-career couples who are satisfied with their lives and with their ability to reach a childbearing decision, the commonly shared element has been their confidence in the lasting nature of their relationship and of their dual-career system. Regardless of the intrapsychic condition, or the level of career achievement, women who believed that their relationship was troubled found it impossible to reach a decision about children. Therefore, although the career and lifestyle pressures and conditions of dual-career couples are dramatically different from earlier generations, in this respect, they are similar to their predecessors. In this respect, predictions about their development as a family system become possible. That is, we know that resolution of marital tension must take precedence over resolution of childbearing dilemmas.

From all the evidence we have, it seems certain that increasingly large numbers of young, well-educated women and men anticipate a dual-career future in which they will undoubtedly try to resolve the dilemma studied in this book. The decision to have children or to remain childless affects not only the couple immediately involved, but also the larger social system as well. As a society, we may be ready (having launched the process of altering the traditional social definition of fully actualized women from one limited to "wife/mother" to one which allows for professional orientation as well) to move on to the issues raised by the childbearing dilemma of the dual-career couple. It is my hope that the ideas explored in this book will not only suggest a framework for helping individuals and couples who feel unable to reach a decision about whether or when to have children, but will also provide some parameters within which we can continue to study this significant, new psychosocial phenomenon.

REFERENCES

1. Kanter, R. *Men and Women of the Corporation.* New York: Basic Books, 1977.
   Hall, D. L. and Hall, F. S. *The Two-Career Couple.* Reading, MA: Addison Wesley, 1979.

APPENDIX A

SOME PERSONAL AND PROFESSIONAL CHARACTERISTICS OF 24 CHILDLESS DUAL-CAREER WOMEN

Category	Group A N = 8	Group B N = 8	Group C N = 8
PERSONAL CHARACTERISTICS			
Average Age	31	30	32
Self as Different	All	All	All
Fluctuating Self-Confidence	All	All	All
Flexibility	Less flexible than spouse	More flexible than spouse	Less flexible than spouse
EDUCATION **Ph.D. or Terminal Degree**	4	0	0
M.A.	2	4	3
B.A.	2	4	5
RELATIONSHIP			
Average # of Yrs	4 Yrs 5 mo	4 Yrs 3 mo	5 Yrs 9 mo
Spouse Seen as Supportive	4	8	4
Satisfied With Level of Domestic Sharing	4	8	6

(cont.)

APPENDIX A (*Continued*)

Category	Group A N = 8	Group B N = 8	Group C N = 8
LIFESTYLE			
Changes Viewed As:	Threatening	Acceptable	Not acceptable
CAREER ELEMENTS			
Average Number of Yrs	9 Yrs	7 Yrs	8 Yrs
Satisfaction Level:			
Not Satisfied	4	0	2
Satisfied	4	8	6
Open to New Career Options	No	Yes	No
CHILDBEARING DECISION			
Approach to Decision	Over-intellectualized	Realistically evaluated criteria	Focused on ways childfree decision set them apart
Adoption Considered	Yes	Rarely	Considered and rejected
RESPONSE TO THE QUESTION: "TELL ME ABOUT YOUR LIFE RIGHT NOW"			
Career focus	4	1	8
Relationship and/or Self-Image	4	7	0

Key:

GROUP A	AMBIVALENT	Those ambivalent about having children
GROUP B	BABY	Those planning to have a baby sometime in the future
GROUP C	CHILDLESS	Those planning to remain childless

APPENDIX B

RESEARCH ON VOLUNTARY CHILDLESSNESS

In 1973 Veevers, wondering about why there was so little research on voluntary childlessness, speculated that the pro-natalist philosophy of our society was so strong that social scientists did not view voluntary childlessness as a valuable area for study. She declared then that childless couples offered too great a threat to established value systems.[1] In a series of studies, Veevers examined individual, medical, and social questions related to this topic.[2] She grouped voluntary childless couples into those who kept postponing children as a way of avoiding the decision, and those who decided even before marriage, or very shortly thereafter, that they wished to remain childless. She discusses four stages in the postponement process in couples who begin marriage not explicitly rejecting parenthood, "but repeatedly procrastinating until a more convenient time . . . " (which never came).[3] These stages progress from initial postponement until some future event happens; (e.g., new job, "right" condition); to a shift to a more indefinite postponement; to a tentative exploration of the possibility of not having children (Veevers calls this the critical stage); to a definite decision. Some couples never reach this last position, i.e., never make a conscious decision not to have children. Many couples go through a period in which they consider the possibility of adoption, which Veevers says is important for its symbolic meaning since it " . . . prevents the childless from being committed to an irreversible state."[4]

You will recall that all the subjects in this study who were either ambivalent or had decided to remain childless stated that at one time or another they had considered adoption as an alternative to childbearing. Group A said they were still considering adoption, whereas Group C said they had rejected the idea. In contrast, none of the women in Group B had considered adoption. According to the research just mentioned, however, it seems the possibility of adoption is frequently held in the back of the mind as an option which relieves some of the pressure to decide about one's own parenthood motivation.

In 1976 Veevers outlined some patterns of voluntary childlessness: 1) couples who idealize the husband-wife relationship and believe that a child would disrupt the balance and interfere with the basic relationship; 2) couples whose occupational commitment is extremely dominant (e.g., some of these couples reported that the " . . . only time they had seriously considered having children was when they had suffered some substantial career setback"); 3) couples who said they wanted to be

293

free to respond to new experiences and opportunities (e.g., travel, transfer); 4) those who believe that childlessness is the best way. to preserve the egalitarian nature of their relationship; 5) those who cherished maximum spontaneity and freedom.[5]

A comparison of attitudes between women who intended to remain childless and those who wanted to have children, yielded the following regarding the childless group: 1) egalitarian attitude re the role of wife; 2) more likely to consider themselves feminist; 3) more career oriented, with higher levels of career aspiration; 4) different in the way they related to their mothers, i.e., this group were not as close to their mothers as those who wanted children, or as apt to see mother as fulfilled by her homemaking role; 5) no differences in perceptions of father.[6]

Gerson studying the attitudes toward mothering in a group of unmarried female undergraduates, found that daughter's perception of her own mother's loving relationship was significantly related to parenthood motivation.[7] This finding, you will recall, was repeated in the present study.

Research on Psychological Issues

Examining the decision to have children, one author said, "As with so many choices . . . the decision may be determined more by unconscious feelings than by conscious planning."[8] Another study exploring the psychological correlates of voluntary childlessness found no differences on CPI and Frank Drawing Completion test measures between women who had decided to remain childless vs. those who were planning to have children.[9] The voluntary childless group appeared somewhat more androgynous on the Bem Sex Role Inventory.[10] The author concludes that there was no evidence that those who support voluntary childlessness were described as evidencing poor social adjustment, poor mental health, or inappropriate sexual identification.[11]

Exploring the psychological basis for the guilt experienced by women considering voluntary childlessness, a recent author states, " . . . The guilt does not arise out of the dual role of women as career person and wife . . . the psychological source of feelings of guilt that so many women experience lies primarily in the relationship to her mother . . . "[12] The decision to be different from mother—to reject mother as a role model—calls into question values incorporated at a very early age from the mother. "It is not that social change (decision against children) causes anxiety in a primary sense, but that when it supports the inner process of separation and individuation, it augments the initial conflicts with parental figures".[13] Menaker's conclusions are close to my own.

Social/Occupational Attitudes

In 1974 Lois Hoffman examined the hypothesis that because working women have fewer children, conditions that encourage female employment will decrease the birthrate. She found that as " . . . incompatabilities between motherhood and employment lessen . . . "[14] the number of children of working mothers may increase. For those whose work provides a high degree of personal satisfaction " . . . childbearing may decrease as career barriers lessen, educational levels rise, and negative societal perceptions of voluntary childlessness are modified."[15] According to the increased number of women who report an intention to remain childless, Hoffman's predictions were very accurate.

Corporations, seeming to ignore the decisions facing young childless professional couples, reflect a "business as usual" attitude that works against couples who want to have children.[16] "We may be facing elective sterilization of the best and brightest among us. Given the present corporate climate, a young woman who is ambitious . . . is placed in an untenable position in regard to the question of motherhood. There is little doubt that career oriented women are penalized for their predetermined biological capacities".[17] This organizational attitude adds another confusing piece to the conflicted messages regarding children which dual-career couples hear. However, for many voluntary childless couples, including those in this study, the choice is clearly satisfactory. In an examination of satisfaction levels among traditional vs. childless couples, it was found that women who were childless by choice scored higher in overall marital adjustment.[18]

In summation, it seems evident that although social attitudes toward family patterns are still heavily traditional, there are some signs of change. Alternate family patterns are predicted[19] which focus on the couple instead of the traditional nuclear family; those who decide not to have children are much more acceptable to their contemporaries than they were 20 years ago[20]; rather than being deviant and "normless"[21] there seems to be evolving a new normative group of voluntary childless couples who could supply the needed reference.[22]

REFERENCES

1. Veevers, J. E. "Voluntary Childlessness: A Neglected Area of Family Study." *Family Coordinator,* April, 1973, 22, 199–205.
2. Veevers, "Voluntary Childlessness." 1973.
   Veevers, J. E. "The Moral Careers of Voluntary Childless Wives: Notes on the Defense of a Variant World View." *Family Coordinator,* October, 1975, 24 (4) 473–487.
   Veevers, J. E. "Life Style of Voluntary Childlessness." In *The Canadian Family in Comparative Prospective.* edited by L. Larson. Toronto: Prentice Hall, 1976.
3. Veevers, "Voluntary Childlessness." p. 359.
4. Ibid., p. 362.
5. Veevers, "Life Style of Voluntary Childlessness." p. 400.
6. Toomey, B. "College Women and Voluntary Childlessness: A Comparison Study of Women Indicating They Want to Have Children and Those Indicating They Do Not Want to Have Children." *Dissertation Abstracts International,* 1977, 38, (11-A).
7. Gerson, M. J. "The Lure of Motherhood." *Psychology of Women Quarterly,* Vol 5 (2) Winter, 1980.
8. Rosenkrantz, P. "Egalitarian Families: Some Clinical Observations." In

Women: Resources for a Changing World. Conference at the Radcliffe Institute, Cambridge, MA April 1972.

9. Teicholz, J. "A Preliminary Search for Psychological Correlates of Voluntary Childlessness in Married Women." *Dissertation Abstracts International,* 1977, 38 (4-B).

10. Bem, S. L. "The Measurement of Psychological Androgyny." *Journal of Consulting and Clinical Psychology,* 1974, 42, 155–162.

11. Teicholz, "A Preliminary Search for Psychological Correlates of Voluntary Childlessness in Married Women."

12. Menaker, E. "Some Inner Conflicts of Women in a Changing Society." In *Career and Motherhood,* edited by A. Roland and B. Harris. New York: Human Sciences Press, 1979. p. 96.

13. Ibid., p. 96.

14. Hoffman, L. W. "The Employment of Women, Education and Fertility." *Merrill-Palmer Quarterly,* April, 1974, 20, (2) p. 109.

15. Ibid., p. 118.

16. Gurtin, L. "Dual-Career Families." *Journal of College Placement.* Spring, 1980.

17. Ibid.

18. Houseknecht, S. "Reference Group Support for Voluntary Childlessness: Evidence for Conformity." *Journal of Marriage and the Family,* May, 1977, 285–292.

19. Slater, P. *Footholds.* New York: D. P. Dutton, 1977.

20. Dowan, E., Veroff, J., and Kulka, R. Study on Staying Single and Childless. University of Michigan Institute for Social Research, Ann Arbor, 1979.

21. Epstein, C. *Women's Place.* Berkeley, CA: University of California Press, 1970.

22. For example, the National Organization for Non-Parents. (NON)

APPENDIX C

SENTENCE COMPLETION FORM

1. The most important people in my life support my complicated lifestyle by . . .

2. In terms of sharing household tasks . . .

3. The hardest times for me are . . .

4. The major trouble with my career/family life is . . .

5. I feel that all this pressure is worth it because . . .

6. Our biggest arguments are about . . .

7. My spouse . . .

8. I believe that having children . . .

INDEX